Sailing Pickle round Great Britain

Sailing Pickle round Great Britain

with family, friends, and bees in my bonnet

Charles Warlow

Published in 2022 by Charles Warlow

6 South Gray Street
Edinburgh
EH9 1TE

charles.warlow@ed.ac.uk

Copyright © Charles Warlow, 2022

All rights reserved

The moral rights of the author have been asserted

Publishing services provided by Self Publishing House

Maps by Steve Druitt
Illustrations by Charles Warlow
Cover design: 'Pickle sailing in the Sound of Jura' by Lucy Warlow

Hardback ISBN: 978-1-7396874-2-7
Paperback ISBN: 978-1-7396874-3-4
eBook ISBN: 978-1-7396874-4-1

For the crew — past, present and future

Contents

Foreword and acknowledgements   ix

Chapter 1:   Planning plan A   1
Chapter 2:   Approaching plan A
              — from licensed doctor to unlicensed sailor   15
Chapter 3:   Leaving behind the world of work   31
Chapter 4:   From Ardfern to Maryport in Cumbria,
              via Northern Ireland   51
Chapter 5:   From Maryport to Milford Haven,
              via the Isle of Man and Ireland   93
Chapter 6:   From Milford Haven to Poole   135
Chapter 7:   From Poole to Harwich   175
Chapter 8:   From Harwich to Edinburgh   227
Chapter 9:   From Edinburgh to Orkney   265
Chapter 10: Round Shetland and back to Orkney   301
Chapter 11: The final leg,
              to Dunstaffnage (and Ardfern)   337
Chapter 12: Epilogue   371

Glossary   383
References   391

Foreword and acknowledgements

'There is a wonderful difference between being outward bound for pleasure, and homeward bound of necessity.'
R. T. McMullen in *Down Channel*[1]

This book is primarily meant as a discursive account of the mostly ups, and occasional downs, of a sailing cruise around Great Britain with my family and friends in 2012, in a well-found and comfortable sailing boat. It is, I hope, a book that will entertain and inform anyone interested in sailing — cruising, definitely not racing — and who might also be curious about the state of coastal Britain in the early 21st century, as well as in a few medical issues. Maybe at times my opinions will irritate, but, as Oscar Wilde put it, 'Whenever people agree with me, I always feel I must be wrong.'[2]

Do not expect a tedious log merely of distances travelled, wind-speed and direction — there is so much more to cruising than those metrics, important as they are. Latitudes and longitudes don't feature at all, nor does wave-height. No records were broken. It is not a how-to-sail-round-Britain book, although there are some tips for anyone following in my wake. Nor is it a tourist guide to the best pubs, historic sites and walks, although I certainly enjoy going ashore at every opportunity, as much to explore as for the exercise that John Inglis commended well over 100 years ago, for 'persons who cruise in small boats, where exercise of the lower limbs is

---

1. R. T. McMullen, *Down Channel* (orig. 1869; London: Grafton Books, 1986), 43.
2. Oscar Wilde, from a speech by Cecil Graham in *Lady Windermere's Fan* (1893).

impossible'.[3] Here and there I draw on memories of a life now mostly lived, a life in which I am fortunate to have had great luck, some inspirational teachers, a loving family, good friends, and the unstinting support from my not very well-off parents. Also, because I worked as a doctor, some medical thoughts inevitably interfere with the sailing, and some political ones too — the bees in my bonnet. This is hardly surprising as I spent my career working entirely in the NHS (National Health Service) and in British universities.

Hundreds of people have sailed around Great Britain before me, but surprisingly few have written books about their experiences, maybe about 25.[4] There are far more books about crossing oceans. Before hesitatingly writing my own book, I did search out as many of the previous round-Britain books that I could, which we in the medical science business call 'systematically reviewing the literature'. However, because the authors seldom cited or acknowledged previous writers, and there is no electronic search facility of the sort we have in medicine, it was not easy to find those books. However, I did at least read the ones I found, unlike some of my old colleagues who were ever eager to adorn their ponderous scientific articles with impressively long lists of references, many of which they had never read (and may have misquoted, even if they had read them).

Naturally I tried to learn as much as I could from earlier writers, like C. C. Lynam, the headmaster of the Dragon School in Oxford, who in 1907 wrote in *The Log of the 'Blue Dragon'*, 'For my part, I buy and read every record of actual cruising that I hear of or see advertised. The interest of such publications (which are astonishingly few in number) very largely depends on their simplicity and good temper ... constant grumbling, generally at the weather or the natives, is another characteristic that spoils them.'[5] I have tried not to grumble too much, at least not about the sailing, or the not particularly good weather, or the 'natives' who were generally friendly. But the state of the world is certainly worth more than an occasional grumble.

I cannot ever forget, or fail to acknowledge and thank, all the various crew who joined me for one or more of the eight two-week legs. I couldn't have done it without them. If I had tried I would have failed, and it

---

3. John Inglis, *A Yachtsman's Holidays or Cruising in the West Highlands* (London: Pickering and Co., 1879), 19.

4. Charles Warlow, 'Circumnavigations of Britain', *Marine Quarterly*, 28 (2017), 98.

5. C. C. Lynam, *The Log of the 'Blue Dragon', 1892–1904* (London: A. H. Bullen, 1907), xi.

certainly would not have been nearly so much fun. And thank you to all the others who have allowed me to use their names and ideas, who have helped in many ways, and who put me right when I made mistakes. Thank you one and all, including: Hamish and Freda Bayne, Jake Broadhurst, Eileen Brolls, Nicky and Chris Brooker, Averil Campbell, Peter Cardy, David Dick, Bridget Drasan, Catherine Druitt, Steve Druitt, Barbara Farrell, Stu Fisher, Mark Fitzgerald, Patrick and Lisa Fox, Sophie Hambleton, Sylvia Harris, Peter Hatfield, Sandra Hollingdale, William Jeffcoate, David Lea, John Paul Leach, Jenny Lewis, Nadina Lincoln, John Lytle, Olivia Lyttle, Ilona McDowell, Neil MacLennan, Klim McPherson, Anne McQuade, Greg Moran, David and Maureen Morgan, Pauline Monro, John and Miranda Myers, Ivan Pawle, Richard Roberts, Martin Rossor, Peter Rothwell, Catherine Royce, Rustam Salman, David Simpson, Malcolm Stewart, Jon Stone, Irene and Thea Stratton, Edwin Swarbrick, Anne Tait, Kevin Talbot, David Thrush, Nick Tregenza, Jan van Gijn, Ben Warlow, John Warlow, Lucy Warlow, Margaret Warlow, Oli Warlow, William Warlow, Will Whiteley, Roger Wild, and Bob Will. They have read the parts of the book that mention them, and sometimes they have added to my own recollections, or suggested a few deletions too. I am sure to have missed out some other people but I sincerely hope I have not offended them, and if I have then of course I apologise.

Others whose help I also appreciate include all those patient and civil harbour masters who guided us in and out of their harbours; the yacht clubs that made us welcome; the people who fixed broken things for us; the Ardfern Yacht Centre who in the end got the boat ready on time; and, of course, Cathie Sudlow, my wife, who kept the home fires burning, did the washing up, looked after our children, checked the epidemiological parts of the text, and even managed her day job too while I was away. Thank you to Rachel Atkins from Self Publishing House who patiently guided me through the whole process of publishing a book. And a huge thank you to Ingalo Thomson who was a kind, persistent and sometimes a necessarily fierce editor.

And finally a thank you to the good ship 'Pickle' that looked after us, as one would expect from a Rustler 36, a Bermudan sloop designed by Holman and Pye in the 1980s, 35ft overall.

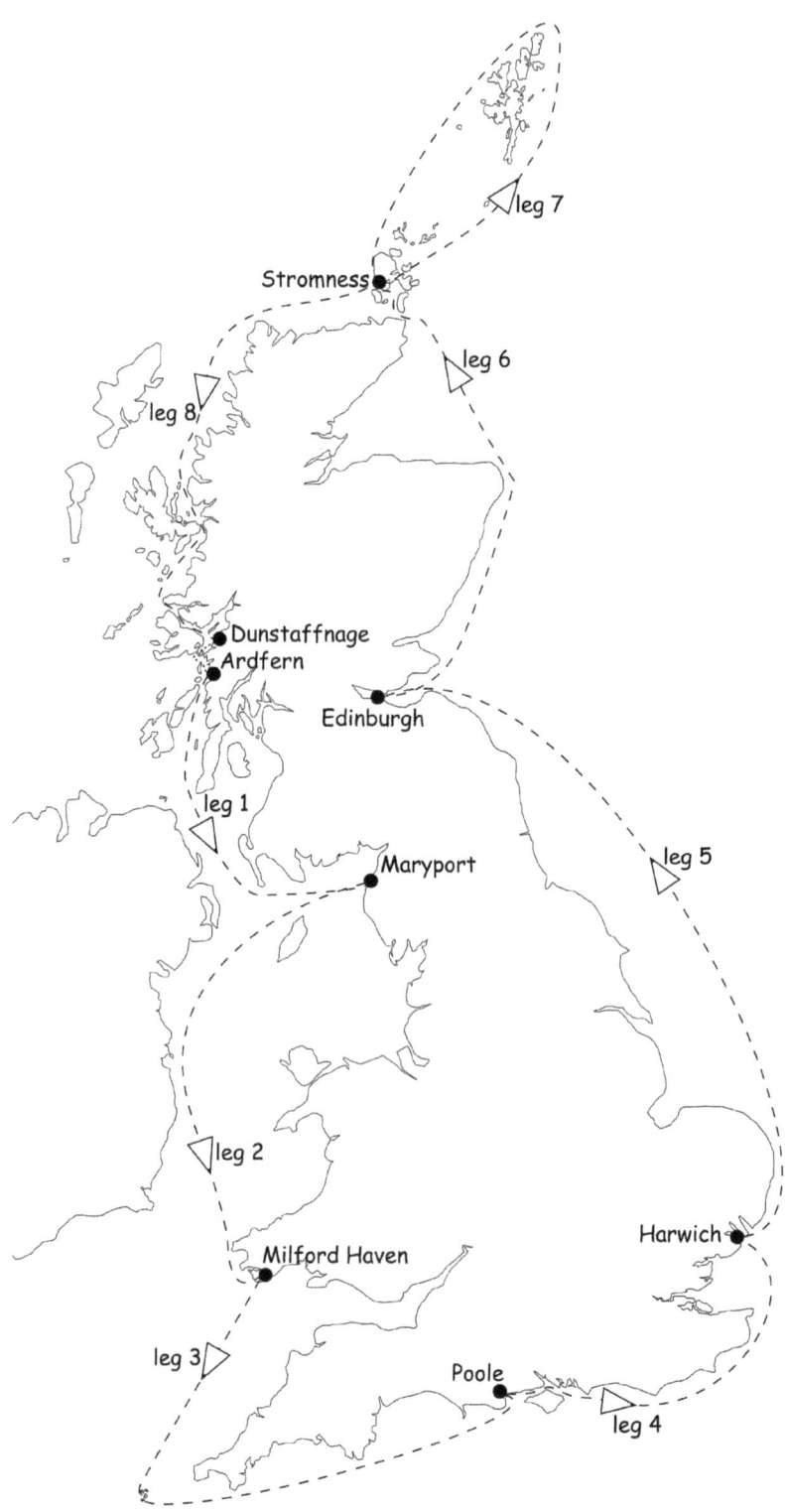

An outline map of the cruise around Great Britain

Chapter 1

Planning plan A

Why? Round what exactly? Which way round? When? With who? These could be the headings on an introductory slide for a lecture about my sail around the British coast in 2012. After 40 years at the NHS coalface as a doctor, and for nearly as long as a medical researcher and teacher at the universities of Aberdeen, Oxford and finally Edinburgh, it is impossible to get out of that PowerPoint way of thinking. Bullet points, visual impact, font size and colour, background. But no longer did I have to care for patients, teach medical students, nurture young neurologists, or present research at scientific conferences. No more grant applications, no more scientific papers to write. A new project beckoned — a few months sailing around my country, with family and friends.

Fortunately, my wife Cathie gave me permission to be away from domestic duties, even though she was working in a very full-time job as a neurologist and epidemiologist, and our two children, Lucy and William, were only eight and four at the time. 'An exeat' as my posh schools would have called it. Luckily, she was hugely supported by her fit and active parents who also lived in Edinburgh, our Polish cleaner, our very good child carer (a Polish student doing an MSc in the psychology of language no less), and Jarek who cut the grass (also Polish, by coincidence). But internet food shopping didn't help much, particularly when in her first order Cathie got the decimal point in the wrong place and ended up with 1 kg of salami, unexpected for someone so numerate.

Why?

Sailing around Britain is hardly novel. Coastal sailing for fun started in the 19th century. At first it was a manly activity for so-called Corinthian sailors, amateurs — almost all male — who managed their boats alone or with other amateurs, without the assistance of 'a hired man'. The first to write about his circumnavigation was probably the Reverend Robert Edgar Hughes who described his seven-week cruise from Lowestoft in 1852, in *Hunt's Yachting Magazine*.[1] He did however have a professional crew of two, as well as his brother, so not quite a Corinthian. The eccentric Lieutenant Empson Edward Middleton, ex of the Indian Army, wrote the first actual book about a circumnavigation, *The Cruise of the Kate* published in 1870.[2] He managed single-handed, hugging the coast in a 23-foot gaff yawl while, according to Jonathan Raban, his 'head was peppered with stings from the swarm of bees that he kept in his bonnet'.[3] Some have written 'how to do it' books like Sam Steele's *UK and Ireland Circumnavigator's Guide*.[4] Ron Pattenden circumnavigated on (hardly in) a Laser,[5] Tim Batstone on a windsurfer,[6] while the tetraplegic Geoff Holt triumphed single-handed in a 15-foot trimaran, albeit with a large but very necessary support team.[7] Slightly surprisingly, the one early account that best described and illustrated the coastline was not of a real cruise at all, but an adventure story for boys by William Kingston, published in 1870.[8]

Others have written very thoughtful books based on their voyage. My

---

1. Robert Edgar Hughes, *Hunt's Yachting Magazine*, 1 (1852).

2. Empson Edward Middleton, *The Cruise of the Kate* (London: Longmans, Green and Co., 1870).

3. Jonathan Raban, *Coasting: A Private Journey* (orig. 1986; New York: First Vintage Departure Edition, 2003), 29.

4. Sam Steele, *UK and Ireland Circumnavigator's Guide* (2nd edn, London: Adlard Coles Nautical, 2011).

5. Ron Pattenden, *Land on my Right: A Sail round Britain Single-Handed on a Laser, Unsupported* (self-published, Lulu Enterprises Inc., 2008).

6. Tim Batstone, *Round Britain Windsurf, 1800 Miles on a 12ft Board* (Newton Abbott: David and Charles, 1985).

7. Geoff Holt, *Walking On Water: A Voyage round Britain and through Life* (Rendlesham, Suffolk: Seafarer Books, 2008).

8. William H. G. Kingston, *A Yacht Voyage round England* (orig. 1870; London: The Religious Tract Society, *c.*1879).

favourite is the first one written by a woman, *One Summer's Grace: A Family Voyage round Britain* by Libby Purves, in which she describes the difficulties — and joys — of her 1988 cruise with her two small children as well as her husband.[9] In *Coasting*, Jonathan Raban treats his 1980s mostly-solo cruises as therapy, exploring his rebellious childhood, angry-young-man early adulthood, and fraught relationship with his vicar father.[10] Being the same generation and with a not dissimilar background, I rather feel for him, but he does push it a bit far in telling his father to 'fuck off'. Mind you, my own father, probably like his, muttered more than once, 'You're going to have to learn that the world doesn't revolve around you.' In desperation I suspect, my parents dispatched me, aged 17, to the Ullswater Outward Bound School for a month, to be sorted out. Maybe I was. The experience certainly instilled a lifelong love of mountains, and of the Lake District, but I didn't enjoy the compulsory and stark-bollocks-naked jumps into the lake at 7am every morning in early April.

The most amusing book about a circumnavigation is surely by Shane Spall who, with her actor-husband Timothy, cruised round Britain off and on over a few years, albeit in small steps and in a sea-going barge rather than a sailing boat.[11] There were plenty of cock-ups, and much champagne was drunk. Swimmers, canoeists and kite-surfers have all made it round our coastline, and at least one paddle-boarder, and many have written books about their experiences, but their challenges were different to mine.

I had thought my own idea of a circumnavigation emerged at about the time of my retirement from clinical work in 2008, but friends can remember me talking about it in the early 1990s. Maybe I had even caught the idea long before, from my father who dreamed of owning a boat and sailing round the world. In neither ambition was he remotely successful, much to the relief of my mother who had suffered more than enough Norfolk Broads sailing holidays in faithful support of him and our family.

The 'why do it?' question clearly went back a long way, unconsciously if not consciously. I think the eventual answer was something to do with wanting to see our British coastline from the deck of my own boat during a continuous journey — to get a better feel for its scale, its geology and

---

9. Libby Purves, *One Summer's Grace: A Family Voyage round Britain* (London: Grafton Books, 1989).

10. Raban, *Coasting*, 165.

11. Shane Spall, *The Voyages of the Princess Matilda* (London: Ebury Press, 2012; rev. edn 2013) and *The Princess Matilda Comes Home* (London: Ebury Press, 2013).

geography, its history, its character, and the connectivity by sea between Lerwick in the north, Falmouth in the south, Lowestoft in the east, and Belfast in the west. As Hilaire Belloc wrote, 'Nowhere does England take on personality so strongly as from the sea.'[12] I was going to check out that English personality, and that of Scotland, Wales and Ireland while I was about it.

I wanted to approach our coastal towns and cities as they are surely best approached, from the sea into the security of a harbour. Certainly not by driving on crowded roads, stuck in traffic jams, waiting at traffic lights, navigating roundabouts, passing industrial estates, caravan parks and drab suburban houses, and finally trying to find somewhere to park. In 1982 the American travel writer Paul Theroux walked and took trains and buses round our coastline, but admitted that everywhere 'looked better from the water'.[13] Maybe he really wanted to be on a boat. Of course, he was hardly the first to take the land route. Daniel Defoe did it several times in the early 18th century, describing the geography, weather, poverty, country houses, farming and more: 'My business is rather to give a true and impartial description of the place; a view of the country, its present state as to fertility, commerce, manufacture, and product; with the manners and usages of the people…'.[14]

Boswell, during his tour of the Hebrides with Johnson in 1773, recorded a conversation in which Johnson declared: 'it is surprising how people will go to a distance for what they may have at home.'[15] Although this referred to finding a wife, it surely also applies to discovering new places. A century later, the Edinburgh advocate and amateur sailor Archibald Young also found it 'somewhat strange, that whilst long voyages are undertaken to distant lands, some of the most picturesque scenery on our own shores should be comparatively neglected'.[16]

---

12. Hilaire Belloc, 'Off Exmouth', in *On Sailing the Sea: A Collection of the Seagoing Writings of Hilaire Belloc* (London: Hart-Davis, 1951), 201.

13. Paul Theroux, *The Kingdom by the Sea: A Journey around the Coast of Great Britain* (orig. 1983; London: Penguin, 1984), 122.

14. Daniel Defoe, *A Tour through the Whole Island of Great Britain* (orig. 1724–6; London: Penguin, 1971), 446.

15. James Boswell, *The Journal of a Tour to the Hebrides with Samuel Johnson, LL.D.*, ed. R. W. Chapman (orig. 1785; Oxford: Oxford University Press, 1970), 352.

16. Archibald Young, *Summer Sailings by an Old Yachtsman* (Edinburgh: David Douglas, 1898), 2.

I have always wanted to get to know my own country better before trying any 'distance', in other words 'abroad'. My first effort was as a late teenager when — much against my parents' wishes — I hitchhiked chastely round England with my first serious girlfriend and, among other things, saw the brand-new Coventry Cathedral as well as the older ones in York and Ely. My father even recruited my vicar cousin Philip to try and talk me out of it, presumably on religious and moral grounds. My girlfriend's parents were more accommodating.

On Mull, Johnson himself reflected: 'All travel has its advantages. If the passenger visits better countries, he may learn to improve his own, and if fortune carries him to worse, he may learn to enjoy it.'[17] For him, Scotland and the Hebrides were undoubtedly other countries. Luckily he had Boswell, a Scotsman, to accompany him, but neither of them could speak the Erse, an early name for Gaelic. This must have limited their contacts with the 'lower classes' if not the land-owning but English-speaking 'upper classes'.

My cruise was nothing to do with testing myself physically or mentally. Indeed I rather hoped I wouldn't have to be tested. And I certainly wasn't interested in the manliness so admired by the late 19th-century Corinthian sailors. I wasn't like Middleton wanting to boast of 'the splendid constitution that nature has bestowed upon me'.[18] Nor was I out to impress. I didn't want or luckily need any sponsorship like ocean racers with corporate logos plastered all over their hulls and sails, and the trip wasn't to raise money for charity.

Finally, the cruise was not only to do myself good, as recommended by Frank Cowper in 1892 — 'There are few adventures more likely to do a man good and set him up generally than a cruise among the many creeks and land-locked inlets which indent the shores of Great Britain south of the Humber, and so round, by South and West, until the East is reached again by North'[19] — I also wanted to have fun, see lots of places (some new to me, some not) and enjoy being with family and friends. It was to be what Catherine of the last leg called 'the best gap year idea of the third age' she had heard of. Cheeky, even if I was 68 years old. Indeed, to my horror, a month before we set off, and for the first time ever, a young man offered

---

17. Samuel Johnson, *A Journey to the Western Isles of Scotland*, ed. R. W. Chapman (orig. 1775; Oxford: Oxford University Press, 1970), 125.

18. Middleton, *The Cruise of the Kate*, 123.

19. Frank Cowper, *Sailing Tours: The Yachtsman's Guide to the Cruising Waters of the English Coast*, part 1: *The Coasts of Essex and Suffolk* (London: Upcott Gill, 1892), 1.

me his seat on a bus and refused to accept my assurances that I was just fine leaning against a pole reading the *Guardian*. I was so embarrassed I got off at the next stop and caught the following bus.

Round what exactly?

Sailing around Great Britain does not of course include Northern Ireland, while around the UK would include it if there wasn't a land border with the Republic of Ireland (much to the irritation of the swivel-eyed Brexiteers who have wrenched the UK out of the European Union). A few sailors, like Lieutenant Middleton, cheated grossly by going through the Forth and Clyde Canal connecting the east with the west coasts of Scotland across the central belt. More have cheated, but not quite so grossly, by using the Caledonian Canal further north between Fort William and Inverness; this is what the Reverend Hughes did, admittedly at a time when yachts off the north Scottish coast could be delayed for weeks by poor weather. Besides, he reckoned rather reasonably that '300 miles of difficult and tedious coasting are avoided, and to those who sail for pleasure, the change of scene in passing from the restless ocean to the peaceful lake and the novelty of the whole thing are most fascinating'.[20] Geoff Holt had no option other than to go through the Caledonian Canal so he could get home before winter, having been delayed by such bad weather earlier on. However, using either canal misses the best cruising in Britain — most of the Inner Hebrides, all the Outer Hebrides, the northwest mainland, Orkney and Shetland. Robert Buchanan, in his panegyric to Argyll and the Hebrides, introduced his 1871 The Land of Lorne, including the Cruise of the 'Tern' to the Outer Hebrides with 'How little do mortals know of the wonders lying at their own thresholds! — so true is it that travellers and tourists, all sorts of Englishmen, are better acquainted with Tenerife or Patagonia than they are with our own Hebrides'.[21] Indeed, so true.

Some people worry about being anywhere near Scotland in the summer because of the dreaded midges, and plan accordingly. But midges are not marine animals. They do not go to sea and are not a problem, even in July, unless you take the inland route through the canals (another good reason not to). Circumnavigators see much more by sailing round the north

---

20. Hughes, *Hunt's Yachting Magazine*, 1 (1852), 443.

21. Robert Buchanan, *The Land of Lorne, including the Cruise of the 'Tern' to the Outer Hebrides*, vol. 1 (London: British Library, Historical Print Editions, 1871), 3.

coast of the Scottish mainland, often with at least one stop in Orkney. Surprisingly few take in Shetland and Muckle Flugga (the most northerly tip of the UK, bar Out Stack), and only Henry Reynolds, a schoolmaster who frequently lapsed into Latin, wrote a book which included getting as far as Lerwick.[22] Having previously got as far as Lerwick myself, I certainly planned to round Muckle Flugga.

I wanted to include Northern Ireland as part of the UK, but not the west coast of Ireland which would have bypassed Wales, another part of the UK. I didn't fancy the Channel Isles, which might have meant missing out much of the south coast. To sail all the way round all the British Isles, one would have to take in some of the very distant and uninhabited Scottish Islands such as North Rona, the Flannan Isles and St Kilda — including them on this cruise would have taken more time than I had available.

Rockall is very familiar as one of the sea areas in the BBC shipping forecast, but I was certainly not going out to that isolated rock in the Atlantic 200 miles west of the Outer Hebrides. In 1921, on his way round the British Isles, the ophthalmologist Claud Worth claimed to have sailed there, but in such poor visibility he never saw the rock for certain.[23] In 1955, during his National Service, my older brother John photographed Rockall from the deck of HMS Vidal, the survey ship whose crew annexed it for the UK by landing a helicopter to plant, or more likely screw, a Union Jack to the rock. The orders from the Queen were: 'On arrival at Rockall you will effect a landing and hoist the Union flag on whatever spot appears most suitable or practicable, and you will then take possession of the island on our behalf.'[24] But our ownership, with the possible riches in the surrounding seas, is disputed. The rock may actually belong to Ireland, or Iceland, or Denmark. Or nobody, if you follow the UN Convention on the law of the sea: 'Rocks which cannot sustain human habitation or economic life of their own shall have no exclusive economic zone or continental shelf.'[25] Or is the rock actually an island? No, because one definition of an island is that it has to support at least three sheep, or maybe two, which Rockall clearly does not. More people have been into space than have landed on Rockall.

---

22. Henry Reynolds, *Coastwise—Cross-Seas: The Tribulations and Triumphs of a Casual Cruiser* (London: J. D. Potter, 1921).

23. Claud Worth, *Yacht Navigation and Voyaging*, chap. 31: *From Hampshire to Rockall and Round the British Islands* (London: J. D. Potter, 1928).

24. A. Robertson, 'Flotsam and Jetsam', *Marine Quarterly*, 35 (2019), 13–15.

25. The United Nations Convention on the Law of the Sea, 1982, article 121.

My plan then was to sail around Great Britain, and to call in on Northern Ireland. Of course all this pedantry of place would be thrown into extreme confusion if Scotland had voted for independence from the UK in the 2014 referendum. If independence does come to pass one day, which it probably will, what, I wonder, will we call the remaining bits of the UK? Certainly not the 'Former UK', like the Former Yugoslavia. The acronym would not amuse. Maybe the 'Rest of the UK' (RUK) would do. If Ireland then reunited we would be down to England and Wales, and if Wales left, what then? Little England, all alone out of the European Union, buffeted by the greater powers of the USA, China and Russia, still nursing imperial dreams of a long-lost empire. How to redesign the union flag would be a problem.

A rather attractive thing about Great Britain is that it is just the right size to sail round. Not too big like Australia, not too small like Malta, and not too daunting like Iceland. It can be done at a leisurely pace, in weeks or months — it doesn't need years. Moreover, it can be done almost entirely in daylight, bearing in mind that in summer in the north of Scotland it is light for most of the night. It surprises many people that you can do this circumnavigation in day-sails — with the exception of the Bristol Channel if you sail straight across the entrance, and the Wash that has very few tenable anchorages or harbours to break the long jump between Norfolk and Lincolnshire or Yorkshire. After all, Lieutenant Middleton managed mostly with day-sails, and lived to tell the tale.

The circumnavigation can take little more than a week if you are racing. But I absolutely would not be; I don't do that sort of madness. Nor did Hilaire Belloc, whose first advice, or rule, for the man who is 'too poor to sail a big boat, or is not such a fool as to desire one … say, boats from seven tons to twenty' was 'Cruising is not racing … For no one can doubt that the practice of sailing, which renews in us all the past of our blood, has been abominably corrupted by racing. I do not know whence the evil came, but I suppose it came like most evils, from a love of money. The love of money made men admire the possessors of it, and so they came to think of sailing as they do of riding horses, or of any other sport — as something to be tested by what the rich man could do.'[26] The corruption of sport by money is nothing new; there just seems to be a lot more of it about these days — certainly money, and also I imagine corruption which tends to follow the money.

You would need several years if you wanted to see absolutely everything

---

26. Hilaire Belloc, *The Cruise of the Nona* (London: Constable & Co. Ltd, 1925), 309.

on a round-Britain cruise, if indeed you ever could. And I didn't have the time, or domestic permission. A few months over the spring and summer of 2012 was to be a good compromise. Enough time to see a lot, but not too long to be away from the family, bearing in mind I planned to include two family holidays on the boat — at Easter for the first leg, and in the summer in Orkney. And I thought I had better get home a couple of times as well, to make sure the washing up had been done.

Which way round?

Which way round was obvious. I had kept a boat on the west coast of Scotland since 1988, most of the time at Dunstaffnage just north of Oban, on a summer mooring under the castle, and, in the winter, at Ardfern 24 miles south of Oban. Setting off clockwise and heading north to Orkney and Shetland early in the season would have been asking for weather trouble, whereas anticlockwise would get us nicely past the south coast of England before the summer over-crowding, and marina over-pricing. Furthermore, tacking back and forth down the Irish Sea between Scotland, the Isle of Man, Wales and Ireland against any southwest prevailing wind seemed a much more interesting prospect than having to make tacks out into the North Sea and back to the east coasts of Scotland and England. Even worse would be tacking down-channel along the south coast of England. So anticlockwise it was.

Because many of my potential crew could not be away from work or family for long, I split the cruise into eight two-week legs with enough wriggle room between them to be fairly sure where each leg would start and finish, irrespective of storm, fog, damage, illness or mutiny. The exact start and finish points needed to be easy for crew changes by public transport, and be where we could conveniently park the boat for a bit of rest and relaxation, and re-victualling.

I decided that the first leg was to be from Ardfern to Maryport in Cumbria, the second to Milford Haven in Wales (the train journey to Milford for the crew was somewhat lengthy, but at least scenic). The third leg would be to Poole where I hoped my good friend David Morgan, who was going to be on that leg, could find me a mooring at his yacht club while I went home for a fortnight so Cathie could go off to a stroke conference in Lisbon. The fourth leg was to be to Walton-on-the-Naze in Essex where my parents used to live, and the fifth up to Edinburgh where I could be home for a week. The sixth leg would take us to Orkney for the two-week family holiday, the seventh round Shetland, and the final leg back down the west coast to Dunstaffnage. Later, a couple of days would complete the circuit to Ardfern. I didn't think to avoid a long first day-sail on each leg so new crew could find their sea legs, but even though difficult to achieve I should have done, particularly for the Bristol Channel and the north coast of Scotland.

When?

I could never have taken several months off work until I retired. As professor of medical neurology at the University of Edinburgh I had to look after patients, teach, and do research. There was not much administration in those halcyon days before universities became full-on businesses, controlled by an increasing number of administrators bearing clipboards and spreadsheets (my contribution to administration was correctly described by one colleague as 'imperceptible'). Fortunately I was working mostly before the advent of the extraordinarily burdensome Research Assessment Exercise (now rebadged as the Research Excellence Framework, perhaps to confer some sort of higher respectability and ambition). This requires universities to waste a staggering amount of staff time collecting vast amounts of data on their research grants and papers, as well as assessing the wider impact of their research, and then to be judged by panels made up of more university academics wasting even more of their time. Naturally, the universities sex-up their income and research output to improve their place in the inevitable league tables, and so attract more funding. Even before I retired, research quantity had begun to trump quality, and competition between universities had become far greater, making research collaboration more difficult when we should all be making it easier.

Mine was a full-on job that I had hugely enjoyed; indeed, I can't remember a day when I wasn't happy to go to work. I was fortunate to have worked mostly with people I liked, many of whom became friends. I can't imagine working with anyone who might try to undermine me, like politicians seem to have to (and some academics, I'm afraid). Medicine is a matey profession. You make friends with people you work with. You share the adversity of being a junior doctor with others as your paths intersect moving from job to job around the country (this happens less often now). These friendships can last forever.

I am certainly one of the lucky ones. Lucky to have survived colon cancer that was removed in 1995. I had felt guilty to be strangely excited, as well as nervous, on the morning of surgery. When I half-awoke from the anaesthetic to discover I didn't have a urinary catheter I assumed the worst, that the surgeon must have just opened me up, seen lots of secondary deposits, and done nothing more. 'Oh no,' said the surgeon when he saw me a few hours later. 'We never use catheters these days; you must be remembering what you learned as a medical student.' Lucky as well to have survived several other less-threatening ailments, and to retire at the conventional age of 65 (willingly giving way to the younger generation before passing my 'best-before' date) — and still fit enough in mind and body to go sailing.

I was also lucky to have had a well-enough paid job to afford to share a sailing boat with my neurologist friend, and former 'junior' colleague in Oxford, Richard Roberts, ever since we coincidentally moved to Scotland in 1987 — me to Edinburgh, Richard to Dundee. We discovered that we had both been saving for a boat for several years. Each with about £10,000, we had enough for two second-hand 26-footers. But how much better it was to combine forces and buy a second-hand Contessa 32 — Calypso.

And later, when I retired, I was again lucky because I had a big enough lump sum from my pension to buy a Rustler 36, while Richard went Swedish and bought a Hallberg-Rassy 372. This meant we could both do more sailing, and at times to suit ourselves. In 2009, given the banking crisis, it seemed crazy to put any lump sum in a bank, and I have never trusted or even understood stocks and shares. I was also uneasy about buying a country cottage that would exacerbate the troubling problem of rural depopulation. So, instead, by buying a boat built in Britain I would be helping prop up the economy of Cornwall where Rustlers were and still are built. Furthermore, 'At our age,' my friend Lindsay Haas, a wonderful New Zealand neurologist, had said to me, 'a pound saved is a pound wasted.' Sadly he died in 2011 from secondary melanoma, too young to have spent very many of his own pounds.

I am indeed of that lucky, lucky generation that saw the introduction of the NHS in 1948 making healthcare for everyone in the UK free at the point of need. But then witnessed its sad decline, at least in England under the 2010–15 Tory government propped up by the Liberal Democrats until their well-deserved electoral wipe-out in 2015. The Tories have carried on trying to dismantle the NHS unhindered in England, while fortunately in Scotland the SNP (Scottish National Party) government has mostly eschewed the privatisation agenda. My generation also benefited from free university education, and we never had to go to war or even do National Service. We saw the liberalisation of the laws on abortion and homosexuality, and the abolition of the death penalty. We have decent pensions, certainly those of us in the public sector, and I was lucky as a student to be able to hitchhike round Europe to see the classic sights before they became too expensive and too over-crowded. Others took the bus to India to smoke dope, and to meditate.

Of course when I was a teenager there were no lattes or cappuccinos — just coffee bars that didn't have proper coffee on offer, although by then there were jukeboxes. I don't think I had enough money to go to a restaurant myself until I was over 20. There were no clubs in the modern sense, but the Bromley jazz club was a bus-ride away from my teenage home in Beckenham, full of cigarette smoke and possibilities while Chris Barber and Acker Bilk played their New Orleans trad-jazz revival stuff. We certainly didn't buy bottles of wine when I was young. And thankfully we were not bombarded by and addicted to social media. To talk to my girlfriend I had to find a telephone box, put coins in, then press button A when she (hopefully not her parents) answered, or button B to get my money back if there was no answer.

Despite the lack of many of the things that teenagers now take for granted, I was extraordinarily lucky to grow up in the 1960s. There was excitement as we broke out from the post-war austerity of the 1950s when my older brother had been brought up. Even though we are only seven years apart in age there seemed almost the gulf of a generation between us. 'Beyond the Fringe', one of the first shows I saw in London in 1961, emphasised the watershed between the 1950s and 1960s: four Oxbridge graduates with their sharp-elbowed satire, and lampooning those in authority. Unforgettable. It was a far, far cry from the more gentle and genteel musical comedy of Flanders and Swann. I am of the Beatles, the oral contraceptive, and the mini-skirt generation. The one serious downside was living with the possibility of Mutually Assured Destruction (MAD) and a nuclear winter. Luckily they didn't happen, although they still might. The even bigger threat of global warming may have started by then, but no one I knew was talking or worrying about it. I will have been lucky, too, to avoid the direst consequences of global warming because it will not affect my generation; sadly the problem will be for future generations.

But back to my boat. Precisely when to start the cruise of several months' duration needed to be as early in the year as was sensible, giving as much time as possible before any autumnal gales. And I didn't want to rush it. April it was to be, at the beginning of the Easter school holidays. I planned to finish in August.

With who?

With who was fairly obvious too. With anyone I could get to help, provided they had some sailing experience and I knew them well enough to have an inkling of what they might be like on a small boat. I didn't want to advertise, and picking up any old crew lounging about on harbour walls did not appeal. And I was certainly not going to sail alone. I can't understand why some people enjoy sailing single-handed, but I can understand why some are driven to it for lack of crew, or irritation with previous crew (an irritation which can be mutual). In any event, I wanted to share the experience — and hopefully the fun.

Nor did I fancy the sheer effort of single-handed sailing — and, even more so, the stress of single-handed pilotage into unfamiliar harbours. Also, given my incompetence at arriving and leaving marina pontoons, the more help the better. Furthermore, as I age, and most of my crew age with me, we have all become increasingly resistant to making that sporting leap for a pontoon while clutching a mooring rope (Bridget of the first leg more recently had to be fished out of the water after foolishly responding to my premature command to 'jump'). We west coast of Scotland sailors may know about anchoring, but not so much about approaching pontoons and harbour walls in good order, and getting off them in an unfavourable wind direction. I didn't have windvane self-steering in 2012, just an electric tiller-pilot that sucked amps out of the batteries, and so human help to hold the tiller on long passages was eminently sensible.

In 2011 I made a list of about 40 people, as well as my immediate family, who might be interested, and who might be tolerable. The original plan was to contact them all simultaneously to find out who wanted to do which leg. But I thought better of that in case I got too many for one leg, and not enough for others. Instead, in the autumn, I emailed just one person at a time, to try and bring together for each leg a suitable crew — socially as well as in their sailing competence. For Shetland I needed a strong crew, for the south coast of England a less strong crew, and for the east coast something in between.

Some people said yes at once, others said no at once, and a few were uncertain for a while. Steve Druitt, an Edinburgh friend, wanted to come on more than one leg, which was helpful because he got to know the boat, he had a lot of sailing experience, and he was excessively keen on cutting up rubbish into tiny pieces so it could be stored in a smaller space before a rubbish bin was found ashore. A few people agreed but later pulled out for mostly medical reasons — broken wrists (yes, both of them in the same person at the same time), frozen shoulder, father-in-law's health. Some wanted to bring partners, and one brought her daughter.

Coastal sailing with very few night-sails required enough of us to sail the boat and share the watches, but not so many that we all tripped over ourselves in the saloon or the cockpit. Ideally I thought we should plan on four for each leg, one sleeping each side of the saloon, one in the forecabin, and one in the quarter berth. That would allow for an occasional last minute no-show due to work commitments, illness or whatever. The minimum would be two, and the maximum five.

My crews eventually included my three older and two younger children, my brother, Cathie, and 22 friends of whom Steve came on two legs, while the rest came on one or part of one leg each.

There was no real Plan B. Plan A was going to have to be flexible enough to get us round on time, and in good order.

Chapter 2

Approaching plan A
— from licensed doctor to unlicensed sailor

Licensed to practise medicine

I have lost count of the exams I have had to pass. Exams to get into first one school and then another and another, exams to get into university, annual exams at university, exams to qualify as a doctor, and finally an exam before I could start training as a neurologist. At least I didn't have to take yet another exam to qualify as a consultant neurologist, but trainees do now. And happily I was not required to keep an over-lengthy ePortfolio to record all my various training experiences, and to document the minutiae of my reflective practice (in the bath, on the toilet, sailing the sea, wherever). How many reflections does one need before breakfast? Which too-honest reflections after something has gone wrong might compromise one's licence with the General Medical Council (GMC)? And when does reflection sink into obsessive rumination? I trained in less complicated times.

After becoming a consultant there are no more exams. Maintaining and improving one's competence and knowledge largely depends on voluntarily keeping up-to-date. There are plenty of opportunities for Continuing Professional Development (CPD), as it has become known: weekly meetings for discussing patients with colleagues in one's own department, and hospital-wide so-called Grand Rounds where patients from any department are discussed. Sadly the latter are increasingly less well attended, partly because everyone is too busy, and because of the most unfortunate view that without any direct personal gain there is no point going. What selfish tosh. Everyone is supposed to put their expertise *into* the meetings, for the benefit of all. There are also national and international meetings where speakers strut their stuff and research results are presented, with educational programmes mixed in. Towards the end of my career we were all supposed to keep a CPD diary, but I never did, and no one found me out. Ever since I signed into anatomy lectures in Cambridge as a medical student, and then walked straight out again, I have had contempt for any system of regulation that relies on self-reporting. It is far too easy to cheat. I'm sure many do.

In recent years, to try and tighten up on their competence and knowledge, doctors have been formally appraised. This has too often been an annual farce of box-ticking overseen by another clinician who may not even be in the same speciality, and by a manager. Better would be a discussion with a senior colleague in the same speciality to discuss how one is getting on, how to improve, and how to overcome what barriers there might be to that improvement. The current system is largely a waste of valuable professional time. Unfortunately, most doctors have reacted with shoulder-shrugging indifference, rather than with suggestions how to carry out more effectively what should be a useful professional exercise.

Then, in 2012, in their wisdom, the GMC started rolling out revalidation of all doctors. Every five years. This involves collecting feedback from colleagues (you scratch my back, I'll scratch yours); collecting patient feedback (gifts, as well as the occasional nice letter, binning the less-than-nice ones); checking annual appraisals have been signed off (with all their faults); collecting evidence of quality improvement or audit activity (persuade a medical student seeking preferment to do a trivial audit); a discussion of any complaints (not too awful hopefully) and compliments (there must be some); a self-declaration of health (don't mention the booze or anti-depressants) and probity (no overt bribes from the pharmaceutical industry); evidence of continuing professional development (checking emails during clinical and educational meetings in between naps); and ensuring that doctors are properly reflective about their practice (management-speak for thinking, hardly novel).

All this appraisal and revalidation requires a lot of preparation time, involves a ludicrous amount of red tape, is easily manipulated, is very expensive (£1 billion over 10 years[1]) and time wasting, takes doctors away from being doctors — and still may not protect patients from incompetent,

---

1. V. T. Brown et al., 'Appraisal and Revalidation for UK Doctors—Time to Assess the Evidence', *BMJ*, 370 (2020), m3415.

or even rogue doctors. It is potentially all to no effect because doctors are far from stupid and can still get away with poor practice. Like any other diagnostic test, revalidation has to be sensitive enough to identify the bad doctors (i.e. not too many 'false-negatives'), perhaps only 1% of the total depending on how 'bad' is defined. At the same time the test must not be so sensitive that it entangles doctors who are perfectly competent — revalidation needs to be highly specific (i.e. few 'false-positives').

Measuring outcome and performance

Along with appraisal and revalidation, quality improvement and safety initiatives have mushroomed, generally aimed at detecting 'poorly performing' surgeons and hospitals. More and more metrics are collected to record surgeons' (and indeed hospitals') performance — and implied competence. The idea of course is that 'poorly performing' surgeons, and hospitals, will surely be identified and sink to the bottom of a league table. Patients can then choose the 'best' surgeons and the 'best' hospitals.

However, making a fair comparison between different surgeons' outcomes is not trivial. One needs to take account of, and adjust, the outcome — for example, death — for the patients' characteristics that influence their chance of dying irrespective of the surgeon's competence. A good surgeon operating on sicker or older patients will otherwise appear 'worse' than a poor surgeon doing the same operation on healthier or younger patients. Making fair comparisons of overall death rates between hospitals with all their variety of patients is even more problematic.

Some performance metrics still use death at hospital discharge as an outcome, simply because it is easier to identify than death at a particular time period after surgery when the patient may have gone home. Unfortunately, it is all too easy to 'game' by discharging or transferring post-operative patients with indecent haste, to keep one's statistics looking good, a fine example of 'when a measure becomes a target, it ceases to be a good measure'.[2] To add to the complexity, some deaths are unavoidable and, moreover, surgical outcomes do not just depend on the surgeon. What about the anaesthetist, the cleanliness of the operating theatre, the quality of the nursing, the availability of intensive care? If comparing outcomes between surgeons is tricky, imagine doing this for neurologists, who look

---

2. Marilyn Strathern, '"Improving Ratings": Audit in the British University System', *European Review*, 5 (3) (1997), 305–21.

after patients with neurological disorders from the never fatal (migraine) to the always fatal (motor neurone disease).

Another challenge is taking account of, and recording, outcomes that are not apparent in the short term, such as a heart attack many years after the insertion of a stent (a small device placed into a coronary artery to open it, and keep it open). This requires long-term follow-up which is only just beginning to be achievable with routine NHS data, provided the data can be collected reliably using electronic health record systems, collated nationally, and made available for analysis without breaching data privacy regulations.

Ideally we should take account of outcomes that are of most concern to patients, and these may not necessarily include death. For example, pain, poor quality of life, unhappiness even. But which outcomes to choose, and how on earth to collect them from patients cared for across all specialities in all hospitals, before even starting on general practice? Whatever else, doctors — like students — should never mark their own homework. If they do they will, consciously or unconsciously, record better outcomes than an independent assessor.[3] In any event, poor doctors, and poor hospitals, are probably more likely to be first revealed by observant and caring local staff — if their managers listen to them — than by statistics. The clinicians in the Stafford Hospital knew there were problems long before the unusually high death rates were reported in 2007.[4]

I once wrote to my medical director expressing concerns about a surgeon who was privately regarded by his immediate colleagues as hopeless if not dangerous. Nothing happened. Naturally I didn't refer any of my patients to him, but others not-in-the-know presumably did. Annual appraisal didn't seem to have any effect on him. Would he have been pulled up by routinely collected surgical outcome metrics? Maybe, but we already knew he was hopeless without any metrics. Of course, incompetence is much easier to spot in a surgeon than in a physician whose mistakes can be more subtle than a botched operation leaving the patient paralysed from the neck down.

Mandating doctors to take a regular exam might work better than metrics. However, knowledge is much easier to assess than what really counts — competence. And what if a doctor failed? Presumably he or she would be suspended, at least for a while during some sort of remedial training. But

---

3. P. Rothwell and C. P. Warlow, 'Is Self-Audit Reliable?', *Lancet*, 346 (1995), 1623.

4. Denis Campbell, 'The Mid Staffs Hospital Scandal: The Essential Guide', *Guardian*, 6 February 2013.

given the shortage of GPs and consultants in some specialities, who would look after the patients?

Unlicensed to sail

Although UK doctors all have to be licensed to practise medicine, no one has to be licensed to sail for pleasure. Sailing is joyfully unregulated. Why so? Perhaps because sailing misdemeanours would be difficult to police, and if sailors foul up they are unlikely to hurt anyone but themselves, plus maybe one or two crew. In this over-regulated and risk-averse age it is rather remarkable that yachtsmen have avoided the dead hand of compulsory examinations and licensing, but they have — so far.

I have sailed since I was eight years old. My father taught me during our annual one-week family holiday on the Norfolk Broads. He spent so much on my school fees that he couldn't afford more than that brief summer holiday. I went on learning from unstructured and sometimes unwise experiences, making mistakes, sailing with more competent friends, and from reading books and yachting magazines (no YouTube tutorials then). Many sailors, perhaps most these days, take the voluntary RYA (Royal Yachting Association) exams — practical as well as theory — which may well be a useful check on competence, and act as an incentive to learn and improve. I don't think these exams existed when I was young. As a result I have no formal sailing qualifications, and never took any exams except for my VHF radio users' licence which is compulsory.

There are not even any alcohol regulations for amateur yachtsmen, although if there were I have no idea how they would be enforced. Maybe the skipper would be held responsible for any crew drunkenness. My own view is that excess alcohol is more of a problem for motorboaters who can and often do go far too fast. Rather surprisingly, lifejackets are not compulsory in the UK — although they are in Ireland for children under 16, and for anyone on a boat under seven metres in length. I don't wear mine enough, despite repeated pleas and reminders from my wife and all my children who have been known to force one into my hand. Like condoms, lifejackets are 'Useless unless worn', as the RNLI (Royal National Lifeboat Institution) slogan rightly warns us.

My old man, being the generation he was, refused to have anything to do with engines on boats. So naturally we all hurled abuse at motorboats on the Broads, usually under our breath (this probably explains my long-embedded anti-motorboat bias). When there was no wind, we quanted with a long wooden pole which we trailed in the water as we walked forwards to near the bows, stuck the pole into the riverbed mud, pushed on it as we walked back along the side-deck, and then with a deft twist of the wrist to detach it from the mud lifted it out of the water and walked forward again (sometimes the quant got so embedded in the mud that it was wrenched out of our hands as the boat moved forwards; some people made the mistake of not letting go). The Broads taught me how to tack up narrow tree-lined rivers with the advantage of forgiving reed-banks on either side to mitigate any damage — although we did once poke our bowsprit through a motorboat's window on the very narrow River Ant.

Sailing on the equally narrow and tree-lined River Lea in Hertfordshire at secondary school was another learning experience. My brother John had preceded me to Haileybury, a second-division public boarding school near Hertford that was then all-boys (motto, *sursum corda*, meaning lift up your hearts we learned). These institutions are of course far from public, they are private. My parents paid a lot for their very dubious advantages, unless you count 'fagging' (younger boys acting as unpaid servants to prefects who competed for the prettiest boys as their fags), and surviving bullying by older boys. Naturally the new boys had to light the coal fires in the common rooms, and favourite 'fun' was forcing a new boy to hold a full bucket of coal in each hand while his tormenters held red-hot pokers under his outstretched arms. Did I, in my turn, bully the new boys? I don't think so, but maybe I have suppressed an embarrassing memory.

The school's main old-boy claim to fame was not mentioned when I was there — one Clement Attlee, perhaps the most reforming prime minister of the 20th century. As a Labour PM he was presumably regarded as one short step from being a communist. It was not until 1987, 20 years after his death, that the school inaugurated the Attlee memorial lecture. There is now even an Attlee Oak, and an Attlee Room. Nor any mention of Erskine Childers who wrote one of the best-ever sailing novels, *The Riddle of the Sands*, which warned of the dangers of a German invasion across the North Sea, presumably because he was later executed as a traitor during the Irish Civil War in 1922. Of much more interest to me at the time was Cliff Richard who had been brought up in a council house in Cheshunt seven miles down the road, and was edging up the hit parade with 'Living Doll', an inspiration to us public-school rockers.

One advantage of public schools is said to be mixing with contemporaries who might one day be influential in one's career. My own friends were a varied bunch — they became an English teacher, an Oxford philosopher, a musician, a submariner, a maths teacher, and an art historian who was a notorious paedophile who jumped in front of a train after he was let out of jail (his was the first proper electric guitar and amplifier I ever clapped eyes on). The 'old school tie' didn't do anything for me, maybe because medicine is a more enlightened and progressive profession than, say, banking, law or insurance.

Brother John was particularly good at ball games, so it came as a shock to the school to find I was particularly bad at them. To escape his First Eleven shadow I opted for sailing in the summer term rather than cricket. Unfortunately in the winter there was no escape from rugby, which I hated. The Combined Cadet Force was little better, although I did learn how to assemble and reassemble a Bren gun, and, when crawling through the undergrowth by muttering under my breath 'shape, shine, shilhouette and shilence' to avoid detection. Later I escaped into the military band to play the trombone (not very well), and joined the RAF section for some real flying, and even to go solo as a glider pilot.

After school my sailing was on pause, to accommodate university, medical school, and the busy years as a very junior hospital doctor. But I was able to start chartering keel-boats in the 1970s when I lived in land-locked Oxford, with Edwin Swarbrick, a medical school friend and dinghy sailor, along with other less competent friends. In the first year Edwin and I skippered together on the forgiving Clyde. The next year, after evening classes in navigation and seamanship (but no exams), we co-skippered again but on the Scottish west coast from Loch Melfort in Argyll which is rather more challenging. After that, for several years, we each skippered Rival 34s from Ardvasar on Skye which was within range of the Hebrides, Orkney, Shetland, and St Kilda — and explore all of them we did. After that, occasional chartering in Greece, the Whitsundays and Vancouver Sound never provided such good cruising despite being warmer (verging on the far too hot in Greece). I did once sail in the Caribbean, with Cathie's Uncle John, but it was too crowded for my taste.

Rather cleverly I thought, I managed a career move in 1987 to Edinburgh which, although on the rather dull (for sailing) east coast of Scotland, is not far from the country's west coast, which I and many others regard as the best cruising area in the UK, if not the world. It has all that the cruising yachtsman could possibly desire — charmingly unpredictable weather (who wants a blue sky all day and every day?); very little fog; usually a decent wind; certainly never too hot but not all that cold in summer; the incomparable scenery of the islands, lochs and mountains; abundant wild life; hundreds of un-crowded anchorages within easy reach of each other; always somewhere nearby to shelter in a gale; and almost no over-priced commercial marinas. Furthermore, by far the best way to see the west coast is from the water, preferably under sail, and best of all in your own boat.

Despite being unlicensed to sail, and notwithstanding the occasional nudge with a rock, before my planned cruise around Britain I had never come to grief or called the coastguards for help. I have since (just the once), due to an embarrassing lack of battery amps to start the engine off Kinsale in southern Ireland. The coastguards on the VHF radio (and my mutinous crew) insisted the lifeboat towed us in, even though I was sure we could manage under sail in what little wind there was. It was most embarrassing. 'Ah, don't you worry yourself,' said our rescuer cheerfully as we approached the marina. 'No one knows you round here.' The silver lining was provided by the lifeboat mechanic who met us on the pontoon, came aboard, quickly found the very obscure and well-hidden blown fuse which had prevented my batteries charging from the engine, replaced it, and left me with a handful of spare fuses. No 'salvage' is demanded these days, but a voluntary and hefty donation to the RNLI was of course appropriate.

Only once have I had a man overboard, and that was 40 years ago. We had gybed rather gently, but unexpectedly (my excuse is that I was not on the helm). The boom knocked the man standing by the shrouds overboard along with his camera. We already had the engine running to enter an anchorage, so with a sturdy crew it was easy to get the poor wet fellow back on board, and warmed up. His camera was not so lucky.

Increasing anxiety

I kept telling myself that I was merely setting off on a connected series of day-sails, almost all within sight of land, with only occasional night-sails. And that I had sailed — without any dramas — my newly built boat from Falmouth up to Scotland in the autumn of 2010, as well as off the west coast of Scotland for a full season in 2011. And that I had already skippered or crewed along much of the British coast. But I was still anxious, nervous even, tending to wake at night worrying. This got much worse in the weeks before leaving and was exacerbated by obsessional reading of yachting magazines which, as ever, were packed full of disaster articles: picking up a man overboard (almost impossible when the sea is rough); going aground (possible disaster); failed bottlescrew (mast collapses); failed chain-plate (mast collapses); shroud snaps (mast collapses); crashing into harbour walls (embarrassing and damaging); fire on board (catastrophic); chafed mooring ropes (irritating and sometimes dangerous); propeller trapped by a poorly marked lobster pot (very tiresome, possibly requiring rescue); corroded seacocks (which then fail suddenly, and let the sea in); dragging or irreversibly stuck anchors (the first more disastrous than the second because stuck anchors can always be abandoned); deteriorated sacrificial anodes to protect more important metal fittings (propeller disintegrates); gas leaks followed by explosion (that happened to two people I know, fortunately without death or serious injury); diesel bug (stops the engine dead); osmosis (hull wrecked; very expensive to put right); collision with whales (not unheard of); life rafts and how to get into them (with great difficulty); and what to keep in your grab bag (don't forget the Kendal mint cake, baby wipes, and a waterproof notebook). I went out and bought a grab bag for the first time.

More disaster articles described medical emergencies in lurid detail. This should have concerned me less, although it had been a long time since I had to deal with any except neurological ones. There were worrying articles about fog, my worst fear, and about sandbanks, neither of which are at all commonly experienced by west coast of Scotland sailors like me. I imagine Solent sailors worry about the Scottish strong tides, unmarked rocks, the Corryvreckan 'whirlpool' between the islands of Jura and Scarba, the Pentland Firth which can definitely be sporting, and a general feeling of isolation with so few marinas to lurk in.

This anxiety was crazy. I had a chartplotter to show me exactly where I was (like a car satnav); a mobile phone with all the UK coastal waters charts on it as well as easy access to weather forecasting; a hand-held GPS (Global Positioning System) giving exact latitude and longitude; and an EPIRB (Emergency Position Indicating Radio Beacon) as well as a PLB (Personal Locator Beacon), both of which, at a touch of a button, could transmit an emergency signal and my position to the coastguards. A few years earlier I'd had none of these, and yet had survived perfectly well. Libby Purves had none of them either, and Frank Cowper could not have dreamed of them when he wrote his magisterial five-volume *Sailing Tours* in the 1890s, the first sailing directions for amateurs.[5] I would only be a mobile phone call from the NHS if anyone got seriously sick (some of us were pensioners after all). The VHF radio would keep me in touch with the coastguards,

---

5. Frank Cowper, *Sailing Tours: The Yachtsman's Guide to the Cruising Waters of the English and Adjacent Coasts*, parts 1–5 (London: Upcott Gill, 1892–6).

night and day. The RNLI lifeboats cover the entire coastline of the British Isles. Why the worry?

Nonetheless, fearing the worst, and accompanied by Cathie, I took a one-day RYA sea-survival course. After a morning in a classroom we repaired to the local swimming pool to practise jumping in using the approved method (one hand holding nose, the other across the chest), swimming in an inflated lifejacket, and then turning an inverted life raft the right way up by oneself (nearly impossible even in a flat-calm swimming pool). When did anyone cruising — not racing — off Britain with our wonderful network of coastguards, lifeboats and helicopters last have to use a life raft? It must be very unusual: probably only needed after fire, gas explosion, or being holed by a half-sunk shipping container.

I should have done that course years ago. It was extremely useful, thought-provoking too. I was astonished that the 30ish-year-old instructor could hold our attention non-stop for a whole day. During my career I had managed to give lectures for 45 minutes at most, while the medical students paid attention for about five minutes at most. How school teachers, like my eldest son Ben who teaches physics, can front up to a class of teenagers day-in day-out and keep their attention I have no idea. They are remarkable, and so very poorly paid.

And, something else I should have done years earlier, I organised a two-hour one-to-one tutorial on my own engine with the Ardfern engineer. When it comes to things mechanical, even a bicycle, I am a complete wimp, always expecting to fail. Too often I find myself left with a nut in my hand after apparently completing the job. Would I remember how to use my brand-new filter-wrench if ever I had to? Possibly.

Still I worried. I worried about the boat — and about making a fool of myself. Of course the solution was to get going because, as ever, the boat would float, and the crew would make do with what there was on board even if the corkscrew had been left behind. There should be no problem with a Rustler 36, a renowned seagoing boat with a 30-year-plus track record. Many Rustlers have been sailed not just round Britain but across every ocean on the planet. Indeed, they came first, second and third out of the 18 yachts that started in the 2018 re-creation of the 1968 single-handed non-stop Golden Globe round the world race. Long keel, comfortable in a seaway, very strongly built. And — on top of these rather essential qualities — they are beautiful to look at, inside and out.

The Rustler joinery is superb, there is a proper chart table and a good-sized galley, it is cosy down below, and absolutely practical. I had read almost every manual about all the boat's bells and whistles (of which there were far more than on Calypso). We had an electric anchor-windlass to spare the back-breaking effort of raising the anchor by hand. There were no electric winches for hauling the sails in — too expensive — but maybe they will come with my older age. For steering I had opted for a tiller rather than a wheel, which made the cockpit comfortably spacious enough for family and friends. Besides, I prefer the better feel of a boat you get from a tiller, and being able to steer 'hands-free' by holding it between my legs.

The boat was built by Rustler Yachts to their usual high standard. Indeed, in that 2012 spring there was no serious problem, just a few niggles. The batteries were not reliably charging, and I wasn't sure the expensive feathering propeller was developing enough power. However, we could do a comfortable 6 knots at 2500 rpm. I was also increasingly worried that the Ardfern yard was not going to complete the few remaining bits and pieces by the end of March, although eventually they did, more or less. I simply could not have afforded to start late — it would have thrown out the whole plan.

Naming the boat

Why did we call the boat 'Pickle'? First off, the name had to be easy to say, to hear, and to spell when talking to other boats and the coastguards on the VHF radio. This cut out a lot of Gaelic names that are so often unpronounceable, even by many Scots let alone an Englishman like me. It should surely not be a jokey name that inevitably wears thin, like 'Rogue Trader', 'Aquaholic' or 'Breaking Wind', or a pun like 'Why knot', 'Me two' or 'Miss Adventure'. Nor should it invite mishearing, like 'Kippa' (is it 'Kipper'?) or 'Starkle' ('Sparkle'?). And it surely should have some resonance for the owner — hence I suppose the large proportion of boats with girls' names, because most boats are still owned by men, and because 'boat' is traditionally a female noun in English (although that tradition is now being challenged).

Some years earlier we had acquired two kittens the day after seeing the stage musical of *Mary Poppins*. As a result the first one was called Poppin, and the other Pickle because the names alliterated rather well. Sadly, a few months later, Pickle walked off never to return, so we called our boat Pickle, partly in his memory. I also rather liked the many meanings of pickle — from 'in a pickle' (that I hoped not to be in) to 'pickled' (drunk if a human, preserved if a vegetable). Furthermore, Pickle's hull is British racing green, just like a green pickle, and chosen as an attractive colour as far removed as possible from the boring and ubiquitous white of so many production boats. (Green, however, is awful at showing the scratches collected by my more than occasional unplanned contacts with harbour walls and marina pontoons.) And the final reason — His Majesty's Schooner Pickle had been the speedy topsail schooner used for carrying dispatches between larger ships, and was the second-smallest British ship at the Battle of Trafalgar. She was chosen by Lord Collingwood to take the news of Trafalgar and Nelson's death to England[6] and was commanded by Lieutenant Lapenotiere (apparently he never used a grave accent on the second 'e', maybe because it was embarrassing then to have a French name). That famous Pickle landed at Falmouth on 4th November 1805. After a 37-hour dash by mail coach and horse to the Admiralty in London, the exhausted lieutenant blurted out, 'Sir, we have gained a great victory, but we have lost Lord Nelson.' Our own Pickle was built in Falmouth. QED, I would say.

A quirky historical aside. During the battle, HMS Pickle rescued 160 French and Spanish sailors who had escaped their sinking and burning ships, including a naked woman. Jeanette, the wife of a French sailor, had torn off her clothes before leaping off the burning Achille, and was found clinging to an oar. This event is illustrated in a large painting that, most surprisingly, hangs in a very prominent position behind the till in the men's department of Fortnum and Mason in Piccadilly.

I have often wondered if there is a systematic difference between the names given to sailing boats and to motorboats. Are the former ever called 'Get Knotted' or the latter 'Primrose'? To test this hypothesis, I thought I might present some boat names, selected at random in a marina, to some 'blinded' observers and ask them which they thought belonged to sailing boats and which to motorboats. If there was a definite difference in the direction I expected, I would surely send off an enthusiastic article to *Practical Boat Owner* for publication. But would I be so keen if there was no difference? Probably not, and probably the magazine would be less likely to publish the 'negative' article even if I did submit it. This is so-called publication bias — positive results of a study are more likely to see the light of day than negative results.

In medical research, not submitting, or not publishing, well-executed studies with negative results distorts the evidence on which doctors rely.

---

6. Peter Hore, *HMS Pickle: The Swiftest Ship in Nelson's Trafalgar Fleet* (Stroud: The History Press, 2015).

Dead-ends may be explored again and again simply because earlier papers whose results were negative were never published. Another problem is that publishing positive but not negative drug trials can benefit the scientific journal, because the drug company often buys thousands of reprints to distribute as part of their marketing strategy.

Publication bias is a huge problem, particularly as a paper reporting positive results which may be due to chance (or occasionally fraud) can lead to an over-enthusiastic press release by a university seeking kudos, splashed around by the media (sometimes even before the paper has been peer-reviewed and published), and then acted upon before anyone realises the results may not be quite as positive as once thought. This sort of hype is expected from politicians announcing funding for a new hospital that never gets built, or for some 'world-beating' test for the Covid-19 virus, but not from scientists. Sadly, even some quite eminent scientists see no point in bothering to submit negative findings to a journal, because they are 'just not interesting'. A friend of mine — a Fellow of the Royal Society no less — was astonished at my suggestion that it was not just misleading but immoral not to try to get well-conducted but negative studies published.

Final preparations

March 2012, and some of the best spring weather ever. Ideal for driving from Edinburgh to Ardfern and pottering about on the boat, making lists, making lists of lists, chasing up the workshop to finally fix the battery-charging problem which was something to do with the battery management system — whatever it was, it had to be changed. (In the good old days batteries simply charged, or not; there were no systems.) There was just one other problem. All three reefing lines that are used to reduce the mainsail's size in strong winds run from the mast to the cockpit, which is convenient. However, I had inadvertently pulled too hard on the line that takes in the first reef which then disappeared inside the boom, lost for the time being as I didn't have the time or knowledge or tools to fish it out. And I didn't want to distract the Ardfern workshop from more important issues.

When equipping Pickle in Falmouth in 2010 I had found the various online chandleries exceptionally easy to deal with, and also helpful when they didn't have something. So was John Lewis where I bought all the galley equipment, and the excellent Ardfern chandlery when I needed to top up the final bits and pieces for the cruise. By March I had mostly what I needed, even a cheap 12-volt hair-dryer that would be handy for the long-haired (and more boatie things, as I later discovered). I treated myself to some brand new waterproof tops and bottoms at huge cost, but still wonder whether they are worth the money. Might simple and robust fishermen's gear be just as good, at less than half the price? At least those expensive waterproofs should see me out, even if I keep sailing into my 80s.

I had of course to lay my hands on all the charts and Sailing Directions for UK waters. I was certainly not going to rely entirely on the electronic wizardry of my chartplotter. As luck would have it, I had many of the charts already, although some were 20-or-more-years old, and had not been kept up-to-date. However, with the 2012 Reeds Almanac I would have all the information I needed about lights, tides and the main harbours, but unlike Timothy Spall I did not keep it by the side of the bed to read before falling asleep.[7] Other charts I borrowed, and some I bought in the form of the very handy Admiralty Leisure Chart Folios. Being definitely more soluble in seawater than the much more expensive regular paper charts, they have to be kept in a clear plastic folder, and they are not good for pencilling one's position on, but who does that these days? Some Sailing Directions I already had, some I borrowed, and some I bought new. Already I had a large ring-binder full of articles about various UK harbours and anchorages, culled from yachting magazines over many years. And of course I had read as many books and articles about sailing around Britain as I could lay my hands on.

The one surprisingly difficult thing to find was a decent wall-map of the UK for Cathie to plot my progress at home and, by showing the children where their Daddy was, to teach them some geography as well. Difficult, because almost every map moves the Shetland Islands south into a box, well away from their correct position, and some even abuse the Orkney Islands in the same way. Failing to find anything on the internet, I went to the mecca of maps when passing through London, to Stanfords in Long Acre. Just one suitable map was available, and even that had to be ordered. It all seems a bit hard on our Northern Isles. I hoped to get to them, and round them too.

Finally — something else I had never done before, but should have — I laminated paper notices to stick up in prominent places around the boat: how to make a mayday call in an emergency; last-minute things to grab before abandoning ship (first-aid kit, binoculars, etc.); personal things to

---

7. Shane Spall, *The Voyages of the Princess Matilda* (rev. edn, London: Ebury Press, 2013), 72.

grab (mobile phone, spectacles, etc.); and safety rules (one hand for the boat when on deck, and below deck in rough weather, etc.). I even made a list of what I should include in the safety briefing for each new crew, regrettably another first for me. And of course there were instructions about how to pump out the heads without blockage or other catastrophes. 'Heads' is the name we sailors give to toilets on boats. Maybe it should be 'head' — because we only have one toilet. Or is an apostrophe missing — should it be 'head's', i.e. of the head (bow) of the boat, where sailors of old went to relieve themselves so their excreta could be washed away when the bow crashed into the waves? Whatever, the plural 'heads' is the convention, even though the singular 'head' would do, too.

The one thing I didn't worry about, or even consider, was keeping the crew happy. Perhaps I should have done, though I think I managed all right.

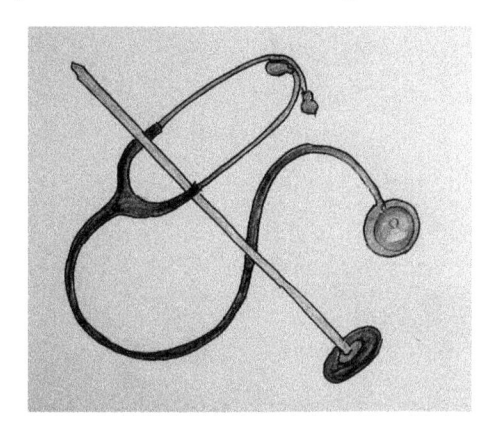

Chapter 3

Leaving behind the world of work

I retired in 2008 and stopped seeing patients, teaching and research. However, although I continued doing some other sorts of work, by early 2012 everything had been wound down. And in the spring sunshine thoughts of any kind of work at all were rapidly fading as I concentrated on the voyage ahead, carefully timed to fit in with my almost complete and final disappearance from the medical scene.

Practical Neurology

I had given up editing *Practical Neurology*, a review journal I had started 10 years earlier. Originally I wanted to call it the 'Journal of Jobbing Neurology' (the shortened 'J Job Neurol' had a nice ring to it) but the original publishers, Blackwells, regarded that as much too frivolous even though it described exactly who I was aiming at — neurologists up and down the land toiling away in outpatient clinics, not the rarefied academic neurologists in their laboratories. My second choice, *Practical Neurology*, was the title of a small but classical neurology book, written by my boss and mentor in Oxford, the late Professor Bryan Matthews.[1] Using the same title — with his blessing — was a nice way of acknowledging all his help and advice. Another idea was 'The Ladybird Book of Neurology', definitely far too frivolous. At the time, neurology journals were full of papers describing original research that were not easily understood by the jobbing neurologist,

---

1. W. B. Matthews, *Practical Neurology* (Oxford: Blackwell, 1963).

including me. We all needed easy-to-assimilate how-to-do-it review articles that digested original research and then suggested ways to incorporate the results into very ordinary (i.e. 'jobbing') clinical practice.

I never allowed *Practical Neurology* to have a so-called journal 'impact factor'. This is actually a citation-ratio — the ratio between the number of times papers from a particular journal are cited in the medical literature over a period of time (usually one year), and the total number of articles published in that journal over the same time period. Unfortunately this miserable metric is not necessarily related to any useful 'impact'. One of several unintended consequences is that a notoriously bad publication, such as the paper suggesting that the triple vaccine for mumps, measles and rubella caused autism,[2] can increase the journal's citation-ratio because people writing about bad medical science so often cite it (as I have just done). That paper certainly had a massive but very negative impact, and even now it is still used to bolster the anti-vaccine movement. On the other hand, a paper that is mentioned in a book, newspaper, or on the radio or TV, or that influences government policy, isn't counted towards its 'impact' when clearly it should be. Wikipedia claims that the 'Impact Factor is not a perfect tool to measure the quality of articles but there is nothing better and it has the advantage of already being in existence and is, therefore, a good technique for scientific evaluation.' It is strange that 'impact factor' morphs into a 'good technique' simply because 'nothing better' is available.

This dreadful citation-ratio metric is used by researchers when picking a journal to (hopefully) publish in, and eagerly anticipated by journal editors who panic when their impact factor goes down and crow loudly when it goes up. Depending on the journal in which they publish, the metric can even affect a researcher's salary and job prospects, as well as their future research funding success.

In *Practical Neurology* we wanted our articles to be read widely, not cited. Our real impact would surely be better assessed by how often the journal is seen on a neurologist's desk or how often one of its articles is used to help understand a case during a clinical demonstration. But the more important things are so often much more difficult to measure than the less important. This has repeatedly been stressed over many years, eloquently by Simon

---

2. A. J. Wakefield et al., 'Ileal-Lymphoid-Nodular Hyperplasia, Non-Specific Colitis, and Pervasive Developmental Disorder in Children', *Lancet*, 351 (1998), 637–41.

Jenkins: 'In an attempt to make the important measurable, we have instead made the measurable important.'[3]

Research ethics

In March 2012 I took the train to London for my last meeting as a member of the National Research Ethics and Advisors' Panel,[4] a role I had been pushed into by colleagues. They hoped I could help stem the tide of over-regulation stifling medical research that involved patients, so-called clinical- or practice-based research. I was and still am exasperated by an extraordinary double standard. On the one hand, I have to seek — quite rightly — a patient's consent to be randomised in a well-organised, ethics committee-approved, trial comparing a new treatment, however trivial and unthreatening, with a current standard treatment. In contrast, in routine clinical practice, patients can be treated with any new drug, surgical operation or device (like a new type of hip joint), regardless of whether there is satisfactory evidence of effectiveness; while patients must still be asked to consent to the intervention itself, they may not appreciate just how little evidence underpins it. To make matters worse, the outcome of treatment may be compared merely with the results in apparently similar previous patients, but those patients might well have been rather different in various ways, including in their outcome (i.e. prognosis). Like is not reliably being compared with like.

With the rare exception of a really big treatment effect (e.g. hip replacement), this 'non-randomised' approach generally does not provide reliable information about whether a treatment works, only anecdotes. 'The plural of anecdote is not data', quipped Henry Barnett, the Canadian neurologist. Randomly allocating patients to either the new or the standard treatment is the only way to ensure that the two groups at baseline are the same in their prognosis (i.e. what happens to them) and in all other ways, *unknown* as well as known. Then, any definite difference between the outcome of one group compared with the other *must* be due to the treatment being tested. Like is definitely being compared with like.

---

3. *Guardian*, 26 October 2018.

4. The 'National Research and Ethics Advisors' Panel' provides advice to the UK Health Research Authority and covers a wide range of human research from medical to social care. When I was a member there were eight of us. By 2020 it had ballooned to about 50 members.

Another ethical roadblock is that when bona fide researchers are searching for new knowledge (i.e. doing research) it is very difficult to obtain ethics committee approval to track patients' health to find out what happens to them by looking at their medical records without their explicit consent. The alternative of bringing patients repeatedly back to clinics for no other purpose would be over-burdensome on them and totally unaffordable by the NHS. Worse, if we are forced by well-meaning ethicists to only follow up those who consent to their records being used, we may get completely the wrong answer because those who consent are likely to be systematically different in all sorts of known and unknown ways from those who don't consent, including in their outcome.

Astonishingly, if *exactly* the same follow-up through health records is rebadged as 'audit' to evaluate the consequences or costs of patients' 'routine care', no consent at all is required. In my hospital, the patient information booklet compared research — 'if it involves you personally you will be contacted and asked for your consent' — with audit: 'we are obliged to act on refusal to participate if possible.' Opt in for the former, opt out for the latter — another outrageous double standard. In 2004 the 91-year-old Sir Richard Doll, the eminent epidemiologist who discovered the link between smoking and lung cancer, declared publicly that he 'would without doubt be willing to break the law and go to jail' if he thought his research was being compromised by time-wasting and unnecessary over-regulation.

A good example of this double standard comes from the Scottish Intracranial Vascular Malformation Study (SIVMS) set up by Rustam Salman as a research project to find out what happens over decades to the 100 or so patients diagnosed every year with an intracranial vascular malformation: a tangle of blood vessels in their brain. Changes in research regulation forced him to rebrand the project as SAIVMs, the Scottish *Audit* of Intracranial Malformations (SAIVMS). Same study, same methods, same staff, but now emphasising the audit — not the research — objectives. Legitimate search for new knowledge was, and still is, being seriously hampered by well-meaning but over-intrusive and highly bureaucratic regulation.

Extreme over-indulgence in — and misunderstanding of the principles of — data protection to preserve privacy can be extraordinarily counterproductive. In a recent example, in 2020, during a televised press conference, the Chief Nursing Officer for England declined to say how many NHS staff had died of Covid-19 'because we haven't got necessarily all of the position across England with all of the people's families giving us permission to talk about them.'[5] Yet simply providing the number had absolutely nothing to do with patient and family privacy.

I don't think my time as a National Research Ethics advisor changed anything. I just became more and more irritated and upset. I shouldn't have done it. Like Japanese knotweed, over-regulation continues to strangle the good things; getting legitimate clinical research through ethics and other regulations takes far too long, and as a result the research can be delayed not by weeks or months, but by years. Or never done at all. To the detriment of future patients. However, the trips to London for the meetings did allow me to nip down to Falmouth to check on the building of Pickle, and to catch up with friends in the south.

After my last meeting I wandered from Tottenham Court Road through Mayfair to the Naval Club to meet Nicky and Chris Brooker (definitely not sailors these friends, but Chris's father had been in the naval reserve, hence his membership of the club, now defunct). I kept wondering why in the middle of what was the worst recession for decades there seemed to be so much money around. Crowds busy shopping in Oxford Street, drinkers spilling out of pubs on to the pavement. The further west I went, the fancier the car showrooms became. The opulence in Mayfair was quite staggering, the size of the cars, the bored chauffeurs lounging in attendance. Clearly we were not 'all in this together' as the then Prime Minister David Cameron and his Chancellor George Osborne would have us believe. Maybe they and their like were fine, but tell that to the 'left-behind' people who live in places like Maryport or Hartlepool, as I would discover on the cruise. It was bad enough in the early 1980s when Paul Theroux wrote, 'There were no secret places in Britain that I had seen, there were only forgotten places, and places that were being buried or changed by our harsh century.'[6] It is surely worse now, more than 40 years after Margaret Thatcher started, or maybe just encouraged, the rot, on becoming prime minister in 1979.

I found myself looking up at the Hilton Hotel on Park Lane, one of the early high-rise buildings in London, at the top of which there was a bar with a grand view. I know because I had been a student at St George's Hospital for my clinical training in the 1960s when the medical school was still mostly at Hyde Park Corner — well-placed for a lovely morning stroll across Hyde Park from my shared and rented flat in Bayswater,

---

5. *Daily Mirror*, 10 April 2020.

6. Paul Theroux, *The Kingdom by the Sea: A Journey around the Coast of Great Britain* (orig. 1983; London: Penguin, 1984), 159.

unaffordable for students these days (I'd really wanted to live on a narrow boat in Little Venice). Since then the whole medical school has migrated to Tooting where, unlike at Hyde Park Corner, there are people who use the NHS — indeed, need the NHS. Not many in Tooting can afford to go private. As a student I visited that Hilton bar occasionally, but if it still exists it would now be far too expensive for medical students.

After three years of pre-clinical medical science at Cambridge, before the university had a proper medical school, we all had to move for our three years of clinical training. Almost everyone went to London, a few to Oxford. I opted for St George's because it was small. There were only about 50 students in my year, which was quite wonderful. We knew our teachers and they knew us. It is so very different now with hundreds of students in almost every medical school. Another reason was that an ex-girlfriend lived just round the corner near a rather cosy pub, and Belgravia was at the time an attractive part of London, not yet bought up by the mostly non-resident super-rich (mostly non-resident foreigners I am told). Indeed, with Fortnum and Mason close in one direction for tea, and Harrods in the other for the occasional shirt, it was all remarkably genteel and at that time not outrageously expensive.

On one ward we had regular coffee breaks in the tiny Sister's office looking down through the portico at the military monuments stranded in the middle of the huge roundabout. These were not just social gatherings, but a time when doctors and nurses could discuss the management of patients with us students in wide-eyed attendance. At night, we climbed up on the roof of the hospital to hurl condoms filled with water onto the pavement below. The roof also provided a short-cut between 'the cottage' (where we had rooms when we 'lived in' and were on call) and the hospital wards, via a window into the nurses' toilet (polite to tap first). Halcyon days. That fine old hospital building has now been converted into an extraordinarily expensive hotel. When I last walked past I noticed a very flashy sports car outside, with the number plate 'HOR 1D'. Says it all, really.

Healthcare Improvement Scotland

By the end of March 2012 I had also had my last meeting as neurology advisor to Healthcare Improvement Scotland,[7] a depressing business for

---

7. Health Care Improvement Scotland was set up in 2010. It attempts to do what it says on the tin, by helping health and social care services to improve, and by regulating

which I was hardly suited. Rather than sitting and listening to people prattling on about 'improvement' tools (whatever they are), it is far better to just get on with it and struggle to improve ourselves, and in my case our neurology service. This whole 'improvement' bureaucracy is expensive, made even more expensive by hiring management consultants who first have to find out what the workers already know. Then those newly informed consultants tell the managers what the workers already know but have dared not say for fear of losing their jobs. A completely unnecessary gravy-train which sucks money out of the NHS. Its only justification is that management consultants are at least independent of local rivalries and other competing interests.

Many people just do what they are told — however daft — by the next person up the food chain, too frightened to tell the truth to those above them who then haven't a clue what is going on at the coalface. The lower orders are somehow not allowed, or maybe are unable without encouragement, to express their ideas, knowledge, skills and enthusiasms. All very top-down, rather than bottom-up, which could be achieved by managers — not management consultants — asking those they manage how they would improve the service and what the barriers to improvement are.

Most doctors want to improve, but they do need to be given time to think and not be flagellated day and night to see more and more patients. It is manifestly barmy to appoint consultants to posts which require them to front up to patients for 90% of their time, leaving just 10% for administration, continuing professional development, teaching students, training younger colleagues, thinking — and improvement. That leads to burnout, early retirement and one less pair of hands to look after patients. A possible solution is a four-day working week, using the other days to get fresh air and exercise, do some DIY, and read a good book. This is what my teacher son Ben does, my mechanical engineer son Oli, and my GP daughter Margaret.

There needs to be a much more serious academic approach to health improvement. Outcomes must be robust and tested properly, preferably with randomisation, and certainly with decent sample sizes to ensure precision, and without the potential bias which so easily arises if the researcher knows which health improvement strategy has been allocated to an organisation, and happens to already favour it or, equally, hate it.

---

these services, licensing drugs for use in Scotland, and providing guidelines.

Science, scepticism, screening and incidental findings

Science is a radical business. It modifies how we think the world works, sometimes completely rejecting very entrenched ideas. Unsurprisingly, scientists are not too good at uncritically believing what they are told, at least not without good evidence. I had form on this from an early age, having constant arguments with my father about the existence of God. I was a terribly argumentative and rebellious teenager. But I really did try to believe in God. I read books about God. I started but didn't get very far reading the entire Bible. I went to chapel every day at school (compulsory). My parents dragged me to church on Sundays in the school holidays. I listened to sermons at school, and in the holidays. I subjected myself to confirmation in the Church of England. But I wasn't convinced. And I soon worked out that fear of God, along with the threat of hell with eternal fire and damnation, was a very good way of keeping the lower classes in order. The promise of the pleasures of heaven to make up for a wretched and impoverished life on earth never convinced me.

My constant questioning of my father must surely have led to my scientific and medical scepticism, encouraged later by many of my teachers. How do we know this treatment works? Who says it works? Are they believable? Has anyone paid them to promote the treatment? When should we stop it? Why are we using it? And what about doing a test — is it really such a good idea? Is it accurate? Will it change the management of the patient? How much will it cost? Can we afford it? Should we spend the money on something more useful? Is it risky in the short term (e.g. spinal nerve injury from lumbar puncture, where a hollow needle is advanced between the bones of the lower spine to collect some of the fluid surrounding the spinal nerve roots), or in the longer term (e.g. radiation risk from CT scans)? Is any risk worth the benefit? Will the test waste the patient's time? Have the doctors even got the time to consider the results of all the tests they order? What if a test reveals something that may be nothing to do with the patient's problem? How do we know if that something is irrelevant? Or serious? Over-diagnosis is a problem as well as under-diagnosis; both are potentially harmful.

Over-diagnosis is even more problematic when it comes to screening of the 'worried well'. Unfortunately, and seldom acknowledged by the screeners, screening may not be sensitive enough to reliably identify the disease being screened for (too many 'false-negatives'), while the more sensitive it is to picking up real disease the more likely there will be unnecessary alarms ('false-positives'). Telling the patient good news that although a test is abnormal it may be of no consequence is as difficult as telling bad news. There are courses for the latter, for what they are worth, but seldom for the former. And it may not be possible to treat the disease even if identified reliably, however early it is picked up — Alzheimer's disease for example. There are only five conditions that are generally agreed to be worth screening for in UK adults: cervical cancer, abdominal aortic aneurysm, bowel cancer, diabetic eye disease, and breast cancer.

What if screening, for example with imaging or now increasingly often a genetic test, reveals something we don't want to know about because nothing can be done about it, or because it is never likely to cause a problem — a so-called 'incidental finding'? Should we tell the person who is then converted into a patient? One more anxious patient, possibly for ever, perhaps with both life and travel insurance compromised. Yet another burden on the NHS as they hurry off to consult their GP who never ordered the screening in the first place, and yet has to deal with the fallout.

The combination of an anxious 'screened-positive' patient with a GP worried about complaints (or even litigation) can lead to more and more tests and treatments, some invasive. Then, perhaps, unnecessary referral to a specialist who may be equally worried, more over-treatment with drugs, and even surgery — for example, removing an asymptomatic breast lump found by screening that was never going to cause trouble despite its 'cancer' moniker. Breast cancer screening with mammography, notwithstanding its apparent attractions, remains controversial because the undoubted benefits may not exceed the undoubted harms.

I don't like acronyms that mostly serve as a kind of secret language for a brotherhood of cognoscenti, but I do like 'VOMIT' (for 'Victims of Modern Imaging Technology') to describe over-tested and over-diagnosed people. Some may even die as a result of unwise treatment of their incidental finding, many will be inconvenienced. Moreover, there is a cost to the health service in terms of more and more tests, and unnecessary treatment. The opportunity cost rankles — more important things don't get funded. Occasionally an incidental finding can be both serious and successfully treated, but not very often. The trouble is that these 'triumphs' are the ones reported in the media under the banner headline 'Medical MOT saved my life!!'.

Many people have no idea of the risks of screening because they are seldom told about them. Any advantages can be exaggerated by guidelines written by professionals with a competing, if not conflicting, interest —

not just doctors, but nurses, dieticians and pharmacists — individually, or through their professional bodies. Screening may be urged on by patient groups that themselves receive industry funding, and by glossy brochures pumped out by the proliferation of commercial screening organisations that charge handsomely for their mostly unnecessary tests. Sorting out these screening controversies will not be at all easy. For a start, 'experts' with any competing interest should be excluded from guideline panels, and not invited to write review articles in medical journals (although they will still be sought out by the general media without anyone even considering a competing interest). Unfortunately, 'clean' experts are hard to find because so many have consultancies with industry and/or have accepted lavish hospitality, but we must try. Competing interests are not just financial. Some guideline writers over-emphasise their own publications or own institutions at the expense of others, and there can be interpersonal rivalries that no one is necessarily aware of.

Screening has three other unintended but foreseeable consequences. Firstly, early cases of a disease brought to light by screening before symptoms arise will live longer — so-called lead-time bias. Clearly we cannot know the screened patient's prognosis because years need to go by to find out. All we know is that it will be better than patients diagnosed *after* symptom onset. The second consequence is that diseases will appear to become more common because pre-symptomatic cases are now detected, as well as symptomatic ones. Finally, while effective treatment can be started earlier (which can be a good thing), many early cases of a disease don't need treating at all because they will never be symptomatic, or because the patient dies of something else first.

Another problem. Treating asymptomatic *people* with something only hitherto tested on symptomatic *patients* may tip the balance away from benefit to harm, due to the complications of the treatment and longer-term side effects in someone who is likely to do well anyway. Nowhere is this more obvious than for prostate cancer when the widely used PSA (prostate specific antigen) blood test picks up small 'cancers' that are never going be a problem. And yet hundreds if not thousands of men have had their prostates removed and been rendered incontinent of urine, impotent, or both … for ever. No wonder patients survive longer in the USA, where PSA screening and subsequent over-diagnosis and unnecessary treatment are so common, than in the UK. But the *number* of patients who die every year from prostate cancer is the same. The intuitively attractive old aphorism 'prevention is better than cure' is not always true.

Unfortunately, scepticism confuses medical students who want certainty painted in black and white (as I did), and yet scepticism is the sine qua non of scientific and medical progress. This is why I used to bang on about it during our weekly departmental journal club when young and old discussed papers from the medical literature (accompanied by food — Bryan Matthews told me that he had never known a successful journal club that didn't also lay on food, but not of course funded by a drug company). Don't believe anything until you check. Were the methods OK? Was the data analysis sensible? Were the conclusions justified by the results? Do we know anything about the authors, which is tricky these days when a paper can be 'authored' by more than 100 people jockeying for position to be either first on the list (regarded as the one who did the work) or last (the leader of the project or lab, probably) and so improve their promotion and grant-getting possibilities? Did anyone pay the authors to say nice things about a treatment or a test, might the whole thing be hyped-up to impress, was there even fraud? What about any competing interest? It is very difficult to tell when the list of all possible interests at the end of a paper can be so extraordinarily long, but without any quantification — presumably a free ham sandwich would have less effect than an all-expenses-paid one-week 'conference' (aka holiday) in Lanzarote.

There is nothing new about the advantages of scepticism. Francis Bacon got it right 400 years ago: 'If a man will begin with certainties, he shall end in doubts; but if he will be content to begin with doubts, he shall end in certainties.'[8]

The Association of British Neurologists

I had also been very involved with the Association of British Neurologists (ABN) to which all but a few UK neurologists belong. We neurologists deal with migraine, epilepsy, strokes, multiple sclerosis, Parkinson's disease, dementia, muscle disorders, brain tumours, and a host of rarities, along with people who have neurological symptoms but no identifiable disease (so-called functional neurological disorders). Of course we overlap with other specialities — for example, geriatricians see as many or more strokes than we do; like us, psychiatrists claim the brain as their organ. Sadly, and I believe quite inappropriately, UK neurologists have been over-eager to deflect elderly patients with more or less any neurological problem to the

---

8. Francis Bacon, *The Advancement of Learning*, book I, v, 8 (1605).

geriatricians; rehabilitation of neurological patients to rehabilitationists; and anything which may disturb their sleep or weekends to the acute physicians. This is an unfortunate hangover from the days when there were so few neurologists that we simply had to limit our workload. And when we regarded ourselves as rather an elite speciality.

Neurologists are often confused with neurosurgeons, particularly by the media. But we neurologists do not operate — we are far too cautious and some would say far too uncertain and intellectual. People think we know how the brain works but I for one don't. Basic neuroscientists in their laboratories seem more confident, although their theories seldom survive tomorrow's even more confident neuroscientists' assertions. I am much more interested in the rather more tractable problem of what stops the brain working — like a stroke, and usually 'at a stroke'.

In the UK, the speciality of neurology emerged from general internal medicine in the early 20th century, usually based in large, mostly teaching hospitals and alongside the neurosurgeons. However, patients often had to travel long distances to see us, maybe for no more than a ten-minute follow-up appointment. From the 1950s, with increasing consultant numbers, the more enlightened neurologists started outpatient clinics in District General Hospitals (DGHs) surrounding their centre, seeing patients referred by local GPs and helping with neurological problems on the wards.

However, this 'hub and spoke' model still left DGHs without a neurologist based in the hospital, available 24/7 to look after neurology patients. As a result, sub-centres with their own neurologists — but still well-connected with the neurology/neurosurgery centre — gradually evolved in places like Reading, and then almost everywhere. Liverpool and Glasgow were exceptions: their increasing number of neurologists remained cloistered in the centre with just day-trips to the surrounding DGHs. (Perhaps they were too daunted by the real world in Bootle and Airdrie, or of somehow being 'downgraded' to mere DGH rather than superior teaching hospital consultants.) This model runs counter to the principle that, if reasonable clinically, patients are best looked after as close to where they live as possible. At the same time, services requiring a lot of expensive and complicated kit, and where various specialists need to interact with each other, have to be centralised and inevitably at some distance from where many patients live.

It is simply unaffordable to provide absolutely everything for modern healthcare on every patient's doorstep, however much local people and local politicians want it. There wouldn't be enough doctors and other medical staff. In Lanarkshire, with a population of less than 700,000, there are three DGHs, not very far apart, each with A&E and an intensive care unit. This is surely crazy, but the politicians keep them all open when one major hospital would do, and be more cost-effective. As long as services that don't require patients to travel far can be provided locally, most people will accept the necessity of getting to a distant centre for more complicated and specialised treatment. With proper care, planning and public information and involvement, there does not have to be a huge political storm to achieve this. When the DGHs in Falkirk and Stirling were closed in 2010 and replaced with a new hospital in between them, there was no fuss, and no headlines in the national press.

Unfortunately the Thatcherite craze for competition between hospitals to improve efficiency — a very debatable outcome — has meant that some very sensible mergers were blocked, for example between the hospitals in Poole and in very nearby Bournemouth. In the 1990s when Edinburgh was considering future hospital provision, the one option we were not allowed to discuss was a single hospital to house all the inter-related specialities. This was not because of the distance some patients might have to travel, but to encourage competition between the three existing main hospitals. Such was the madness of the Thatcherite model, which still lingers. Competition between healthcare providers does not sit comfortably with our medical tradition of collaboration, and I am not convinced it is more cost-effective.

Outsourcing from the NHS to private companies in competition with the NHS is another horror. In 2019 a profit-motivated private company was awarded the contract for PET-scanning cancer cases in Oxford (PET — positron emission tomography — scanning is a method of imaging with radioactive isotopes, particularly suited to tracking down primary and secondary cancer). Patients would no longer have their scans in the Churchill Hospital but go by ambulance to a distant scanner. Face-to-face discussion between clinicians and radiologists would certainly be compromised, and so would the training of radiologists. Quality was being ditched in favour of cost-cutting which may have turned out to be more apparent than real. After huge protests the decision was reversed, more time having been wasted pursuing flawed Tory dogma.[9]

To get even closer to where patients live, and taking the lead from Chris Allen in Cambridge, some hospital-based neurologists now do clinics in GP surgeries. There are a lot of advantages: generally no car-parking problem for either patient or neurologist (in 2019 it took patients an hour just to get

---

9. *Guardian*, 27 March 2019.

into the John Radcliffe Hospital car park in Oxford); no getting lost along miles of hospital corridors; no queuing in clinics; and patients are more relaxed on home territory. Fortunately, unlike many other specialists, in outpatient departments we neurologists seldom need help from nurses, or a lot of gear — just a bag containing a tendon hammer, ophthalmoscope, pins, a tuning fork, and a sandwich for lunch. Not many neurology outpatient referrals need to travel to a distant centre (for example for a brain scan or other complicated investigation); most can be sorted out by a competent neurologist near where the patients live.

Of course, this distributed approach does require the neurologist to get off his or her bum and travel, rather than compel patients to make their way to a distant clinic. My colleagues thought it very strange when I started a regular outpatient clinic on the edge of Edinburgh. If patients from that area were to see me in hospital, they might have to travel for maybe an hour there and another hour back. For me to travel to see them, however, all I had to do was read a newspaper on a bus for half an hour before sitting down in a well-appointed GP surgery. The hospital managers thought it was an excellent idea until they started worrying about my travel costs, my salary being already paid by the university. They were so delighted to hear I had a free bus pass, being over 60 at the time. It was sad, and rather typical, that they were energetically counting the pennies while looking a gift horse in the mouth, to mix a couple of metaphors.

The Department for Transport

Chairing the Medical Advisory Neurology Panel to the Department for Transport had been interesting. Twice a year we brooded on which categories of patients should be stopped driving, and for how long, on account of any residual effects of a relatively static neurological condition, like after stroke or head injury (as we did for patients with progressively disabling conditions such as motor neurone disease and Parkinson's disease). Another panel dealt with the elephant in the room — dementia. Essentially we tweaked the well-documented and long-standing regulations in the light of increasing knowledge. It was of course impossible to consider each individual driver. Clearly everyone cannot be tested on the road, and in any case how and what to test, under what weather and road conditions, in daylight or darkness, is controversial. We had to make general rules, and allow individuals to appeal if they felt hard done by.

More difficult was dealing with the risk that a sudden and brief 'attack', especially an epileptic fit, might cause a driver to lose control. Over the years the rules have been relaxed, in part because they were far too draconian, in part because the rights of individual autonomy began to overtake those of society, and in part because we have got better at estimating and understanding risk. We had a rather arbitrary benchmark: to put a car driver off the road, more than 20% risk that an 'attack' might cause a crash at some point in the next year; for a heavy goods vehicle or bus driver, more than 5%.

As for what to do about elderly but otherwise healthy drivers — that was firmly in the too-difficult box, and still is. Calls to test everyone on the road who is over the age of 75 are totally unrealistic, and would be a logistical nightmare. And how often to test? Every year, every five years? Fortunately, the elderly don't tend to drive far, they often avoid driving in the dark, and they don't drive fast. Moreover, they are less likely to be involved in a serious accident than young males, and no one is testing *them*. Leave us ancients alone to dwindle gracefully, I say.

The number of fatalities and seriously injured on our roads has been steadily declining in the UK. Although it is surprisingly difficult to be sure, very few seem directly caused by a medical condition. So we are probably getting the regulations about right, although they could still be too harsh. In our attempts to minimise risk we may be denying too many people the right to drive. Maybe driverless vehicles will solve the problem, as cleverly adapted vehicles already have for many of the physically disabled.

The Lancet

The *Lancet* is the premier British medical journal of international repute. But not of high enough repute for many UK medical scientists who fancy themselves and want to impress their universities by submitting their papers to the *New England Journal of Medicine*, which has a higher citation-ratio (aka impact factor), that horrible metric already discussed. Personally, I think it is treasonous for British scientists to send a paper to the American premier medical journal unless it has been rejected by the British premier journal.

For some years I had been Ombudsman to the *Lancet*. In fact there had not been much to do because the role was definitely not to calm aggrieved authors whose submitted papers had been turned down (we have all been there), but to try and resolve the occasional dispute about the editorial process between authors, readers and the journal. For example, if anything was published which was perceived as pro-Palestinian I was immediately inundated with more than a hundred complaining emails using essentially the same words, as well as the same arguments. A paper supporting natural birth rather than Caesarean section for non-medical reasons also caused a fuss, which may still rumble on. And almost anything to do with chronic fatigue/myalgic encephalomyelitis was guaranteed to cause complaints.

The *Lancet* is of some emotional significance to me because it published my very first scientific paper, during my second junior hospital doctor job at the now flattened Birmingham Accident Hospital, well known in its day (there I saw that internationally recognised trauma care can be provided even in a decrepit building). This was again luck. I had failed to get a job in Cambridge with Roy Calne, one of the first transplant surgeons, where I would probably have been worked totally off my feet. In Birmingham, on the other hand, I found myself off-duty every other afternoon, which was most unusual in those days, so I learnt to glide (for the second time) over the Warwickshire countryside, a skill that sadly I have not kept up.

As an aspiring physician in essentially a surgical hospital, I naturally became interested in the myriad of non-surgical complications that can occur after trauma, particularly when I found myself treating epileptic attacks in young children with relatively minor burns. The surgeons didn't seem to know why they occurred, and I wasn't content with the nurses' view of 'oh, we see these things all the time', especially as some of the children died with cerebral oedema (swollen brain). I'm not sure we know now, or whether like many conditions the problem has disappeared, but I went for advice to Pam Hinton, the medical registrar and only physician in the hospital. When more cases emerged, Pam and I wrote them up,[10] and I was rather proud of writing what must surely be a general truth in medicine, that this complication of burns was 'not a rare condition which is commonly fatal, but a relatively common condition which is rarely fatal'. Almost all 'new' illnesses seem to take this course — for example, AIDS was initially regarded as quite rare and always fatal, but we now know that the infection is much more common as well as controllable. I am quite sure we were not the first to think of this truism. We should all know perfectly well that as we get better at diagnosing a particular disease over time we will detect milder cases — so the disease will inevitably appear to become more common, and less serious. One can but hope that this will happen during the Covid-19 pandemic.

---

10. C. P. Warlow and P. Hinton, 'Early Neurological Disturbances following Relatively Minor Burns in Children', *Lancet*, 2 (1969), 978–82.

Apparently the Birmingham 'Accy' had been a hotbed of communist doctors during the second world war and it still retained a very left-wing tradition. None of the surgeons did any private practice, not even the plastic surgeons. What's more, the consultant on call was around in the evenings and weekends, seeing patients and teaching us (unheard of in London). Like John Hicks who built an ingenious little model of the ankle joint to show us junior doctors where and how fractures occurred, and how to put them to rights.

A few years earlier, as a medical student doing an elective at the 'Accy', I went out with the ambulance drivers to see what they did. A call came in from New Street Station; a young woman had collapsed off the London train. Diagnosis? The ambulance drivers knew before we got there: she was probably back from an illegal, possibly back-street abortion (this was before David Steel's abortion act of 1967). Correct. Another example: as we were speeding along one side of the inner ring road the driver spotted the casualty lying on the other side. 'Fractured femur,' he said. Right again.

Ever since my six months in Birmingham I have realised that every career setback has a silver lining, if you look for it. For example, in 1987, I didn't get the chair of neurology in Oxford when Bryan Matthews retired (chairs then seldom went to insiders like me). In a slight huff, and avoiding the common academic fate of getting trapped in Oxford to grow fat on free college dinners, I left for the first chair of neurology in Edinburgh which is a much more interesting and attractive place to live, with a better quality of life too. Less traffic, and further away from Margaret Thatcher. And so very much closer to the Scottish west coast for sailing. Friends from Oxford used to phone to inquire solicitously whether I was enjoying Edinburgh. 'Yes, very much,' I replied. 'More than Oxford?' 'Yes, of course.' Silence from the south.

A common southern misconception is that we all fly from Edinburgh to meetings in London. Nonsense, of course; there is a very comfortable train which passes wonderful scenery north of York, and only takes four and a bit hours to deliver you to the centre of London, about as quickly as flying and far more pleasant, and kinder on the environment. On the early train there is plenty of time to read the papers for a meeting later in the morning, and catch up with the emails. No endless queues for security, no herding through over-heated and deeply unpleasant retail areas, no sitting hunched up in an uncomfortable aeroplane seat, and then ending up at Heathrow from where you still have to toil in to central London. Now, during the Covid-19 pandemic and the rise of internet-enabled 'face-to-face' meetings on a laptop in the comfort of one's own home (or boat), almost no one has to catch a train, let alone a plane, to attend a meeting. Hopefully, this will to some extent continue, again to the advantage of the environment, and to family life.

Good to go

By the end of March 2012 I was as well prepared for the cruise as I could be, or would ever be, and completely disconnected from work. But I did suffer from some wistful nostalgia. I was no longer part of a professional team doing a useful job, in the thick of it, helping patients, interacting with the younger generation of doctors, teaching medical students, working with colleagues all over the world, and taking responsibility. But I didn't have much nostalgia for research that had become so difficult because of over-regulation, endlessly competing for grants, keeping up with the burgeoning medical literature, and feeling obliged to attend tedious conferences in distant parts of the world. Besides, I had increasingly realised that most research is of very low quality, and I was getting bored with it.

Handing over a department has its emotional problems. If the new head runs it better than you did you may feel diminished, and if worse you may feel disappointed. Naturally I am critical of my successors in some ways, but they have had to adapt to a very different world. Sadly, the world of consultants in the NHS (primarily looking after patients, not expected to do research, and being a bit grumpy about teaching) is drifting away from the world of clinical academic doctors in university medical schools (lots of research, and as little teaching and looking after patients as they can get away with).

As head, I was left to do what I thought best, but nowadays universities harass their senior staff with targets which require metrics (them again), performance-related pay, spreadsheets and line-managers, all unwisely taking their management model from business. Bonuses even. It should not be a surprise — although it was to me — that most UK universities, including Edinburgh, are members of the Confederation of British Industry (CBI). Everything in universities is now all much more top-down than bottom-up; they have become businesses rather than seats of scholarship and learning. To add to the business 'gloss', leaders of big research teams are now often badged as Chief Executive Officers, CEOs if you please. Depressing. And even more depressing is the widespread gobbledegook picked up from business practice like, from Deloitte, working 'on an agile basis' with 'dedicated layer leads from NHS T&T … defining the customer segments and support articulating volumes; articulating an improved and simplified customer journey … a channel approach … compiling an as-is organisational baseline + "factpack"'.[11] And so on, and on. All bollocks.

Never mind — all this was nothing to do with me anymore. I really was leaving behind the world of work. What I was setting off to do would involve some responsibility, the crew would be a team that needed building and nurturing, and sometimes teaching. But I was hardly contributing to society anymore. To my 40-year ingrained work ethic, this all seemed deeply irresponsible. I had to get over it. And enjoy myself.

---

11. *Private Eye*, 1556 (Sept. 2021), 10.

Chapter 4

From Ardfern to Maryport in Cumbria, via Northern Ireland

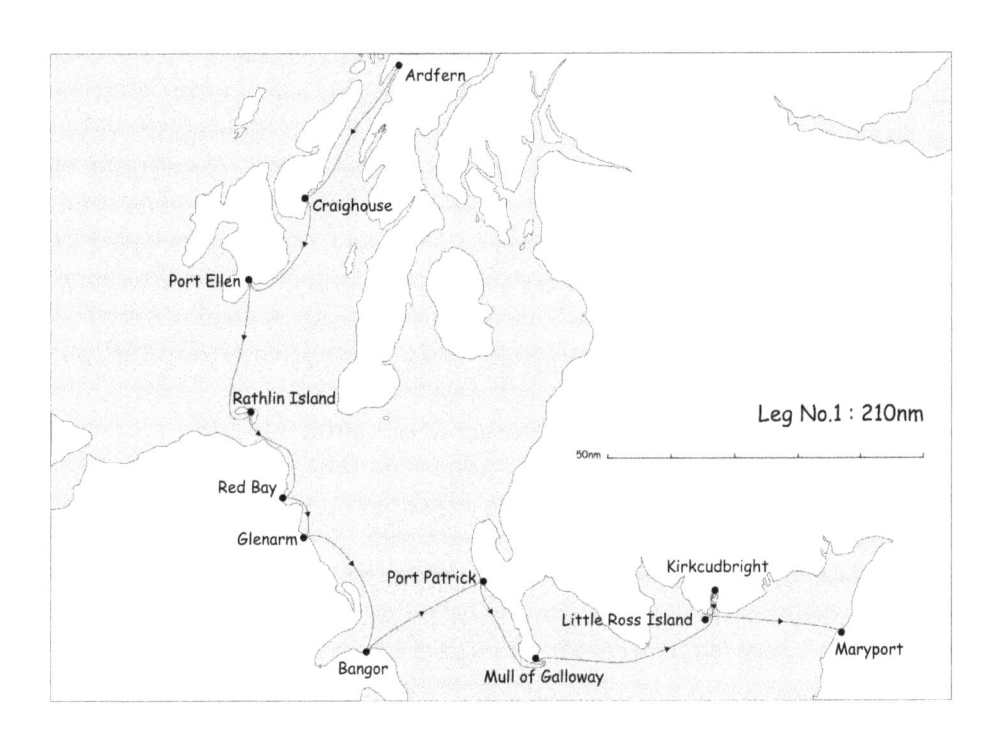

Waverley station, Edinburgh, Saturday March 31st, 11am train to Glasgow Queen Street. Change for Oban by one of the most attractive railway journeys in the UK. Skirting the north shore of the Clyde, past Gareloch which hosts our unpleasant nuclear-armed submarines, above Loch Long with views of the curiously shaped summit of the Cobbler, across to Loch Lomond, a pause at Crianlarich, and then onwards skirting Loch Awe by

Kilchurn Castle to Loch Etive, and finally the sea — the west coast. The family were reasonably well behaved, and not half as nervous as I was. Cathie was in her familiar role combining mothering with checking emails on her phone (thankfully she had left her laptop at home). Lucy looked as engaging as ever; at the time she was drawing a lot, an early hint of more serious art at high school. While William energetically tried to escape whatever restraint we could dream up, he was at the stage of learning letters and counting up to 100. His maths talents had appeared early when he tried to work out what relation he was to Ilona, my first wife. After giving the problem some thought, he declared decisively… 'She is my quarter mother.'

Then, shock horror, halfway to Oban, I realised I had forgotten my camera. But within minutes I had it sorted. Although one of my future crew, Steve Druitt, would not be travelling from Edinburgh to Craighouse on Jura anytime soon to see his daughter who lived there (our planned first stop), he phoned her and she volunteered to lend me her camera until I could get hold of mine. Meanwhile Bridget Drasan, who was to join us in Belfast, was organised via Cathie's parents in Edinburgh to pick up my camera from our house. What would we have done before mobile phones? This was to be a recurring question during the cruise, and not just about phones but about all the other electronic wizardry that our sailing forebears had never even dreamed of when they sailed around Britain in the 19th and 20th centuries.

The west coast was looking spectacular in the spring sunshine. This made up for shopping in the hot, overcrowded and visually confusing Tesco supermarket in Oban, although convenient for provisioning the boat. At least I had done most of the shopping the week before in the Co-op supermarket next door. Then off we went by taxi to Ardfern and on to Pickle looking clean, tidy and ready to go after all my anxiety-driven efforts in March.

We were all very familiar with the Ardfern Yacht Centre after so many years of wintering there. It was a delight to be on Pickle again, among the knobbly and exquisite scenery of Argyll, close to the handy chandlery, the Crafty Kitchen for delicious homemade lunches (sadly no longer there, and replaced by 'Lucy's'), and the Galley of Lorne for a satisfactory pint and pub supper. In the summer we are not at Ardfern because Dunstaffnage is 45 minutes closer to Edinburgh by car, we can also get there easily by train or bus, we had a mooring in the bay, and the lack of tidal restrictions means quick and easy access to the open sea with a huge number of weekend cruising options. Turn right for Lismore, left for Luing and the other 'slate islands', or straight ahead for the Sound of Mull and the delights of Tobermory.

To Craighouse on the Island of Jura

I am not one for a complicated and written passage-plan, at least not for most coastal day-sails. It was quite simply in my head that 'tomorrow we will leave, sail to Craighouse on Jura, have dinner in the hotel, then onwards to the south, and keep turning left'. So off we went on Sunday April 1st in a convenient and modest northwest wind, bowling along at up to 7 knots over the ground, to arrive at Craighouse — the 'capital' of Jura, population of humans about 200, of deer about 6000 — in just four hours for the 25 miles. But sadly not in sunshine, and it was chilly enough for gloves.

Interestingly, I developed my familiar but infrequent migrainous headache, presumably due to the anticipation and stress of the situation, and responsibility for my small but growing second family, no easier than when I had been responsible for my first family (perhaps because I was a couple of decades older). Neurologists are said to be more prone to migraine than others but this is almost certainly because we are likely to recognise the symptoms for what they are — the recurrent headaches and often nausea, with or without preceding flashing lights in the corner of one's eyes for a few minutes. If the episodes (hardly meriting the sobriquet of attacks) are infrequent with little or any headache, and start in middle to old age, most people don't even think migraine. But we neurologists do.

It is not essential, but it is definitely best to sail with rather than against the tide down the Sound of Jura, looking out as you go for Barnhill, the isolated house on Jura where the ailing and tuberculous George Orwell wrote *Nineteen Eighty-Four*, his final book (streptomycin might have cured him if he had been able to tolerate the side effects; he stopped taking it and donated the rest of his supply to two other patients who were cured). As we were very early in the season we saw only four other sailing boats, and there was no one on the 16 Craighouse moorings as we approached under engine. Indeed, the moorings were still without their pick-up buoys. This caused some consternation on the foredeck, and shouting from me on the helm, as we were not prepared with our own ropes.

I knew the anchorage backwards from having competed in about 20 of the annual Scottish Islands Peaks Races with Richard Roberts, along with various fell runners and sailors. It starts in Oban, with Craighouse the second of three stops, the others being at Salen on Mull, and Lamlash on Arran. These may be stops for the three sailors, but not for the pair of runners in the team of five who essentially have to run three mountain marathons in about 48 hours — Ben More on Mull (22 miles and about

3000ft of climbing), three of the Paps of Jura (a mere 14 miles but about 5000ft of climbing with no discernible tracks and a lot of horrible scree), and Goatfell on Arran (18 miles and again about 3000ft of climbing, but along an easy-to-follow tourist path). Finally, there is a short 15-mile sail to the finish in Troon. The runners, who like to add what they call 'the boat race' to their CVs, are often serious amateur athletes, training every day, competing all round Scotland and northern England, in a sport that is little recognised.

In comparison to the running, the sailing is relatively easy, about 150 miles in total from Oban to Troon. However, if there is no wind one has the tedious option of rowing which we have done for hours at a time, with long sweeps of the sort used by rowing eights, pivoted on the stanchions. We could manage a steady one-knot in the Contessa 32, two for a quick burst. Once we even rowed through the Corryvreckan (which is not really a whirlpool but it does get extremely rough when the flood tide meets a big Atlantic swell). Of course we were rowing with the tide in a flat calm, in sunshine — definitely no heroics.

Another reason for knowing Jura so well was that the only hotel on the island had been run since 2010 by Steve Druitt's daughter Catherine and her husband Andy. In their early 30s, they were just the right age for the full-on, full-time task of re-energising the hotel. To help, Andy's brother was a builder so quite quickly the grey hotel was painted a more welcoming white to match the distillery behind it. Then they refurbished the bedrooms, upgraded the shower facilities for campers, and built a home for themselves on the back. All most energetic and impressive.

The hotel has the island's only bar, where a rather interesting old painting of a group of local people hangs. They have all been identified, except one — the mermaid with long dark hair sitting on a barstool. She certainly looks quite like Christine Keeler and it could well be her because it was apparently to his estate on Jura that she was taken by Lord Astor to avoid the outcry and scandal during the Profumo affair in 1963.

The bar didn't, and still doesn't, have what I would call proper beer pulled out of a barrel, the real ale of the sort I had first illicitly drunk as a schoolboy at Haileybury, out on my bike with my mates around the Hertfordshire countryside. (McMullen's it was, brewed up the road in Hertford.) Unfortunately, on Jura not enough people drink real ale before the barrel goes off and the beer becomes undrinkable, suitable only for slug traps.

In 2012 Jura had two problems. Like most of the Highlands and Islands, the large estates on the island are owned by very rich people who usually don't live on them, indeed may scarcely visit. Many owners are not even British. Jura is no exception. On only one of the seven estates are the owners in residence all year round, and it shows. The Fletchers from the Ardlussa Estate started the monthly Jura Jottings, and with three local women now distil Lussa gin with considerable success. In contrast, the Ardfin estate was bought in 2010 by an Australian hedge fund manager. He has hardly ever been there. It is rumoured that he had to downsize his executive jet so he could land at the nearest airport, on the adjacent island of Islay. On buying the estate he immediately closed the wonderful Jura Gardens to the public, claiming health and safety issues that he would resolve. He hasn't. The gardens are still closed. They had been open to the public for years and were an important tourist draw to an island with a very marginal economy. He then built his own personal 18-hole golf course, but is now commercialising it for high-end clients (£20,000 for Jura House and the golf for one night). In 2022 he bought the hotel.

I have no idea whether rich incoming estate owners who treat the land as their personal leisure parks have any idea of what damage they do to the local communities, or what good they could bring if they put their minds and money to bear. Their sometimes acquisitive and selfish behaviour is an apt metaphor for the rise of individualism and the decline of communitarianism — accompanied by tolerance of the extraordinarily wealthy who avoid paying their full taxes — that was ushered in by Prime Minister Margaret Thatcher in the 1980s. And, to their eternal shame, this philosophy, if not encouraged, was at least tolerated by the Labour Party when it returned to power in 1997, and then accelerated again under the Tory government in coalition with the Liberal Democrats from 2010. Unfortunately, the SNP does not seem to have the stomach to do much about land ownership in Scotland, despite having been the governing party since 2007. They may talk left, but they don't walk very far on the left. Maybe the 'coalition' with the Scottish Greens after the 2021 Scottish election will provide a stimulus to do better.

The second problem on Jura was the loss of their GP, forced off the island by a stupid and vindictive resident complaining to the Health Board that it was dangerous to leave dispensed prescriptions out in the open for patients to collect. Drugs might be stolen and used inappropriately, he claimed. The pathetic Health Board took the inevitable risk-averse option and agreed, even though this practice had been going on for years without any problem. I remember doing exactly the same when I was a GP locum in Tongue on the north coast of Scotland in the 1970s.

Finding and retaining GPs in the Highlands and Islands, with small populations and difficult access to schools, particularly high schools, is very problematic. Jura was left without a GP for months. Nor is rural practice an easy job, particularly on small islands. Without the backup of a hospital down the road you have to be able to turn your hand to much more than an urban GP does. And you shouldn't summon the lifeboat or even a helicopter to take a patient to hospital without very good reason.

Distance and accessibility are such important medical considerations. When I was in Tongue I was called to a 'sudden death'. A middle-aged servant to a shooting party from England was found dead in bed in a pool of vomit. The procurator fiscal (coroner in England) to whom I reported the death by telephone told me in very short order that it was unrealistic to ask for a postmortem to establish the cause of death: 'That would mean transporting the body 90 miles to Inverness, partly along single-track roads,' he said. As a young doctor trained to complete death certificates accurately, I was shocked. But, feebly acquiescing, I signed the servant out as a heart attack, the most common cause of sudden death, but by no means the only one. No wonder heart attacks appear so common, according to death certificate data. At least I turned the man over to make sure there wasn't a knife sticking out of his back, but I couldn't check if he had been poisoned. Against the odds, given that the practice population was only a few hundred, there was another sudden death the next week. By then I knew exactly what to do, but that time it almost certainly was a heart attack. An elderly shepherd was seen to fall down dead while loading sheep onto a truck.

As well as how-not-to-fill-in death certificates accurately, I learned from the incumbent Tongue GP, before he went on his holidays, about two common problems that I had never seen. What to do about midge bites? Not many midges near my medical school at Hyde Park Corner. Answer: antihistamine cream, which he kept in a very large tub from where smaller tubs could be topped-up. And what about a fish-hook snagged in the face? No salmon in the Serpentine, I believe. Answer: cut through the shank of the hook with pliers and then ease out each half separately. In two weeks I had to deal with both problems.

Jura had made do with a succession of GP locums for several months while the post was advertised in the medical and national press, but to no avail. Eventually, the islanders took matters into their own hands and shared the problem on Facebook. This attracted the attention of national journalists who always like quirky stories about small remote Scottish communities hanging on by the skin of their teeth, probably imagining the natives huddling in front of peat fires and surviving on potatoes and porridge. What these journalists often don't realise, particularly if they work in London, is that many of the people of these communities are highly educated and well in touch with the world, as they were before the internet made them even more in touch. Happily, the media coverage did the trick. Several doctors applied, and a husband and wife team from the Midlands was appointed.

Rather to my surprise, Catherine Druitt said she had no trouble with GP locums, as long as they stayed a year or so. After all, she said, 'I almost never saw the same GP twice when I was living in Edinburgh.' What an indictment of general practice. As a patient, I have really valued seeing the same doctor, someone to whom I didn't have to give my medical history on each visit. It's called continuity of care, and it works. Ironically in the last 30 years, while many more NHS consultants and specialist nurses have been appointed, but hardly any more GPs, it has become easier to provide continuity of care in hospital just at the time that so many GPs have abandoned it, even though they recognise its value. Perhaps this is for lack of staff or the practice getting too big, perhaps due to part-time working, or centrally imposed excessive bureaucracy.

I myself have had far longer continuity of care from the garage that services my car (16 years) than from any GP. And from the barber who cuts my hair (27 years), the dentist who looks after my teeth (8 years), the boatyard that looks after my boat (20 years), my window cleaner (18 years), my solicitor (22 years) and my accountant (17 years). Like any change, discontinuity is unsettling, even a quite small change like the editor of *Practical Boat Owner* changing (and more importantly his really helpful secretary changing, she who was so good at looking after my occasional offerings). Continuity of care from a good doctor leads to a more satisfied patient who is then more likely to accept medical advice and less likely to be admitted to hospital; it may even lead to lower mortality too. But choosing the good doctor is a problem. There is no *Which?* guide, no Tripadvisor. Relying on metrics recording patient satisfaction is a waste of time. After all, Harold Shipman satisfied his patients, until he plied them with a little too much morphine.

I was shocked on arriving in Edinburgh in 1987 to find that patients with chronic and lifelong conditions, such as epilepsy, had been seen for follow-up by a different junior doctor every six months, often for years, without any recorded consultant involvement. At the time this was not unusual in the NHS, which is one argument used in favour of private practice where patients do see the same consultant. 'Private' is such a charmingly British misuse of words, like 'public' schools, a tendency well known to Humpty Dumpty: 'When I use a word ... it means just what I choose it to mean — neither more nor less.'[1] Commercial practice is the appropriate term, not private. Money changes hands — sometimes a lot of money on a fee-for-item-of-service basis that is guaranteed to lead to too many 'items' being clocked up, often unnecessarily. Another shock in Edinburgh was to find patients being told by the outpatient nurse to undress and don a white gown before seeing me. This was in 1987, not 1887. This demeaning and unnecessary ritual was stopped at once.

Counter-intuitively, follow-up patients are more challenging in neurology practice than new patients. The latter can often be seen first by a trainee neurologist before the consultant is brought in for definitive diagnosis and advice. Follow-ups should not be left to a junior doctor, but so often they are. If 'easy', these patients should not be followed up in hospital at all, but by their GP. My own criteria for follow-up were on-going conditions which were treatable, or at least manageable to some extent, but too tricky for a GP to deal with (difficult not easy epilepsy, difficult not easy Parkinson's disease); rare conditions with which GPs could have little experience (a GP might see one new patient with motor neurone disease every 33 years); and patients whose diagnosis was entirely unclear but who were increasingly disabled by whatever was going on. However, a problem is that junior doctors don't get any experience of following patients up — and a feel for the ups and downs of a chronic condition over months and years.

A diversion into General Practice

Maybe my view of general practice is hopelessly idealised and unrealistic but, unlike I suspect most consultants, I have done GP locums. As well as in Tongue, I had a couple of weeks in Luton single-handed in the winter of 1969 during a strike at the Vauxhall car company, the biggest employer in town. Oddly, I was befriended by the local Rabbi who invited me to his family dinners on Fridays. (I had not eaten gefilte fish before, nor have I since.) These days I would not be allowed to do locums because only trained GPs can do so. That seems reasonable although I don't think I did more harm than good. Mind you, in Luton I was once asked to proclaim

---

1. Lewis Carroll, *Through the Looking-Glass and What Alice Found There* (London: Macmillan, 1871).

on the virginity of a teenage girl who had been dragged in by her mother. Best to say she was a virgin, I thought — and as far as I know she didn't return pregnant.

As a consultant, I have sat in with GPs from time to time, to find out more about what they do, and to understand better their stresses and strains. In South Queensferry I was told of the retired senior partner's useful tip, 'If you get called twice in 24 hours to a patient with the same symptoms, admit to hospital!' Fine, provided that on the second visit, likely nowadays by a different GP working for an on-call organisation, this second GP realises that someone else had seen the patient in the previous 24 hours. How this works now that patients may have to phone an anonymous helpline is quite beyond me.

My medical school didn't think GPs had anything useful to impart to us students. Fortunately, John Fry had been our GP in Beckenham when I was a teenager. He was an astonishing man who was not just a GP but a writer of medical books; he was on the GMC, and a founder member of the Royal College of General Practitioners. It was obvious that I should sit in with him for a week, even though I had hated Beckenham, a boring suburb in south London (but at least it was a quick train journey into London and the book and record shops in the Charing Cross Road). Later, I spent another week with a very rural GP in Hutton-le-Hole on the North Yorkshire Moors. He was a Theakston, the family of brewing fame. At the time I hadn't heard of the beer. He showed me how to burn heather on a grouse moor, and he regarded cats as vermin; any in his garden, he told me, were shot on sight.

John Fry insisted that he was a family, not a general, practitioner. He would only take someone onto his list if he took the whole family, so keen was he on the idea that the dynamics within a family had an important impact on individual health. As their doctor he needed know about those dynamics. To a hoity-toity London medical student, brought up to believe that GPs were failed hospital consultants who couldn't possibly teach us anything, I was suitably chastened when he told me that the consultants in his local hospital were his 'ancillary workers' (I'd thought the ancillary workers were porters and cleaners). And quite right, too — GPs are the people who should know *all* about our health, not just the neurology bit or the cardiology bit. This is a huge challenge for them.

For John Fry, his surgery was a continuing follow-up clinic. He may not have seen patients for more than a few minutes at a time, but over the years as they returned with their various ailments, serious but more often not so serious, those few minutes added up to hours, days and weeks, to a complete picture of their health and indeed sometimes their whole life. He didn't have to dredge back through other doctors' notes to find out what had been going on, and he was practising in the days before doctors gazed at their computer screens rather than at their patients. Continuity of care at its very best. My late medical school contemporary and good friend, Ian Campbell, was rather similar. When I once sat in with him he told me what was wrong with each patient before they even came through the surgery door, so well did he know them.

John Fry somehow found time to record every consultation using a punched card for each patient (no computers in those days). At the end of every year, armed with his pile of cards, and by poking a knitting needle through the appropriate hole, he could extract and then count the frequency of the common diseases he saw, many rarely seen in or recorded by hospitals — such as 'catarrhal children' and 'acute urinary infections'. In 1966 he published all this information in a small but brilliant book.[2]

I had gone to him for advice when, as a 17-year-old schoolboy doing physics, chemistry and maths (because those were what I was best at), I had decided that my future in science looked unlikely, especially after a school visit to United Steel in Sheffield where I saw scientists measuring the breaking strain of various steel alloys. I asked one whether it was not really boring. I can't recall his reply but the work looked boring to me. Besides, those of us public-schooled in the south were brainwashed to be scornful of the industrial north of England where most of the steel industry was, so I certainly didn't want to live there. In any case I was not good enough at maths to do high-level science. So what about medicine? I had no doctor relatives to consult. John Fry's advice then is still relevant now: 'If you do medicine you will always have a job, and probably a well-paid job. But more important than that, you don't have to decide exactly what you are going to do for another five or six years because there are so many different sorts of medical opportunities once you are qualified as a doctor. Medicine is not like being taught to be a pilot where you are being trained just to fly. In medicine you might end up as a surgeon which is completely different from cutting up dead bodies as a pathologist, or looking after the health of your community as a public health physician.' Back at school, I did a crash course in biology.

But returning to Jura where the husband and wife GPs are still there,

---

2. J. Fry, *Profiles of Disease: A Study of the Natural History of Common Diseases* (Edinburgh and London: E. and S. Livingstone, 1966).

now with two children to join the nearly 40 under 18-year-olds on the island — an encouraging number. Hopefully their professional isolation will not lead to the fate of some remote GPs in the past: incompetence, laziness and alcohol. The challenge will be to keep up their competence when there is rather little medical care to be provided for just 200 people, along with not that many summer tourists coming to climb the Paps and peek at Barnhill. But not to visit the Jura House gardens anymore, unless the hedge fund manager has a change of heart, or goes back to Australia and stays there. One day I really must try to understand what hedge fund managers do, and how hedge funding contributes to society.

To Port Ellen, Islay

Monday April 2nd dawned drizzly, but after we had let the children loose in the play-park and the tide had turned south in our favour, the sun came out. The wind was still in the northwest giving us another pleasant sail on a beam reach for the 19 miles to Port Ellen, in four hours. Whisky lovers would appreciate our route that day, sailing along the southeast Islay coast past three famous distilleries in full view — first Ardbeg, then Lagavulin, then Laphroig. There were five others on Islay at the time but as I personally don't like peaty whiskies, typical of Islay malts, they are not of much interest to me. Well, in fact one of them was — Bruichladdich — because before it went bust it had sponsored the Scottish Islands Peaks Race. The distillery was bought some years later by private individuals who turned it into one of the very best in Scotland. It was a small company, nimble on its feet, locally based — exactly the sort of enterprise we should encourage in these days of greedy international corporations and crooked bankers. But, sadly, like so many small and successful companies, it was swallowed up by a big international organisation, Rémy Martin, with all the profit that means for the original owners, and all the risks for the local community if Rémy Martin closes down the distillery as a small 'inefficient' cog in a much bigger international wheel.

There were new pontoons at Port Ellen. But only just beyond them were far too many mooring buoys as well as shallow water, making turning a Rustler 36 into a finger-berth difficult, and getting out likely to be well-nigh impossible. Motoring Pickle backwards is perfectly doable. But backwards in the right direction is almost random because of the long keel, unless by first edging forwards you can get the bow swinging before reversing (impractical when stuffed into a finger-berth) — or you are lucky enough to have the wind on the bow to turn the boat in the required direction. Often I end up going backwards in the direction the boat decides, while smiling in a haughty complacent sort of way as though the direction was my plan all along.

The water was shallow as we motored in towards the pontoons so naturally we went aground, albeit briefly, my excuse being that the marker buoys had not been laid for the season. Embarrassing, but there were scarcely any witnesses, and it was reassuring to see a dredger doing helpful things just close by. At the same time as all the huffing and puffing to get us afloat again, the children started behaving badly. Young children, particularly siblings, have this uncanny knack when coming into a marina or anchorage. They sense the end of the journey is in sight, stop playing nicely or reading quietly down below, poke their heads up from the cabin to look out into the cockpit, nudge each other for a better view, then kick each other, after which war breaks out. At this point I lose my cool, call for their mother who is trying to untangle the mooring ropes, scream at the children, shove them down the companionway, and slam the hatch shut. And so we arrived at Port Ellen. There were just two other boats already on the pontoons, the first we had seen all day.

By then I had discovered what I should have anticipated. Planning this sort of voyage is far more anxiety-provoking than actually doing it. When planning there are any number of anchorages, marinas, headlands, lights, rocks, sandbanks and tides swirling around in one's head. Out on the water there is only one passage to think about at a time, the one that you are on — far easier. And the one harbour to aim for, and swot up in the Sailing Directions. (Plus something of a plan B in case of adverse weather, illness, or crew mutiny.)

The next day was not a sailing day, certainly not for the family. There was far too much wind, it was extremely cold, and there were snow showers. Thankfully the cabin-heater did its job brilliantly, so it was very cosy down below. April can provide the best and worst of sailing weathers in Scotland. Because Port Ellen seemed to have little to offer, we caught a rattly and bumpy bus to Bowmore which gave us a view of what, in the mid-sixteenth century, Donald Monro described as an island which was 'fertil, fruitful, and full of natural grassing, with maney grate diere, maney woods, faire games of hunting beside everey toune ...'.[3] Bowmore is a much more animated sort of

---

3. Sir Donald Monro, *Description of the Western Isles of Scotland called Hybrides* (Edinburgh: Birlinn Edition, 1994)[combined with 'A Description of the Western

a place than Port Ellen. It has the island swimming pool which we enjoyed before, a round church of architectural note, and an excellent bookshop with a large selection of sticker books which were ideal for William.

The last scheduled bus back seemed to be at 5.10pm, so to get more time in Bowmore we later took a taxi, as ever an interesting experience on an island. I already knew there was unhappiness at the tiny airport (briefly famous in 1994 when Prince Charles pranged his aeroplane on landing, and him an RAF 'group captain' too). Despite only a handful of flights a day, there was over-intrusive security, as though the next terrorist attack on the UK was being planned right there on Islay. It turned out that the woman in charge of security was an ex-girlfriend of the taxi driver. She was widely known as Madam Hitler.

To Northern Ireland

Wednesday April 4th was a lot better. Although still cold, it was one of those bright blue cloudless spring mornings when the world seems full of possibilities, as it was for Mole after he had 'scraped and scratched and scrabbled and scrooged' his way up into the sunlight in *The Wind in the Willows*. Unfortunately, poor William was much troubled by eczema and a night-time chesty cough, a typical combination in kids that they usually grow out of (as William has). I had it myself quite badly as a child. Indeed one of my earliest memories is scratching the eczema on my arm so much that to stop me it was put in plaster. Not that it did stop me — a knitting needle surreptitiously pushed down inside the plaster made a pretty good scratcher (and possibly scrooger, too).

My mild asthmatic tendency last emerged as a medical student when I got seriously short of breath at night after being in the dissection room and exposed to the formaldehyde used to preserve the cadavers. That smell — even now — takes me straight back to those bizarre days when six of us clustered round a corpse trying to understand how it was all put together. Today's medical student seems to do very little dissection, learning from just looking at dissected specimens. Perhaps it's better than the old system. Instead of the overload of anatomy that I had to put up with, students are now often taught at great length how to be nice to patients — something my generation was able to sort out for ourselves, or so we believed.

Getting out of those Port Ellen pontoons was, as predicted, a nightmare.

Islands of Scotland Circa 1695' by Martin Martin], 493.

The wind had gone round 180° and was blowing up our stern. There was no way I could reverse out and reliably turn the stern to starboard and then go ahead to escape through the small gap between the ends of the finger-pontoons to starboard and the shallow water and moorings to port. Instead, I hatched a cunning plan of warping (nautical-speak for using ropes) the boat round between the two finger-pontoons enclosing Pickle so that we could head out pointing in the right direction. Pacing it out told me there was enough room. Indeed, the boat just fitted between the two finger-pontoons. But all this was easier said than done in a 15-knot wind with two small children and just their mother for help. Luckily, a neighbouring crew came to our rescue. We got away intact apart from a slightly shortened ensign staff which had snapped off at its base when we hit something. How I hate pontoons.

After that trauma we had a splendid genoa-only five-hour run for the 24 miles down to Rathlin Island, in sunshine with a view of snow on Goatfell, the highest peak on Arran, visible over the Mull of Kintyre. (An urban myth relates that this droopy-down bit of southwest Scotland was once used by the BBC as a guide to the maximum angle of penile erection that could be shown on TV.) Goatfell was the first mountain I had climbed, aged about 14, during a family holiday on Arran with my Scottish cousins from Glasgow (all Glaswegians holidayed on Arran then; I imagine many still do). I also attempted my first clumsy kiss on Arran, in the bushes around the Corrie Hotel. She came from Bearsden, the rather posh Glasgow suburb. Where is she now, and what was her name? Pat, I think.

I wondered yet again what the point was of the rule of having to sail at right angles across the traffic separation zone between the Mull of Kintyre and the Northern Irish coast, outward-bound vessels to the northeast, inward-bound to the southwest. Admittedly it is only 11 nautical miles across at its narrowest point so there is not much room for large ships, and there is a strong tide. But on the many occasions I have sailed through there, I have hardly ever seen a ship of any sort. I must admit that in good visibility I don't necessarily follow the right-angles rule — bad nautical behaviour you absolutely would not get away with in the English Channel.

I'm afraid Lucy is very prone to seasickness. She threw up twice, after which her cheeriness was immediately restored. William threw up once, largely because he was still coughing a lot which we realised was probably more to do with a chest infection than asthma. Lucy proclaimed the grand total of three crew vomits. In that fairly cold weather the children tended to want to stay warm and cosy down below which of course makes any seasickness far worse unless you lie down and close your eyes. Even R. T. McMullen, the hardened Corinthian sailor, was badly affected in the Irish Sea in 1871: 'No amount of motion on deck affects me, but battened down below with the charts and books, bending over the table, and clinging to it for support in a small vessel sailing 7 knots in the trough of a heavy sea, is a position that would severely try the arch-enemy himself, even without the additional discomfort of wet clothes, and privations of all sorts that poor mortals have to endure.'[4]

There were no other sailing boats out, and only a few fishing boats. Nor were there any on the Rathlin pontoons, or anyone to collect money from us, just a lot of eider ducks and seals. The cooing of eider ducks always takes me back to my rather lonely days in Aberdeen in the 1970s, wandering on the Forvie sands by Newburgh, which is where I first recognised an eider duck, and heard their typical calls. While so many of my friends were by then married, I was not.

Most people probably don't know exactly where Rathlin Island is, although some over a certain age may have a vague memory of the name. This is probably because they remember Richard Branson (one of the few businessmen anyone has heard of), ditching his hot-air balloon into the sea off the island at the end of his Atlantic crossing in 1987. No one alive will remember the first-in-the-world commercial wireless link that Marconi made from Rathlin to Ballycastle six miles away on the Irish coast in 1898. Maybe this route was partly chosen because although Marconi was Italian he had an Irish mother from the Jameson whiskey-distilling family.

But seafarers have known for centuries about Rathlin because it was such a useful stopping-off point between Ireland and Scotland as sailing ships returned from the Americas to ports like Liverpool. And because, although the island is only about four miles long, such is the strength and complexity of the surrounding tides that it has three lighthouses (a mecca for pharologists, the word which I understand refers to those who study lighthouses). But what we as a family will all remember is the drama of Lucy locking herself in the public toilets, screaming the place down before we heard her (she tended to be histrionic at the best of times), and finally climbing over into the next cubicle to make good her escape. Most impressive initiative. And I can remember successfully springing Pickle out backwards from the pontoon, a useful trick I was learning (and still am —

---

4. R. T. McMullen, *Down Channel* (orig. 1869; 3rd edn, London: Horace Cox, 1903), 88.

with the gradually disintegrating how-to-do-it instructions from *Practical Boat Owner* clasped in my hand).

There is absolutely no point trying to sail along the northeast coast of Ireland against the tide; it is far too strong. If you sail at 5 knots over the 14 miles to Red Bay, and the tide is 2 knots against you, it will take about five hours. Family fed up. But if the tide is with you, it will take two hours. Family delighted. The next day, having done the tidal calculation, we lazed about and wandered around Rathlin in — by then — warm sunshine. It was strangely warm, given that the snow ploughs were out on the east side of Scotland and friends on skis texted us from the Cairngorm mountains only 120 miles northeast of us.

Again, being so early in the season, there was almost no one around. More or less everything on Rathlin was shut. Even the pretty Protestant church was locked, but not the more worker-day-looking Roman Catholic church. No doubt there would be trippers coming over on the Rathlin Express, the fast catamaran from Ballycastle. This quick and easy 25-minute ferry ride has certainly enhanced the island's tourism, and maybe saved it from being abandoned because even now the population is only about 100, having been over 1000 in the 19th century.

During the afternoon, given the strong tide and notwithstanding the very light northwest wind, it took us only two-and-a-half hours to sail, or rather drift with the tide, under the impressive cliffs of the Antrim coast to anchor off Waterfoot village in Red Bay. This didn't seem the most fascinating anchorage to explore, but as it was evening when we arrived anyway, we stayed on board and didn't bother blowing up the inflatable dinghy. Once again there had been no sailing boats out, and nor were there any on the moorings off the Cushendall Sailing and Boating Club.

To Glenarm

Good Friday, April 6th, another short family-friendly hop, a mere eight miles. A two-hour easy sail in a 10-knot northwest wind to the small marina at Glenarm, run by the local council and not by some pricey private outfit of the sort I was to find further south. Feeling guilty about all the family seasickness earlier, I was deliberately taking it easy, which was part of the plan anyway as we didn't need to get to Belfast until the Sunday. From the sea, Glenarm is a bit battered-looking dominated by the remains of I think a cement factory. In contrast, it has a beautiful limestone harbour in which the marina sits — the oldest harbour in Northern Ireland. The harbour master was as friendly and helpful as he had been 18 months earlier when we sailed Pickle up to Scotland from Falmouth. And, like then, there were no other visiting boats. Loads of space for us, and a few black guillemots. This was the perfect place to commandeer the marina laundry and catch up with our washing.

The village is a short walk inland. It is partly pretty, partly boarded-up in those times of recession (although much of Northern Ireland had been a depressed area for many years), and partly spruced-up. And even though a bank holiday it was very, very quiet. Fortunately, this was the first day of the season that the teashop in the castle garden was open, with excellent cakes served up by the extraordinarily friendly people I had come to expect in Northern Ireland from many previous visits. How do they manage to be so friendly to strangers, despite this part of the UK having been such a troubled place for so long? The centuries-old strife between the Protestants in most if not all the positions of power and the down-trodden Roman Catholics had boiled up during the troubles which had begun in the 1960s. With all the violence, sectarian killings, and the army as well as the police on the streets, it had been more or less a no-go place for outsiders. Indeed, when I first went to Belfast in 1980 to visit one of the hospitals in our UK-wide trial of aspirin to reduce the risk of stroke, no one I knew had ever been to Northern Ireland unless they came from there.

Paul Theroux at the time described Belfast as 'an awful city'.[5] Indeed it was. I remember the checkpoints to get into the centre of the city, army vehicles on the streets, police stations protected by huge mesh-steel grills, Union Jacks flying far more prominently than in England, red, white and blue-painted kerb-stones, and the notorious Maze prison where Joe Lyttle took me to view the outside. Joe, who has since died of a brain tumour, was a lovely Northern Irish neurologist, as aghast at the troubles as anyone — and superficially as unaffected as others in the middle classes because most of the violence had been in the poorer areas of the cities, and in parts of the countryside. Interestingly, his brother had been the senior pilot for Aer Lingus, the Irish National Airline, and might have expected to fly the Pope to Ireland for his visit in 1979. But no, as a Protestant he had to give way to a junior Roman Catholic pilot. This stark religious divide was astonishing to me, and so complicated that even now I hardly attempt to read about Northern Irish politics. They seem to make so little sense.

---

5. Paul Theroux, *The Kingdom by the Sea: A Journey around the Coast of Great Britain* (orig. 1983; London: Penguin, 1984), 230.

At least Northern Ireland is calm these days, more or less, since the Good Friday agreement of 1998, almost normal and able to rebuild its tourist and other trade with the rest of the UK and further afield. Provided Brexit doesn't wreck the place. How ironic that the geography of Ireland, which has been so badly treated by England over the centuries, nearly rescued us from falling out of the European Union in 2020 because of the logistic, social and political difficulties of a customs barrier at the land border between the Republic of Ireland and Northern Ireland (difficulties which still have to be resolved even after Brexit). In 1998 Cathie and I cycled from Edinburgh to Belfast where there was not even a policeman let alone a soldier on the Catholic Falls Road, or the Protestant Shankhill Road. Progress, thankfully.

To Bangor (the Irish not the Welsh one)

Saturday April 7th. Up at 7.30am to catch the tide south with a nice wind from the northwest, and sunshine. Excellent bacon butties for a quick breakfast as we set off. It was to be another short hop. Although it is 21 miles to Bangor, it only took four hours such was the speed of the spring tide. The sea was a bit bumpy in parts so Lucy was sick again, just the once.

Bangor, full of Easter weekend holidaymakers, was somewhat dispiriting and run-down with boarded-up shops and a distinctly cavernous and rather empty-shelved supermarket. There was a huge gap-site overlooking the marina. My Northern Irish friends tell me Bangor had been like this for many decades, its heyday as a holiday destination for Belfast people long gone, being no competition for the Mediterranean and the availability of cheap flights. This problem is shared with so many seaside resorts in England and Scotland, but maybe their time will come again if the climate emergency persuades us to give up flying off to warmer resorts for our holidays. The marina felt somewhat 'industrial', mostly catering it seemed for large white-hulled yachts, with no Contessas or Rustlers to be seen. And by then we were far enough south to see many more oversized and underused bling motorboats.

Despite Bangor's unfavourable impression, once again the people were wonderfully friendly, for example when we were served up outstandingly good steaks in a most unpromising-looking restaurant. We were at that stage in family life when in restaurants waiting for food we needed to entertain restless children (with miniature Happy Families, Snap, Uno, anything portable). The Family Fun Park right by the marina is excellent for children too; ours certainly enjoyed it, in particular the pedal-operated swans on the big pool. And there were dodgems, a miniature train, and ice creams to help maintain control, harmony and family happiness.

Easter Sunday April 8th dawned still on the cold side, and somewhat overcast. Belfast, and the rest of the UK, and the world as far as I knew, was in a frenzy of Titanic history. It was coming up to April 14th, the centenary of the incident of the iceberg in the night. The brand new Titanic museum in Belfast had just opened to great acclaim, so great that there was no possibility of us getting tickets. In these hyped-up days it is billed as 'an experience': the 'World's largest Titanic visitor experience'. Funny that — the Titanic herself was billed as the largest ship afloat at the time, and unsinkable. Hype is not new, but there seems to be a lot of it about, far too much.

Odd how a city can celebrate such a disaster. However, the Titanic was built in Belfast by the Harland and Wolff shipyard. As much to be celebrated in the 'experience' as the Titanic is that very shipyard, which was still just about there in 2012 having provided jobs since 1861. But no longer — it closed in 2019 to join the long history of great British shipbuilding, now almost no more. I have visited the Titanic 'experience' twice since then and it really is a magnificent museum in a magnificent building with bang up-to-date facilities, and full of interest. How many eggs were on board? Answer: 40,000. How many men built her? 3000. How many rivets did they use? Three million. A future visit to Belfast must include HMS Caroline, the 1914 light cruiser that is the last surviving ship from the 1916 Battle of Jutland, and which since 2016 has been open to the public.

In 2012, instead of the 'experience', we contented ourselves with a 15-minute (and brand new) train to Cultra between Bangor and Belfast to see the outstanding Ulster Transport Museum. Lots of old steam trains, trams, cars, and aeroplanes. And some Titanic stuff that Lucy found particularly fascinating, so much so that she picked the Titanic for a school project when she got home. Sadly we didn't have time to see much of the adjacent Folk Museum; we had to hurry back to Bangor to greet Bridget.

To Portpatrick

I have always been rather impressed with Bridget Drasan, a primary school teacher. I have not had any other crew who has sailed round the world, even to the Antarctic in her case (without a cabin-heater, she claims). And she can fix things like troublesome winches. She has often been on our boat, not just as a very competent crew but also as a good friend to our children. Clearly she was ideal for the cruise along a coastline that was new to me, the exposed north shore of the Solway Firth. It helped enormously to have her take the pressure off Cathie who could then see to the children, or the boat, but not both at the same time.

Bridget arrived in the afternoon, off the plane from Edinburgh, weighed down by luggage and thankfully my camera, noisily as usual. And off we went across the sea back to Scotland. I don't think she had been to Northern Ireland before, but we could only give her 20 minutes to savour it, such was our need to get away in good time. It was drizzly and roly-poly across the North Channel in a following 10–15 knot wind from the west, for all of the 22 miles to Portpatrick on the Rhins of Galloway, the bit of land shaped like a hammer-head that pokes down from southwest Scotland into the Irish Sea. Surprisingly no one was sick. This route does seem to be going backwards but I was keen to see Portpatrick for the first time, we had the rest of the week to meander towards Maryport, and we were in no hurry, which was the whole point of the cruise. It was definitely not a race.

The sun appeared for our arrival in the evening, but so did rain squalls during which the wind gusted up to 20 knots, not exactly ideal for a narrow harbour entrance facing southwest with no port of refuge for many miles north, and nothing at all appealing to the south. I had been warned: 'Entering Portpatrick for the first time at dead low water is a sporting enterprise', observed Libby Purves.[6] It is crucial to recognise the day-marks, a very clear orange-painted line on the harbour wall in line with a less clear orange-painted line on a building set back from the harbour. Fortunately there was a photograph of the lines in the Sailing Directions, so we knew what we were looking for. It was not quite low water that evening, and luckily we found a gap in the weather as we very cautiously puttered in on the engine. Not cautiously enough. We went aground, briefly. This time because I didn't recognise the port-hand buoy to turn around — at low tide it looked just like a fender lying well up on the rocks.

In 1693 the hydrographer Captain Greenvile Collins published the first 'pilot', or what we would now call sailing directions, as well as the first reasonably accurate charts of Britain.[7] Interestingly he did not include Portpatrick or indeed anywhere else on the west coast of Scotland. At the time this was very much terra incognita and of no great interest to either the Royal Navy who were concerned with attack from mainland Europe, or

---

6. Libby Purves, *One Summer's Grace: A Family Voyage round Britain* (London: Grafton Books, 1989), 109.

7. Greenvile Collins, *Great-Britain's Coasting Pilot* (London: 1693).

mariners from Europe who sailed round the north of Scotland or down the English Channel to reach the Atlantic. The Orcadian Murdoch Mackenzie, originally a teacher at Kirkwall Grammar School, was the first to properly chart the Scottish west coast, and provide sailing directions. In the late 18th century he described Portpatrick as merely 'a small dry harbour, open to the westward, and without the conveniency of a kay to shelter boats or vessels that come into it ... small vessels must go in at high-water ... the ferry boats that cross between Scotland and Ireland sail from this place.'[8]

Once again we were the only visiting boat, so there was plenty of harbour wall to tie up to. I had almost forgotten how to do this, so long had it been since the last time. However, with much shouting and muddling of warps, and positioning of a fender-board, we got ourselves sorted out, with care because it was by then dead low water and there was going to be an 11ft rise in water level during the night. My son Ben's gift of a redundant climbing rope was particularly useful, largely because it made such a long warp (nice and springy, too, as climbing ropes have to be to arrest the falling climber).

Bridget was rather more bothered about the warps than I was, and as the tide rose she got up several times in the night to adjust them, while I kept my head down — apart from one time when maybe she was pretending to be asleep and I did get up. But I soon stopped worrying once confident that with long warps and a well-placed fender-board (hardly necessary now most harbours have solid walls rather than piles) all would be well without constant fiddling. Harbour walls may be romantic and more authentic than pontoons, but this one did require the ever-mobile and squirming William to be strapped firmly into a safety harness attached to a rope to haul him up a slimy ladder to dry land. The brand new lifeboat in the harbour was a reassuring presence. Less reassuring was the large noticeboard with a map of all the wrecks around the local coastline.

Easter Monday, April 9th was drizzly. We planned to get up late, breakfast at 10am, and then have a day to look around, and generally avoid the unpleasant weather at sea that was forecast. The harbour master was as helpful as I was beginning to find harbour masters generally are. Not being used to the breed, who hardly exist where we normally sail, I didn't have any particular expectations. However, I became more and more impressed by their knowledge of local conditions, professionalism, advice, friendliness, and their help which included catching mooring ropes when I failed to get

---

8. Murdoch Mackenzie, *Nautical Descriptions of the West Coast of Great Britain from Bristol Channel to Cape-Wrath* (London: 1776), 25.

close enough for crew members to jump for the shore. A mobile phone or VHF call to the harbour master was to become a helpful prelude to arriving without too much fuss, anxiety and tension. Harbour masters usually told us in advance which side of the boat we would be moored up, and tried to accommodate our request to have a berth from which we could exit easily, bearing in mind our long keel and difficulties in reverse. Maybe they were different in the 1930s, when one of Belloc's crew Dermod MacCarthy later wrote, 'The Old Man began to revile all harbour masters again, and ended with an aphorism: "People of no education put in a position of absolute authority, invariably abuse it."'[9]

Like many other small harbours, Portpatrick had definitely seen better days. It had even once been the main ferry port to Northern Ireland, before the much better sheltered Stranraer took over, now superseded by Cairnryan. Within living memory Portpatrick did have one brief glimmer of glory, as a strike-breaking port for ships to Ireland during the seamen's strikes in 1966 and 1970. I have never really thought about to whom harbours belong; on the Scottish west coast we don't have many. I probably imagined they were a public good to which users contributed with harbour dues. But someone must have gone to the trouble and expense of building them, expecting a return on their capital. In recent years Portpatrick harbour had been owned by some private and uncaring individuals, and allowed to run down. However, in the week before our arrival it had been taken over by a local community trust with plans to raise money to buy and improve it. Good luck to them.

Portpatrick itself is charming and touristic with pubs, cafés and gift shops (the RNLI shop was the best). The tourists arrived in mid-morning and were mostly gone by late afternoon, leaving the place to snooze under the emerging sunshine. Of course all this would have changed if Boris Johnson's dotty idea of a bridge across the Irish Sea, or a tunnel under it, had not been scuppered by sensible engineers and almost everyone else. Access would have been awful — one long traffic jam along the busy and narrow road between Portpatrick and the M74 motorway between Glasgow and Carlisle. It already takes at least two hours.

By the evening the wind had gone round to the southwest and swell was coming straight into the outer harbour. It was a good thing we had decided to come over from Bangor the day before, a decision much aided — as was to become usual — by xcweather, the brilliant forecasting website easily

---

9. Dermod MacCarthy, *Sailing with Mr Belloc* (London: Collins Harvill, 1986), 87.

available on mobile phones. I find the Met Office forecasts broadcast by the coastguard, and on the internet, generally rather too pessimistic and conservative, and so I suppose 'safer'. And long ago I stopped listening to the shipping forecast on BBC radio. Before there was any alternative, back in the 1970s, I and the rest of the crew always fell asleep before their late-night forecast got around the coast to our local areas of Malin and Hebrides. In the morning we all had to confess we hadn't a clue what the forecast had been. The wonderfully mellifluous tones and lilting rhythms of the forecasters were far too soporific.

Suggestion, placebos and hypnosis

Over the years Bridget had been plagued by various symptoms — sounding minor to me, but not to her. This time she was very troubled by knee pains. She had to perform elaborate daily exercises in the cabin involving elastic bands, recommended by a physiotherapist, without which she could hardly walk any distance. Although this sort of therapeutic response could easily have been a placebo effect — an effect unrelated directly to the treatment itself — I would not knock it, provided no one was spending a lot of their own or the NHS's money.[10] After all, as an occasional hypnotherapist, I am all for the power of suggestion, and therefore influencing a patient's expectations and thus their outcome, which is presumably how placebos work in ameliorating symptoms such as pain. They don't *directly* affect any underlying physical disease, although various hormonal and other chemical changes do occur. So beware the placebo effect before proclaiming a direct curative effect of, for example, a surgical operation (or any other 'impressive' and complex intervention) on a subjective outcome such as pain or depression — which is absolutely not to downplay the importance of these symptoms to the patient.

A famous randomised trial in the 1950s compared ligation of the internal mammary artery — a frequently performed and apparently successful operation at the time — with just an incision in the skin over the chest but nothing else (i.e. sham surgery) to relieve angina chest pain due to coronary artery disease.[11] There was no difference in outcome! Whether a

---

10. L. Colloca and A. J. Barsky, 'Placebo and Nocebo Effects', *New England Journal of Medicine*, 382 (2020), 554–61.

11. L. A. Cobb et al., 'An Evaluation of Internal Mammary-Artery Ligation by a Double-Blind Technic', *New England Journal of Medicine*, 260 (1959), 1115–18.

research ethics committee would approve such a trial design in this day and age I rather doubt — but without that trial it is conceivable that a useless operation would still be performed today. Clearly using sham surgery to allow for the placebo effect of real surgery is a major ethical issue for randomised trials of surgical procedures, from the relatively banal (knee surgery for arthritic pain) to the decidedly risky (transplanting cells into the brain to relieve Parkinson's disease). Of course, whoever is assessing the patients' outcomes must have no idea whether sham or real surgery was used (i.e. is 'blinded'). This is because not even the most scrupulous observer is completely unbiased in their hopes and expectations for a particular treatment, certainly not if they have anything to gain from its success (kudos, fame, fortune, share options, career advancement, etc.).

My own most vivid experience of the power of suggestion was in 1993. It was the day after a surgeon inserted a long nail down my broken tibia, the result of slipping on ice in the carpark after a walk up Ben Ledi in the snowy Trossachs. Lying in my hospital bed after surgery, there was a lot of pain and swelling in my injured leg. I was scared stiff that I had a blood clot in the leg veins that would surely break off and float into my lungs to kill me (a deep vein thrombosis, DVT, followed by a pulmonary embolus). I was more scared than most doctors because my research degree had been on this very topic back in the early 1970s in Aberdeen. Too much medical knowledge can be very disquieting. The consultant orthopaedic surgeon came round in the evening, glanced at my leg and proclaimed it was just fine, exactly as he anticipated. My pain vanished within minutes. Surgeons are ever optimistic and certain — such useful aids to suggestion. The late Henry Miller, the charismatic Newcastle neurologist who was not beyond using suggestion himself, observed — perhaps with some envy — that his surgical colleagues had 'that innate physical energy and joie de vivre that so often distinguishes the surgeon from his more debilitated medical colleagues'.[12]

That orthopaedic experience changed my own clinical practice because I decided that sick neurology inpatients should be seen by their consultant every day, not just twice a week as was the general pattern of consultant care at the time. A daily visit by a junior doctor, however charming and competent, or a chat with a sympathetic nurse, is no substitute for the consultant — the boss — at the end of the bed every day, explaining and reassuring, their very presence exploiting the power of suggestion.

---

12. Henry Miller, 'Facial Paralysis', *BMJ*, 3 (1967), 815.

However, in Edinburgh, a daily neurology consultant presence could only be achieved by consultants taking it in turn to look after inpatients on the ward, and for their on-call week or month to be freed up of anything that might take them outside Edinburgh — outpatient clinics in surrounding towns, meetings in Glasgow and London, or invited lectures. The obvious disadvantage of this 'attending' system is potential loss of continuity of care for those inpatients who stay for weeks rather than days, which put some consultants off the whole idea. Fortunately I had enough like-minded colleagues to make it work, while others stuck with their old-fashioned habits. Not for the first time my experience of being a patient proved helpful to me as a doctor.

Of course, suggestion doesn't just apply to surgical interventions. For a physician prescribing drugs there are two contrasting approaches which surely affect patient expectations and so outcomes: 'I suggest you take this drug which should help, although it doesn't help everyone, and do watch out for the side effects like this that and the other thing. You will find them all listed on the package insert, or you can look them up on the internet'; versus 'Take these tablets, which will help you get better. If you don't, or if you notice any new symptoms, let me know.' And suggestion is not just confined to medicine. At school I had a holiday job in a swish shop in Piccadilly; when a customer thought his new shoes were a bit tight, my superior took the shoes round to the back of the shop to 'stretch them a bit', waited a couple of minutes doing nothing, and brought them back to the customer who proclaimed them 'a perfect fit'. Harnessing the power of the mind, which is surely how suggestion works, is not to be ridiculed, it is to be exploited. Which brings me to hypnosis.

When I was a medical student, a physiology lecturer illustrated the role of the sympathetic nervous system in the 'fear, fright and flight' reaction by asking the whole lecture theatre of 100-plus students to feel and count our wrist pulses. Without warning he whipped out a starting pistol and fired it — BANG! Never forgotten, that immediate increase in heart rate. Later one evening he gave some of us an amazing off-piste demonstration of hypnosis, convincing a student that he had walked upside down across the ceiling.

Naturally, I rushed off to try hypnosis for myself. The results were astonishing, but I think pure beginner's luck. The friend sitting in front of me whom I was trying to hypnotise (look at this pencil above your head, your eyelids are getting heavy, very heavy, etc., etc.) remained hyper-vigilant, while the friend sitting behind me, Robin Preston, lapsed into a trance and was easily taught how to self-hypnotise. He was clearly a 'good subject', as they say in the trade. Under hypnosis he performed some rather extraordinary suggested feats, including pretending to stand on a letterbox while singing Irish songs. Robin was from Enniskillen in Northern Ireland, and has remained one of my closest, but non-sailing, friends ever since. (Like many of the Northern Irish who were able to, he escaped to England never to return to his Irish roots.) Some years later, as a lecturer in medicine in Aberdeen, I demonstrated to friends that it was quite possible to persuade people under hypnosis to do things they would not normally do, by suitable framing: 'It is getting terribly hot in here, maybe you would like to take your jersey off. It is getting much hotter, so maybe take your shirt off too … and your bra'. And so on. Except we never reached the bra stage.

As for the power of suggestion, on which hypnosis relies, and on which the placebo response presumably depends, I had been shown how to use it by John Fry. He gave a so-called 'tonic' to many of his patients with minor problems that were mostly going to get better by themselves. It was a revolting brown fluid — Mist. Gent. Alk. — which contained a mixture of gentian, an alkali, and chloroform water. The formula is still available in a pharmaceutical dispensing guide.[13] When I asked him why, he told me it was to make his patients feel better, which it did. It was a placebo, whose effect was no doubt helped by the tendency of many patients to get to their GP just as their symptoms are about to resolve spontaneously. In resistant cases Dr Fry was not beyond an intramuscular injection of vitamin B12, entirely harmless, cheap too, and a hopeful colour — pink. It suitably impressed, and pained, the patients when injected into their buttock. A more powerful placebo.

These days many would regard this sort of doctor behaviour as dishonest, with patients now expecting to take decisions about their treatment. 'No decisions about me without me', as the slogan has it, is absolutely right when a patient has a serious disease, and when very heavy drug treatments are needed or surgery is contemplated. But for minor ailments that are probably going to get better without treatment, I don't see any harm in a bit of paternalistic subterfuge, as long as it works. By 'works' I mean it gives patients reassurance, makes them feel better, has no side effects, and provides them with a safe inexpensive intervention (which is what they mostly hope for, anyway). In other words, a placebo — surely better than a

---

13. *Pharmaceutical Compounding and Dispensing* (2nd edn, London: Pharmaceutical Press, 2012), chap. 2 'Solutions'.

drug with side effects, particularly one with addiction potential like valium or antidepressants, and certainly opioid analgesics. Whether a placebo works if the patient knows it is a placebo seems unlikely, although some say it will. If true, that may be one way to escape the ethical jam of being 'dishonest' with the patient.

Maybe in these more politically correct days we can only use words of reassurance —convincing and kind words. No placebos, no subterfuge. This has got to be better medicine than the advice I got from the departing GP in Luton when I was about to do his locum in 1969: 'Every patient when they leave the surgery must have a diagnosis, and a prescription.' By prescription he certainly didn't mean a cheap placebo. And he didn't much care for my question, 'But what do I tell patients when I don't know what's wrong with them?' 'Fibromyalgia', he replied. This common but often very disabling condition may well be a functional disorder in the sense of not being due to any structural disease that can be seen on a scan, or even on a biopsy, or confirmed with a test. This sort of doctor is responsible for the huge amount of over-treatment we have to grapple with, on the back of what is now called 'disease-mongering': claims that problems such as male-pattern baldness, insomnia, muscle aches and pains, hypoactive sexual desire, premenstrual dysphoric disorder, and the menopause are 'diseases' which can and should be treated, usually with drugs — real drugs with side effects, and costs. A similar and emerging problem is that people without any symptoms at all, but whose test results are slightly outwith the 'normal' range, should also be treated (for example, for 'kidney failure' or an 'underactive thyroid gland'), and so be transformed, perhaps permanently, from people into patients. And there are people who *do* have symptoms, but their abnormal test result may be entirely irrelevant. Deciding whether it is or not requires clinical judgement, not yet another test.

Naturally the pharmaceutical industry is not averse to disease-mongering. The media jump on the bandwagon with anecdotes of cured 'patients', and politicians panic and succumb to Big Pharma as well as to lobbying by patients and their organisations. We have come to live in a culture where far too many patients want 'a pill for every ill'. Without mandatory disclosure (not achieved at present), one does not necessarily know that a patient organisation is funded by industry,[14] with the inevitable result: more and more lobbying for more and more drug 'treatments'. How is it possible

---

14. Piotr Ozieranski et al., 'Exposing Drug Industry Funding of UK Patient Organisations', *BMJ*, 365 (2019), l1806.

that almost half of those over 65 in the UK are taking five or more different drugs?[15] Such polypharmacy must surely be pharmacological lunacy, as well as pharmaceutical company profit, which can then fund 'educational' courses for doctors, medical journal supplements, and conferences in exotic places that are so often just advertising.

And for good measure, psychiatrists have expanded their original diagnostic categories of, for example, anxiety and depression, so that almost everyone now seems to have a mental health problem, requiring treatment, very often with drugs — new drugs still in patent and therefore expensive. As a medical student I saw the demise of barbiturates as 'non-addictive' sleeping pills that were obviously addictive, and then the rise of valium that was 'non-addictive', or so we were assured. It was simply not true. Now we have moved on to the problem of getting patients off anti-depressants (astonishingly, prescribed to 17% of the English population in 2017–18).[16] Yet another win for the pharmaceutical industry.

John Fry would have had none of this over-treatment. He had a charming habit of nodding his head reassuringly when patients were telling their story; his empathy was obvious. Maybe he knew about the great, late 19th-century Canadian physician William Osler's three simple actions which can make all the difference: 'the kindly word, the cheerful greeting, the sympathetic look'[17] — actions that will surely add to any suggestion that all will be well. None of this is new. Patrick O'Brian, in his well-researched historical novels, and knowing all about the Napoleonic period, gave Jack Aubrey's ship's surgeon Stephen Maturin the words 'For you must know, gentlemen, that when the mariner is dosed, he likes to know that he has been dosed: with fifteen grains or even less of this valuable substance scenting him and the very air about him there can be no doubt of the matter; and such is the nature of the human mind that he experiences a far greater real benefit than the drug itself would provide, were it deprived of its stench.' And what was this valuable and smelly substance? Asafetida — 'by far the most pungent, the most truly fetid, variety known to man'.[18]

---

15. James Le Fanu, 'Mass Medicalization Is an Iatrogenic Catastrophe', *BMJ*, 361 (2018), k2794.

16. *Dependence and Withdrawal Associated with Some Prescribed Medicines* (Public Health England, 2019).

17. Mark Silverman, T. Jock Murray and Charles Bryan (eds), *The Quotable Osler* (Philadelphia: American College of Physicians, 2008).

18. Patrick O'Brian, *The Commodore* (London: Harper Collins, 1995), 98.

Another of my own experiences of the power of the mind came shortly after my colon cancer had been removed in 1995. I became more and more convinced that the niggling pains in my chest were due to secondary cancer. After worrying for some weeks I finally asked a radiological colleague for a chest X-ray. It was normal, and the pains vanished overnight. I clearly had a functional problem: symptoms — quite obtrusive symptoms — but no physical disease; the *structure* of my body was fine, my mind was in overdrive.

Although people may have never heard of functional disorders, they account for about one third of outpatient referrals to neurologists.[19] And probably for just as many in other specialist clinics, and even more in general practice. These patients certainly have symptoms, often several at the same time — weakness, fatigue, pins and needles, blurred vision, headaches, muscle pains, blackouts, poor memory. In some cases these may be wrecking their lives. Maybe they can't even work, many are on benefits, and some remain disabled for years, occasionally for as long as or longer than patients with a 'real' disease such as multiple sclerosis.

Contrary to popular prejudice, and the opinion of some doctors, these people are seldom 'making it up' or consciously feigning illness. The symptoms are as real for them as the symptoms from a serious disease, like stroke, and yet they have no recognisable disease. Indeed, they often have typical signs of a functional disorder. Their weak leg, to take an example, can be made strong again by various methods, including hypnosis, which would certainly not be possible after a stroke. Not surprisingly, many are anxious and depressed as a consequence, not as a cause of their symptoms. Also not surprisingly, some unsympathetic doctors refer to these people as 'heart-sink patients'.

Functional problems are not mental disorders like depression or schizophrenia, nor are they necessarily due to some deep and dark subconscious Freudian subterfuge. We simply don't know the cause in most cases, but we do know we don't have a drug treatment that will help, and there is nothing for a surgeon to cut out or cut off. Under these circumstances doctors have two options. Some tell the patients they have medically unexplained symptoms, there is no physical disorder, they don't have x, y or z, and there is nothing anyone can do about it, often with the verbal or facial implication of 'you are making it all up and I can't be bothered with you.'

---

19. Jon Stone, Chris Burton and Alan Carson, 'Recognising and Explaining Functional Neurological Disorder', *BMJ*, 371 (2020), m3745.

The better option is surely to explain that the problem is very real, that it is called 'functional', that it is well-recognised and common, and that we don't exactly know why the symptoms arise. And put a stop to an endless string of normal tests. Patients prefer to know what they have wrong, not what they don't have wrong. It hardly helps to be told that the tests are all normal, that there is no evidence of multiple sclerosis or whatever, and yet the symptoms are 'unexplained'. Breaking good news that a test is normal, that there is no 'disease', can easily seem like bad news to patients, unless it is done well. Quite often, patients ask for, even demand, yet another test, with an escalating risk of revealing an incidental finding which has absolutely nothing to do with their symptoms. This must be kindly and firmly resisted.

I have sat in countless meetings being shown radiological images of normal spinal cords and nerve roots of patients admitted urgently to neurosurgery with low back pain and inability to pass urine. They clearly do *not* have what doctors rightly worry about, compression of the nerve roots in their lower back which needs urgent surgery. There is nothing to operate on. And yet so often they are sent home with 'nothing we surgeons can do about it' ringing in their ears or, worse, 'nothing wrong', when there clearly is. Many are quite likely to have a functional neurological disorder — symptoms, certainly, but equally certainly no disease. They mostly get better, and — as with other functional disorders — it is almost unheard of for a relevant diagnosis of a physical disease to emerge.[20]

Explanation may be all the treatment required for functional symptoms, along with calm and kind reassurance from someone who knows what they are talking about and has seen lots of it before. I often used the analogy of a clock that has stopped — the symptom. Either the mechanism is rusted up which would be equivalent to a physical disease, or the clock needs a new battery, equivalent to a functional problem.

For tougher cases one can try hypnotherapy although I personally have not had a lot of success. Maybe I expected too much, although one success for maybe 5–10 failures might be regarded as quite a good track record. Or one can get help from a physiotherapist who is as well signed-up as the doctor to the notion that the patient has a real and pressing problem, a *functional* disorder. The physio can provide a programme of physical exercises to re-establish normal movement patterns if that is the problem,

---

20. I. Hoeritzauer et al., 'Scan-Negative' Cauda Equina Syndrome: A Prospective Cohort Study', *Neurology*, 96 (2021), e433–e437.

as well as encouragement. After all, the functional patient with physical symptoms such as a weak leg rather logically anticipates a treatment that is physical — not something prefixed by 'psych'.

Admittedly it can sometimes be very unclear whether a neurological problem is functional or there is an identifiable underlying physical cause, particularly with some of the odd movement disorders. As a young consultant in Oxford I had a patient with torsion dystonia — his arms, legs and trunk were almost constantly twisting into distorted postures. None of the recommended drugs for what was widely regarded as a physical disease had any effect. The patient himself suggested hypnosis and I discovered a local GP who offered hypnotherapy. After a few sessions the patient was back to almost normal. I took the 'before and after treatment' videos to a neurology meeting in London full of movement disorder experts, many internationally renowned. After the first video they all agreed the man had torsion dystonia. After the second video I asked them what the successful treatment had been. No one got the answer right. When I revealed the truth they were most discombobulated.

To the Solway Firth

Considering how worried I had been before we started, there were at this stage only two problems with the boat. Firstly, the electric automatic bilge pump wouldn't switch itself off, but I could disable it and just turn it on when needed, which was hardly ever as the bilges seldom contained much water. And there was nothing wrong with the two hand-operated bilge pumps for back-up. Secondly, there was no first reefing-line because it was still buried inside the boom, but I could make do with the traditional method of lashing the luff and leech down to the boom. Modern conveniences are fine as long as you know what to do without them — a problem for the younger generation, not so much for ancients like me.

On Tuesday April 10th we left Portpatrick at 7.15am, planning to head south and catch the tide off the Mull of Galloway. Our exit required the usual shouting match between the slightly deaf skipper (me, since my fractured base of skull two years before, of which more later) and the crew who as ever thought they were more competent than I thought they were, which in truth they mostly were. Of course my bad skippering is always worse when I'm nervous, which I certainly was looking at the very bumpy sea at the harbour entrance at low tide with a 20-knot westerly wind blowing in. However, with a reliable engine to force us out there was no problem. It is extraordinary that sailors coped in the old days with no engines at all, or later with unreliable petrol engines. They probably didn't even try going out to sea in these conditions, or they attempted to row out, or perhaps got a tow from a fishing boat that did have an engine.

Once out at sea we had a wonderful sail, wind on the beam, and in sunshine, albeit accompanied by some vomiting by both Lucy and William. They were very good about it, tucked up in the pipe-cots each side of the saloon from which they couldn't really fall out, along with suitably sized vomit bowls that I emptied over the side as they filled them up, while Cathie complained about the cold. Poor Cathie, like her father, has a hopeless blood supply to her peripheries and gets Raynaud's phenomenon very easily, a propensity for the blood flow in one or more often several fingers to close down so they go white and numb, and then blue and painful when the hands warm up.

We got to the Mull in a couple of hours, by which time the wind had eased — thankfully, as I was a bit worried about the tide race which extends a couple of miles offshore, though not completely. The Portpatrick harbour master had told me to hug the coast right under the lighthouse where impressively we found no race at all, even though we could see it disturbing the water just a hundred yards further out. We anchored in East Tarbet Bay, just round from the lighthouse, in a flat calm, open but protected from the west, at 10.15am. A quick and easy 18-mile sail, and not too bad for the family. It was definitely good to be out and about early in the season. Harbours and marinas are not stressed-out by too many boats, and nor are their staff battered by the demands of the summer crowds. Not that there are many summer crowds in Scotland, although there are summers, contrary to the belief of some.

The old slipway in the bay was built to supply the lighthouse and was good for landing in the dinghy. Otherwise there were just a couple of ruined cottages. We had a beautiful late-afternoon walk in the warm sunshine up to the lighthouse from which you get a fabulous panorama of the Irish Sea, with a surprisingly close-up view of the Isle of Man — and an even closer-up view of the tide race with the strip of calm water at the foot of the cliff. Clustered round the base of the lighthouse are the old lighthouse keepers' cottages (which can be rented), and a café and a small museum which were both closed by the time we got there. As had the lighthouse itself, which was a pity because it is one of the few UK lighthouses that you can visit and clamber right up to the top. Everyone else had driven off in their cars, leaving just us with the views and the birds.

Like almost every Scottish lighthouse, this one was built by the Stevenson dynasty of engineers who had so successfully cornered the market after their early success with the Bell Rock lighthouse off the Firth of Tay.[21] Robert Louis Stevenson was the black sheep of the family, preferring to write, but like his relatives he too left a wonderful legacy. Who has not read *Treasure Island*? And how spine-tingling is the panegyric to his family, inscribed at the entrance to the Northern Lighthouse Board in Edinburgh? 'Whenever I smell salt water, I know I am not far from one of the works of my ancestors. The Bell Rock stands monument for my grandfather; the Skerry Vohr for my Uncle Alan; and when the lights come out at sundown along the shores of Scotland, I am proud to think they burn more brightly for the genius of my father.'[22]

By the time we got back to the dinghy the tide had fallen further than I had expected. Embarrassingly, the dinghy had been suspended by its painter until the restorer of one of the cottages had very kindly rescued it. Interestingly, and somewhat unusually, the children had walked well without complaining, almost certainly because Bridget was with us. She seemed to be walking fine too, thanks to the elastic bands. Naturally she was as stubborn as ever, reversing our Pickle order of dealing with dirty dishes: wash, drain and dry from left to right across the two galley sinks. Not, repeat not, right to left. A minor sin, which I tolerated with kindness and understanding — most of the time.

To Kirkcudbright

Wednesday April 11th, another sunny day, albeit with some hail off-and-on — to be ignored. The sea was flat with a good wind behind us as we sped eastwards across Luce Bay. Perfect, and we were so lucky with the wind direction as this coastline is completely open to the south with hardly any harbours of refuge. Right in the middle of the bay we passed close to some nasty unlit rocks, the Scares — Big Scare and Little Scare, such apt names dreamed up by the old seamen and cartographers (although conceivably 'scare' is a witty Anglicisation of the Gaelic *sgeir*, meaning rock). They are easy to avoid in daylight, but not so easy in the dark without a chartplotter.

---

21. Bella Bathurst, *The Lighthouse Stevensons* (London: Harper Collins, 1999).

22. Robert Louis Stevenson, 'Memoirs of Himself', book 1, p. 149, in *Memories and Portraits, Memoirs of Himself, Selections from his Notebook* (orig. 1887; London: William Heinemann, 1924).

I had planned to stop at the Isle of Whithorn where I could have tried drying out against the harbour wall (for the first time in Pickle). This is more or less unnecessary now there are pontoons to tie up to almost everywhere. But it wasn't so long ago that leaning a boat with a single keel against a harbour wall at high tide and letting it settle at a slight angle on the ground at low tide was an important skill to acquire. It would not do to let the boat topple over away from the harbour wall. However, given the excellent sailing conditions, we decided to press on to Kirkcudbright, 34 miles away. I'm afraid that Lucy was cheerfully sick again, twice. I can but hope she will not be put off sailing as a result. Cathie didn't help by being very negative about the Irish Sea, the short waves, and its reputation for invoking nausea. I suspect this rather unwanted message for the children contributed to their seasickness (suggestion again).

But then Cathie is always trying to protect our children from, if not harm, then at least from being unnecessarily uncomfortable. She is the good guy who craves short sails in a beam wind in perfect weather with no swell — me the bad guy who wants to get places, almost come what may. I am often asked if the children enjoy sailing, but have always thought it best not to enquire, in case I get the answer I don't want to hear. (David Cameron foolishly asked the UK whether we wanted to leave the European Union in 2016; he should never have asked.)

No one has written better about the problems, horrors even, of sailing with small children than Libby Purves in *One Summer's Grace*. However, she also pointed out the obvious, that for children it is a magical experience, all the wild life, being on the ocean. And it surely must bring a family closer together, huddled in the saloon playing Ticket-to-Ride or Uno, something we almost never do at home. We are too busy with our separate lives — working, homework, computer games, guitar practice, football, drama club, gardening. On the boat we set up the children with their books, music and stories on their CDs or other devices, and drawing materials. And we can slip reading, writing and arithmetic into everyday life as we explain the charts, the compass, the depth of water under the keel. Plus a bit of spelling practice.

Mind you, my own spelling is awful. When I started research on aspirin as an antiplatelet drug to reduce the risk of heart attacks and strokes (platelets are very small structures which circulate in the blood and are a key part of blood clotting and of thrombosis) I was blissfully unaware of the 'i' in the middle of aspirin, and the 'e' in the middle of platelet. My deficiency was spotted very early, in a school report at the age of ten when the teacher wrote: 'I am astonished to find what a weak speller he is.' How informative, brief and to the point school reports were back then. And at the age of 13, perhaps prophetic for anyone reading this book: 'Some ideas and interest, but not much stylistic polish or accuracy at the moment.' This is so unlike the uninformative and over-long verbiage I get about my children now. I may be told at length what they were supposed to have done, but generally have no idea whether they are doing so well I don't need to worry, or so badly I should employ a tutor (that irresistible fall-back for a state-school parent able to afford one).

We all have to get on with each other on a small boat, help each other and, to an increasing extent as the children — and I — get older, rely more on each other. On a small boat the family becomes a team, a real team. Not like some disparate bunch of demoralised healthcare workers sat in a room attending yet another useless team-building course. Or being harangued by a tedious manager responding to the next manager up the food chain chasing some ridiculous target set by a politician who has moved on by the time it all goes pear-shaped. It is no surprise that all the military services, not just the navy, use sailing as a team-building activity.

One of the truly awful changes in hospital medicine in the last couple of decades has been the loss of the coherent medical team at ward level, the so-called 'firm'. Once upon a time there was a consultant or two who worked with and supervised a senior registrar and a registrar; below them were maybe a couple of senior house officers, and a newly qualified houseman (in those days we never used the term housewoman, even though there were a few). All these terms are slightly dated now, with unappealing or at least unmemorable numbers and letters having taken their place. The firm did regular ward rounds together on 'their' ward with 'their' patients (a downside, though, was that we weren't always too good at respecting patients' privacy). The team drank coffee and ate buns together in the Ward Sister's office. We all had lunch together in the days when hospitals still had a doctors' mess (later abolished as too elitist). The firm stayed together for perhaps four months, after which those below the registrar rotated on to the next part of their training, while the registrars generally stayed for longer. Medical students were part of the firm too, maybe for a month or more.

We 1960s housemen all lived in the hospital and were on call for months at a time, but it was not that bad. At least we knew all the patients we were called to see, and we could knock off for the occasional night or even a weekend with cross-cover from a friendly colleague. We watched a lot of

TV; some played bridge. At night or weekends we didn't have to cover wards full of patients we didn't know, staffed by nurses who didn't know us. It is now far more difficult to deal with problems over the phone, because the doctor and nurse don't know each other, and the doctor doesn't know the patient.

We worked closely with the nurses on our ward — occasionally slept with them too, and sometimes married them in the days when doctors were mostly men and nurses mostly women (staggering on to the ward in the morning after not much sleep, I will never forget the smell of toast being made by a sympathetic nurse). We all knew each other, we went out for meals and to the pub together, and often we went round to the consultant's house for dinner, or for tennis if he (no 'she' at St George's then) was rich and lived in a big house. I was once taken to Glyndebourne (never went again; opera is not my thing). We knew each other's strengths and weaknesses. We knew whom we could rely on. We supported each other, we felt as though we belonged, and were valued. Often we made lifelong friends. We could spot colleagues getting stressed out and do something about it. We could avoid burnout. Unlike nowadays, we were not commuting shift-workers, with nowhere to sit down at work, or have a cup of tea. In 2019 the GMC national training survey found that over half of the trainees didn't receive their on-call rotas with six weeks' notice, so how were they supposed to book holidays, weddings and other important events? We were professionals. I certainly never felt like an employee. We thought for ourselves, and weren't handed a set of tasks to tick off (so meaningless unless one knows the patients). Fixed rotas and unsympathetic or indeed any sort of managers were almost unheard of, at least at junior doctor level. It is quite different now, so brutally as well as wittily described by Adam Kay, who abandoned his own medical career, in *This is Going to Hurt*.[23]

Nowadays consultants often have to work with junior doctors they hardly know, or who may be away on yet another course, or having time off after an exhausting night on call in a completely different part of the hospital. The rotas are very rigid with little give and take. Part of the reason is the European Working Time Directive which so limited the hours we can work, although apparently it could have been somewhat circumvented, and in practice has not affected consultants, nor I suspect plumbers and fishermen.

---

23. Adam Kay, *This is Going to Hurt: Secret Diaries of a Junior Doctor* (London: Picador, 2017).

Sadly, at the time I was close to retiring, a junior doctor, when asked to present a patient on a ward round, often had to read me notes written by another doctor who was no longer around. More than once I snapped, 'I can read these notes for myself, thank you.' Of course the modern managers, and educationalists, are very keen on teaching team-working, but they have ignored the teams that really worked — the medical 'firms'. Maybe the new-in-2018 post of 'Chief People Officer' for the NHS in England will help. In Walsall they have gone one step further with a Director of People *and* Culture. Pigs may fly too.

Another difficulty is the modern insistence on so much formal training instead of the relaxed, even matey informality of the old teams where we learned almost without knowing it. Mind you, the 'see one, do one, teach one' mentality was seldom appropriate. As a student I was not even taught properly how to take blood — a nurse thrust a syringe into my hand and told me to get on with it. Manikins had not yet made their appearance to spare patients' orifices from the prods and pokes of young doctors and medical students, nor had 'how to do it' videos on YouTube. However, somehow my generation learned lots, and it was even quite fun, notwithstanding the long hours. Of course we whinged a bit, perhaps a lot, but today's junior doctors have a right to whinge far more: they have a harder life and without the support we had. And now they can do so much more for patients in the way of drips, monitors, drugs, and procedures, their life is much busier than mine was.

At one of our departmental quizzes just before I retired a slide was shown with 10 faces on it. The consultants were asked which five had been our junior doctors in the last year, and what their names were. Unsurprisingly we did not do very well. In contrast, I am still in touch with one of the last surviving consultants I worked with when a very junior doctor; she is now nearly 90. Pauline Monro was the first woman to be appointed as a consultant at St George's Hospital. So unusual was this in 1969 that when she very nervously asked at the reception desk where the interviews were for the consultant neurology post, the man behind the desk looked her up and down, frowned, examined his list, and then asked her if she was sure she didn't mean the post of domestic supervisor. For a fleeting moment it passed through her mind that maybe he was right!

In the current generation I don't see these sorts of friendships. We can't even select our own junior staff now; they are selected for us by national committees who know nothing of the local situation and likely success of on-the-ground interpersonal and professional relationships.

Nonetheless, today's enthusiastic junior doctors have somehow adapted and they get through their training, but it can't be half so much fun — or as professionally satisfying — as it was for my generation. Not that I would want to go back to being on call every night and day for weeks at a time. But there must be a middle way. Regrettably, there is nothing I can do about this in retirement, and nothing I could do even when it was all changing. The Association of British Neurologists had no executive power — we were at the mercy of the politicians and the rather too acquiescent Royal Colleges of Physicians (it should be a rule never to elect a President of a Royal College unless they already have a knighthood). So, back to the sailing.

A big tide under us across the Solway had us arrive too early to catch the rising tide up the River Dee to Kirkcudbright. As advised by Murdoch Mackenzie, we waited for 'the tide, by dropping anchor between the Island Little Ross and Torres Head, on three and a quarter or four fathoms water'[24] Then, after some lunch, we motored for an hour up the shallowing and narrowing river, following the modern Sailing Directions with some care. As ever, it was much easier than it had seemed when reading about it beforehand, although one must always be prepared. The smells wafting from the land changed from seaweed, to trees and fields, to mud. There was a surprising amount of mud at low tide, the navigation buoys were dried out at the edge of the steeply dredged channel — most unlike the mainly rocky shores of the rest of Scotland.

Once tied up to the local authority pontoon in Kirkcudbright aided by the friendly harbour master, we could have been on an inland river rather than the sea — if not for the rise and fall of the tide. There weren't many fancy boats up here (in fact rather downmarket boats), but that was just fine. Some scallop boats were exporting their catch to France and Spain. It is weird to think that more than half of the seafood we catch is exported, while more than half of what we eat is imported; at least, that was the case before the chaos of Brexit. I was surprised to hear that there was a long waiting list for pontoon berths, presumably because this is the only deep-water and safe mooring spot on the north Solway coast. However, there seems to be almost nowhere to cruise to, at least for weekends.

Kirkcudbright turned out to be a charming town of narrow streets, Georgian and Victorian houses, and small friendly shops, but with only one pub that we could find — the Masonic Arms — which did not admit children. What a daft rule that is, and one which varies so much from place

---

24. Mackenzie, *Nautical Descriptions*, 22.

to place, and pub to pub, depending on the licence category. The town was all very quiet, and rather deserted. There were surprisingly few decent cafés, and as far as we could see not many restaurants, but we were probably not looking hard enough. However, there was a swimming pool, a good Co-op supermarket a few minutes away for morning croissants and stocking up, a funny little place down a lane to get laundry done, and nice (as well as less nice) galleries because, after all, Kirkcudbright does badge itself as 'The Artists' Town'.

Broughton House, looked after by The National Trust for Scotland, is the attractive former Georgian home of the artist E. A. Hornel, one of the 'Glasgow Boys'. Not all artists were impoverished like Van Gogh, and Hornel certainly wasn't. He seems to have churned out paintings and made good money from them. The castle is another Kirkcudbright attraction, an impressive 16th-century ruin bang in the middle of town, more of a fortified L-plan house than a defendable castle, I think. It was good for the children to run around in, and play hide and seek.

Before we left Kirkudbright I fixed the rim of the top-loading fridge which had descended away from the galley work-surface to which it had only been glued, a surprisingly feeble arrangement for a Rustler. After a quick mobile phone call to Rustlers in Falmouth for advice, I glued it up with araldite. Not having any clamps, I had to weave a spider's web of ropes to pull the rim up underneath the work-surface while the glue dried overnight. It worked and, to my surprise, was still intact at the end of the cruise (it collapsed later and is now fixed with araldite *and* screws). I never had this problem on the Contessa 32. No fridge. As a child, I can remember my father bringing home araldite, a new and miraculous glue in two tubes, the contents of which had to be mixed together. He told me sternly never ever to put the wrong cap on the wrong tube or he would never get it off. I tell my own children the same, sternly.

A less fixable problem was my intermittent vertigo. In 2010, near the Crinan Canal, I had tripped and plunged headfirst into the cockpit of Richard Robert's boat, briefly knocked myself out, and woke up surrounded by a very worried crew. There was a lot of blood coming from a cut earlobe. What I didn't know until I coughed was that blood was also squirting out of my ear, a sure sign of a fractured base of skull. So off by taxi I went to Lochgilphead to the Mid Argyll Community Hospital and Integrated Care Centre (with the delightful acronym of MACHICC) where the medical care was exemplary. No waiting in A&E, an attentive local GP, my cut ear glued up, a quick skull X-ray which looked normal, and into bed to be monitored overnight by local nurses and fed with local food. There was no point sending me all the way to Paisley for a CT brain scan, an odd destination anyway as the neurosurgeons (if anyone was needed it would be them) were just up the road at the Southern General Hospital in Glasgow. I did have the scan the next day back in Edinburgh where my neuroradiological colleagues eventually found the fracture. My favoured neurologist (carefully chosen of course) and then neurosurgeon both said there was nothing to be done (I knew that already) and that I would almost certainly get better, which in a few weeks I did. The headache, unsteadiness, sore ear, poor concentration, listlessness, fatigue and general malaise all faded away. This was surely a fine example of distributed but joined-up healthcare extending from a GP in a distant community hospital to a neurosurgeon in a very specialised department 100-or-so miles away.

Irritatingly, I was left with some deafness, hardly surprising as the fracture went through my inner ear. And with brief attacks of irritating but intermittent vertigo over periods of days or sometimes weeks, because I had presumably dislodged little bits of stuff in the tiny tubes in my inner ear that control balance. This unpleasant feeling of my head spinning round very fast was accompanied by equally fast jerky movements of my eyes, called nystagmus. Typically for this condition, my attacks were brought on by certain head positions, and lasted seconds. In between them, I also had a vague feeling of imbalance, which was annoying but not really disabling. Again, typically, this all settled down in a few weeks. Until, on this cruise, I slipped on the Kirkcudbright pontoons, and landed with a bang on my bum. The inevitable jerk of my head was enough to set off another bout of vertigo.

One must never waste experiences like this so I wrote up my own case of post-head injury vertigo in *Practical Neurology*, in the 'Me and my Neurological Illness' section.[25] There is nothing so educational and illuminating as a neurologist telling the story of their own neurological illness, as many have done before me and after me. The neurologist as patient sees the world very differently from the neurologist as doctor.

To Maryport in England

It's tricky sailing the 25 miles from Kirkcudbright to Maryport. There is not enough depth of water to leave Kirkcudbright until near high tide, so it will

---

25. Charles Warlow, 'A (So-Called) Mild Head Injury', *Practical Neurology*, 13 (2013), 260–2.

almost inevitably be near low tide on arrival off Maryport, sailing at 3–4 knots. There you would have to heave to or anchor and wait several hours for the lock to open around the time of the next high tide, about 12 hours after leaving Kirkcudbright. The solution was to take the evening ebb tide to Little Ross Island five miles downriver from Kirkcudbright for an overnight stop, and then in the morning set off at low tide and sail to Maryport to arrive at high tide. The harbour master tipped us off about a useful mooring buoy by the island that was seldom used by the boat monitoring the nearby firing range. We tied up to it on a sunny evening with views across to England and the mountains of the Lake District, and had supper.

Friday April 13th, another sunny day, with enough time to go ashore and explore the small island. It was clearly privately owned, but only later did I discover who had rented it for 25 years — Roger Wild, the radiologist who in 1995 had run his ultrasound scanner over my liver to look for any secondary deposits from my colon cancer (there were none). How very tense that moment had been for me, and probably for him too. It is not easy looking after a colleague.

Roger and his family had done good things on the island. They had restored the lighthouse keepers' cottages which were no longer needed after the light was automated, installed solar panels and a wind turbine, and got vegetables going in the old walled garden which had been built for the keepers. Not that long ago, in 1960, one of the keepers murdered the other one; maybe it was all too much living at close quarters with no one else around. Curiously, Hamish Haswell-Smith, an architect by profession but who could turn his hand to more or less anything, did not describe this island in the first edition of his magisterial and now classic book about Scottish islands.[26] It was too small to be included — given his arbitrary criterion of less than 40 hectares.

We had a perfect afternoon sail to Maryport on a flat enough sea for the family to be content, even though we were close-hauled on the port tack in an east and then northeast wind. It was even flat enough to sail across the rather ominously named 'Two-foot bank' as well as the less worrying 'Three-Fathoms Bank', naturally with help from the chartplotter. We passed quite close to the Robin Rigg offshore wind farm completed only two years earlier. I don't have a problem with wind farms, onshore or offshore. Given that we must abandon fossil fuels and generate renewable energy to reduce the hazards of global warming, the turbines seem a small price to pay. They

---

26. Hamish Haswell-Smith, *The Scottish Islands: A Comprehensive Guide to Every Scottish Island* (Edinburgh: Canongate Books, 1996).

are not ugly, in fact they are rather elegant, and can be dramatic to look at, in the right scenery. Nor in my experience are they unpleasantly noisy (at least not the three on the Island of Gigha where we had stayed in a cottage right by three of them — nicely named Faith, Hope and Charity, now joined by Harmony). Objecting to them because they slice up birds that haven't learned to avoid the slowly revolving blades, as the RSPB has done, is ridiculous. There won't be any birds to slice up if even more serious climate change takes hold. It is estimated that between 10,000 and 100,000 birds in the UK are killed by wind turbines every year which sounds a lot. But not compared with the 55 million killed by domestic cats[27]. Does the RSPB intend to shoot cats, like the good Dr Theakston of Hutton-le-Hole? I would far rather have wind turbines than nuclear power stations with all their risks, and the problem of disposing spent nuclear fuel rods, or coal-fired power station chimneys belching carbon dioxide into the atmosphere.

We arrived off Maryport early, an hour before the lock gates were due to open, but we were soon tied up in the half-empty marina for afternoon tea. Why Maryport? It might seem a diversion in a sail south down the Irish Sea, and hardly a hot tourist destination. But there was a very good reason. Had I arrived in the late 19th century, my great-grandfather would have been looking out for me from his big house overlooking the Solway Firth.

THE MULL OF GALLOWAY

---

27. BBC Science Focus Magazine, 15th February, 2022.

Chapter 5

From Maryport to Milford Haven, via the Isle of Man and Ireland

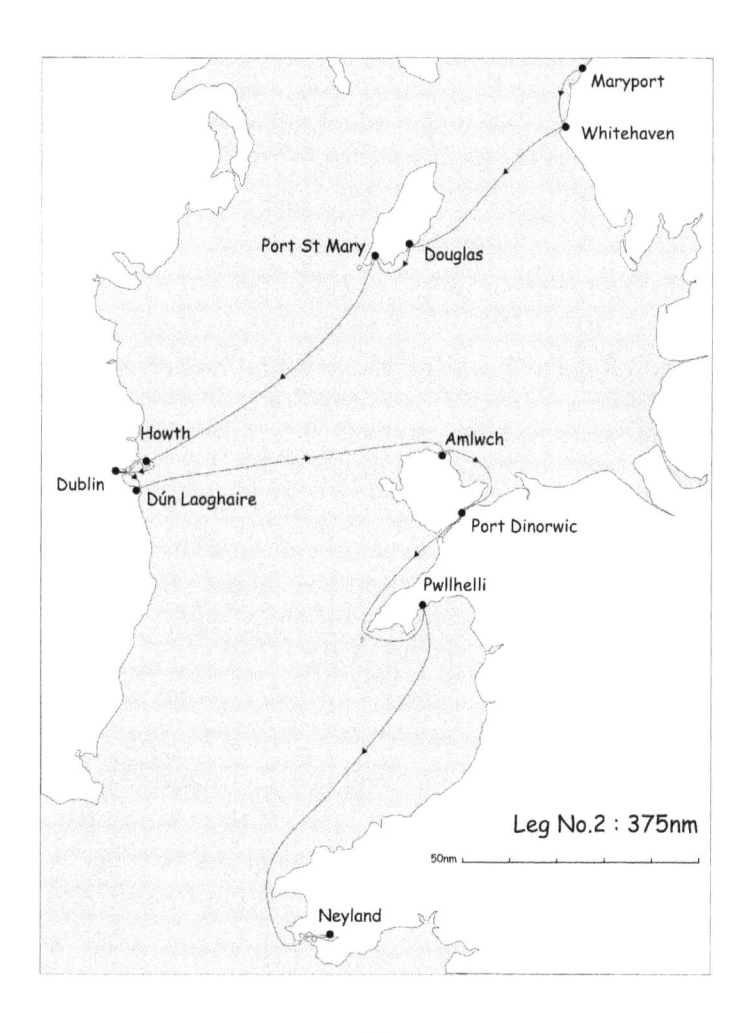

Leg No.2 : 375nm

We tied up to a pontoon in the very same dock from where my great-grandfather's ships had sailed the world in the late 19th century. Unable to pay its creditors, his company — the Holme Line — went suddenly bust in 1907, after which Maryport gradually declined to the sad state it is in today. Alfred Hine, my mother's grandfather, had died in 1902 at the age of 61, before the disaster. His business partner, his older brother Wilfred, had to sell everything, including his own house. He later retired to London to live in what was described as 'genteel poverty' by Ian Hine in *A Cumberland Endeavour*.[1] None of the wealth that Alfred and Wilfred Hine must have accumulated trickled down to the subsequent generations. It all went we know not where.

The docks finally closed in 1962 and eventually the whole area was cleaned up, landscaped, grassed over, memories faded and buried. There is no sign of the rail tracks to the dockside along which so much coal, iron and steel was once delivered by the Maryport and Carlisle Railway to the Holme Line for transporting to Australia, South America, Canada and the United States. There had even been a Maryport shipbuilding industry, although the river is so narrow that ships had to be launched broadside.

The old dockside buildings are gone, some replaced with not bad-looking 'waterside apartments' under which there must have been plans for shops and restaurants which have not materialised. We found the whole place to be very quiet indeed, more or less silent, just an occasional child in the play park. There were no bling motor cruisers in the less-than-full marina, nor even many of those mass-produced yachts for the charter industry, rather a more down-at-heel and eclectic selection, with, pleasingly, one Contessa 32. The local council owned the marina and I imagine had very little money to spend on it. It had not been particularly well maintained; only a couple of years earlier the lock gates had collapsed to let in a mini-tsunami from the Solway Firth which did for the pontoons as well as the boats attached to them.

What were those highly religious, Baptist, teetotal, Victorian entrepreneurial Hine brothers like? My ancestors. Were they hard-hearted gang-masters, or kindly Quaker-like employers? Did they drive their sea captains too hard? Is that why so many of their ships foundered, or was that just how it was in those days? They were not themselves seamen, but businessmen immersed

---

1. Ian Hine, *A Cumberland Endeavour — Hine Bros. of Maryport: The People, the Ships, the Town* (Words by Design, 2012).

in ship ownership and management, brokerage and marine insurance. Why couldn't they pay their creditors? We don't really know.

Alfred's son, my mother's father, John McLennan Hine, trained as a marine engineer, and worked initially for the Holme Line before setting up his own company. He had married well, to Lydia Booth, in what must have been a very grand Edwardian wedding at Plashwood Park in Suffolk. Their family left Maryport in 1907 and moved to Luton, and then to Nottingham, where John Hine worked for an insurance company. I should have paid far more attention to my elderly relatives' stories when I was younger, particularly to Great Aunt Ethel (John's sister) and to Mary her daughter, who both lived in Beckenham. If only I could ask our dumb late 18th-century grandfather clock, made in Whitehaven, which was passed down from my grandmother to my mother and chimed away the hours during my and my children's childhoods. What has that clock seen over the centuries?

To help me understand at least some of my family history, and to join the crew, my brother John arrived the day before our arrival. He had been staying in the Sailor's Return, a remarkably inexpensive bed and breakfast establishment by the harbour. We all found exceptionally friendly people and a good pub supper in the Lifeboat Inn, and very inexpensive real ale at £2.40 a pint.

Saturday April 14th was the day for our local exploration. It was beautifully sunny but still cold — cold enough to value the cabin-heater for a quick blast of comfort in the evenings. As in the pub the night before, the people in the small shops were wonderfully friendly. It was a delight to shop in them. The hardware and DIY shop was outstanding. Up the hill away from the dock, John and I came across the surprise of Fleming Square, a quiet and elegant domestic Georgian and Victorian backwater. Further up still we found the pair of very large semi-detached houses that the Hine brothers had built for themselves. They are mirror images of each other — Park Hill for Alfred, Camp Hill for Wilfred. From both they would have had a fine view of the sea and their ships appearing over the horizon, no doubt bringing home their fortunes. These are still among the largest houses in the town which otherwise seemed to consist mostly of neat Victorian terraces in the centre with an outer ring of run-down modern estates with, we were told, huge unemployment and drug problems. But what is there to do here in the way of work? It seems too far away to commute easily to Carlisle to the north or to the nuclear industry in Sellafield to the south; maybe a few have jobs down the coast in Workington or Whitehaven, or in tourism.

The small Maritime Museum had relatively recently reopened and was run, as these places so often are, by a band of volunteer enthusiasts. And what a delightful place it was, well laid-out, and with excellent activities for children. Here they could learn about the code flags, spelling out their names with them, and look at the games that sailors used to play on board ship, like deck quoits. Not surprisingly, the museum staff were interested to hear about our connection with Maryport — we were even interviewed by a journalist on the local paper (not that anything much was actually published). It is almost impossible to imagine how busy the harbour must have been in its heyday. All we could do was look at the black and white photographs in the museum, and wonder. Perhaps Maryport will decline even further and revert to the drying harbour where in the late 18th century Murdoch Mackenzie found there were 'twelve feet of water, at high-water, with ordinary spring-tide, and eight with neap-tide'.[2] I came away feeling incredibly sad, thinking of what Maryport once was, helped along by my ancestors, compared with what it now is — forgotten, ignored, washed-up. Almost nobody I know has a clue where Maryport is. I wonder if my mother's second name of Mary came from here.

By late afternoon it was time to say goodbye to Cathie, Bridget and the children who all left by train for Edinburgh, leaving me and John to have another meal in the Lifeboat Inn before returning to the silent marina for the night.

Sunday, April 15th, and the arrival of the rest of the new crew: Jake Broadhurst and Greg Moran, fit and eager young men in their 40s, which was ideal given that I didn't really fancy the Irish Sea with just my ageing brother and my slightly less ageing self. Jake was an administrator drumming up international business for Edinburgh University. He had done a lot of crewing on various keel-boats, and racing, so he was for ever fiddling with the sails. 'Trim, trim' was his favourite expression, while I yawned and leant on the tiller for support. Greg was much more laid-back. He had recently bought a Contessa 26, a classic small yacht from the 1970s that he sailed on the Forth, handy for day trips from his home in Edinburgh. He had been a colleague, a clinical neurophysiologist, a specialist in recording and measuring the electrical activity of the brain, nerves and muscles to help diagnose what is going on in patients with various neurological symptoms. Is it epilepsy, a damaged nerve in the hand,

---

2. Murdoch Mackenzie, *Nautical Descriptions of the West Coast of Great Britain from Bristol Channel to Cape-Wrath* (London, 1776), 23.

an inflamed muscle? Clinical neurophysiologists have fairly stress-free days of nine-to-five. They seldom get involved with managing patients. They are diagnosticians, like radiologists with their X-rays and scanners. For some reason, it is not an attractive speciality. It is hard to recruit and even retain staff, notwithstanding the very respectable consultant salary. A few years after our cruise Greg himself more or less retired, at the age of 50, leaving no permanent consultant clinical neurophysiologist in Edinburgh for several years (why Glasgow had five was quite beyond me).

To Douglas, Isle of Man, via Whitehaven

After going through the safety briefing (well done me for remembering to do this) we set off as soon as the lock gates opened, at 6pm on a beautiful sunny evening. I was eager to get the 11 miles down the coast to Whitehaven before dark. It would then be a somewhat better angle to the wind for the Isle of Man the next day, forecast to come from the south. That evening what wind there was came from the southwest, against us to begin with, so we made rather slow progress, assisted by the engine for a while. As we passed the industrial coastal scenery of Workington with its many wind turbines, the wind picked up from the west, and we arrived off Whitehaven at 9.30pm. Fortunately, the entrance was quite easy, even in the dark, although we had to get the tidal timing right for the lock gates that were opened for us. The lock-keeper threw down a package of papers which showed us where to go. In we went to tie up to one of the pontoons in the large marina within the huge old dock, another relic of the coal-exporting age. Like Maryport, Whitehaven had been cleaned up and is adapting to the leisure industry — adapting rather well given the £27 a night marina charge compared with about half that in Maryport, £15. But there was no extra fee for opening the lock gates out-of-hours, unlike some marinas (Liverpool, and Limehouse in London, come to mind).

Unfortunately we didn't have much time in the morning to explore the town that is bigger, and looks more prosperous, than Maryport, and has quite a maritime history too. Not least it was the target of the only American naval raid on Britain led by one John Paul Jones in 1778. Luckily he failed, otherwise we would all be in a rather different situation — Prime Minister Donald Trump perhaps. Engraved into some paving stones we found 'Here in days of old, voyage deals were struck over a firm handshake and a piece of gold. Pigtails and rum-soaked buckled shoes brought home the recent foreign news. Memories of this small piece of ground, fluted iron stubs, a lock-up and a lamp were taken to many a sailor's grave.' We made a quick dash to the Tesco supermarket that was very close to the marina, and another quick dash to look round the town, completely missing at least two butchers, a greengrocer and a baker (all of which I found on a later, more leisurely visit). Too bad — we wanted to be sure to get to the Isle of Man 39 miles away before the Douglas harbour flap-gate shut, two hours either side of high water. There was no gate in 1776, just a drying harbour described by Murdoch Mackenzie: 'A vessel that draws ten feet of water may go into Douglas Harbour at about high-water with neap-tide, a ship that draws fourteen may have water to go in about high-water with spring-tide.'[3] We left Whitehaven at 10.30am as soon as the tide was high enough for the lock gates to be opened.

The sail to Douglas was close-hauled, almost all on one port tack, in a rising wind up to about 25 knots in the end. It was quite tough; certainly Jake found it so because he spent a lot of time being sick, noisily. Nor was brother John too good. He was not just sick but needed to use the heads quite often. This was awkward in a tossing boat — so much so that he dislodged the toilet seat, something which had often happened before and was easily put right in Douglas. This got me thinking about ageing, again. Would I be like John when I am his age? Would I cope with sailing Pickle? Will we both fade like our father who managed to disguise his cognitive decline in his 70s behind the sharper wits of my mother, even after a stroke damaged her language abilities? After she died in 1987, he went rapidly downhill and died a year later. Not that John or I had any obvious memory problems, we were just frailer than we used to be, stiffer and slower, easily thrown across the cockpit by a big wave — he is just seven years further along the track than me. This is sad when I remember how athletic he was, playing cricket, racquets, and squash to just under a Cambridge half-blue level.

How much longer have I got, I wondered. Will my brain go before my body, or my body before my brain? Not that we have any choice in the matter, any more than we can choose the manner of our eventual death, as the writing on one of my coffee mugs reminds me: 'Beware the deadly donkey falling slowly from the sky. You can choose the way you live my friend, but not the way you die'.[4] My brain seemed OK but the body was

---

3. Mackenzie, *Nautical Descriptions*, 21.

4. The ditty on a mug designed by Edward Monkton, the pen name of Giles Andreae (b. 1966), writer, artist, illustrator, humourist and Old Etonian friend of David

not in full working order what with the intermittent vertigo, and a general feeling of imbalance. In addition, I was very aware that I was not as strong as I had been, not so nimble, although being on boats a lot over the years does help. John suggested that I should look at him and then imagine myself when I got to his age. Well, as I write this I have passed that age, and am certainly more hesitant on stairs than I was, tending to hold a bannister if there is one, and consciously preparing to step down or up. But still sailing Pickle, for now.

As we got closer to the Isle of Man we were reminded it was not part of the UK when Greg's mobile phone, without apparently being used, informed him that he had racked up a £20 charge. And then £30! Something to do with a fancy smartphone quietly doing its own thing, even if you don't think it is (this was before roaming charges in Europe were abolished in 2017, but thanks to the Brexiteers are now back). So we had to beware in foreign countries, but hadn't thought the Isle of Man was all that foreign. Wrong.

Luckily we only had to make one final short tack to arrive off Douglas in reasonable time, at 7.30pm. But we then had a very rough sail across Douglas Bay against a strong wind with waves rushing into the harbour, a lot of spray, and rain too. Rather strangely, we could only make 2 knots over the ground, even with the engine to help, presumably against some sort of tide. We had a second reef in the mainsail, and maybe another one should have been put in. I am rather bad at reefing in good time — ideally, reefing needs to happen before one really has to, when it is easier to achieve. But who reefs when they are supposed to, in other words when you first think about it? Maybe I get away with my lack of diligence because Pickle, as a quite heavy displacement boat, doesn't really need reefing until the wind gets up to 15–20 knots.

Under the circumstances it was a horrible entrance, and somewhat alarming. So it was with some relief that we motored through the open swing-bridge into the marina and tied up out of the wind. That evening I certainly agreed with Heckstall Smith, writing in the 1930s: 'I know of no place like the cabin of a well-found yacht where this feeling of content is so strongly emphasized, especially after a hard day's sailing.'[5] It hadn't been that hard for us, just a bit unpleasant.

Cameron.

5. S. Heckstall Smith, *Isle, Ben and Loch, from the Clyde to Skye* (London: Edward Arnold, 1932), 123.

A tour of the Isle of Man

Douglas is an odd place. Jonathan Raban was struck by 'its miniature railways, its miniature roads, its miniature landscape and its miniature news' with which 'it was clear that the Isle of Man was not so much itself as a scale model of something bigger'.[6] Notwithstanding a large yacht named 'A-Crewed Interest' (oh, how very funny), my own first impression from the marina was rather good, a sort of Copenhagen-like waterfront with historic houses lined up behind the pontoons. But beyond them came the banks for the rich people in which to conceal their money from the UK taxman. It is not surprising that smuggling was a major industry here in times past. Further behind the banks is a somewhat decaying Victorian seaside resort, but with a grand promenade. The traffic-free cobbled main street was rather attractive, and the crew told me the local museum was excellent. However, the people seemed glum and not that friendly, in stark contrast to the much more downmarket Maryport.

The Isle of Man has a reputation for being old-fashioned, stuck in a 1950s time-warp. 'We never had the sixties here,' said a resident to Libby Purves, 'Not sure we've had the fifties yet really.'[7] Luckily, I had local friends to show us round, William Jeffcoate and Nadina Lincoln, who were to join us on the next leg. They lived partly in Nottingham and partly on the Isle of Man, largely because William was in love with the island where his mother had come from. Indeed she had been born in one of the houses near Douglas Harbour. So off we all went in a charming tram that has been running since the 1890s. The Isle of Man had to generate its own electricity to power it, and any surplus electricity was used for their first electric streetlights.

Our objective was the 19th-century Laxey wheel, the largest working waterwheel in the world. Not that it actually works anything anymore — rotating waterwheel would be a better description. It was constructed to drive the pumps to keep the now-closed lead, zinc and silver mine dry. The island has no coal, and in fact much of that was imported from Maryport, hence the need for local hydropower. The Laxey miners had a terrible life, in the morning climbing down hundreds of feet by ladder with just a candle stuck on their helmets for light, then back up again in the evening.

---

6. Jonathan Raban, *Coasting: A Private Journey* (orig. 1986; New York: First Vintage Departure Edition, 2003), 66.

7. Libby Purves, *One Summer's Grace: A Family Voyage round Britain* (London: Grafton Books, 1989), 100.

The man who designed the wheel, Robert Casement, was from the local village, and a self-taught engineer.

This got me thinking about why we encourage more and more school leavers to go to university, particularly to do what seem rather useless degrees and in such large numbers that they cannot possibly all get jobs for which some degrees are overly specific (the numbers are capped in medicine to match the need for doctors, but they are not in sports management and media studies). So often today's graduates land up in jobs that never needed a degree in the first place, working in bars, restaurants and shops, on Deliveroo bicycles, in call centres, Amazon warehouses and, most dispiriting of all, in those airless, windowless and over-priced retail mazes that you are forced to walk through before boarding an aeroplane. And even if they could find a job they would be saddled with thousands of pounds of debt because in 2012 the Tory government, propped up the Liberal Democrats (who should have known better than to renege on their pre-election promises), dramatically increased university tuition fees in England from about £3000 to £9000 per annum; in Scotland there are still no fees at all. To add insult to injury the so-called top universities are nowadays mostly interested not in their teaching, but in their research prowess and income, which I first realised in 1998 when an academic colleague's research income was praised in her funeral eulogy.

In an attempt to improve their balance sheets, universities now offer a proliferation of postgraduate degrees to make their graduates even more 'educated', but not necessarily more employable. Yes, we need a knowledge-based economy, but we also need to be able to make things, and to fix them rather than throwing them away. John Gardner's remark sums it up: 'A society which scorns excellence in plumbing simply because it is plumbing, but rewards mediocre philosophy simply because it is philosophy, will soon become a society in which neither its pipes nor its theories will hold water.'[8]

After leaving school, what is so wrong with, for example, an apprenticeship in plumbing, of course with an educational component mixed in? You get paid while being properly taught along the way — and you do a job that actually exists, not educated to do a job that may not exist. You can go to university later, part-time or full-time, if you want to, and if you can afford the fees.

Barbara Farrell had no degree and not much experience either, except of quite a difficult life, when she became a clinical trial manager with me in Oxford. By her retirement she was the doyen of trial managers,

---

8. John Gardner, in a letter to the *Lancet* in 1961.

much sought-after for her advice and training, including by the Medical Research Council. Mark Fitzgerald, married to a neurologist friend, left school without any qualifications at all, become a joiner, thought better of it, joined a small investment firm in Northern Ireland and then Barclays on the bottom rung of the ladder (in the Isle of Man as it happens), and soon became a big earner in the City of London. But, as he told me, he had a hunger to succeed, a quality not necessarily reflected by having a first-class degree from a 'top' university. Perhaps most remarkably, Godfrey Hounsfield, who invented the CT scanner, never went to university but that didn't stop him getting the Nobel Prize for Physiology or Medicine. It is difficult to imagine today's schoolkids taking his advice on accepting the Nobel Prize — 'Don't worry if you can't pass exams, so long as you feel you have understood the subject.'[9] Pushy parents wouldn't agree either, and I might find it difficult too, even though I entirely approve of the sentiment.

To redress the overemphasis on research, universities have more recently been assessed on their teaching, but the metric does not inspire confidence — the Teaching Excellence Framework. It has been seriously suggested that in part it should take account of graduate salaries. Universities will then be sorely tempted to abandon degrees leading to lower-income careers — like creative arts, nursing and teaching — and work up degrees in medicine and anything which might lead to a lucrative job in finance (sadly where so many maths, physics and engineering graduates currently end up, making money rather than useful things — it must be so boring).

In the UK, universities are still easier to get into if your parents are rich, and on the whole graduates have a better chance in life than non-graduates. Poor kids living in poor areas, with maybe just one parent struggling to cope, who go to poor schools, have far less chance of getting to university. State schools simply don't have the funding to pull up even bright children from deprived backgrounds and to close the 'attainment gap' between the rich and poor.

When I was a medical student, nurses came straight from school and learned on the job. These days they go to university, if they can afford to. Unfortunately, once qualified for a few years, many now move from the stress of the wards to where the money is, becoming specialist or research nurses, and managers. Doctor training has moved somewhat in the opposite direction. I spent three years learning the basics of anatomy, biochemistry and physiology with no patient contact at all. Only then was I let loose on patients. Nowadays patient contact is much earlier, often in the first year.

---

9. Godfrey Hounsfield, obituary, *BMJ*, 329 (2004), 687.

But without the old apprentice system when clinical students were attached to a 'firm' with a consultant at its head, consultants now haven't a clue who the students are, in contrast to my staying in touch with several who taught me. How memorable they all were, even the bad teachers from whom one learned how *not* to do it. Once, at the end of a teaching ward round, the rather short urological surgeon jabbed his finger at me standing at the back of the group of eight or so students:

'You!' he shouted, going red in the face.

'Me?'

'Yes, you,' going even redder, maybe purple. 'Remember, truculence is no substitute for diligence!'

I had only asked an innocent question. That surgeon was awful. He shouted at male patients on the ward in public, about quite private things (well, their parts). He sent medical students to run round the block if they answered a question wrongly. He inspected our fingernails, which maybe was a good thing. He was not a friend. But I will never forget his admonition, and how *not* to teach.

It is from the best teachers that one learns how to teach, at least bedside medicine — and not from the proliferation of formal courses. Mike O'Sullivan, who always got the most complimentary student feedback in Edinburgh neurology, learned to teach from observing his own best teachers when a medical student in Cork. He also had the advantage of being a surgeon, a neurosurgeon. Surgeons tend to think in black and white, which is much more popular with medical students — including me when I was one — than physicians' shades of grey punctuated with uncertainties (dithering, as the surgeons would say).

A stereotype not a million miles from the truth is that when a surgeon is not sure whether to do something he — and increasingly she — will tend to do it, while a physician tends not to. So many of my best teachers at medical school were surgeons, and usually not consultants but registrars, and more often working in the NHS than in universities with their over-emphasis on research (big grants in, lots of papers out). Peter Lord was so popular as a senior registrar that when he got a consultant surgeon post in Chertsey we asked him to give us St George's students teaching rounds, which he did even though we had to travel 24 miles to attend them.

A major difficulty when learning clinical medicine is that you don't start with chapter one of a textbook, you are confronted with a patient with a problem. This requires pulling in knowledge from all over the place, hence the quite reasonable fashion for 'problem-based learning' that I had seen being pioneered at McMaster University in Canada in the early 1980s. Mind you, it can be taken too far if students are left to explore the various available resources without guidance, so-called FoFo learning (Fuck off and Find out). You still need a framework of anatomical, physiological and biochemical knowledge from somewhere — usually learned in the first few years during the pre-clinical course. As a student, learning *clinical* medicine seemed to me like putting together a 1000-piece jigsaw with no edges and, worse, as soon as you had sorted out one area the picture expanded and more pieces were thrown onto the board. No wonder I nearly gave up and dabbled with becoming a photographer, going so far as to talk to the photographic editor of the *Sunday Times*. I showed him my portfolio. He flicked through it, sighed, and handed it back. 'Photographers,' he said. 'But'n pushers. Stick to medicine, my boy.' So I did. It was good advice — there can only be so many David Baileys.

From Laxey we drove past the not particularly inspiring scenery to Peel, a charming small town but deadly quiet. A chilly walk around the outside of the castle overlooking the harbour was followed by excellent ice creams, something of a Manx feature. Not that it is quiet during the TT motorbike races in the summer when the place is full of ageing, overweight, tattooed bikers in black leathers who, despite their alarming appearance, are generally friendly. I have always thought appearances are deceptive. A suit does not necessarily cover an honest person, while jeans and a T-shirt can be worn by the best of doctors.

To round off the Manx day, we had a delightful dinner at William and Nadina's 18th-century converted millhouse nearby, a real bolt-hole for William who would live there permanently if he could. Nadina is a restraining influence.

To Port St Mary

Wednesday April 18th — sunshine and a strong northeast wind as we puttered through the swing-bridge at 12.15pm for a short and pleasant coastal hop to Port St Mary on the south coast of the island. Twelve miles in two-and-a-half hours. But not before my usual incompetence with pontoons, requiring two attempts at leaving. Fortunately we were rescued by the marina manager who released our mooring ropes for the successful third attempt. I had bought a large spherical fender that very day, for just such an occasion. I now have three, and need every one of them.

On our way out we spotted the sad and rusting hulk of the Solway Harvester leaning against the harbour wall. She had been a scallop dredger out of Kirkcudbright which in 2000 had sunk in severe weather off the coast of the Isle of Man. This may have been due in part to a lack of proper maintenance, which resulted in a lengthy legal case against the owner. Eventually the case collapsed. She had been hauled up from the seabed with the seven drowned crew still on board, all of them from the small community around the Isle of Whithorn in Dumfries and Galloway. She has now been scrapped.

The visitor moorings at Port St Mary were too far out from the pier for a convenient dinghy trip, at least using oars, but needs must. John had great difficulty getting in and out of the dinghy over the side of Pickle — even using the ladder I had thoughtfully added to the boat as an extra, thinking of the older person's potential problems (i.e. mine). And he had difficulty getting up from the low sitting position in the dinghy when we arrived at the pier. I shouldn't have been surprised — that's just how it is when you get older. I now have a knotted and fixed rope for dangling over the side of Pickle for the elderly to pull on while pushing themselves up from the dinghy. For this leg of the cruise I resolved to avoid using the dinghy if possible.

Nadina met us by car and, as we didn't like the look of Port St Mary very much — Libby Purves described it as 'genteelly moribund'[10] — we drove off to Port Erin which is set on a lovely sandy bay in the southwest of the island (but when we anchored there in 2018 it looked awful from the sea, with huge white buildings standing out like sore thumbs). We had more ice cream in the sunshine while watching a fat man in a fancy open-top car trying to impress his fancy lady. No doubt he was a financial type from Douglas. Or a smuggler. Maybe there is not much difference. Then to Castletown which was charming (we should have anchored there), and to an excellent pub with Manx real ale. Libby Purves got it right again: 'The Isle of Man was altogether the least American place I had ever been to on the surface of the earth, except perhaps one small village in Communist China.'[11]

To Howth, in Ireland

An early start on Thursday April 19th, 6.30am, needing to get to Howth 63 miles away. John stayed in his bunk which was fine. We certainly don't need four people to get Pickle going — two is enough, and one can be OK

---

10. Purves, *One Summer's Grace*, 102.

11. Purves, *One Summer's Grace*, 99.

from an anchor or a mooring (and even from a pontoon on a good day with plenty of room, and no wind or tide). Unfortunately when John did get up he felt so seasick he couldn't contemplate the lunch of delicious mixed salad with warm potatoes, made by me. The reputation the Irish Sea has for causing seasickness may well be justified. Greg and I were pretty relaxed about the motion of the boat, and Jake kept himself on his toes with sail trimming, so maybe avoiding his own seasickness. Like most sailing racers, he gets quite shouty on the helm. Maybe I should shout more, but I am no racer, just a cruiser.

For me, sailing is a pastime not a sport, more of a means to an end, rather than an end in itself — and all the better when shared with family and friends. I enjoy arriving at places from the sea, and exploring them. Not for me the superhuman toughness of sailing non-stop round Britain and unassisted in an open 16-foot Wayfarer dinghy, as Will Hodshon and Rich Mitchell did over two weeks in 2019. They wouldn't have seen anything of our coastal communities, but I suppose the compensation is setting a Guinness World Record (and raising £10,000 for the RNLI and Surfers Against Sewage).

It was good to get back into the rhythm of sailing on the open sea again, one hour on watch and two off. The wind was in the northwest, 15–20 knots, so with a couple of reefs in the mainsail we made good progress under overcast skies. By 4pm we were approaching the Irish coast, the sun was out, the wind had moderated and moved into the north, the reefs were released and we hoisted our Irish courtesy flag to the starboard crosstree. In theory we could have flown the yellow Q free-of-a-quarantinable-disease flag (maybe with both Ireland and the UK in the European Union at the time there was no need).

Ah, the complex formalities of ensigns and flags, a true paradise for dyed-in-the-wool traditionalists and nerds. I had bought the courtesy flags of various countries around the British Isles, and some coastal counties too, such as Cornwall and Shetland. And the flag of St George for England which, as a Scottish sailor, seemed to me just one more nation of the UK to be acknowledged as we passed by. But to my surprise I was told by Colin Mumford — a very non-nautical work colleague who knows all about flags as well as many other unlikely subjects (and is one of those irritating people who follow you into a rotating door and come out in front of you) — that I should never ever fly this as a courtesy flag as I already fly the Red Ensign. He was right.

The main rule is that the Red Ensign should be flown as near the stern as possible by all UK-registered vessels (as we do). Flying the Saltire (the Scottish flag) as an ensign may be practised by some Scottish nationalists and romantics, but is not strictly legal. The flag of St George will have to remain in its packet until such time as Scotland becomes independent when we will fly the Saltire as our ensign, and the flag of St George at the starboard crosstree when we visit England.

Vexillology had me beat, a word I never knew before, and meaning the study of flags, from the hated Latin. I had to do Latin to get into Cambridge; it was also meant to be important for medicine. Fortunately I was not thought clever enough to be forced to learn Greek as well. All the Latin I can remember is 'Hic and illi, this and that, went to buy a cricket bat'. Not much medical there.

We arrived on the Howth Yacht Club pontoons at 5.15pm. Ten-and-a-half hours sailing, no engine needed. Like many in the UK I get a bit romantic and dreamy about Ireland. Never mind that it was one of the first countries to suffer from the financial crash in 2008, and never mind the corrupt politicians — concentrate on the literature, the friendly people, and draft Guinness. So off we went to search out a pub for that Guinness. We found one where everyone sounded and looked as though they were in a Sean O'Casey play (more romantic tosh on my part). Then, having been tipped off by a Dublin neurologist some months earlier, we headed back to the harbour to find the brilliant Octopussy seafood tapas bar. Small, informal, food cooked right in front of us. Goodness knows how many courses we had, but I did count the bottles of wine — three. It was there I first realised that the crew on this trip were mostly on holiday and would want to go out eating and drinking every evening, which for 16 weeks would be expensive and over-indulgent for me. No matter, I intended to join in. After dinner John and I left Jake and Greg to go out on the town while we went to bed. Younger men in search of fun.

I have never found Howth to be particularly interesting; there is not much of it, just a few shops and a load of pubs. The yacht club is too slick and swish for me. And it has shallow patches to contend with as well as its pontoons. However, it is not just getting Pickle onto and off pontoons that troubles me, but with half a colon I sometimes had to get up two or three times at night and it is annoying to walk for what can be quite a way along a pontoon to find the toilets. In pyjamas. In the cold night air. At anchor or on a mooring I just stagger the few feet to the heads.

To Dublin

Friday 20th April, sunshine, breezy, and nothing to detain us in Howth. After the tumble a week earlier I still felt a bit vertiginous looking up, and when walking, but this seemed to be settling down. Checking the wind direction by looking at the arrow on top of the mast was not a good experience. Luckily the information is transmitted electronically to the wind instruments at eye level.

We had a grand five-hour 11-mile sail round Howth Head where we took the relaxed opportunity to try out the new cruising chute for the first time, all green, to match Pickle's green hull. Of course, despite tips from Owen Sails who made it, and reading various how-to-do-it articles, we twisted the sail around the forestay a couple of times before we got the thing up. Then off we went. Most satisfactory. We even managed to gybe the sail without problems, largely because Jake was jumping around on the foredeck keeping things right. More practice was clearly needed with the chute, as would become obvious later off Dartmouth.

Against the westerly wind we were soon doing long and delightful tacks into Dublin Bay, edging in towards the well-known landmark of the two high chimneys at the mouth of the River Liffey. Then a motor up-river against wind and tide, aiming for the pontoons more or less in the middle of the city, just before the first of the Dublin bridges. However, they were shut, so we ended up a little downstream at the Poolbeg Yacht and Boat Club pontoons on the south shore, opposite the docks. Very different to Howth. Downmarket boats, downmarket clubhouse and bar, but much more friendly, and a higher average age. Not flashy at all. Slightly alarmingly, huge ships were turning in the river right by us to get into the docks — most impressive and far more under control than I can manage the 35 feet of Pickle.

There wasn't anything obvious to see and do in the immediate vicinity so, by now in the rain, we took a 45-minute stroll into the centre of Dublin. Friday night, packed, noisy people spilling out from bars, restaurants full although we managed to squeeze in to one for a meal. Vibrant. This did not seem like a country in the middle of the worst recession for decades. But the centre of a capital city, with its core of rich people, seems to survive better than the periphery. It all proved irresistible to Greg and Jake who disappeared after dinner to find some action that they recorded on their smartphones while John and I took a taxi back to the boat. Whether they sent the photos to their wives I cannot possibly say. This was the first evening it was warm enough to sit out in the cockpit under the stars listening to the buzz of the docks, which were alive with ships and cranes — again, a surprise in the recession, but I suppose it is here in Dublin along with Belfast and Larne where so much comes in and out of Ireland. I took the chance to make a few phone calls. Cathie seemed to be coping OK at home.

Saturday was another sunny day so while the crew went off to explore Dublin I busied myself with boat jobs. There are always boat jobs. I prefer to be alone doing them, pottering about, stroking the interior joinery and admiring the teak in the cockpit, interspersed with dealing with emails and generally tidying up. Jake was by then on his way back to Edinburgh where his wife has more control over him than Greg's wife has over Greg.

But dear oh dear, as we motored down the Liffey in the afternoon, the battery alarm was constantly sounding. The batteries were clearly not charging off the engine's alternator. Flat batteries would mean no lights, no chartplotter, no engine starting, no VHF radio, no anchor winch, no phone charging. Those Corinthian sailors never had this problem — no batteries. Nonetheless, the five-mile sail to Dún Laoghaire was a delightful but brief two-hour genoa-only reach across the bay among the yachts out racing, the first time we had seen large numbers sailing.

We were soon tucked up on one of the pontoons of the incredibly friendly Royal St George Yacht Club. It's odd, that 'Royal' adjective in the Republic of Ireland — as with the RNLI which covers Ireland as well as the UK without anyone worrying that the R refers to a UK Royal Highness. We were the first visiting boat of the year. The manager provided an astonishingly long line for 240v shore-power, showed us round the clubhouse, the bar, the library, the toilets, and invited us to the barbecue but not the later black-tie dinner. 'Make yourself at home,' he said. The place was alive with keel-boat and dinghy racers coming in and sorting out their boats, chatting over hamburgers, drinking, relaxing in the sunshine for probably the first time that year.

Having got the phone number of a mechanic who said he would come to sort out the battery charging, we waited. And waited with rising anxiety about what was wrong. Would it delay us? Could it be fixed? Eventually he turned up at 7.30pm, by which time we were in the bar halfway through our first pint of Guinness. He was middle-aged, rather round, chatty, and friendly. I told him we had no euros but I would nip to the bank to get some, or use a credit card.

'No cards,' he said, as he set to work with his voltmeter. 'We'll sort it out later.'

As I told him about the problem he muttered: 'Boat owners, they always claim there has never been a problem before, always that they service their engine regularly.'

As a matter of fact I do, but his remark reminded me of patients who claim they have 'never been ill, fit as a flea, drink almost nothing'. Of course, for the mechanic (these days they call themselves engineers) the engine and the battery-charging behaved perfectly. No alarm sounded. I suspect this was because we probably still had the shore-power turned on, something neither he nor I realised at the time. After nearly an hour of fiddling about he said he thought it was an alternator problem, and I could perhaps get a replacement from Nani, the maker, under the guarantee. How long would all that take, I thought to myself? As he was packing up I asked him how much he would like.

'Nothing,' he said. 'Don't worry about it — welcome to Ireland!'

Astonishing — called out on a Saturday night too. Nonplussed, I managed to think to give him the one note I had, £20 which he could change into euros. The problem was apparently fixed, or maybe not.

Later that evening Greg and I left John to go to bed while we went off to find a pub. It was surprisingly difficult, but eventually, having walked up the very quiet main street and looking around a bit, we did. Not that the pub was very exciting in itself, but the barmaid was. She was so impressive, over 6 feet tall, well-built rather than obese, short dyed hair, strangely sexy. And totally in command. She could easily have been the bouncer as well. Greg still reminds me about her each time we talk about Dublin.

To Anglesey

On Sunday April 22nd we were up at 6am in the sunshine to slip quietly off the pontoon. But not that quietly. Greg had gone ashore to return the swipe card for the club toilets. Not finding the correct locked door to slip it under as instructed, he climbed up to a half-open window and pushed it through — and set off the alarm. There was not much we could do about it at that time in the morning, we said to each other, the piercing noise receding the further we sailed away (in some embarrassment). I haven't been back but I hope they will have forgotten about us when I do.

With sunshine and a brisk breeze from the west it should have been a straightforward sail. But it wasn't. By midday the wind had dropped and we were motoring, but even so we were too late to catch the east-going tide by the skerries off Carmel Head, the northwest tip of Anglesey. We would have got there sooner had I not, as usual, left it far too long before giving up on the sailing and switching on the motor (my father's anti-engine influence, I suppose). Eventually we did get more wind, as well as the tide along the north coast of Anglesey, to find ourselves off the small town of Amlwch at 8.45pm, a 14-hour sail for the 66 miles, about a third of the time under engine. There was quite a cross-tide running when we edged into the narrow harbour entrance, but luckily no wind to push us even further off course.

It was getting dark early under the overcast sky so the whole place had an even more dreary and gloomy look than perhaps it deserved. And it was unpleasantly smelly. Luckily we found a work-boat to tie up against in one of the pens which apparently are reserved for fishing boats. This saved us having to worry about the rise and fall of the tide against the high harbour wall. Greg being Greg headed off to find a pub after our sausage casserole aboard. He wasn't gone long. He came back and said it was all very bleak, including the pub. For Greg to say that, the pub must have been very bleak indeed.

It still looked bleak when we got up at 6am the next morning. Again it was overcast and again there was no wind. We had to motor a lot — in fact almost for the entire day as the tide took us east into the Menai Strait that separates the mainland of Wales from Anglesey. It was definitely chilly, which was not too surprising given we could see fresh snow on the Snowdonia mountains. Somehow, as we hoisted the rather useless mainsail, the crew managed to comprehensively snarl up the halyard round the winch in the cockpit. This we had discovered tended to happen when putting on three rather than two turns of rope round the winch. Usually it's not a problem because you can get hold of the halyard at the mast, yank the sail up a bit more, and so take the pressure of the halyard at the winch and unloop the jammed rope. But not if the sail is more or less at the top of the mast, which on this occasion it was. The only solution seemed to be to take the winch apart, which I did for the first time and without losing any of the small bits and pieces inside. Having done it once successfully, I have since had fewer fears when needing to repeat the procedure (usually because I have forgotten to tell a new crew, or remind a forgetful previous crew, to take only two turns on the winch). The problem has now been solved by raising the winch by a couple of centimetres.

It was flat calm in the Menai Strait, and looking all very pretty against the mountain backdrop. We motored along, past Beaumaris to starboard and the old iron pleasure pier at Bangor on the mainland shore, to just short of Thomas Telford's magnificent 1826 Menai suspension bridge. There we tied up to a buoy to wait half an hour for the tide. I had been there before so knew about the handy mooring buoys, as well as the very strong tides. But I had never actually been through the Swellies, the shallow, narrow and very tidal stretch of water under the Menai and the Britannia bridges (the tide is reputed to flow at 8 knots at springs, but I wonder if it really does).

High water slack is the time to tackle the Swellies, according to the current Sailing Directions as well as to Captain Greenvile Collins in 1693 whose view was that 'As many Ships are lost by Ignorance and Negligence, as by stress of Weather'. It took eleven years for him to produce 'Great-Britain's Coasting Pilot' in which he wrote: 'the Rocks in the Swilly are dangerous, the Passage narrow, and the Tides very strong; be sure to pass the Swilly at a slack Tide.'[12] So that is exactly what we did more than 300 years later. In fact we cheated slightly by following two other boats that looked as though they knew what they were doing (a dangerous assumption that is all too easy to make). In truth it was not nearly as difficult to pick up and follow the leading lines as the directions suggested. It is probably a good thing, but Sailing Directions do tend to make things look trickier than they turn out to be, an impression well known to the inveterate Corinthian sailor, Henry Reynolds, who in 1921 wrote: 'many years experience had taught us to discount heavily the pessimistic tone of those invaluable books.'[13] I agree — they are indeed both invaluable, and pessimistic.

The scenery got even prettier as we motored on past Nelson's statue to starboard, and a posh-looking stately home, Plas Llanfair, which now accommodates the Joint Service Mountain Training Centre and various outdoor activities for families. We arrived at Port Dinorwic on the mainland at 12.15pm to lock in to the small and charming harbour, by then in warm sunshine. It had been built in the late 18th century for exporting slate from the local quarries. We smiled at the road-sign 'Caution, slow down, ducks crossing'. Twenty-three miles in five-and-a-half hours, all under engine. The Menai Strait must be a grand area for dinghy sailing on the sheltered, flat water, and with plenty of room. Presumably it is much busier in the summer than it was on that sunny spring morning, empty of boats of any sort.

Diagnosis, prognosis and treatment — of engines as well as patients

We originally planned to stop a little further on at Caernarfon, and even

---

12. Greenvile Collins, *Great-Britain's Coasting Pilot* (London: 1693).

13. Henry Reynolds, *Coastwise—Cross-Seas: The Tribulations and Triumphs of a Casual Cruiser* (London: J. D. Potter, 1921), 269.

attempt drying out as Libby Purves had done. However, by mobile phone we had been able to get hold of the Nani agent in Port Dinorwic. Ever since Dublin the battery-charging alarm had been going off almost continuously when the engine was running. That is maybe why the Irish mechanic hadn't charged us. He hadn't found the cause, the diagnosis as we would say in the medical trade.

The Welsh mechanic arrived by van, along with his assistant, coming to a halt above us on the harbour wall. He leant out of the window and said, 'Tell me the story.' Yet again in my contact with mechanics, I was taken straight back to how we make medical diagnoses. Unless it is a dire emergency (and usually even then), we too want to know the story, how the patient's symptoms came on, what the symptoms were, what the patient was doing at the time, exactly when the symptoms began, how they developed, if anything else happened at the same time. What brought them on, if anything? Were the symptoms intermittent or constant, getting worse, and did anything make them worse — or better, how long did they last, had they happened before, and what happened next? How crucial the story is in making a neurological diagnosis — for example, it is the story of the symptoms of migraine that makes the diagnosis. The same is almost as true for much more serious neurological conditions like brain tumours, multiple sclerosis and strokes, but here the diagnosis is then confirmed by scans or other tests.

In neurology, if not in the more technologically crazed specialities such as cardiology, or in dermatology, with perhaps a rash to look at, the story is far more likely to lead you to the diagnosis than just examining the patient, or ordering a test, or even lots and lots of tests. Maybe we are the last speciality that takes the story seriously, apart from the psychiatrists who don't have anything else to go on. It is distinctly odd that the examination of the nervous system is given far more space in textbooks than getting the story straight, and is usually taught at much greater length (maybe because it is easier to teach). But without the story you would not know which bit of the nervous system to examine, or indeed what test to order or part to scan. Or whether any abnormality — during the examination, or of a test result — is relevant rather than something incidental, nothing to do with the symptoms. Of course we should always examine the patient to some extent, if for no other reason than patients expect to be examined, feeling short-changed if they are not. Moreover, there is definitely something usefully therapeutic — even a bit magical — about the 'laying on of hands'.

Most patients have no idea how important the story is in diagnosis. They never say 'My story was taken extremely well' but rather 'the doctor examined me all over, and so thoroughly, and I had two scans not just one'. I always taught medical students that after getting the story they should know roughly where in the nervous system the problem lies (in the head and which side, in the spinal cord, or in the nerves and muscles in the limbs). And to be able to repeat the patient's story in simple words. Not dressed up with dreaded abbreviations (CNS — central nervous system), acronyms (SOB — short of breath), and professional obfuscations like 'hemiplegia', rather than 'weak down one side' which everyone understands. And spare me from 'cerebrovascular accident' or CVA as doctor-speak for stroke — while some people may think a stroke is to do with the heart rather than the brain, they surely know it is not an accident. There is nothing 'accidental' about a stroke: it has a cause, sometimes more than one.

I told the Welsh mechanic about the intermittent battery alarm. How they had fiddled around in Ardfern, again in Ireland, and how it was now going off almost all the time. The battery was clearly not being charged by the engine — the story made that very clear. The mechanic sat in the cockpit while his assistant went down below to examine the engine under the companionway. Leaning down into the cabin, he suggested to his assistant where to look. Just like training a surgeon. The master and the pupil.

'Try measuring the voltage there, or there, have a look there and there, is there a connection problem deep down behind the alternator? Take it off and have a good look.'

There was a problem. One connection was completely broken, the crimping had detached, a wire was flapping around uselessly. Diagnosis made, prognosis dire without treatment that in this case was easy. Wire reconnected, problem solved — engine cured.

I never had to charge patients in our NHS, but at £42+VAT the Port Dinorwic mechanical cure seemed incredibly good value. Some things do work better in the private sector than in government services — it would be difficult to imagine a national marine engine service free at the point of need. On the other hand, the NHS provides the reassurance and guarantee that whatever goes wrong with you, you will be sorted out for 'free'. Of course it is not really 'free', with the funding coming from taxation, and you may have to wait if your problem isn't urgent. Happily, unlike health insurance schemes, taxation is progressive in the sense that the richer you are the more tax you pay (until you are so very rich that you hide your money off-shore or become a tax exile). The NHS is a beacon of social solidarity, outside the predatory world of the market where every buyer must beware every seller. Introduced in 1948 by the post-war Labour government, it has not been dismantled by even the most rabid Tories, at least not yet. But the dangers of privatisation still lurk.

The NHS remains the pinnacle of the welfare state, and much loved by the British public. I don't think they would tolerate a private alternative which they had to pay for, or insure themselves for. They only have to look at the thousands of people in the USA who cannot afford healthcare, despite that country's attempts to reform its system since at least the 1970s when I was in North Carolina to study how it worked. Besides, without the transaction costs of insurance and private medicine, and the problem of choosing between a multiplicity of providers, the NHS is far more cost-effective — with not nearly so many unnecessary tests just to make money for the doctors. Imagine having to choose which medical insurance company to sign up with, and which private hospital to go to. Trying to navigate your way through incomprehensible tables and bar-charts, unravelling unconvincing metrics, past the inevitable hype and downright lies — it would be worse than choosing your gas supplier. Choice is stressful, and can be irrational too. And yet in England, over-encouraging patient choice in the NHS has become something of a government fad, perhaps fading nowadays, but it was never such a problem in Scotland.

I wish neurology had been as easy as sorting out our engine. Although we can usually make a diagnosis, neurologists have the reputation for not being able to offer much in the way of treatment, let alone cure. Indeed I find it difficult to recall many patients I really cured rather than merely helped, in the way I was not just cured but my life was saved by Graeme Wilson who cut out my colon cancer in 1995, and by James Garden who removed my inflamed gall bladder through a couple of keyhole incisions in 2007. No wonder patients give presents to surgeons. As a physician, the best I ever got was from a butcher whom I saw every six months: a steak on each visit. My gift for Graeme Wilson and his wife was a meal in a very nice Edinburgh restaurant. But I didn't forget the physician who made the diagnosis, so Kel Palmer got the same. It was Kel who wisely chose my surgeon for me. By working with surgeons, his choice of the most suitable surgeon for me was going to be much better than mine. And certainly better than any choice based on nationally collected surgical outcome metrics which may well be subject to poor data collection, small numbers, and gaming to improve the surgeons' place in the league tables. Not surprisingly, surgeons may avoid operating on patients likely to do badly, while inflating any comorbidities on those they do operate on — both resulting in their surgical death rate being adjusted favourably. A cynical view, yes. Realistic, often yes too.

This 'physician before surgeon' principle was probably first formalised at the justifiably renowned Mayo Clinic in the United States in the early 20th century. It still largely persists there, except for trauma admissions where the patient goes direct to a surgeon without first passing through physicianly hands (connected to thoughtful brains); it leaves the Mayo surgeons to do more of what they really like doing, and are so good at — operating. Sadly this model of care is more or less non-existent in the UK. Our surgeons have to spend far too much of their time in outpatient clinics where many or even most patients will never need surgery. And far too little time enjoying what they do best, honing their really important skills in the operating theatre. Our Edinburgh neurosurgeons only get one day a week in the operating theatre, plus emergency work one day in eleven, and some operating in the private sector if so inclined. Surely their skills would be better maintained by more operating time. If yearning to operate you will get far more experience as a dentist, five days a week.

Teaching

Another similarity between mechanics and doctors is how we learn our trade. Some theory of course, but essentially we are best taught on the job, gaining experience at the feet of the master (or mistress). At the same time being helpful, doing the simpler things like removing the alternator, or sewing up the abdomen. Preferably one-to-one, by the engine, or at the bedside, solving the diagnostic or management problem, live problem-based learning — not a paper exercise in the classroom, as valuable as that can be. Nor indeed learning merely from books. I don't know if William Osler was a sailor, but his nautical aphorism is apt: 'He who studies medicine without books sails in an uncharted sea, but he who studies medicine without patients does not go to sea at all.'[14]

A seldom acknowledged advantage of bedside rather than classroom teaching is that it is not just the students who learn. The Dinorwic experience taught me, as well as the mechanic's assistant, about alternators and their connections. Likewise, I always structured my own bedside teaching to help the patient understand what was going on. I wasn't just talking to the students. We were all having a conversation together, for everyone's benefit, the patient's included if I discovered something relevant about the patient I or others didn't already know. Of course, along the way, one has

---

14. William Osler, 'Books and Men', *Boston Medical and Surgical Journal* (1901).

to be sensitive to the patient's concerns, privacy and comfort. I insisted that students had a chair to sit on, as I did, so we were all at the same level as the patient, not towering above him or her, as I remember as a student (besides, I had been exhausted and got sore feet standing for hours during teaching ward rounds).

Richard Smith, a past editor of the *BMJ* (*British Medical Journal*) — a major UK medical journal, containing a mixture of news, politics, research and education — rightly said that teaching is a branch of the entertainment industry (perhaps not coincidentally, his brother Arthur is a well-known comedian). The students have to be engaged, it has to be fun for everyone — as well as serious. In a lecture about how to encourage patients to take what they are prescribed, in the context of drugs to suppress epilepsy, John Paul Leech (once a part-time stand-up comedian but now head of medical education in Glasgow) discussed the usual trio of compliance, adherence and concordance with treatment — then, after a dramatic pause, added … '*and* obedience'. A joke of course, but it stuck in my memory, and made me think. But never ever laugh at the patient, only with the patient.

Our mechanic and his assistant were perfect examples of how to teach and be taught. Unfortunately these days, when medical schools are so huge, it is not so easy to achieve such one-to-one apprentice-like teaching. I was in a class of only 12 in my third pre-clinical year at Cambridge and was personally taught the then new technique of tissue culture by Robert Edwards. Unbeknown to us, he was working towards in vitro fertilisation (IVF) that he later perfected with the obstetrician Patrick Steptoe who in Oldham was developing the technique of laparoscopic ('keyhole') surgery to collect human eggs (Louise Brown was born in 1978, the world's first 'test tube baby'). In 2010 Edwards was awarded the Nobel Prize for Physiology or Medicine, but it was too late for Steptoe who had died. Jean Purdy, the third person in the IVF team, didn't share the prize either and has almost been forgotten, maybe because she was a woman and 'merely' the nurse, but perhaps, like Steptoe, because she had died before the award was made. And yet Edwards regarded her as much an equal contributor to IVF as himself. Not that I have much respect for the Nobel Prize selection process given that Richard Doll was passed over despite making the greatest public health discovery of the 20th century — that smoking causes lung cancer. He had to make do with a knighthood.

After Cambridge, I was in a year of just 50 clinical students at St George's Hospital Medical School. In Edinburgh, by my retirement in 2008, there were 250 in a year, and the BSc class in neuroscience had increased from less than 20 to more than 60. I had learned neurology with just three other students at Atkinson Morley's Hospital (AMH) in Wimbledon, where we were even given a small house to live in for a month. The teaching was so good that we threw the staff a thank-you party in the grounds with a live band, dancing and fairy lights. AMH was where the first human brain was CT-scanned a few years later, in 1971, by the NHS (not university academic) neuroradiologist, Jamie Ambrose. And yet he found the time to teach us some radiology every morning, interpreting skull X-rays in those days. In contrast, I had to teach neurology in Edinburgh round the bedside to up to 10 students, and to lecture to over 200. As a student, I knew my teachers, and they knew me. To my regret I didn't manage to thank most of them before they died; all it needs is a letter that is always appreciated. My mechanic and his assistant clearly knew each other well: they were a good team, and seemed to be friends. Quite right too, and reassuring.

Continuity of care — again

Although it is more comfortable to learn from other people's mistakes, we learn better from our own, provided we get to hear about them (and there are not too many). I once saw a podiatrist for pain in the ball of my foot while walking — metatarsalgia. He gave me an insole for my shoe. There was no need for follow-up, he said, because his treatment always worked. But if he never followed people up, how could he possibly know? He couldn't, and so he never knew that my foot pain persisted. In fact it moved into both feet before getting better a few years later. Likewise, that friendly Irish mechanic will never know he missed the diagnosis because he did not get any feedback — not his fault, just the geography. Feedback is so crucial in medicine. We need to see patients through their illness to find out what we did right, or wrong. That follow-up may take years rather than days for chronic conditions like epilepsy and Parkinson's disease. This all requires continuity of care.

My worst mistake was missing bacterial endocarditis in a 55-year-old woman with a mild but unexplained stroke, even though we had considered it and asked a cardiologist's opinion. What none of us did, however, was the crucial blood culture for the bacteria that must have been lurking in her circulation. She was recovering well in a rehabilitation hospital when she had a far worse stroke. She was readmitted under me again, when it became very clear that blood clots were forming on an infected heart valve and dropping off to be swept through her arteries into her brain. I might never have known, and learned from that unforgettable mistake, if I had not myself readmitted her. Subsequently I passed on that lesson in all of my teaching — 'do not, repeat not, forget a blood culture in a stroke patient with no obvious cause.'

Another mistake was not so damaging, again coming to my attention through continuity of care. I saw a man, who came alone, with 'dizzy turns' that I couldn't make much of despite trying to understand exactly what he meant by 'dizzy' (which might mean anything from feeling faint to off-balance to a sensation of spinning, from trouble in the head to trouble in the legs). I thought his dizziness was probably of no consequence, so I reassured him. A few years later he had a minor car accident during another 'dizzy turn' and came back to see me. This time his wife was with him. She told me that in the 'dizzy turn' he had gone deathly white, gripped the steering wheel tightly, stared straight ahead, ignored her shouts of alarm, and was unresponsive for several seconds. When I asked her, she also told me that during previous 'dizzy turns' he had been unresponsive and white, and looked 'far away while slowly raising one arm into the air'. Clearly a form of epilepsy. On his first visit my mistake had been not to question a witness to the dizzy turns — a witness can be so crucial in diagnosis. Even phoning his wife after the clinic visit would have revealed the truth. Without continuity of care I would not have learned the error of my ways.

I am not sure if I have ever made the opposite mistake, diagnosing epilepsy in someone who had just a simple faint. Not a fatal mistake maybe, but one that would keep the patient off driving for months (perhaps compromising their job). And have them take drugs unnecessarily, also for months but more likely years because so many patients whose attacks have stopped don't want to come off medication — for fear of having another fit.

The current pattern of shift and part-time working makes continuity of care almost impossible. Young doctors now learn less from their own experience and rely more on a tsunami of guidelines and algorithms to help them do — we hope — the right thing. As a consequence, I think, they have become more risk-averse. They order more tests. Just in case. They refer to other doctors. Just in case. Maybe they admit to hospital. Just in case. They can't 'wait and see' because their shift will be over in a few hours, and the next doctor may not have time to take over properly, or have a coherent idea of what the patient was like some hours earlier. This all adds up to spending more money to compensate for the loss of continuity of care.

When my daughter Margaret was a junior doctor in acute medicine and discussed occasional patients with me, I used to ask her what became of them, what the scan showed, and so on. Sadly she often didn't know, as she had gone off-duty and by the time she returned a day later the patient had been handed on to someone else in another part of the system.

I am not asking for a return to the (good?) old days when we were sometimes on call for days with very little sleep, often alone. Some consultants were simply unavailable when we needed help, and our careers depended far too much on who we knew rather than what we knew. But I definitely am asking for junior doctors to work in a team whose members can easily communicate with each other, who know each other's strengths and weaknesses, with a consultant leader, and not be constantly off the wards for yet more classroom teaching, a fire-fighting course, or whatever.

Back to the cruise. I had by then really appreciated just how friendly and helpful harbour masters are. In Port Dinorwic, after admiring Pickle, our man pointed us towards the shops, the pub, the showers and the laundry facilities — the essentials of life ashore, making the perfect marina for the cruising yachtsman. We made use of all these essentials during the rest of the day, a lazy day in spring sunshine. Once again we were complimented on Pickle, not I think because she was then still a relatively new and shiny boat, but because Rustler 36s are so good-looking, proper boats, with a proper-boat shape. Maybe we were also helped along by the colour I had chosen for her hull — that British racing green. Smart.

To Pwllheli, but only just

Tuesday April 24th, a beautiful morning. We locked out of Port Dinorwic at 11.15am, intent on catching the tide through Bardsey Sound some 30 miles to the southwest. The little wind we had was against us so we motored past the impressive-looking Caernarfon Castle and out of the Menai Strait. Then over the rather anxiety-provoking Caernarfon bar that moves about so much that you must follow the buoys, not the chartplotter. But there was a problem. I don't know why I looked over the stern, but shock horror, no seawater was coming out of the exhaust — the water that is sucked in to be pumped around the engine to remove heat from the sealed freshwater cooling system. Greg opened the cockpit locker and was immediately enveloped in steam; there was no freshwater left, it had all boiled away. Quickly turning the engine off, we opened up all the hatches to let the whole thing cool down.

What had happened? Diagnosis? First things first. Was the seacock to let in the seawater for the cooling system closed, or was it blocked? Dear oh dear, it was closed. I had closed it the day before when we were sorting out the alternator, and had forgotten to reopen it afterwards. I hadn't done what I should have done, and normally do. Always, but always, each and every time you turn on the engine, look over the stern to check that plenty of cooling seawater is coming out with the exhaust. I thought I had looked, and if so what I had seen perhaps had been condensation being blown out of the exhaust. Luckily, the engine restarted easily, and it seemed that we had got away with it.

Up with the sails, and off we went alongside the beautiful Lleyn Peninsula on a fine fetch, calm sea, mini-mountains to port, green and largely empty of people, making about 5 knots over the ground. It was sunny, warm even, and yet looking back there were still some patches of snow on Snowden, the last of winter. All was extremely well with the world even though someone had managed to block the heads that morning (I decided to wait until we were at anchor before fixing the problem). At 3.30pm the wind dropped so we had to use the engine. At 5pm we could just about sail again, but were very conscious that if we didn't get a move on we might not make it through Bardsey Sound before the tide turned against us.

There had been white smoke from the exhaust, for reasons unknown, but I should have been more inquisitive. However, the engine seemed to be working fine and water had been, I thought, coming out with the exhaust. At about 6pm when the light wind turned against us, we started motoring again. Within minutes the engine coughed, and stopped. There were clouds of black smoke in the engine compartment. The engine must have been overheating again, or so I presumed. But much more considered thought was required. I kind of unconsciously clocked that the engine did not seem all that hot, and if it had been overheating it should have been very hot indeed. I checked the seawater-entry seacock again, but that looked fine — open, not clogged up with anything. And there was plenty of freshwater in the cooling system. Next along the cooling line I checked the impeller, the small circular rubber part of the pump which pushes the seawater around the engine. It seemed OK to me but I am no expert. I changed it anyway, and successfully put it all back together, as I had been taught by Steve in Ardfern. Yet still the engine wouldn't start. Clearly the cooling system was fine, which I should have realised, given that the engine hadn't overheated. In the stress of the moment I was definitely not thinking straight. I had succumbed to that awful doctor tendency to too easily make the same diagnosis as the last apparently similar case.

Luckily the wind got up again, it was turning into a lovely evening, and the sea was flat. So amid all this diagnostic confusion we could carry on sailing slowly south. I opened up all and every hatch around the engine, and cleared out the cockpit locker so I could clamber into it and see what was going on with the engine. It seemed too much of a coincidence to think the problem was not something to do with the overheating earlier. Aided by a torch and with much poking about, the penny dropped. A connection between two sections of the exhaust pipe had fallen apart, just where it went through a bulkhead. A broken jubilee clip was lying underneath it, probably because the earlier overheating had distorted it. The cooling seawater had been going around the engine alright which is why it was not overheating, but then it had gone straight into the bilges — not out at the stern along with the smoke from the exhaust which then enveloped the engine. That is why it had stopped. Even I knew that a diesel engine needs only three things to keep going — fuel, water and air. There was no shortage of fuel or cooling water, so presumably the problem was something to do with the exhaust smoke depriving the engine of air. A diagnosis!

A notion which still lingers among non-neurologists is that we neurologists may be very good at making diagnoses but are hopeless at treating anything, largely because so much of what we see is incurable. In 1999 Richard Smith described the neurologist as 'a brilliant, forgetful man with a bulging cranium, a loud bow tie, who reads Cicero in Latin for pleasure, hums Haydn sonatas, talks with ease about bits of the brain you'd forgotten existed, adores diagnosis and rare syndromes, and — most importantly — never bothers about treatment'.[15] His tongue-in-cheek stereotype may once have been true, but there are now as many or more women than men training in neurology; I personally do not have a bulging cranium and have never worn a bow tie except unwillingly with a dinner jacket; I nearly failed O-level Latin which I loathed; I can't sing and can barely hum; I am not very good at neuroanatomy; and I was much more interested in common diseases like stroke and functional disorders than rare genetic syndromes. Furthermore, neurologists can now at least help people with Parkinson's disease by alleviating their symptoms (though not curing them); they can suppress migrainous headaches, and control epilepsy to some extent. Sadly there is still nothing for Alzheimer's disease or motor neurone disease.

While we do not have many cures in the sense of getting rid of a disease completely, nor do many other physicians. Who has *cured* chronic

---

15. Richard Smith, 'Neurology for the Masses', *BMJ*, 319 (August 7th 1999).

bronchitis, heart failure or kidney failure? Managed, yes, maybe for years, but cured — no. These diseases are seldom gone for ever, they are just kept under control for as long as possible. If you want *cures* you have to look to surgeons who can transplant lungs, kidneys and hearts, replace opaque cataracts, and cut out cancerous colons. And to antibiotics which see off many bacterial diseases, but are no good against viruses. And to nurses who restore hearing in an instant, just by removing earwax.

Greg, armed with a new jubilee clip between his teeth, a screwdriver in one hand, and long arms, got his head into the engine compartment, and with much huffing and puffing managed to fix together the two parts of the exhaust pipe. And bingo, without being enveloped in oxygen-depriving exhaust smoke, the engine started, with water coming out of the stern exhaust pipe as it should, and no white smoke (even as a non-believer I always say a little prayer as I press the starter button, and thank someone for miracles when the engine starts). Off we went through Bardsey Sound, a benign piece of water that evening, not the rushing torrent it can be, and was when Hilaire Belloc unwisely sailed through with a gale of wind and against the tide in 1914: 'a confusion of huge tumbling pyramidical waves, leaping up, twisting, turning and boiling in such a confusion as I had never seen … the painter which held the dinghy to the stern parted, and that boat, a good and serviceable one, was lost.'[16]

Turning slightly to port along the coast we had the southerly wind on our beam for a delightful evening sail, but not to anchor in Aberdaron Bay as I had planned. It is exposed to the south, and a southeast gale was expected. We needed more shelter, and maybe a mechanic to check we had done the right thing by the engine. (In fact we didn't bother, and ten years later the jubilee clip is still there.) There always should be a plan B. Ours was to press on towards the shelter of Pwllheli marina, where we arrived in the dark. At the harbour entrance there was a multitude of flashing red and green lights on buoys to guide us in. On the west coast of Scotland we are not used to such aides, which can be confusing if there are a lot of them. So we motored slowly and cautiously towards the pontoons where even at 11pm there was a man waiting to guide us to a berth, which was very kind of him. Safe at last. And a relief to be able to go down below and have the supper I had cooked along the way. Lamb burgers. We had arrived, 51 miles, no harm done, and luckily the weather had been kind. Diagnosis and treatment would have been more difficult in the rain, and definitely in a rough sea.

---

16. Hilaire Belloc, *The Cruise of the Nona* (London: Constable & Co. Ltd, 1925), 5.

A pause in North Wales

As forecast the weather was vile when we woke up on Wednesday April 25th. Rain and lots of wind, all coming from where we wanted to go — south. These were not good conditions in which to judge the marina but it did seem very soulless. Too many rather large motorboats. No one was around. I wondered where the boat owners lived, presumably in the Midlands mostly. The town centre was too distant and didn't sound the sort of place for coffee and a bun. Fortunately, David Lea had driven over from his home near Porthmadog to take us on a tour. He was to join us later for the Shetland leg.

I have known David since I was a medical student, before he moved from London to north Wales to set up his one-man architectural practice, and develop a smallholding. He once had a rather wonderful old wooden sailing boat, a Tumlare — 'Schnapps' — berthed in Porthmadog, but she was really too much to maintain. Sticking with wood, he then bought a 'Loch Long' for day-sails, and now has a pretty 'Ness Yawl', an Iain Oughtred-designed boat, also wooden. I think we have both been rather fascinated by each other's professions; certainly, I have always been interested in architecture. Maybe it would have suited my science background and artistic pretensions but it was never raised as an option at school. Instead, when I was 17, after filling in some questionnaire, a so-called career advisor suggested that I go into the oil industry. I ignored him. I do wonder if these advisors get their recommendations right, but it would need 10 years or more of follow-up to find out.

First off was to David's local pub at Llanfrothen for lunch. Then to Ogoronwy, his smallholding and office, for coffee. He is quite a well-known architect, not in the Norman Foster megacorporation sense, but for designing beautiful and energy-efficient buildings like the conference facility at the Centre for Alternative Technology near Machynlleth. He takes a serious ecological approach and has always been very environmentally minded, from his days working with John Seymour who wrote the highly influential 1973 book *Self-Sufficiency*. Not that John Seymour was all that self-sufficient himself. When he ran out of money he wrote another book. This however is how it has to be. On a smallholding you can never grow enough to sell to then be able to buy things like laptops, and presents for the children. Crofters in Scotland knew that: they had several part-time jobs as well as their land for crops and an animal or two. David had more or less retired and was turning his hand to designing himself a boat, of course in a traditional shape, and of course made of wood.

David, who is English, had been married to Welsh-speaking Irene but despite his best efforts had never learned to speak Welsh himself, unlike their two children who are brilliantly bilingual. What a surprise it still is to me to hear them speak with a perfect English accent one minute, then instantly switch into what I presume is a perfect Welsh accent the next. The Welsh have kept their language far more successfully than the Scots, by which I mean the Gaelic-speaking Scots of the highlands and islands (not the Scots in Edinburgh who never spoke Gaelic, nor anyone in Orkney and Shetland where Norse was spoken before they switched to English).

I had been to Ogoronwy many, many times over the years. It was good to be back. It is off the sealed roads, through a couple of farm gates, on a hillside facing south with a view of distant Tremadog Bay. In the early days, David had tried to grow vegetables but didn't really have the time. This was when the self-sufficiency movement was getting going and we all wanted allotments. There were, however, still sheep around, looked after by Irene, and lots of woodland, with bluebells. Not surprisingly there were solar panels too. An attempt at a build-your-own hydro plant in the stream had not worked out. And there were lots of memories. Like when the screams of my son Ben, then aged ten, had us all rushing down the hill past the sheep to find he had fallen off a rope-swing into the stream, but was unhurt. Years before visiting Ogoronwy, I had come with university friends to north Wales in the Easter vacations to work for exams, and later by myself to an earlier and even more remote place of David's to revise for membership of the Royal College of Physicians. Being in a beautiful place and taking breaks to admire it, and go for walks, certainly helped me get work done. And still does.

After lunch we all piled into David's car for a slightly damp tour. We took in Tremadog where I had rock-climbed on the low crag that was always a good alternative to the mountains when the weather was bad, and Black Rock sands where during those exam revision times we had done a ton in a friend's 1930s Lagonda. I only owned a 1936 Morris 8, and then a 1935 Austin 10 with a delightful 'dickey seat' instead of a boot for at least a partial Toad of Toad Hall 'poop, poop' experience. Then to the late Clough Williams-Ellis's house and lovely garden with its 'lines of view' through the topiary, accompanied by the sound of tinkling water. He it was who owned so much land round here, and designed many of the houses, including that strange confection of Portmeirion, all with their woodwork painted the same shade of blue.

Meanwhile I again brooded on the obvious. Looking after the crew during a voyage round Britain is just as important, and in many ways more challenging, than looking after the boat. This brooding coincided with a rather whingey phone call home. I was fed up with some of the boat issues. The reefing line, and the heads. I was fed up with my vertigo and imbalance. I was also worried about John who didn't seem well. (I must remember to find out about future crew medical problems in advance, discreetly — particularly given my usual crew's average age.) I had no idea at the time that John's problems had been going on for nearly three years, but then I myself had had symptoms for three years before doing anything about my colon cancer. Like many men, John and I tend to avoid going to doctors, even when there is something quite obviously wrong.

A long hop to Milford Haven, briefly via Skomer

By late afternoon the wind had died down, was forecast to move to the northwest, and the rain had stopped. After Greg's signature dish of spaghetti bolognese, we left at 10pm, aiming to cross Cardigan Bay and arrive off Ramsey Sound 70 miles away when the tide turned south (I had a passage-plan after all). Our exit was as careful and as slow as our entry, bearing in mind all those lights to sort out, and because the marina was gradually silting up. Greg and I took two-hour watches through the quite short night, leaving John to sleep.

Despite some drizzle it was a very reasonable passage. The wind started off light in the northeast before gradually strengthening and moving round to the northwest, perfect for where we wanted to go. We made about 4–5 knots, up to 7 at times. I was quite impressed with how our electronic tiller-pilot coped (not that we used it much, given its drain on the batteries). I thought that one day I should get vane self-steering, a plus being that it may be a lot better at steering in a straight line than some of my crew. In 2014 I did, and it is. I bought the Neptune system, designed and built by Trenchard Bowden, a South African living in Wiltshire. Sailing to the Faroes that year in Pickle, Steve Druitt remarked that it was worth every penny. It really does steer Pickle in a straight line, and provides endless fascination as one watches the vane swinging gently from side to side to maintain the same angle to the wind, with just one rope and four pulleys moving the tiller to keep us on course. So simple and yet so effective, and needing no energy other than the wind.

By midday we were off St David's Head going at 7 knots, a grand sail. But it was still overcast and a bit drizzly. I impressed myself — and Greg —

by arriving at the north end of Ramsey Sound at precisely the right time, as the tide turned in our favour at 12.47pm, high water slack, brilliant. By then we were running with the genoa furled away and the main held out by the preventer, so we could whiz through the sound in style, past the Bitches, rocks which poke into the sound from the west. They are easy to spot, and avoid. Not such a big deal really, despite the Sound's reputation and Hilaire Belloc's description: 'The water roared and thundered over the rocks inshore for all the world as though we were not upon the sea at all but upon the lower reaches of a tidal river.'[17] But then he was sailing on the full ebb, and not at slack water. I suspect he was better at writing about sailing than actually sailing and getting the tides right.

John had stayed mostly down below because he was feeling so wretched. To make matters worse we all had to use a bucket because the heads were playing up so much. With his family history of colon cancer (i.e. me), could that be his problem, I wondered, and more than hinted as much to him.

There were no other boats around; indeed, we had seen none all the way from north Wales. This was not too surprising given it was still early in the sailing season and the weather was hardly appealing. In fact, it was getting greyer and greyer, gloomy, and rather unpleasant. So even though the wind was in the north I abandoned thoughts of anchoring at Solva in St Bride's Bay. We carried on. I didn't fancy tangling with Jack Sound, and anyway I wanted to look at Skomer Island where we could have a tea-stop and a nap in the southern anchorage, and look at the birds. Lots and lots of birds. There were puffins everywhere — on the water, in the air, on the cliffs. A wonderful sight we had all to ourselves. I don't know why, but in 1869 the opinionated Lieutenant Middleton thought the puffins on Skomer were 'pugnacious, pompous, stupid, selfish, brutally-quarrelsome dirty little birds'.[18]

I also failed to get to Solva in 2015. The anchorage is some way from the village and the tempting pub where friends were expecting us for dinner. We set off rowing in the Tinker inflatable dinghy, which I knew was a bit leaky. It was, after all, 20 years old, but much loved. And, more importantly, it was easy to row with proper oars, not the vestigial paddles most modern dinghies have because they are designed to be driven by outboard engines. Rather suddenly a slightly worn seam in the floor fabric ripped wide-open and we began to sink. In something of a panic I rowed briskly to a nearby

---

17. Belloc, *Cruise of the Nona*, 62.

18. Empson Edward Middleton, *The Cruise of the Kate* (London: Longmans, Green and Co., 1870), 167.

beach, at which point I had a shower of bright floaters in my left eye, which persisted. I imagined I had a retinal detachment (serious), but it turned out to be a vitreous detachment (not serious), diagnosed that evening during a phone call to an ophthalmologist friend (just from the story again), and later confirmed by a Welsh optician in Aberystwyth. Meanwhile there was no way we could get off the beach, as the cliffs were too steep. Fortunately there was a mobile phone signal. After a plaintive call to our friends on the harbour wall who couldn't see us, and who had no idea where we had got to, they summoned a passing boat and we were returned to Pickle. We couldn't then get ashore without a serviceable dinghy, so — no pub dinner.

Back to this cruise. We had arrived at Skomer at 3pm and set off again at 5.30pm, aiming for Milford Haven, the large and deep estuary off the southwest tip of Wales. A safe haven indeed, as it has been since, and presumably well before, Greenvile Collins described it in the late 17th century as: 'certainly the Best harbour in the 3 Kingdoms, there being no manner of danger in sailing in or out of the Harbour, so that you need no Pilots, and may turn in and out very safely with contrary Winds, taking the Tide, as well by Night as by Day.'[19]

The five-mile sail across to St Ann's Head guarding the west entrance to the Haven was a splendid broad reach. Then, as the evening wore on, we sailed leisurely up the estuary on flat water, peace and quiet at last. Well, not that quiet when we nearly hit a sandbank. I wasn't paying enough attention out in the cockpit while down below John wasn't paying enough attention to the chartplotter. The estuary was not as industrial as I had anticipated; in fact, it was remarkably rural, the oil refinery and chemical works not intruding too very much. Libby Purves had the same feeling 30 years earlier: 'We passed miles of oil-refinery staging: Gulf, Esso, Texaco; monstrous creations that would have wrecked a gentler coastline, but which looked oddly insignificant next to the rugged, wooded, ancient glories of the Haven itself.'[20]

Because we needed to sort ourselves out and change crew, anchoring just inside the entrance of the Haven at Dale would have been no good. Back home, Cathie — my one-woman support team — had discovered that I could get the help I needed for the heads and the lost reefing line not at Milford itself, but a bit further up river at Neyland Yacht Haven. This we found tucked into a narrow valley under a high modern bridge carrying a

---

19. Collins, *Great-Britain's Coasting Pilot*.
20. Purves, *One Summer's Grace*, 62.

busy main road. After a 20-hour 94-mile sail, and no need for the engine except to approach the pontoons, we tied up at 8.30pm, only just in time to catch a meal in the rather good marina restaurant, and a pint at their bar. What did we do before mobile phones? How did we book a table in advance from out at sea? We didn't — we just turned up and hoped for the best.

And so to bed, after a whisky with Greg who was leaving for home in the morning. I was going to miss him. He had been an excellent crew, largely because he is not just an experienced sailor and strong, but because of his constant enthusiasm — about the sailing itself, the scenery, the birds, everything. Sitting on the foredeck admiring the view he often remarked, 'What's not to like about all this?' Like me, he had been taught to sail by his father, who had had a catamaran in the not very appealing Bristol Channel with its strong tides, brown water, and paucity of safe harbours and anchorages. Sadly his father died out at sea, alone, and presumably suddenly because he was discovered in his catamaran. He had been a steel erector, as are Greg's three brothers. Greg is the odd one out because he went to university and medical school.

Greg has strong opinions, many of which I rather approve of. He could see no advantage in his children going to a private school when like me he lived in a pleasant part of Edinburgh with excellent state schools, and with reasonably well-behaved neighbourhood children. Not a view that many of our neighbours, or indeed doctor colleagues, shared. Their children, not mine, can mix with the children of those yummy mummies driving ridiculously large cars, and dads who appear once a year to strut their stuff at sports days. They can pay many thousand pounds a year for what Greg and I get for 'free', although to be fair (through gritted teeth) the private schools usually have much better sports and music facilities. This 'private must be best' attitude at least keeps pressure for places off our full-to-bursting Edinburgh state schools. The solution is for private schools not to be abolished but to be absorbed into the state system, as my children's school was — James Gillespie's High School. Muriel Spark, its most famous old girl, based Miss Jean Brodie on Christina Kay, one of her teachers.

Greg also insists that all his family eat together in the evening. No chicken nuggets or turkey twizzlers, the same adult food for one and all. Not so difficult for him to get home in time because of his nine-to-five working hours. Many doctors don't get home until after their children are in bed. Unfortunately he votes Conservative, I think (irrelevant in our south Edinburgh constituency with a huge Labour majority). I'm not so sure about his pipe smoking, all that ash scattered about, but he has since given that up — in favour of cigars. He departed by taxi leaving one sock, and he thinks his pipe, which we never found but maybe we didn't look too hard.

Without him I couldn't have coped, what with Jake's seasickness and my brother's health problems, and his frailness because after all he was 76. Now at 78, I too am frailer and seldom sail without a younger crew, particularly on longer trips.

A rest

Friday April 27th. I saw John off from Milford station in the morning. He was unusually effusive in his goodbyes, perhaps out of worry about his health. It was then good to be alone for a bit, to have a wander around the marina. Like many marinas in old docks, Milford's is surrounded by new flats and retail units, many of the latter unlet. Judging by the café where I found some lunch, the whole place appeared classier than it actually was; certainly the marina charges were far less than at Neyland.

However, the Milford Haven Museum was a real treat. I was buttonholed by a knowledgeable local volunteer who gave me a potted history of the Haven, and then showed me round the historical sequence of Vikings, oysters, a safe haven, pirates, whaling which flopped, coal mining, lime kilns, boat building, the port and then dockyard which was never used for the anticipated transatlantic trade, fishing which came to the rescue and was huge for a while, the arrival of the railway, two world wars, and finally the post-second world war oil and liquefied natural gas industry. But then what for Milford? Between the two world wars Hilaire Belloc found the Haven to have 'no industrial hinterland … half dropped out of men's memories'.[21] Maybe it will drop out of memories again, once we have abandoned fossil fuels. And who will care, bearing in mind the lack of care for our towns and cities devastated by the loss of coal mining, steel making and shipbuilding in the late 20th century?

For me it was a day for catching up, sorting out, and having a break from the open sea. And in particular dealing with the heads and the mainsail reefing line, both tasks clearly beyond my meagre capabilities but well within those of the two men who Cathie had discovered would do the necessary. The fact that it was still grey and overcast, and a bit chilly, didn't really matter to me. Nor did the floods in Yorkshire. After all, we were not going to sea again quite yet, and Yorkshire was a long way away.

---

21. Belloc, *Cruise of the Nona*, 71.

I simply had not been able to get the plastic pipes off their connections to the toilet bowl. The plumber knew how. Warm them up, the plastic softens and then the pipes are easier to wrench off. Of course he had the right tool, and so did I, as it happened — the hair-dryer that we had never used for its intended purpose, and still never have. The heads outlet valve turned out to be blocked with paper and scale, and the plumber sorted it all out. Along the way I had a useful one-to-one tutorial on how to unblock the heads. This was the sort of personal teaching that these days is a rarity in most universities that are so flagellated by the government to produce high impact research (often rushed and not necessarily of even modest quality) that they have ignored, or at least reduced, their major role in teaching.

The rigger was equally informative, and successful. He fished out the lost reefing line from inside the boom using a long bendy rod with a hook at its end — simple but effective. And he taught me how to properly attach the reefing lines to the boom so the mainsail leach could be pulled down really hard. He had a surprisingly English accent. Here in this part of Wales he told me everyone has an English accent. He had been born here. I am not sure if this accent is because much of the population has come from England in the recent past, or because in so-called Little-England-beyond-Wales — South Pembrokeshire and southwest Carmarthenshire — English is what people have spoken for centuries, rather than Welsh. My father's ancestors had come from these parts, where Warlow is such a common surname that I didn't have to spell it out.

Unfortunately, there hadn't been time for John and me to explore the area for our father's family history, and we hadn't been able to hire a car anyway. Our ancestors had probably moved from Germany to southwest Wales some centuries ago. The Warlows had in some way got muddled up with the Pictons, although Picton Castle up the River Cleddau from Neyland is nothing to do with our branch of the family. General Sir Thomas Picton is, however.[22] We are descended from his sister. He was a soldier and the first British governor of Trinidad, at the time a lawless colony. There he fathered four children by a local mixed-race lady, one Rosetta Smith, but was forced to resign under a cloud and return to Britain, for too much flogging and too many executions and torture it seems (he left his mistress and children to fend for themselves).

After impressive service with Wellington in the Peninsular War, and a

---

22. Robert Havard, *Wellington's Welsh General: A Life of Sir Thomas Picton* (London: Aurum Press, 1996).

short spell as a Tory MP, he was persuaded back from retirement to serve directly under Wellington at the Battle of Waterloo. This was a mistake. He was too old at 56. Moreover he was ill and concealing a painful wound to his ribs from the preceding Battle of Quatre Bras which he had not even told his surgeon about. It is said that his luggage had not arrived in time, so he fought at Waterloo wearing his civilian clothes and a top hat which, when he was leading a charge, clearly could not deflect the bullet to his head that killed him. Apparently he is the only Welshman buried in St Paul's Cathedral, a singular honour bearing in mind that Wellington referred to him as 'a rough foul-mouthed devil as ever lived' but softened a little by adding 'no man could do better in different services I assigned him'.[23] Sir Thomas did think to leave £1000 to each of his four children. I was pleased to see there was a Picton Road in Neyland. At least there was on the map, but no apparent sign on the road itself. But maybe, after his activities in Trinidad became more widely known in 2020, the name will be erased from there, and from other roads, and towns like 'Picton' in New Zealand. His statue in Cardiff City Hall has already been concealed in a box. I doubt if this will do much for the problem of modern-day slavery and racial discrimination.

With the two boat problems fixed I felt a lot better. My mood improved amazingly. I sorted out the charts for the next leg, and found myself looking forward to the arrival of the new crew. But I was still picking at the dry skin on my thumb, a horribly antisocial activity I have indulged in for years when anxious. It's not good. The skin starts to bleed, and doesn't heal up; when it does the skin is dry, begins to flake off, needs a bit of a tug to help, and more tugging, bleeds again, and so on. And then the skin cracks open and the thumb gets sore. (TMI as the younger generation would say.) This habit probably arose when I used to get pompholyx, those itchy blisters on hands and feet. This once got so bad when I was a junior hospital doctor that I had to stop inserting cardiac pacemakers — which I was not properly trained for, and which I hated. Those blisters must have been a physical response to my undoubted stress, worsened by feeling unsupported by my senior colleagues. Pacemakers were then in their infancy and St George's, an early centre for pacing, received patients from as far away as Hull and Plymouth — to find little junior doctor me. But those blisters did the job, the treatment of lashings of steroid cream and plastic gloves putting paid to any more pacing.

---

23. Royal Collection Trust, description accompanying Picton's portrait.

I felt even better when I had got the boat well cleaned-out, and tidied up, with everything back in its right place. John had helped but was not very good at cleaning, like many other crew. Maybe this is just a man problem, or maybe it is because he had not been bossed around and castigated by Cathie who is an outstandingly good cleaner, but so obsessional she takes forever and never finishes. She hasn't read the legendary McMullen's 1869 *Down Channel*, but surely agrees with him that 'if things are not washed up when used, it is not deferring the cleaning to a more convenient time, but paving the way for habitually using them dirty'.[24] McMullen was a difficult skipper by all accounts, well able to handle his boat alone after sacking his crew for not attaining the perfection that he rather unreasonably demanded. He was one of the first to abandon the notion that yachting was a kind of social affair for posh, rich people, and more a kind of man-alone against nature activity.

During the day I also had time to sort out my emails — not anymore on a laptop with a rather feeble dongle to connect to the internet, but easily on my iPhone, a hand-held computer of amazing power compared with what was available only a few years previously. Mind you, the emails were mostly spam, plus an unwelcome request to write a foreword for some document I was involved with for Healthcare Improvement Scotland (far enough away in time and place to be ignored). The weather forecast was there on the phone too, as long as I had a decent signal, which one usually does around most of our coastline. I presume the forecasts have got so much more accurate because computer modelling has improved over the years, along with more and better real-time data collection from all round the world. With their instant availability the forecasts have become a lot more useful for planning voyages, particularly forecasts giving very local information, and for several days ahead. Sitting in Neyland, I could see from xcweather that a southeast gale was on the way in a couple of days, worth a thought for the Bristol Channel ahead.

Another extraordinary advance was being able to download all the charts of the British Isles on to my phone. The locating, so-called GPS, facility was then not quite good enough for serious navigation (it is now), but the electronic charts were certainly detailed enough to use if all the paper charts got blown overboard, and the chartplotter packed up or the boat batteries went down. That phone had been so handy for planning cruises as I sat at the back of boring lectures during international stroke conferences.

---

24. R. T. McMullen, *Down Channel* (orig. 1869; London: Grafton Books, 1986), 214.

Another advantage I had no idea about was Spotify, until Greg showed me. Fancy being able to summon up any tune you want to listen to, in my case tested with Humphrey Lyttelton, and then 'Smoke Gets in your Eyes' by the Platters (my age was telling). I have yet to explore the phone's video possibilities, and still hardly use the camera facility, largely because I prefer my Olympus digital camera, bulky as it is.

The end of leg two left me thinking about a few things, as one does on a boat in ways one does not at home. Maybe because there is more time for sitting about, and because most of the problems are within a few feet of one's nose, usually within reach too. When was the weather going to warm up? Why was there some blue engine coolant in the engine bilge? How did some of it get into the vegetable locker? Why wasn't the electric outboard motor battery charging properly? Probably something to do with the connection from the charger. (How I hate outboards. Rather than repeatedly wrenching on a starter cord, or reaching for the starter button, I prefer to row — also an essential skill to teach children.) Which way were we going to cross the Bristol Channel? Would we make Lundy Island, or Padstow, or have to go direct for Land's End? The wind was forecast from the southeast, which was good for Land's End but nowhere further east. Maybe the Scilly Isles would make more sense. Hopefully the new crew would be up for whatever lay ahead.

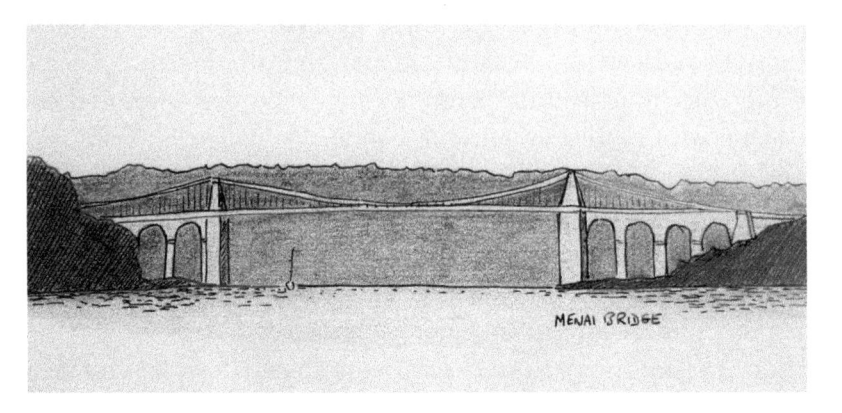

MENAI BRIDGE

Chapter 6

From Milford Haven to Poole

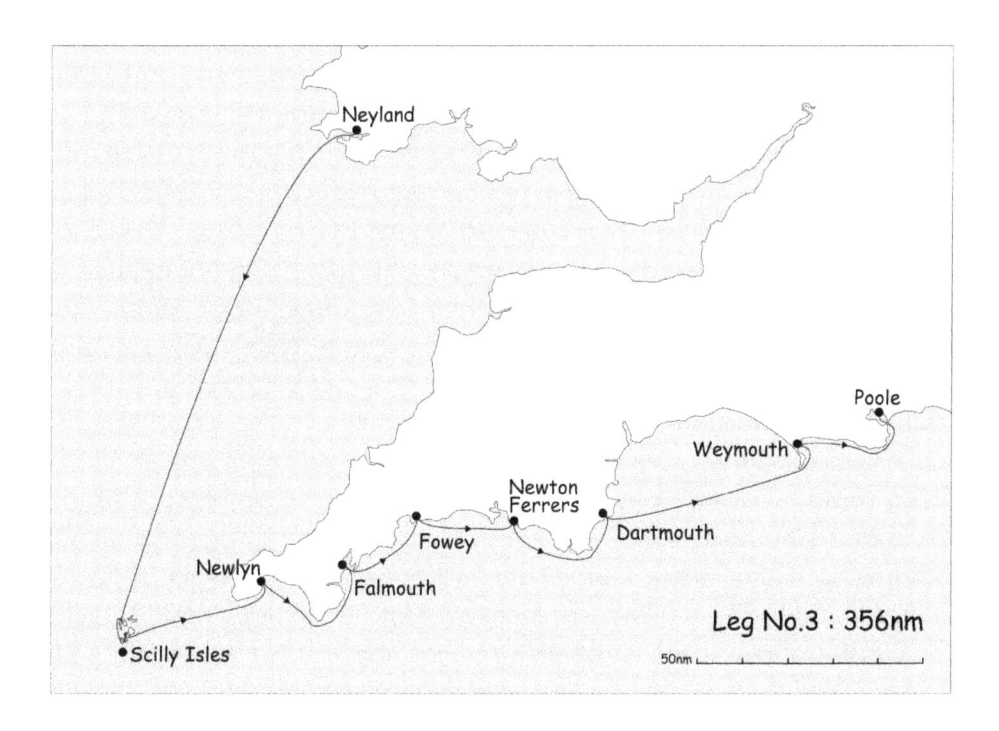

Saturday April 28th — still no sign of the sun, and I was having a lot of brief bouts of vertigo, with a nasty feeling of imbalance and nausea in between them. This became particularly bad during a wander around Neyland, when I even had to hold on to the occasional lamp-post. Most embarrassing, but there was hardly anyone to see me weaving about in what seemed a rather nondescript and grey little town (only on my next visit did I discover the cosy Neyland Yacht Club). This culminated in an awful attack of vertigo in a newsagent's when I looked down at the pile of newspapers on the floor. Everything was going round so fast that I had real difficulty picking out the *Guardian*. Clutching the paper, I staggered back to the boat and, for the first time, was violently sick in the heads. Strangely, the really bad vertigo never recurred during the rest of the voyage, the imbalance gradually almost disappeared, and all was eventually well — and still is. Slightly counter-intuitively, a sailing boat is not a bad place to be if you are off-balance because you are always holding on to something anyway, or should be. 'One hand for the boat' and all of that. It feels much safer than crossing the road, or a large room, with no means of emergency support.

Another irritating health problem declared itself in the shower. Unlike in a bath, which I much prefer, in a shower one is standing and has to look down to find the errant soap that has slipped out of one's hand and is slithering around on the floor. Looking down that morning I was astonished to see a swelling in my right groin. I poked at it. Squishy. An inguinal hernia! A piece of my gut trying to push its way out of my abdomen! Where had that come from? When did it happen? Why? Maybe because I had been coughing a lot in the early part of the voyage, due to some sort of respiratory infection that had taken weeks to shake off. The 'thing' wasn't painful, just unsightly. I guessed it would get worse, and eventually need operating on. And so it was, in 2014, by John Casey who took a break in between transplanting livers. I didn't fancy a truss: only old men wore trusses in my limited medical student experience. All this made me feel old, again.

However, undaunted by the old and new medical problems I set off to Milford by bus. There was a Tesco supermarket by the station for loading up with all we would need for a few days. I keep several copies of a victualling list on the boat, an aide-memoire. It wouldn't do to forget a basil plant for example — not that Tesco had one. Just as I was studying the feeble selection of red wines, Steve Druitt appeared off the train carrying the *Guardian*.

Steve is English but had lived in Edinburgh for decades, and ran a small company devoted to traffic planning. I had known him for years, as part of the south Edinburgh bourgeoisie that sends their children to the local and very good state schools. His wife had died of breast cancer the same month as I had my colon cancer out, in 1995, leaving him with three teenage children. He never remarried but had attracted a selection of girlfriends, consecutively and concurrently. One of the most memorable was Elizabeth, a feisty lady then in her 20s who had been one of the 11 competitors in the second Big Brother reality TV series, and she nearly won it. Steve was a good sailor. Like me he had learned as a boy, in dinghies off the coast at Margate. He had also co-owned a Sigma 33 that he cruised off the west coast of Scotland, and a Hunter 707 for racing on the Forth, and he had crewed with me many times over the years. We loaded up all the food and wine into a taxi and set off back to Neyland. It was good to see him and catch up with the gossip.

David Morgan arrived next, carrying yet another *Guardian*. He and I had been close friends since medical school. He was one of the few in my class who had actually wanted to be a GP, not like the many who ended up as a GP because they couldn't get on with, or just didn't like, any other speciality. Curious really, bearing in mind how rewarding general practice is to do well, and how satisfying it can be. You have to know so much across a huge range of medicine, some of it in depth, from neonates to children to teenagers to adults pregnant and not pregnant, to the very old, and to the dying. Hospital specialists may know a lot but only about a few areas, sometimes just one. How boring it must be to be an oncologist, for example, maybe only dealing with one sort of cancer, and never having to make a diagnosis because they don't see the patients first off. Or a cardiologist pushing their catheters — loads of commercial (aka private) practice, but it's not worth the money they trouser in my view.

David was retired from his practice in Poole where he still lived with Maureen whom he married as a medical student. She was the first person I had known to be on the contraceptive pill back in the halcyon 1960s, that happy gap between panic over missed periods and panic over AIDS. Like Steve, David was an experienced sailor; he kept a Moody 27 in Poole Harbour.

Finally, William and Nadina Jeffcoate appeared in the evening, also carrying yet another *Guardian*. I imagine one is more likely to make friends with people who read the same newspaper (I don't think I know anyone who reads the *Daily Mail*). They had met back in the 1970s in our chartering days from Skye. Nadina was on my Rival 34. She was a friend of Ilona, my first wife, and they were both clinical psychologists in Oxford at the time. On another Rival 34, skippered by Edwin Swarbrick, had been William, a junior doctor in London. Nadina was and still is a very keen dinghy sailor. Quite quickly William had to become equally keen. They became doyens of the UK Scorpion fleet, and their son now keeps winning the national championships. Their engineer daughter is involved in tidal energy, like my son Oli was, and is another keen sailor (racing more than cruising, I think).

Both Nadina and William are quiet but very good company. William is always amusing. He had brought a large jar labelled homemade Pickle-lilli (ho ho), and by my special request a basil plant. I have yet to solve the problem of where to keep a pot of basil on a boat. It needs light, warmth, fresh not salt water, and — crucially — somewhere it won't tip out all over the place. Maybe some dedicated gimbals could be designed. Again, by special request, Nadina was bearing homemade marmalade; mine had run out and I didn't want to resort to the shop varieties that never taste right.

William's clinical and research passion was the deeply unfashionable problems that many patients with diabetes have with their feet. However, in the early years he was more of a general hormone man, an endocrinologist. Seizing a research opportunity during a cruise to Orkney long ago, he took blood from all the male crew every other day and, unbeknown to them, asked the female crew to score each of the males for bossiness towards the rest of the crew. The blood was to measure testosterone as I recall — as anticipated, the level correlated with 'bossiness'. The results were published, although editors now might question why the male subjects had not been fully informed about the experiment's purpose (which would have ruined it as each of us would have upped our bossiness efforts). Such are the problems of contemporary medical research ethics. William's study in his home is referred to as 'The Growlery', presumably because he growls when disturbed.

Steve didn't know the others who were old friends, but he soon became quite jolly like the rest of us, helped along by a gin and tonic on board and then a good meal in the marina restaurant, for the third evening running in my case. And even more jolly later, on board, with a whisky (single malt, naturally). Note to self: buy brandy for Nadina in future, and rum for brother John.

As the wind was light we took the opportunity to warp Pickle round on the pontoon to face the expected gale and make it easier to motor out the next day. I was still very bothered by manoeuvring in marinas, particularly after the Port Ellen fiasco (I still use the shortened ensign staff as an incentive to do better). The weather forecast was vile. And so it came to pass. The next day the wind howled, the rigging rattled, and it poured with rain. Up late, late breakfast, late coffee and cake, late lunch, and a thorough read of the *Observer*. Nadina and William became absorbed on their laptops, the rest of us in our books. Greg and John would not have been good at this sort of enforced idleness. For tea Nadina had found some doughnuts in the local Co-op. Dinner was splendid, cooked by David who had clearly picked up tips from his father who had been head chef at the Cumberland Hotel in London. We laid out the Nottingham 'lace' tablecloth which was an old present from William and Nadina, a decanter of good wine, and ate steak while rain battered on the cabin top. I can't remember the dessert, but there must have been one. All very *gemütlich*, that German word which sounds cosier than our 'cosy', and the briefly fashionable Danish *hygge* — and certainly Visit Scotland's once feeble attempt with the possibly inaccurate Gaelic of *còsagach* which nobody knows how to pronounce (it may mean a small hole where insects live; scholars are probably still arguing).

Across the Bristol Channel to the Scilly Isles

The wind had died down a bit by the next morning, and it was still overcast. I reckoned we should leave if we possibly could. With too much hanging around I was getting bored, and besides the marina was surprisingly expensive at £36 a night. It had been nice to have a couple of days to rest up and sort myself out, days off from sailing. But enough was enough. I had enjoyed revisiting Wales, particularly the north where I have had so many memorable times — rock-climbing when a medical student in London (before the M6 made it easier to get to the Lake District), visiting David Lea over the years, and revising for exams.

We were all avidly watching the weather forecast on our phones. We had been lucky with the wind direction so far, with depressions tracking further south than usual. And the weather was better than on the east side of Britain. It was going to be a strong wind, but from the east or southeast so we should be fine for the Scilly Isles, 121 miles to the southwest. Sadly we had to abandon any thought of getting to Lundy Island, or even Padstow, with that wind direction. And nor could we experience the fascination of sailing up the muddy River Avon under the famous suspension bridge into the centre of Bristol, where you enter the lock into the Floating Harbour. There you are greeted by the lock-keeper, who in 2018 was voted British Marine Lock-Keeper of the year — I'm not surprised, as he is a lovely man. All those places had to wait until my third circumnavigation.

We also knew the wind was expected to moderate. And we trusted the weather forecast. There would be no life worth living without trust. We 'trust' all the time — trust that our pilot can fly an aeroplane across the Atlantic, trust that someone has checked the rails between London and Edinburgh, trust that a beef burger contains beef and not horse, trust that our milk will be safe and free of TB, trust that people tell the truth most of the time, and trust that the tide times in Reeds Almanac are correct. We don't have time to check everything, or indeed the expertise. So we 'trust', because we have to (but maybe not estate agents, second-hand car salesmen and politicians, and particularly not Boris Johnson).

At 11am, with two reefs in the mainsail and no genoa, we set off upriver to explore. It was all rather pleasant, the rural river Cleddau, a bit like Devon, and pretty. Then at 12.30pm we turned to reach very fast, back down to the fairway buoy at the entrance to Milford Haven. By then the wind was gale force and so we tied down the third and final reef in the main. The preventer was rigged to avoid any unexpected gybes and, with a bit of jib rolled out, we were off, bouncing out into a very disturbed Bristol Channel. At least the sun had come out, slightly. All Nadina can now remember about that morning is wishing 'we could wait another day for the wind to abate'. We all probably had the same wish.

I knew the boat would be fine, but what about the crew? Within an hour Steve was the first to disgrace himself. He is very noisy being seasick. Somehow the crew got to ruminating whether noisy vomiting correlated with noisy love-making. Steve informed us not (he should know) and retired to the quarter berth with a bucket conveniently dangling off the companionway grab-handle. William delayed his quiet and restrained single vomit until he made the mistake of grilling bacon in the morning. The rest of us were OK. In truth it was a miserable night — drizzle, rough — and we could only manage soup to eat. I am hopeless at preparing meals, or even thermos flasks in advance, being generally far too optimistic (unrealistic, the crew would say), preferring to cook at sea when a meal is due. But that doesn't work too well when it is really rough. Despite not getting sick, I find it just too difficult to cope in the galley without making a monumental mess, and having to leave the washing up until later when it is a congealed mess.

Like others I have spoken to, I have become generally more anxious about sailing with age, fuelled by too much reading of yachting magazines, and more worried about making a navigational mistake (dementia coming on?) or falling off the boat and not getting back (frailty coming on?). These days I hope I have the sense to be more cautious, and not set off with such an unfavourable weather forecast that we had for the Bristol Channel. But sometimes I still do, and as ever feel guilty about exposing the crew to rubbish weather, frozen fingers, seasickness, and (let's face it) a bit of fear, too. It would surely have been more sensible to avoid a long passage, like across the Bristol Channel, with a new crew. However experienced, they need time to adapt and get into the swing of things.

We saw no other yachts, not surprisingly. However, off the north Cornish coast we spotted a few lights on tankers. They were also revealed by small triangles on the chartplotter from their AIS signals (Automated Information System), dubbed 'triangles of doom' by my son Ben. What a wonderful invention AIS is. By the time of this cruise, all ships of any size had to transmit an AIS signal, and a lot of smaller ones did too, even some yachts. In 2018 we fitted an AIS transmitter so Pickle too started to appear as a triangle of doom. It is useful for family and friends to know where we are (using their phones), and indeed harbour masters on approach to their harbours. (In earlier days Cathie was once so worried about my whereabouts that she phoned the coastguard, just as I was casually entering the Sound of Mull. When I reached Tobermory the harbour master said, 'The coastguards are looking for you!')

So many boats now transmit AIS that the chartplotter can become a confused mess of triangles of doom, particularly in busy places like the Solent. But how very useful to know where boats are when they can't be seen because of poor visibility or darkness — and what sort of boat they are, their name, the number to call them on the VHF, which way they are going and how fast, and the closest Pickle will be to them, and in how many minutes (assuming both boats proceed in the same direction at the same speed). And you can see when a ship changes course to avoid you. It is a brilliant and reasonably inexpensive aid to safe navigation.

More triangles of doom appeared on the chartplotter, pointing in all sorts of directions. These we discovered were fishing boats, presumably out of Newlyn. And in a typically random pattern, which nowadays indicates not necessarily fishing boats, but also support boats clustered around offshore wind farms.

I had decided to stay up until it was light. After all, the crew were new to the boat (apart from Steve who was currently no use) and wouldn't have known how to use the chartplotter, where all the ropes and winches were in the dark, and so on. Thankfully by 5am the wind moderated down to force 6, so I retired as Steve emerged after many vomits to a grey, still drizzly and breezy morning off the Cornish coast. Down below was a bit of a mess, not surprisingly. The water in the heads had slopped out all over the place, and was rather smelly. (Must remember to pump them dry at sea.)

By 9am I was up again to find we were reaching along in a calming sea and the sun was shining. However, in my slightly dopey state a big wave caught me unawares. I lost my grip on the chart table and crashed backwards into the galley, cracking my back and then my head on something hard. I think the bent guardrail in front of the cooker tells the story. My back was extremely painful and for a few minutes I could hardly move. Ibuprofen was required.

The rest of that part of the leg was relatively uneventful. The split-pin fell out of the attachment of the kicker to the mast but that could be bodged up with thin rope. And I finished reading *The Cruise of the Nona* by Hilaire Belloc, published in 1925. He sailed all round this area and his descriptions of sailing alone, drifting up and down with the tide without an engine, are quite lovely. But the interspersed political and other comments can be tedious.

In the old days before GPS, I suspect I would have headed for the north Cornish coast to be sure of making a recognisable landfall, and then turned west along the coast towards the Scilly Isles, making the journey about 15 miles — three hours — longer. However, with modern technology and less navigational stress, we could head straight for New Grimsby Sound in the Scilly Isles, 'a Road, or rather a small Cove between the Island of Tresco and the Island Bryer; there is no Danger in going in. This Place is narrow, and only fit for small Ships. You anchor before the castle in five, six or seven fathom water', according to Greenvile Collins in 1693.[1] There was no danger back then, and none now, and visitor moorings mean you don't even have to anchor. It was easy to approach from the north, and well sheltered from the direction of the wind that morning.

Down with the Welsh courtesy flag, up with the Scilly Isles flag. We arrived at 1.30pm to tie up to a mooring which cost £24 for the night, a sign of what to expect on Tresco. There was just one other visiting yacht — French, and saving money at anchor. We were only the second visiting boat on a mooring that year. Late April and May is definitely the time of year for cruising, at least to places that get packed out in the summer. It was beautiful. Calm, blue, sunny, warm even though it was breezy, while the east of England was being battered by rain. How lucky we had been with favourable wind directions so far.

I confess I was wondering yet again whether I was getting too old for this sort of sailing. Maybe I should stick to light winds and daylight? My balance was not as good as it had been, irrespective of the attacks of vertigo. I was not as strong as I was, which was never very strong. My hernia was just beginning to feel uncomfortable, my teeth were breaking up as usual, my back was still sore, and I was again pulling at the dry skin on my thumb (such a bad habit). Like most people my age, I imagined I

---

1. Greenvile Collins, *Great-Britain's Coasting Pilot* (London: 1693).

might be dementing but probably wasn't. I was certainly frailer, more easily knocked over. At times I was aware of a slight tremor in my right hand when brushing my teeth. Early Parkinson's disease, perhaps?

That said, boats are now much easier to sail, and more comfortable, so one should be able to sail well into one's 80s. On Pickle, like most sailing boats nowadays, we have a furling jib so no scary trips to the foredeck to change the foresail anymore, no undoing and doing-up those metal hanks with frozen fingers. And all the lines from the mainsail come back to the cockpit, so no need to crawl to the mast to reef (I would not countenance a furling main myself for fear of it getting stuck). We have an electric anchor winch, hot running water, a cabin-heater, VHF radio to call the coastguard, GPS, chartplotter, AIS, mobile phone, internet access. None of these conveniences were on sailing boats when I started, and some hadn't even been invented. Why not carry on until I am 80 or beyond? We will see.

Tresco

Not surprisingly we spent the rest of Tuesday sleeping and talking, and eating but not as outrageously as Henry Reynolds back in exactly the same place in 1904. Of his lunch he wrote, 'Strawberry jam with clotted cream upon a foundation of new bread, sent in pursuit of all the lobster one can comfortably swallow, is a mixture calculated to make a dyspeptic shudder, but gives great satisfaction to a robust appetite.'[2] And we reminisced. About the time we got a rope round the propeller while at anchor at St Kilda, not a good place to run into difficulties, especially as the increasingly strong wind had shifted round to the southeast to put us on a lee shore. And when Edwin Swarbrick, in a gale anchored off the Treshnish Islands, rather carelessly tossed our second anchor over the side from the inflatable dinghy only for the anchor to pierce one of the rubber tubes. With air hissing out fast, he only just made it back to the mother ship; the alternative was the hostile shore of Mull some four miles downwind. There were a lot of good things to look back on, and lessons learned. But I was missing the children and Cathie, even though I had left them in Maryport less than three weeks earlier.

Wednesday May 2nd, a beautiful day to explore Tresco, with swallows and house martins swooping over the fields. The harbour master, Henry

---

2. Henry Reynolds, *Coastwise—Cross-Seas: The Tribulations and Triumphs of a Casual Cruiser* (London: J. D. Potter, 1921), 186.

Birch, was delightful and helpful. There were one or two people strolling around, locals or tourists, all very polite. No children that you would normally see in the school holidays, but not many young adults either. The average age was in the 50s and 60s. The upmarket English accents were a bit strange after Scotland and Wales. There were no cars, just electric golf buggies like on Hamilton Island in the Whitsundays. Everywhere was ever so neat and tidy. The pub, The New Inn, was nice but expensive. The final give-away was the 'village shop': unbelievably posh and prices to match, with an extensive wine selection, its own bread and patisserie counter, and a cheese counter too. There must be a lot of very well-off people here in the summer to support this sort of place. The Hebrides it is not. Rather it is Waitrose-on-sea — or maybe Harrods-by-the-sea. Contrary to expectations and first impressions, all was not as remote as one might imagine on Tresco, at least not as regards shopping for food and wine.

However, the sun was warm, the sea sparkled, and the Abbey gardens beckoned, famous for well over a century. In 1870 W. H. G. Kingston's fictional crew all 'agreed that we had never before been in so perfect a garden, so rich with a profusion of flowers'.[3] The entrance fee was so high we nearly didn't go in, but it is fortunate we did. The gardens are superb. Exotic and local plants in profusion, inspired garden design, lovely sculptures, everything blooming weeks before it would in Scotland and probably most of England too. And interestingly, figureheads salvaged from the many wrecks there have been around the Scilly Isles. It seemed like high summer and yet it was only very early May. Much enchanted, we then walked around more of the island, admiring the fabulous beaches, and examining the 17th-century Cromwell's Castle overlooking New Grimsby Sound, built to deter the Dutch. I imagine the whole place must be awfully crowded in summer.

St Mary's

By mid-afternoon it was time to move on. We funked the direct route to the main island of St Mary's across the drying and complicated sandbanks. Our excuse? The tide was falling. Earlier we had been astonished to see the French yacht set off in that direction, and on a falling tide with its sails up. It appeared to get stuck at one point before moving on. Instead, in a

---

3. William H. G. Kingston, *A Yacht Voyage round England* (orig. 1870; London: The Religious Tract Society, *c.*1879), 166.

light northeast wind, we sailed out to sea, turned left and had a delightful two-hour, eight-mile, evening cruise to the moorings off Hugh Town, keeping well away from the ominously jagged rocks that surround the whole archipelago.

Hugh Town was more crowded than Tresco, with not many vacant visitor moorings. Some were far too close together for our 35ft, and the one we found was a long way from the shore, at least for rowing the dinghy rather than motoring. But too bad. The Torqeedo was dead, the battery had not been charging properly, and the cause did indeed eventually turn out to be a loose connection. Ah, the outboard — it doesn't seem to matter whether the dinghy is powered by a clean, green and quiet electric engine like mine, or by a noisy, smelly, greasy, heavy petrol engine. In both cases they don't work for me. They never have, from way back when I chartered a boat with one of those ancient 'Seagull' contraptions clamped to the pushpit. Hugh Town must be a hellish place in the summer — anchoring is prohibited and the competition for visitor moorings must be intense.

At St Mary's we saw the first of many rowing pilot-gigs. It was a couple of days before the World Championships and at least 100 were parked up in the town, crewed by tough and bronzed teams from around Europe, the most notable being a Dutch female crew who all seemed about 7 feet tall. Very scary, rather like that Dublin barmaid. Maybe the Dutch are so tall because the portion sizes in Dutch restaurants are so huge, but if so why haven't they grown sideways as well as upwards? William informed me that some new urinals in Holland are higher than they used to be; he himself once had to stand on tiptoe to relieve himself.

The next day we had a look at St Mary's. Very different from Tresco, it didn't feel so much of an island somehow, with many more tourists. It was a bit down-at-heel but with some attractive buildings and corners in Hugh Town, particularly the 18th-century harbour wall constructed with huge dry-fitted granite blocks. This is where Harold Wilson came regularly to holiday in his modest bungalow, a more authentic Labour Prime Minister than Tony-Iraq-War-Blair who took bling holidays with rich people on expensive yachts in the Mediterranean. The old castle up on the headland is now a hotel. We didn't go in, and just admired the view, preferring to walk around the north side of the island to look at the 16th-century Harry's Walls (remains of an old fort), the prehistoric Bant's Carn Burial Chamber, and the 2000-year-old Halangy village. They were OK but not in the same archaeological league as Orkney. It was even warm enough to have lunch outside in a café overlooking the sea. Well, everywhere overlooks the sea here.

St Agnes

In the early evening we motored the three miles to St Agnes (and were overtaken by those Dutch ladies — rowing), and anchored in The Cove, a south-facing bay. We were the only boat. St Agnes is different again, very different. Quiet, hardly any tourists, unkempt in an attractive scruffy way so very unlike Tresco, lush vegetation, meadows, hedgerows, swallows, and delightful little cottages. Terrific ice cream too, made on the farm on the west side of the island where a campsite overlooks the Atlantic and the surrounding very dangerous-looking rocks as well as the distant Bishop Rock Lighthouse. And close by on the cliff edge is the small Troy Town 'maze' made out of smooth stones from the beach (not as ancient as it looks, it was probably started in the 18th century and remodelled many times since then). The Turk's Head right by the anchorage had decent real ale, and was surprisingly crowded. It was warm enough to sit outside, watched over by a one-legged seagull. By evening it was flat calm. Maybe summer had arrived at last.

I found myself brooding again on age, and was feeling mine. This was getting a tedious habit. I still sometimes had the vertigo turning in bed in the morning, but at least I was now fine in between times, and my balance was restored. However, my back still felt very sore. Steve had lent me his elasticated corset-like belt, which certainly helped. (A strange thing to bring on holiday.) I needed the ibuprofen but could now put on my own socks; only the day before William had to help me, making me all too aware of my handicap. I was being rehabilitated.

In thinking about rehabilitation, there is a helpful distinction between impairment (basically a symptom, like my sore back, or my deafness) and disability (what you can't do, like bend over in my case, or hear the radio). More crucial is the third level, which is handicap — not being able to do something you want or need to because of the disability (get my socks on without assistance, or hear when 'Pickle' is being called-up on the VHF radio). There may be little you can do about impairment or disability, but there should be a lot to alleviate handicap (getting help with my socks from William, and turning up the volume on the radio).

The modern equivalent terms are less intuitive and far less helpful. Impairment is still there, but disability is now inverted to 'activity', while 'participation' is the more politically acceptable opposite of handicap. Who can get these 'improvements' easily across to medical students? Not me.

Rehabilitation is not popular with medical students, probably because it is badged as something removed from the dramas of acute medicine, and often taught separately. It would be taken up more enthusiastically if it became part and parcel of ordinary bedside teaching on the acute ward (and in general practice for that matter). There, as well as discussing the diagnosis and acute treatment of stroke with the exciting-sounding clot-busting drugs, the equally important issue of recovery and rehabilitation can be brought in too. The same goes for the other unpopular-with-medical-students subject — epidemiology (the science of studying populations rather than individuals). Do not hive off epidemiology to be taught in a classroom by epidemiologists but bring it to the bedside, along with rehabilitation. Slip in both of them under the radar where the white-coated stethoscope-wielding students won't notice. When the makers of potato crisps want them to sell well, they improve their taste by sprinkling them with salt before putting them in bags. What they do not do is put the salt in a small blue bag as in my youth, and hope the buyers sprinkle it over the crisps for themselves. Rehabilitation and epidemiology should not lurk in small blue bags — they should be sprinkled into the bigger bag of bedside teaching where they can't be avoided.

Again I wondered how many more sailing years I had in me. Lots, I hoped, it didn't do to be pessimistic. While some of my friends and acquaintances have packed up completely, or bought a motorboat, I prefer the Percy Woodcock approach: 'Sailing is a grand game, the best I know, and I have played it all my life. Now that I am getting long in the few teeth I have left I am still playing it, and hope to continue to do so for some time yet.'[4] To stiffen my resolve I was encouraged by meeting a 92-year-old man at the Scottish boat show who was still sailing a small keel-boat out of North Berwick.

David may have been harbouring similar thoughts. He had a new hip joint and was not nearly as nimble as he once was. A few years after this cruise he fractured his femur, had a complicated orthopaedic repair during which he had a heart attack, and not surprisingly got home in a rather sorry state. What was surprising was how long he took to get going on his feet again. Nearly a year later I went down to Poole to visit him. When he got out of the car to meet me he was carrying a stick, not using it, which seemed a bit odd. In the car I noticed his right hand was shaking.

'David, how long has that been happening?'

'What?'

---

4. Percy Woodcock, *Looking Astern: A Ditty-Bag of Memories* (London: Frederick Muller Ltd, 1950), 176.

'That shake.'
'Oh, I don't know, a while.'
'Have you thought what it might be?'
He paused and looked a bit sheepish.
'It looks like Parkinson's disease to me,' I said. 'Let me have a feel.'

Sure enough, his arm was stiff and he was very slow in moving his fingers, clear signs of Parkinson's disease. On reflection, it was also obvious that his face was slightly immobile, and his walking was typically slow. No wonder he was taking so long to recover from his operation. Thankfully, now on the right drugs, he is much better, and back singing in his choir. He had stopped singing because his throat was uncomfortable, something to do with having a tube put down it during the anaesthetic he rationalised. No, no, that was the Parkinson's disease too. But how was this diagnosis missed? He had seen his GP a few times, and both his orthopaedic surgeon and his cardiologist several times. None of them had noticed the shake, or if they had they must have dismissed it as someone else's problem. Such is the fragmentation of medicine, at least of specialist medicine. A now-retired neurologist in Cambridge was so specialised that he was said to make only two diagnoses — of the very rare Wilson's disease in which he was a world expert, and not-Wilson's disease that was definitely not for him to deal with. We specialists may know everything about our own narrow speciality, but precious little about the others. David's GP, with his broader, but necessarily less specialised, knowledge, could perhaps have done better.

Years ago this fragmentation of medicine was brought home to me when I was training at the National Hospital for Nervous Diseases in London. The hospital only dealt with neurology and neurosurgery so when a patient prolapsed his piles into the bedclothes we young neurologists had no idea what to do. There was no point in calling our consultant neurologist who would have even less idea. In the end we used that most useful instrument, the phone, and got someone over from St Mark's Hospital for Cancer, Fistula and other Diseases of the Rectum (as it said on the tin) to do the necessary.

Another London problem, then and maybe still now, was that a patient might, over months or years, be admitted to several different hospitals with the same underlying illness, for example multiple sclerosis or coronary heart disease. This sort of chaotic healthcare was one reason I escaped to Oxford in 1976, the 'push' to complement the 'pull' of working as a lecturer with Bryan Matthews. Besides, I didn't like the National Hospital's tendency to train you to believe that you should never ever be wrong, and if you are wrong to never admit it.

To Cornwall

Friday May 4th, to Newlyn with a rather fickle east-northeast wind. We had to motor quite a bit, managing the 37 miles in eight hours. Penzance was the other option, with its extremely attractive and friendly harbour in the midst of things. But their dock gates open only for a couple of hours before high tide and one hour afterwards, which is awkward for arrival and departure. Despite the Sailing Directions stating that prior contact with the Newlyn harbour master was essential for all visiting boats, I couldn't raise him on the VHF. Nonetheless, a helpful man appeared on the pontoons to take our lines and charge us a very reasonable £18 for the night. Newlyn is dominated by fishing boats, but is a good option for yachts even though the pontoons are more industrial than would be found in a yacht marina. You could tell the place was not meant for the leisure industry by the state of the toilets: we had to hop over a large pool of water to get in to them.

An important reason for going to Newlyn was to catch up with my very old friend John Rawles and his wife Katharine. John and I had worked together in Aberdeen in the early 1970s. He was the first person I knew who used an electronic calculator, a rather clunky desktop machine with which in his spare time he was trying to work out the mathematical significance of the mysterious Aberdeenshire stone circles. Hand-held calculators only appeared in large numbers a few years later, and proper computers after that. Although highly intelligent and educated, John had always preferred to be on the outer edge, first working in Wick as a junior doctor, and then later at the other end of the country here in Penzance as a single-handed consultant physician. He was retired and had just finished his book *The Matter with Us*,[5] an impressive philosophical and scientific exploration of mankind, which sadly did not sell at all well, presumably because as an unknown he had not been able to find a decent publisher.

Some years previously he had accidentally sawn off a few fingers of one hand, and then in 2010 he had been on his bicycle when he was mown down by a car (ironically driven by an ex-patient with diabetes). He had to have bilateral below-knee amputations but by the time of my arrival was walking reasonably well on prosthetic legs, not bad for over 70 years old. He could drive, walk a mile, and had bought a bespoke tricycle to extend his range. Indeed he had legs for walking, and different legs for cycling.

---

5. John Rawles, *The Matter with Us: A Materialistic Account of the Human Predicament* (Brighton: Pen Press, 2011).

He didn't complain of phantom limb pains, and only later did I discover he was taking medication to keep them more or less at bay. The silver lining for him was that he had arranged with the prosthetic leg-maker to increase his rather short height by a couple of inches. Presumably he can go on surreptitiously growing each time he needs replacement legs, like the tortoise in Roald Dahl's *Esio Trot*.

Coincidentally, John and Katharine knew a local friend of David's. Jenny Lewis had trained as a nurse at St Thomas' Hospital in London in the 1960s. (Nurses then were a bit scary and had to be taken very seriously by young, as well as older, doctors.) Another of David's friends to join us was Nick Tregenza, a GP by training, no longer a doctor but an inventor. Brought up in Mousehole just along the coast, aged 14 he had invented very long shoes with flaps underneath and walked Jesus-like on the sea to the island off Mousehole harbour, in danger of doing the splits all the way. They didn't catch on. Later he came up with a forward-facing rowing boat with a wave-piercing bow and a scary urge to start surfing. It languishes in his back yard. More recently he invented high-tech pods to lower into the sea to listen to the voices of whales, dolphins and porpoises. These were viable and are now in use on every continent, monitoring beleaguered dolphin and porpoise populations, and all made in Mousehole.

Amusingly, I inadvertently locked up Pickle with Nadina still on board (clearly I was not yet used to having a larger boat than a Contessa 32). Ever resourceful, she opened the forehatch, climbed out and, much to my surprise, appeared walking along the pontoons just as I was asking, 'where's Nadina gone?' All nine of us then went off for a very jolly dinner at the Smugglers Restaurant overlooking the harbour, with its friendly owner and staff.

There was much talk of local affairs, in particular the extraordinary news that the important helicopter service between Penzance and the Scilly Isles was closing down. The Penzance council had done a deal with Sainsbury's who were going to build a supermarket on the helipad, even though the town already had Morrison and Tesco supermarkets. Maybe there was more to it than that, I don't know. Because the passenger ferry between Penzance and the Scilly Isles does not run in winter, the islands would become far more isolated. Yes, they would still have the aeroplane but that goes either from the middle of nowhere (Land's End airport), or from Newquay (not all that helpful), or from far-away Exeter. The good news is that the all-year helicopter service resumed in 2019. The bad news is the adult single fare now starts at £134, for just 30 miles in 15 minutes. More bad news is that some flights will land on Tresco to spoil the peace and quiet — but then, Tresco is just the sort of place that people who can afford the fare will want to go to, direct to 'Harrods-by-the-sea'.

To Falmouth

Saturday May 5th, an overcast, grey, and chilly day. Nadina and William were away home on the train, probably to some crucial Scorpion dinghy race they could not possibly miss. Their commitment to their local sailing club, while admirable, did mean they could only come for a week, which had been tricky to orchestrate given the uncertainty of wind and weather. They thoughtfully left the basil plant for us to cherish.

I hadn't expected much of Newlyn, essentially I imagined a fishing harbour with a smattering of tourists, but little did I know. However, as well as the small Co-op supermarket there was a very good fishmonger, a pasty shop, a butcher, a lovely cheese shop, and an excellent café for coffee and a bun. Altogether a neat little town. Later, I discovered that my parents had spent half their honeymoon here, in 1931.

How interesting it is to be able to eat local food, rather than some ubiquitous international brand — Cornish pasties here in Cornwall, Stornoway black pudding in the Outer Hebrides, smokies in Arbroath, butteries in the north of Scotland, Guinness in Dublin (not quite a food), and lots of clotted cream in Devon to smear on scones with heaps of jam — preferably homemade.

My back was definitely on the mend, there was no vertigo or imbalance, the boat was going well, and a new split-pin had arrived via John Rawles but as it was too big we continued with the rope bodge-up to secure the kicker. But the heads were still giving me grief, something to do with the seawater inlet it seemed. Should I have chosen the easier-to-understand Jabsco toilet, which has no vacuum arrangement to confuse the crew and for me to worry about? Maybe our Lavac would be more understandable, we fantasised, if the toilet bowl and pipes were transparent so we could actually see the poos being pumped out, while seawater is sucked in by the vacuum (provided the lid is closed). A slightly uncomfortable fantasy. (Nowadays I have simple instructions for the uninitiated, stuck to the bulkhead above the toilet bowl.) And I worried about the other problem, the loose connection to the battery charger for the Torqeedo outboard that I was not in a position to do anything about without a soldering iron.

The sail to Falmouth was frustrating. We left after lunch, planning to have the tide with us off the Lizard. But we got there too soon and the easterly wind against the ebb tide made for discomfort — indeed it was quite rough. There was a lot of motoring, for about half the time, too much. The 34 miles took eight hours, so it wasn't till 8.30pm that we tied up to the town pontoons (where a couple of years earlier I made a fairly disastrous attempt to turn round my freshly minted and so-difficult-to-steer-backwards boat). Those pontoons can certainly get crowded. Often as not you have to raft up which is generally fine by me, as we did on that May Bank Holiday weekend. Naturally we inspected the plaque on the harbour railings commemorating the arrival of HMS Pickle bearing the news from the Battle of Trafalgar.

I think this is the best place to stop in Falmouth, in the middle of everything, right by the venerable Chain Locker pub and the fabulous chandlery in a low-ceilinged Aladdin's cave (alas, it has now moved into the main street and become more a clothes shop than a useful chandlery). And the town pontoons are close to the local shops. Pendennis Marina seemed too posh for us and rather soulless, and I had not been impressed with the less than helpful receptionist I once encountered there. The Falmouth marina is too far up river, but is nice enough when you get there, and handy for visiting the Rustler yard.

Falmouth was fun — so much more fun than the bleak and grey town it was when I had crewed a small yacht down the English Channel in 1962. It is now an exciting place with real shops, not just Tesco, and an excellent hands-on maritime museum. There were loads of tourists but that made for a reasonably good atmosphere. And of course Cornish clotted cream to spread thickly on scones, on top of a thick layer of jam (cream before jam in Devon). As Libby Purves remarked: 'Falmouth is the Piccadilly Circus of the coast. Stay here long enough, tied up to the town pontoons under the Custom House, and friends will appear, expected or unexpected, from land or sea.'[6] Disconcertingly there seemed to be a high proportion of Americans, explained later when we saw a huge cruise ship, as big as a castle, anchored off Pendennis Point. This is presumably good for the tourist industry and the local traders, not so good for the environment, or for passengers if they fall victim in their hundreds to some contagious microbe.

I began to form a vague plan for the following year. Sail down the Irish Sea to Cornwall with friends, be joined by the family for a couple of weeks'

---

6. Libby Purves, *One Summer's Grace: A Family Voyage round Britain* (London: Grafton Books, 1989), 43.

summer holiday exploring Cornwall and Devon, then back round the west of Ireland with a fresh crew. But against family sailing along the south coast are the rather long hops between anchorages and marinas, swell, and the exposure to the southwest. Compare that with the west coast of Scotland where there are so many bolt-holes (often easy to enter irrespective of wind direction), but you do have to know how to use an anchor, and to rely on it so you can sleep soundly.

We ate on board that night, a meal cooked by David who had taken over as chief chef — crevettes and excellent Dover sole from Newlyn. We were joined by Anne McQuade, a retired GP friend of David's. She is a hellish-keen sailor, Irish, wanting to know all about Pickle. She had a good poke round, and asked about my passage-plan for the following afternoon. Very disconcerting — 'have lunch, leave, sail to Fowey and have a cup of tea on the way' was my less-than-nautical response.

To Fowey

Sunday May 6th, a summer's day at last, about time too. Rest and relaxation until lunchtime when we set sail for Fowey on a sparkling sunny afternoon. The wind was a satisfactory 15 knots from the southeast so it was a fast fetch to the Dodman, then free to Fowey in four-and-a-half hours, 22 miles. A brilliant sail, a classic south coast experience. Steve felt a bit less sick, maybe thanks to the Stugeron he took, or maybe the sea was just less lumpy. Nor was he so grumpy about the weather forecast that he tends to interpret in a catastrophic sort of way. Quite a few other yachts were about, mainly racing from Falmouth to Fowey to Plymouth, we gathered, but nothing too obtrusive even for us (being used to the empty seas of the Hebrides).

On the way we realised a rescue operation was going on, somewhere around the Helford River. On the VHF radio we could hear not just the coastguards but the 'casualty', a man with a broken leg on board a 33ft motorboat. The lifeboat had arrived, as well as a helicopter to winch him off. The motorboat's skipper had been incredibly calm as he was asked to count to ten over the radio to enable the helicopter to get a good fix on him. Within half an hour the injured man had been parcelled up 'for dispatch', hauled up into the helicopter, which a few minutes later flew past us on its way to Derriford Hospital in Plymouth. Most impressive, and reassuring.

One reason for visiting Fowey was that Steve, whose parents had lived in Cornwall, was keen to arrive there by sea (as ever, far better than driving through dreary suburbs before finding nowhere to park). And it was well worth it. When we motored in, and as the sea settled down between the headlands, we began to see the houses tumbling down (or should it be climbing up?) the wooded banks on either side, Fowey itself to port, Polruan to starboard. As the harbour opened out, the profusion of well-spaced visitor moorings (anchoring discouraged) might have been confusing if not for the harbour master in his launch who came out to guide us in. He provided an excellent guide to the harbour facilities, the telephone number for the water-taxi, advice about recycling and rubbish disposal, and more.

Fowey is such a classic west-country harbour, unspoiled, no marinas by choice. There is a track record here. Between the world wars Percy Woodcock recalled a resident's riposte to his father's remark that Fowey lacked nice beaches. "'Drawback,' snapped the resident. "It's no drawback, it keeps Fowey what it is.'"[7] As does the lack of marinas. The occasional ship taking away Cornwall's china clay doesn't spoil the charm of the place, but too many cruise ships certainly would.

As in Falmouth, there were quite a few traditional yachts around to enhance the scenery. And many flags flying with a black cross on a white background, the Cornish flag, which is very much in evidence everywhere in Cornwall. As in Scotland, where there are also a lot of national flags flying, Cornwall feels itself on the edge, ignored or patronised by London — the flag making a statement about its separate identity, maybe wanting political independence like Scotland but much less likely to be achieved. (No flags in Devon, though, which must be too close to London.)

Monday May 7th was warm and sunny, warm enough to sit in the cockpit and admire the view all around while having breakfast. Even warm enough to soften the butter, but not yet for T-shirts. Then it was by water-taxi to Polruan to wander around the quiet steep lanes. Afterwards back to Fowey by ferry where we were met by Anne McQuade and Jenny Lewis as we stepped onto the harbour wall. Anne was carrying David's wallet. He realised he had lost it somewhere in Falmouth and was resigned to never seeing it again. Fortunately someone had picked it up — in the marina toilets — and phoned the first name on a list in the wallet, which happened to be me, by then at sea. I arranged for the wallet to be handed in to the marina in Falmouth where Anne picked it up. Another triumph for mobile phones.

What did we do before mobile phones, only a few years earlier? As long as you can charge your phone from your boat's battery, texting and emailing are all possible, as well as phoning ahead to the harbour master to sort out

---

7. Woodcock, *Looking Astern*, 103.

a mooring, getting instant forecasting from xcweather or the Met Office, contacting friends ashore and family far away and sending them photos of where you are, and looking things up on Google. I even got a text from my daughter Margaret who, at the time, was an expedition doctor in Nepal. And an email from a future crew enquiring what kit to bring.

Fowey was more animated than Polruan, with some delightful shops, including a proper butcher and several selling decent bread (and cakes). Chelsea-on-sea, perhaps. My favourite for coffee is The Dwelling House, very friendly, and with a shady garden, proper clotted cream, and a spectacular toilet in what could easily be mistaken for a sitting room. Fowey is one of the few places where the RNLI provides lockers for storing lifejackets, an encouragement to wear them in the dinghy but not then have to carry them round the town.

Before leaving Fowey Steve insisted we go to Pinkies for coffee and cake, and I'm glad we did. It is slightly out of the centre of the village, crammed with soft sofas, newspapers and books lying about to read, and curious bric-a-brac. A Posy Simmonds sort of a place, just right for *Guardian* readers who loved her strip-cartoon satirising the English middle classes (people like us). A few years later Steve introduced me to the beautiful 'Hall Walk' by taking the Bodinnick ferry from Fowey across the river, then walking by the high path around Pont Pill to Polruan, and back by ferry to Fowey, and a cream tea. Fowey is indeed 'the harbour of harbours' as Hilaire Belloc called it, 'without any admixture of the modern evil ... all is courtesy ... I suppose when the crash comes, and the ruins have been more or less cleaned up, Fowey will remain to carry on the traditions of a better England.'[8]

To Newton Ferrers

Why Newton Ferrers, rather than the adjacent and much more historic Plymouth? Firstly, because long ago, as a teenager, I remember sailing in here to anchor and being amazed by the steep wooded banks of a classic Devon river, the Yealm (pronounced Yam). I was crewing for Peter Gallichan, a rather ascetic young man with a pipe and a wooden boat — no sprayhood in those days, or stanchions and guardrails to prevent you falling overboard, or jackstays along the deck to clip on to. My brother had sailed with him a few years earlier, having answered his advertisement for crew in the *Times*, on the front page in those days. And secondly to the Yealm because Cathie's

---

8. Hilaire Belloc, *The Cruise of the Nona* (London: Constable & Co. Ltd, 1925), 141.

uncle and aunt — John and Chris Lytle — lived there, as did my old friend from medical school David Thrush and his wife Ruth.

Nowadays there is nowhere to anchor because the whole place is so jammed with moorings, even more so than in 1988 when Libby Purves found: 'There were too many moorings: too much uninhabited and white plastic afloat on the Yealm, but there is still a certain peacefulness even in these over-used, honeypot West Country harbours.'[9] Now, in summer you almost always have to raft up at a couple of floating pontoons. Jonathan Raban noticed 'the silence not of seclusion but of retirement — of childlessness, of pottering about indoors, of watching golf on television in the afternoons and having all the time in the world to read the Radio Times'.[10] Pretty accurate I reckon. Well, both John and David were well retired.

In some ways the Yealm is not that easy to enter. Quite a bar across the entrance means you need to be careful to stick to the leading lines. These are clearly enough marked by beacons on the hillside, provided you can spot them on the sort of murky evening it was when we motored in. It had been a sunny afternoon when we left Fowey, southerly wind, sailing free at 6–7 knots. Perfect. But the wind dropped, the tide turned against us off Rame Head, it started to drizzle, and we had to motor for the rest of the five-hour and 23-mile journey.

However, after rowing ourselves ashore, we were rewarded with a very spirited dinner at David and Ruth's house, along with John and Chris who were just back from the Caribbean where they were then spending the winters on their Bowman 40. Walking into a warm and cosy sitting room, I suddenly felt rather dirty and smelly. Luckily we could all have showers. It was good to be clean, sitting on chairs not bunks, and being well fed by Ruth, a Glaswegian with a typical Glaswegian personality — irreverent, lots of laughs. There was much chat over dinner, in particular about the local vicar who had recently been ousted. The ousting campaign had been led by David who being a vicar's son plays quite a part in the parish (albeit not being such a believer as maybe he once was). David thought the vicar had been lazy and wanted the curate appointed in his place. But there seemed to be some churchy technical problem, not that the curate was a woman, but something obscure that required the Bishop of Plymouth to adjudicate.

---

9. Purves, *One Summer's Grace*, 37.

10. Jonathan Raban, Coasting: *A Private Journey* (orig. 1986; New York: First Vintage Departure Edition, 2003), 112.

There was much banter between David and John who had been colleagues at Derriford Hospital before they retired, David the cautious and reflective neurologist (for whom Cathie had once worked), and John the gung-ho anaesthetist running the Intensive Care Unit (ICU). Both David and I had been house physicians to Professor Tony Dornhorst at St George's, one of whose most memorable harrumphs in the mid-1960s as intensive care units were coming in was 'Intensive care, pah, more intense than careful!'. Both David and I rather agreed, but of course John did not, as it is almost always the anaesthetists who run ICUs. Nowadays they have mostly lost the 'care' bit anyway, and are rebadged as intensive 'therapy' units (ITUs). Dornhorst did not even allow an anaesthetist onto his medical ward; he regarded his clinical physiology skills as far superior. If our patients required surgery, they came straight back to us to be looked after, not to a surgical ward with an anaesthetist in attendance. This just meant that I rang the anaesthetist in the evening to get help when the professor had gone home.

By the time we set off rowing back to Pickle it was dark. We had forgotten to bring a torch, and to turn on our anchor light.

Towards Dartmouth

Tuesday May 8th, 6.30am start, dull with drizzle. At that hour there was no harbour master to see us off, or to collect any money. But, by the time we were abeam Start Point it had turned into a lovely day, shirt sleeves, perfect sailing conditions with a 10-knot southerly wind and no swell — so perfect that in Start Bay we hoisted the big green sail, the cruising chute which we had first and last used off Howth Head. It did not go well when we gybed. Our failure to practise caught up with us. The chute wrapped itself several times round the forestay. David, who knew about these things, suggested we start the engine and turn the boat round in circles to unwrap it. Good idea. But somehow in the confusion one of the chute's sheets went over the side unnoticed, where it found our propeller and wove several turns around it. We discovered this only when we started the engine, and put it into gear — it stopped dead.

Now what? There was no way from the deck that we could disentangle the rope from the propeller; it was jammed solid. At least with the mainsail up we could gybe round in circles to release the cruising chute from the forestay, and then think what to do while we drifted on gently — luckily a good way off the beach. Being the youngest (just), Steve was the first to volunteer to go over the side in his swimming trunks, firmly attached to a safety rope. The wetsuit I carried on board for these emergencies turned out to be too small for him, and so ancient that it split when he tried to pull it on. Notwithstanding the water temperature of a mere 12°C Steve bravely dived down to discover six turns of rope round the propeller. On the second dive he managed to release the sheet, so chewed up that the two ends provided us with two mooring ropes.

We felt ever so pleased with ourselves as Steve dried himself in the sunshine, until he suddenly became distressed and could hardly speak or swallow. But he could indicate that this had happened before, that it would get better, and we were not to panic. It didn't, so I did panic. Lucky we had a GP on board, as choking is well beyond a neurologist's competence. David popped his head out of the saloon to find out what was going on in the cockpit, returned down below and re-emerged with a glass of warm water. 'Swallow that,' he commanded in his best bedside manner, which Steve did. Astonishingly it worked. Within seconds an amazed Steve was back to normal. And mightily impressed, as was I. So what was that all about? Had immersion in the cold water set off some sort of reflex to constrict Steve's throat muscles? But he had warmed up by the time it happened. Besides, the problem had occurred before on dry land and in the warmth. What possible physiological explanation was there? I had no idea but the fact is the treatment worked — indeed a remarkably simple treatment that cost nothing, unlike many of today's clever drugs marketed at extraordinary cost by avaricious drug companies. It seemed a bit too dramatic for a placebo response, but you never can tell; suggestion can achieve some remarkable things.

At the time it really didn't matter why Steve's throat got stuck; what mattered was the empirical fact that he was better. One way or another the treatment had worked. Professor Dornhorst would not have approved of such a slack attitude, so keen was he on understanding disorders in terms of abnormal physiology, and then working out what should reverse them. And yet, arguing from the principles of physiology, Dornhorst taught us that the then new-fangled beta-blockers should never ever — ever — be used if a patient was in heart failure, as they would certainly make it worse. Years later, after randomised controlled trials, the empirical evidence to the contrary is quite clear: beta-blockers are a *treatment* for some forms of heart failure!

This is a good example of empiricism trumping mere theory, or as Thomas Huxley put it: 'The great tragedy of science — the slaying of a beautiful theory by an ugly fact.'[11] Biology is just too complicated for us to always predict accurately what we should do for the best. Physiological understanding is of course important, and at the very least it is hypothesis-generating, but generally not enough for hypothesis-proving. If we can't accept that, we would still be blood-letting to treat typhoid fever, and never have stemmed the 20th-century epidemic of unnecessary tonsillectomies for recurrent sore throats in children.

On that sunny afternoon we were not inclined to trouble our brains with physiology. Instead we took all the sails down and I made a splendid salade niçoise that all three of us enjoyed with a glass of white wine, as we drifted slowly towards Dartmouth. From a recipe by William Jeffcoate who some years earlier had famously prepared this dish on a calm and lovely day, also drifting — off Cape Wrath of all places.

A diversion into evidence-based medicine

So what about the current fashion for so-called evidence-based medicine (EBM) where every treatment has to be empirically justified by a randomised controlled trial (RCT)? And preferably by several which can be put together in a so-called meta-analysis of all the randomised evidence, a technique introduced in the 1970s and then made rather over-detailed and heavy-going by the Cochrane Collaboration database of all the available randomised trials in the world.[12] This inclusive meta-analysis approach certainly increases the effective sample size, making the estimate of any treatment effect more precise, and it takes account of *all* the *available* evidence, not just the evidence that one particular researcher or drug company want to emphasise — or even reveal. The trouble is that the results of any RCTs that are suppressed for commercial or other reasons (and almost always more likely to be 'negative' than 'positive') obviously can't

---

11. Thomas Huxley, 'President's Address to the British Association for the Advancement of Science, Liverpool Meeting, 14 Sept. 1870', *The Scientific Memoirs of Thomas Henry Huxley*, vol. 3 (1901), 580.

12. The Cochrane Collaboration was initiated in 1993 by Iain Chalmers in Oxford. It is hugely ambitious and has been astonishingly successful, no doubt the reason why my friend Iain became 'Sir Iain'. It collects together, synthesises and summarises in systematic reviews all the randomised trials of treatments in medicine, and makes them available as a library on the web (Cochrane.org). It is probably the bible of so-called 'evidence-based medicine'.

be included in any meta-analysis, however detailed. The result? Publication bias, already discussed.

Allocating patients in RCTs at random by a computer ensures that the intervention group and the control group are as similar as it is possible to make them — apart from, obviously, the intervention being tested, whether a drug, surgical operation or device like a new hip joint, or something more complicated like admitting stroke patients to a stroke unit rather than a general medical ward. If the intervention group does better, you can conclude that the treatment works. On average. But you can't tell *exactly* for whom the treatment worked, and more importantly *exactly* for whom it will work in future clinical practice. It won't be everyone. Some patients get better as a result of the treatment — the lucky ones for whom the treatment really does work — yet some get better despite the treatment, and some get worse even with the treatment. Sometimes, a lot of patients have to be treated for just one to benefit, which is fine for the one but not so fine for the others who are exposed to the side effects and hassles of treatment. Hence the metric of 'number-needed-to-treat' for one patient to benefit.

One might ask what does doing or getting 'better' really mean? Exactly what benefit are we talking about? Delaying death for a few months with chemotherapy for cancer may not be 'better' for some people who could be devastated by side effects for the few months they have left. Long-term drug treatment to reduce the risk of a heart attack, even a severe one, might be turned down by a patient to avoid side effects. It is a difficult decision to make when the patient and doctor will never know if a heart attack truly has been prevented by a treatment, or would not have happened anyway. But the patient will certainly know about the side effects of any treatment.

Despite their technological attractiveness, outcomes like reducing the size of a stroke on a brain scan, a cancer metastasis on an MR scan, the number of leukaemia cells in the blood, or getting good results on a memory test, do not necessarily constitute 'doing better' if the patient's quality of life is not improved. These are so-called surrogate outcomes which might, if 'better', point the way to testing treatments against outcomes that really do matter to patients, like quality of life perhaps. But quality of life means different things to different people, and is not easily measured.

Because new drugs have been properly evaluated in RCTs for decades we mostly know their benefits and harms (even though doctors tend to overestimate the former, and underestimate the latter, as I have certainly done). They are also known for some surgical techniques. But medical devices have largely escaped proper scrutiny — hip joints of various sorts, breast implants, heart valves, pacemakers, brain stimulators, knee replacements, various other bits of plastic and metalwork, and the mesh used for women with weak pelvic floors after childbirth, and for inguinal hernias. (Given my own hernias are now controlled, and if true that the risk of a serious complication of hernia mesh is only about one in 500, I can rest easy that I will stay OK.) Simple public health measures like physical distancing and face masks during the Covid-19 pandemic have also escaped proper evaluation. Face masks may reduce viral transmission but they are definitely a hassle. Besides, masks cost money, are far from recyclable, and audiology departments are inundated with people who have dragged off and lost their hearing aids when taking off their masks. No intervention is without potential harms.

The International Subarachnoid Aneurysm Trial[13] is an honourable and remarkable exception. Two different operative procedures for the serious condition of subarachnoid haemorrhage (bleeding around the brain) due to a ruptured aneurysm (swelling of an artery) were compared: surgical clipping of the neck of the ruptured aneurysm (the original procedure), which requires opening the skull followed by at least a couple of weeks in hospital to recover, versus aneurysm coiling, where a neuroradiologist inserts a special catheter into an artery in the groin and leads it up to the aneurysm which is then filled and blocked off with tiny coils of platinum wire. Both procedures aim to reduce the risk of further bleeding from the aneurysm. It turned out that coiling was better than clipping — patients got out of hospital much faster (an average of a few days), were less likely to die, and less likely to end up dependent on others for everyday activities. In short, they did better, at least to begin with, although after coiling there was a slightly greater risk of the aneurysm eventually recurring. Particularly remarkable was that the neurosurgeons with their clips, and the neuroradiologists with their coils, were prepared to be tested against each other — neither of these specialists being known for their modesty.

One difficulty with evaluating devices is that the manufacturers are nothing like as wealthy as pharmaceutical companies and may not have the resources to support large randomised trials. But they are still wealthy enough to employ lobbyists to prevent proper scrutiny of their devices. And, as ever and certainly like pharmaceutical companies, there is the

---

13. A. J. Molyneux et al., 'The Durability of Endovascular Coiling versus Neurosurgical Clipping of Ruptured Cerebral Aneurysms: 18-year Follow-up of the UK Cohort of the International Subarachnoid Aneurysm Trial (ISAT)', *Lancet*, 385 (2015), 691–7.

problem of competing interests, with doctors paid directly or indirectly by device manufacturers to promote their devices. Better evaluation will not happen unless the government or medical charities step in. Using routine NHS data, or funding a decent prospective register that systematically follows what happens to *all* the sometimes thousands of patients treated with a device of some sort, would help to at least assess the size of any risks (and the results should not be kept confidential merely to protect the manufacturers). Of course, it would not do to just count problems, however accurately and without any bias (for example, due to increased awareness in response to media scares) — we also need to know the total number of patients treated with a particular device. Numerators are not informative without denominators. But a better approach would be for government to fund randomised trials of devices *on condition* that none is used outside the trial in routine clinical practice, and this could be achieved in a publicly funded healthcare system like the NHS.

I was very much part of that evidence-based medicine movement (some would say religion), running big trials of thousands of patients across the UK and Europe to test whether aspirin and operating on the carotid artery in the neck reduced the risk of strokes. Both do, on average, but both would be more cost-effective if we could predict in advance exactly who would benefit, reducing the number-needed-to-treat.

However, the only genius I have ever worked with, the statistician Richard Peto in Oxford, was less interested in that *individual* issue than the *public health* impact of treating everyone eligible for an intervention that is beneficial. He wanted to know how many thousands of lives would be saved, or strokes prevented. He mistrusted subgroup analyses (comparing benefits in males versus females, older versus younger, for example) to sort out for whom treatment works best or at all, arguing that inevitably the number of patients in a subgroup becomes too small for precise estimates of treatment effects, and might even get a result which is the opposite of the truth. Particularly problematic is when several subgroups are analysed and yet only the result of the one which suits the investigator's, or drug company's prejudice, is published.

In contrast, clinicians, who have to front up to patients, are far more bothered by exactly which individual should get a particular treatment, which is why one of my previous research fellows, Peter Rothwell, has been arguing with Richard for years and trying to identify the smaller numbers of patients who *will* benefit from treatment, not just the larger number who *might*. This approach would obviously reduce the overall cost of treatment as well as side effects in an unnecessarily large number of patients. I hope Peter's approach eventually turns out to be right, although that might not please Richard.

Richard was not the easiest person to work with, although we did well in combination because he originally didn't know much about strokes, and I didn't know much about statistics. I (and I hope Richard) tried to follow the advice of Austin Bradford Hill, perhaps the first statistician to apply his mind to medicine: 'Without pretending to expert knowledge, the clinician must think statistically and the statistician must think clinically.'[14] One way to achieve that is of course for people from different backgrounds to work together, to combine their different expertise, as Bradford Hill the statistician did with Richard Doll, the clinician. And then Richard Doll linked up with Richard Peto who linked up with many clinicians, including me. In the 19th century Brunel could build bridges (the Clifton suspension bridge), railways (the Great Western Railway) and ocean liners (the SS Great Britain). No one can do all that now, any more than anyone can be both an outstanding clinician and an outstanding statistician. Everything has become so much more complicated, and there is too much to know, even for the multi-talented.

Not one to hold back, Richard once called me a statistical ignoramus after I made some trivial mistake. And he refused to help me understand natural logarithms because, 'If you haven't understood them by the time you are 13, you never will!' All geniuses are difficult for the rest of us to cope with. Richard, who is the same age as me, works on and will work until he drops, like many epidemiologists seem to. 'Our projects last 30 years,' he explained. Just like John Fry's continuing follow-up in general practice to find out what happens to people with not just short-term diseases like appendicitis, but long-term ones ranging from the less serious (like migraine or hay fever) to the more serious (like epilepsy or asthma). In fact, so many worthwhile investigations take years to come to fruition, hence the need for studies like UK Biobank,[15] which is following up half-a-million people

---

14. Austin Bradford Hill, 'Aims and Ethics', in A. B. Hill (ed.), *Controlled Clinical Trials* (Oxford: Blackwell, 1960), 3–7.

15. UK Biobank is a prospective study of 500,000 participants, all of whom had their personal and medical data collected at baseline, and all of whom are being followed up through their routine medical records to determine the associations and causes of common diseases in the middle-aged and elderly (ukbiobank.ac.uk).

(including me); the Million Women Study;[16] and the Framingham Heart Study in the USA that was probably the very first prospective study of a community's health, and which goes so far back that I was taught about it in medical school.[17] Short-termism is truly hopeless when studying diseases that take years to emerge, and then even more years to run their course. We need continuing follow-up of thousands of people in epidemiological studies just as much as we need continuity of care and follow-up of patients in clinical practice.

However, a hard-core evidence-based approach can be taken too far. Some useful treatment effects are blindingly obvious, like removing the tumour obstructing my colon, or using insulin to control Ilona's diabetes. Nor do you need to randomise hundreds of aircrew to jump out of an aeroplane either with or without a parachute to find out if parachutes work (although a randomised trial did *not* confirm that using a parachute prevented death, but then the aeroplane was on the ground, making the important point that the context of a trial is all important in its interpretation[18]).

A series of case reports, even involving hundreds of patients, purporting to support a less-than-obvious treatment effect, will not pass muster without randomisation to ensure that like is being compared with like. This is exactly what happened with surgical unblocking of the carotid artery in the neck to reduce the risk of stroke: occasional case reports over several years; then many series of patients reported over several more years by enthusiastic surgeons unconstrained by sceptical physicians; and eventually large randomised trials which showed that the operation definitely did reduce — though not abolish — the risk of stroke over and above routine medical treatment such as aspirin (but only in patients with a severely narrowed artery). The problem is that this whole process took far too long, about 50 years. Enthusiastic innovators may launch a technique, sometimes with a

---

16. The Million Women Study started recruiting healthy participants in 1996 and is following them up to determine the causes and associations of various diseases in middle age and the elderly (millionwomenstudy.org).

17. The Framingham Heart Study is the grandfather of all prospective follow-up studies. It started in 1948 and involves the residents of Framingham, Massachusetts, and it still continues with their descendants, following them up to examine the associations and causes of heart attacks, strokes and other vascular diseases.

18. R W Yeh et al., 'Parachute Use to Prevent Death and Major Trauma when Jumping from Aircraft', *BMJ*, 363 (2018), 463.

single case report, like Felix Eastcott's carotid operation in the *Lancet*,[19] and this can change medical practice. But they must not stand in the way of us more plodding clinical triallists who want proof. To do him great credit, Eastcott did not; he supported the carotid surgery trials. Of course there has to be serious uncertainty about the usefulness of an intervention to ethically justify randomising patients to no-intervention (control) versus intervention, as well as acknowledgement that the control group may *benefit* by being protected from any treatment-induced harm, unexpected and expected. Benefits always have to be weighed against harms.

Eventually to Dartmouth

Steve has continued to have choking attacks, but the warm water trick has stopped working. The 'cure' off Start Point was either a placebo effect after all, or he was going to get better anyway. Medicines indeed 'do most good when there is a tendency to recover without them,' remarked Sir William Gull in the 19th century when very few medicines worked at all. Eventually, in 2015 Steve had an endoscopy (sticking a long, thin, flexible tube up or down a hollow structure like the bronchus or oesophagus, to be able to look inside it, and take biopsies, photographs etc.). This revealed some of his stomach had escaped from his abdomen into his chest (a hiatus hernia), and there was a touch of gastritis (inflammation of the stomach). Neither could be the explanation for his symptoms that clearly arise near the top of his oesophagus, not the bottom. Nonetheless, he was given omeprazole for 'gastritis', so demonstrating the common mistake of using a test to dictate treatment even though the abnormal test result is nothing whatsoever to do with the symptoms. Of course it didn't work.

It seems far more likely that Steve has an upper oesophageal motility problem; there was certainly no physical obstruction like cancer. However, because his GP thought cancer was a distant possibility, Steve had to be, and was seen, within two weeks of referral. 'Suspect' cancer and hey presto you get attention, fast. GPs play that game to get patients seen quickly. Steve's attacks continue. He could attempt a so-called n-of-one trial, trying warm water for some attacks and cold water or nothing for others, in random order, to see what happens. Curiously it is very difficult to pull off trials like

---

19. H. H. G. Eastcott, G. W. Pickering, and C. G. Robb, 'Reconstruction of Internal Carotid Artery in a Patient with Intermittent Attacks of Hemiplegia', *Lancet*, 264 (1954), 994–6.

that, as they take time and organisation, and are easily confounded if the patient knows what treatment he or she is getting, as Steve certainly would. He decided to just live with his intermittent problem. Very sensible.

With all this drama we didn't cover the 28 miles to Dartmouth until 4.30pm. The entrance to the Dart is a treat, between high wooded banks, so typical of the rivers hereabouts, before widening out to reveal Dartmouth to port and Kingswear to starboard, complete with a whistling steam train on its seven-mile way to Paignton. A salty place indeed, very historic too. Some of my school friends headed here to train as naval officers. More went to Sandhurst and the army, a few to Cranwell and the RAF. The school at the time, after all, was called Haileybury *and* Imperial Service College (the last bit has now been dropped). Of the less militaristic, no one I remember went to a northern or redbrick university — it was to Oxford or Cambridge, medical school, or to Daddy's firm in the City.

We had to first tie up to a pontoon out in the river, waiting for the tide to change direction so we could get on to the main pontoon attached to the harbour wall. The harbour master had suggested we went astern to reach it, in other words in reverse! Madness. With the tide under us and the wind blowing us in, there was no way Pickle of the long keel and impossible steering in reverse could achieve that without catastrophe. This was surprisingly poor advice, although the manoeuvre can easily be done in one of those big white sailing boats with skinny keels (which can fall off), and one or even two steering wheels at the back end, along with a bow-thruster to turn the bows to left and right.

Sadly we didn't have much time to explore Dartmouth. By the time we were settled by the harbour wall not much was still open, so we ended up in the Dolphin pub, one of many scattered around the neat little town with its old houses and ancient church. Given the bad weather expected, we were anxious to get to Weymouth the next day, and had to catch the tide at Portland Bill 44 miles away. It was to be a very early start. So, after supper on board, early to bed.

To Weymouth

At 3am it was dark, dank, drizzly and horrible as we motored out to sea, illuminated by the blinding searchlight of a fishing boat behind us. I understand this was their way of letting us know we had been spotted. As there was no wind, we motored on past the Mew Stone and then headed east. On and on we motored for at least three-quarters of the way across

Lyme Bay. Strictly speaking we didn't have to, but as the wind was very light from the east-southeast, we were not going to catch the tide round Portland Bill that afternoon unless the motor was used. And bad weather was definitely on its way. Fortunately by 10am the wind had shifted to the southwest and strengthened to 15 knots, giving us a splendid sail in the murk around Portland Bill without seeing it; we were going at 9 knots over the ground aided by the fast east-going flood tide up the English Channel. We kept well offshore to avoid the notorious tide race and pressed on east to round the Shambles Bank so we could get a reasonable angle for a port tack into Weymouth, by which time it was raining. There were a lot of very well-handled racing dinghies to be avoided in Weymouth Bay, practising for the Olympics that were to be held there in the summer. Dinghy racing is far too physical for my liking — you can't go down below for a cup of tea. And I had never been any good at it, even when younger. There is also far too much shouting, which goes for keel-boat racing too.

After the 52-mile sail it was a relief to get the sails down and the engine on, and to tie up to the town pontoons by the Weymouth Customs House Quay because by then it was much more comfortable to be indoors rather than outdoors. The town itself looked so very nautical and attractive with charming old houses clustered round the harbour, some with bow windows, one dating from 1600. There were only three other visiting boats, one big advantage of getting round the south coast before the summer crowds. The pontoons were right by the toilets (new for the Olympics) and the harbour master's office. And there were two chandleries on the quay, as well as the Royal Dorset Yacht Club, pubs, restaurants, fish and chips, and the local fishing fleet. All very convenient and scenic. Going further on into the marina itself seemed pointless, although it is a bit closer to the Asda supermarket for supplies.

It was all a long way from home, and very different from Scotland. Not surprisingly, the harbour master had never heard of our home port, Dunstaffnage, when we signed in:

'Where's that then?' he asked with a puzzled look.

'West coast of Scotland,' I replied. 'Near Oban.'

'OK then, we'll put down Scotland as your home port.'

In contrast, the main part of the town was rather run-down and looked short of money, but there are still some very grand Victorian parts of Weymouth. There is the impressive beach too, but in that weather there was no one sitting on it, or swimming off it either. Weymouth was a good place for us to chill out, gather our strength, stock up with this and that, and wander about. In the evening we tried the Yacht Club for a drink but it was almost deserted; luckily one of the pubs was rather more animated. Paul Theroux thought Weymouth was 'grand without being pompous' which gets it about right.[20]

Thursday May 10th was horrible, as forecast. Bad weather had been expected for days, according to xcweather. There was no way we were sailing anywhere given the mist, rain and almost gale-force wind. Instead, David's wife Maureen turned up by car to give us all a tour of dreich west Dorset. The first stop was the newly built marina on Portland Bill, the centre of operations for the forthcoming sailing Olympics and the home of the National Sailing Academy. Notwithstanding the huge and safe artificial harbour, it seemed a bleak, bleak place, with bleak architecture too, certainly not somewhere I would bring a cruising boat unless the weather was desperate, especially with the delights of Weymouth only four miles away.

Then to the lighthouse on the end of the Bill where a few hardy folk were leaning against the wind, one trying to hold down his tripod so he could take pictures of crashing waves and soaring gulls. The impressive tide race extended out into the murk, not to be taken lightly when at sea, dangerous, too, and known for centuries, even before Greenvile Collins in 1693 wrote: 'The Race of Portland is a great Ripling of the Tides, caused by the unevenness of the Ground at the bottom, called Overfalls; and when the Sea is high, and the Tides strong, it breaketh in great Seas, and one that is a Stranger would think that there it was shoal water.'[21] Hilaire Belloc had a lot to say about the Race too, but more poetically: 'it lumps, hops, seethes and bubbles … it is a chaos of pyramidical waters leaping up suddenly without calculation, or rule of advance.'[22] Well so it is on a bad day, but on a good day the race is not so awful and can be avoided completely by sailing very close in to the lighthouse, just a 'biscuit toss' from the shore, to use a dated metric. Or by being three miles out to sea as we had been.

On we drove to West Bay, the port for Bridport. Presumably it was partly the rubbish weather but again I was not encouraged by the modern flats round the harbour, or by the very unstable-looking pontoons bouncing around in the swell. Chesil beach, shingle extending far to the east, was

---

20. Paul Theroux, *The Kingdom by the Sea: A Journey around the Coast of Great Britain* (orig. 1983; London: Penguin, 1984), 98.

21. Collins, *Great-Britain's Coasting Pilot*.

22. Belloc, *Cruise of the Nona*, 203.

almost invisible. I didn't know the sea and the wind graded the stones, small to the west and larger to the east (apparently useful location information for smugglers of old coming in from the sea at night).

Lyme Regis was better, touristy of course but charming. The Cobb harbour wall was well up to expectations from the 1981 film, *The French Lieutenant's Woman*, in a lovely curve. Beautifully cut stones sloping away to seaward to throw off the waves — a wall to walk under, or along, but without getting blown away.

And finally to Poundbury, a new town, a grim pastiche of nostalgic buildings, built on land owned by Prince Charles's Duchy of Cornwall, and designed according to his old-fashioned architectural principles. It is divided up by dull straight roads, like Milton Keynes without the roundabouts. There didn't seem to be a pub, school or shop although presumably they must have been there somewhere. No pubs were mentioned on the 'Discover Poundbury' website, but we were told there was one — The Poet Laureate. Ironic, really. John Betjeman, a real Poet Laureate, wanted to bomb the ugliness of Slough: 'come, friendly bombs, and fall on Slough to get it ready for the plough.'[23] I am sure if he was still alive he would bomb Poundbury comprehensively. To be fair, it was still a partial building site, and would remain so for a few years. Nonetheless, why anyone would want to live here, apparently in the middle of nowhere (although it is kind of an extension of Dorchester), defies my imagination.

Then back to Weymouth for a pub supper and, surprise, surprise, Maureen said she would join us for the sail in the morning, the first time in nearly 50 years that she had come sailing with me. I had sailed all that way from Scotland to persuade her. Maybe it was something to do with the ever-reliable xcweather forecast for the morning. Sunshine!

To Poole

Friday May 11th, sunshine as predicted, and a breeze from the west. Perfect. After refuelling we were off at 11.15am, aiming to catch the east-going tide off St Alban's Head in the afternoon. A brilliant 28-mile sail along the east Dorset coast, with only five other boats in sight all afternoon. As the army were not practising lobbing shells at the Taliban and other enemies from their firing range, we could sail close inshore to admire the geology of those lovely limestone cliffs, as well as Durdle Door and Lulworth Cove

---

23. John Betjeman, *John Betjeman's Collected Poems* (London: John Murray, 1958).

which admittedly are much more impressive from the land than from out at sea. We rounded St Alban's Head followed by Anvil Point where Hilaire Belloc in the 'Jersey' very nearly came to grief — just under the cliff he was unable to tack, 'caught in irons', so his younger crew turned the boat back out to sea by crash gybing with only yards to spare.[24] We were close-hauled past Durlston Head, and on we sailed with Old Harry to port, the very recognisable white chalk-stack that once had a 'wife', but in 1896 'she' crashed into the sea. As Belloc put it: 'now he is alone. He cannot wish to remain so much longer, staring out to sea without companionship. I think he longs for his release.'[25] Nearly a century after Belloc, erosion has not yet done for Old Harry, and happily he is still accompanied by a smaller stack, his 'latest wife'. Then, dicing with the chain-ferry at the narrow entrance, we motored in to Poole Harbour at 4pm. With David's local knowledge from having sailed here for 40 years, we turned to port and motored along to anchor out of the fairway just before we hit the mud of Dorset in South Deep. It seemed an eerily quiet spot for Poole Harbour, with only two other boats in that remote corner. Strangely, we appeared to be in the middle of an oil field with pumps quietly pumping, visible on the land across the fields.

In great contrast, the main part of Poole harbour was astonishing to behold by those of us from the north. There must have been more boats than in the whole of Scotland. Of course, most are parked on moorings or in marinas, but there were still loads of motorboats whizzing around, and yachts everywhere. And dreaded jet-skis too. You certainly have to keep your wits about you to keep out of everyone's way. In 2008, that posey broadcaster and journalist Piers Morgan apparently exclaimed about Poole Harbour: 'My God, I didn't know somewhere as beautiful as this existed in Britain.' He should get out more. Maybe it once was beautiful, before it was ruined by humans and their aquatic toys. However, for us it was a quiet evening, with a last — for this leg — dinner aboard, while I brooded about the next leg, tides along the south coast, the Solent, and on into the North Sea.

In the morning we were edging back to reality. Colin Baigent was on the BBC Radio 4 'Today' programme extolling the virtues of statins to reduce the risk of heart attacks and strokes, for almost everyone over the age of 60 (like me). Colin is an epidemiologist and clinical trialist who

---

24. Dermod MacCarthy, *Sailing with Mr Belloc* (London, Collins Harvill, 1986), 48.
25. Belloc, *Cruise of the Nona*, 219.

had supervised Cathie's DPhil (Oxford-speak for PhD), and an old friend. Clever he is, yes, but surely I don't want to take pills every day of every week of every month for the rest of my life. Colin's strategy could save some 8000 UK lives every year, but that might not include mine. Much more on this during the next leg when two of the crew happened to be taking a statin.

The plan was to leave Pickle on a Poole Yacht Club mooring and for me to head home for a week. I wanted a rest from having to concentrate on keeping the crew happy, and the boat safe. And to sleep in a proper bed. David drove me to Southampton Airport to catch my flight back to Edinburgh, dropping Maureen off at the nursing home of her sadly dementing mother. Yet again I wondered if I too will dement one day. Or will my body crack up first? And to know if I was going to suddenly drop dead leaving an unholy mess in my study for Cathie and the children to sort out — books, papers, photographs, sketchpads, bills, pictures. Or would I decline slowly with enough time to 'get my affairs in order'? At least I had at long last written my will. I simply must get all my papers better organised at home. But how long ahead am I supposed to plan for? The Royal College of Physicians of Edinburgh must know something I don't. In 2018 they offered me life membership for the same cost as my fellow's subscription for just one year. So far so good, for me, but not for the college which by 2020 was in serious financial trouble. But should I renew my old person's railcard at £30 for one year, or for three at £70?

Back home to Edinburgh — by aeroplane

It was strange to be dumped back into Edinburgh, and home, by plane. It seemed indecently quick compared with sailing. It was cold and wet, while Poole had been warm and sunny. There is a rhythm to sailing that I missed on dry land. Maybe it was a mistake to break the voyage. But there were lots of things to do. Make contact with the next crew, think hard about Rye Harbour and talk to the harbour master, go to the dentist (ageing teeth wear away and break off in bits), sort out the garden, do a big supermarket shop for the family, download all the photos from my camera, keep track of our domestic finances, catch up with emails, and collect more Sailing Directions.

As I had been at her age, Cathie was far too busy with work to be able to keep all the household things going from doing the washing to cooking supper to paying the bills, but I did have the time. How a couple with children, both working full-time, can cope is beyond me. As a retired person, I am Cathie's 'Domestic God', or so she claimed in her 2014 professorial inaugural lecture. There are after all some advantages for a full-time working-woman having an older retired husband. Doing my bit for my present family made me uncomfortably aware of how much Ilona had done for my first family. I don't think I even noticed, probably because unconsciously (rather than consciously I hope) I assumed it was 'her job' as a woman and mother, irrespective of the fact that she worked too, necessarily part-time. Like so many men of my generation, I was too busy at work, or so I claimed.

I was very familiar with the Clyde Cruising Club Sailing Directions for the Scottish coast. They are reasonably water-resistant, not too thick, and are spiral bound so can be folded over and conveniently held in one hand while the other holds the tiller — easy to use in the cockpit, particularly for pilotage into tricky harbours. The Royal Northumberland Yacht Club does a very similar production from the Humber to Rattray Head. None of these publications tries to tell you very much about what there is to do on shore, or about local historical and other attractions. That way they are kept uncluttered and a manageable size. It is easy to find the navigational and pilotage information you really need, like how to approach and enter harbours. Where the rocks are do not get mixed up with where the pubs are. You need a different sort of book for the latter, and for other things of interest ashore. I think it is a mistake to combine everything in one book. It gets too big and heavy, more coffee table than chart table.

Maybe the internet will take over from paper Sailing Directions, like so much else in book publishing, but not yet I think. Anyway, at the moment, it is difficult to read a tablet or mobile phone in strong sunlight. Admittedly, it is much easier to keep online information up-to-date compared with a book. But all that takes time, as I know only too well from trying to keep up-to-date the website scottishanchorages.co.uk, my what-to-see-and-do guide for the 250-plus anchorages between the Mull of Kintyre and Skye.

I was missing summer sailing in Scotland. There is little to beat the Sound of Mull, and all the islands. I missed the world of work too, being in the thick of it. I had been at the top of the game in my career as a neurologist, and as a researcher into stroke. No longer — I was out-of-date. In contrast, I still felt somewhere low-down on the sailing learning curve even though I was certainly on the way up it by learning from my several mistakes. I will not forget to open the engine cooling-water seacock again, or fail to notice ropes over the side of the boat, or pull a reefing line right through the boom so far that I can't get it back. These are the vivid memories, and these are what provide the stories back home.

Without the world of work, might I get depressed, like a friend and colleague who retired too early even though he had another life as a jazz musician? What other life had I got? I needed a project as well as sailing; writing this book is one, it seems. Too late to build my own boat as I once wanted to do. Too late for most things. Some days I even feel a bit demoralised, of little use to anyone. After all, Cathie and the children did fine without me. But as she has got busier at work, and as the children come up to exams, I think — hope — that I am still needed after all.

This rumination was not good. I was cheered up by a bike ride with Lucy to Portobello, to Edinburgh's local beach, warm again, hot even, the sky was cloudless. A different sort of sky to the south coast. In Edinburgh we don't seem to get so many of those fluffy white clouds building up over the land, maybe it never gets hot enough. No ships of any kind were to be seen out on the Forth, very unlike the south coast. No swimmers in the sea either, far too cold. I wanted to get back to that coastal subculture where everywhere around our wonderful coastline seems to be connected with everywhere else. Wick and Penzance have so much in common despite being hundreds of miles apart. By the middle of the week I was looking forward to the next leg of the voyage, sailing past some of my childhood memories.

CROMWELL'S CASTLE, TRESCO

Chapter 7

From Poole to Harwich

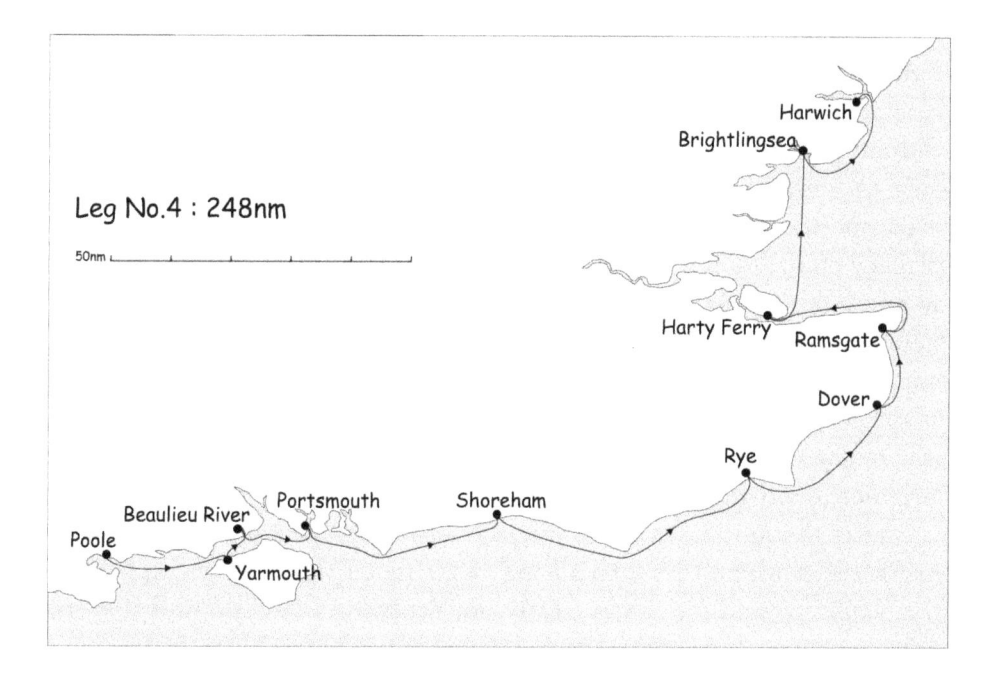

Leg No.4 : 248nm

Friday May 25th — I was on my way back to Pickle, standing on Waterloo Station brooding on the long-gone cartoon cinema and my mother's tears. How so? Waterloo is the London station for the Poole train, which goes through New Milton, between Southampton and Bournemouth. And New Milton is where I and other young boys in our shorts and grey school uniforms got off that train to be escorted to Durlston Court, our boarding prep school (motto: *erectus non elatus*, roughly translated we were told as 'upright not swanky'). Before seeing me off at the start of every term, and to cheer me up, my mother always took me to that cartoon cinema to laugh at Mickey Mouse and other legendary characters, before leaving me on the train and herself on the platform concealing a tear. I was away for many weeks at a time. My parents couldn't afford a car and seldom visited during term time, living as we then did over 100 miles away in Beckenham.

From the age of 8 to 18 I was exiled to private boarding schools, which is what many of the middle and most of the upper classes did to their children in those days. Some still do, even though many, including my parents, make huge sacrifices to pay the fees. As a result I have never known the answer to the question, 'where do you come from?' I never even thought about it until I was first asked, which was on my arrival in Aberdeen in 1971. Unlike me, the Aberdonians knew precisely where they came from. But where *did* I come from? Certainly not Beckenham, which I hated, or Nottingham where I was born in 1943 and can hardly remember. And not Germany where we lived when I was very small; I spoke fluent German only to forget it after we got back to England where my father tried to make me speak it in front of friends and relatives. I became determined that my own children would surely know where they came from by living at home during their childhood and going to a local school, preferably state rather than private. And that is how it worked out, thankfully. They know very well that they come from Edinburgh. Two don't live in Scotland anymore, and none of the older three has a Scottish accent. But Scotland is still 'where they come from', I think. The younger two have never known anywhere other than Edinburgh.

I never thought of myself as 'English' or felt very 'English' until moving to Aberdeen where I became all too aware that I was different to most of the people around me. I was clearly not Scottish. I had and probably still have a quite posh English accent. Fortunately, I prefer living in Scotland, where I feel very much at home. But I shall never be able to shake off my foreignness. I will always be an immigrant from England, very conscious of my English accent. How much harder it must be for immigrants of a different skin colour, or who speak a different language.

When I was at school, as well as no car we had no TV (the wireless and a 78 rpm record player had to do); no washing machine (we did have a mangle); no food processor (we hand-minced the cold lamb from the weekend roast to make shepherd's pie); no fridge (a larder was the thing then); and that single week of family holiday on the Norfolk Broads every year. Not surprisingly, as a boarding school boy, I was bored stiff during the school holidays because I had no local school friends. However, I did usually spend a few days with my mother's sister, Margaret, who had been an illustrator and was just a bit unconventional. Her son, my cousin Jeremy who was paraplegic, perhaps sparked my eventual interest in becoming a neurologist, and in access for the disabled. We used to carry him in his wheelchair up and down many, many steps in cinemas, but on the plus side he did get an edge-of-centre-court place at Wimbledon. Also, I stayed with my mother's brother, my Uncle Alfred, who was a great expert on magnetic compasses. He lived where he worked, in the grounds of the Admiralty Compass Observatory near Slough, a Victorian castle where I could fish in the Victorian moat, but with little success. He wrote the definitive book on his subject, but didn't live to see it published.[1]

I am still careful with money despite having far less need to be than my parents. My mother's words — 'your father says we can't afford it' — forever ring in my ears. Quite illogically, if I can't find my old person's pass that gives me free bus travel in Scotland, I will walk a mile or two rather than pay for a bus ticket (of course, I should walk anyway to combat my increasing geriatric frailty). After my father died I discovered more than one letter in his files asking the headmaster of my school to defer the fees until an insurance policy matured, or he got a new job. Somehow he struggled through while I the stroppy teenager wanted to know what was wrong with sending me to the local grammar school, provided of course I could pass the 11+ entrance exam (I know of at least one professor of neurology who failed his). It would have been free and provided me with local friends during the holidays, as well as term time. And I imagine a perfectly good education. Ungrateful boy that I was.

But back to May 2012. When I got off the train from Edinburgh at King's Cross, I must have been on automatic pilot because I took the underground to Paddington Station, of so many Oxford memories, not to Waterloo of those earlier memories. Maybe I am a dotty professor after all, a figure of fun rather than of respect, which is why on retirement I reverted to the more straightforward appellation of doctor. (Curiously, the shortened 'prof' is a kind of socially acceptable halfway house between surname and Christian name when juniors address their seniors — 'doc' doesn't work in the same way.) Or maybe I headed for Paddington because my unconscious mind found Waterloo emotionally too difficult. Whatever, as I was clearly

---

1. Alfred Hine, *Magnetic Compasses and Magnetometers* (London: Adam Hilger, 1968).

going to miss the train to Poole, there was no need to dash up the escalator in Waterloo and risk a heart attack or more likely a broken bone.

London was very hot and very crowded. I definitely wanted out of it, and back to the sea. The train journey was vaguely familiar from my school days, particularly around Southampton where arms of the sea and the docks intruded on the view. And the New Forest where we were bussed every Ascension Day for a holiday, and catching butterflies. I am ashamed to say we gassed them and pinned them to a display board. I had worked briefly in Southampton as a very junior locum doctor in neurosurgery (every aspiring neurologist should do some neurosurgery, and vice versa — seldom achieved I'm afraid). How useful that Southampton experience was when I became a neurologist, and needed to work with and understand my neurosurgical colleagues. But what I never understood, despite our best efforts and the fact that we worked closely together, was that it was almost impossible to get our neurosurgeons to join us neurologists in meetings to discuss the patients and conditions we shared. Bryan Matthews thought it was because they have an inferiority complex, at least when facing up to neurologists. Maybe we shouldn't try and involve them, and just keep them in their boxes doing the operating.

Neurosurgeons were different then compared with now. There were far fewer of them, and they operated more often. One was John Garfield, a Southampton neurosurgeon who had taught us at St George's when he was a senior registrar. I have ever since passed on to students and young neurologists his advice: 'for neurological diagnosis, the telephone is more useful than the tendon hammer' (used to tap the knee to make the foot jerk reflexly upwards — that defining mark of a neurologist as well as an Ealing comedy doctor). His reasons? Because taking the history — the story — is just as, if not more, important than examining the patient (and needs even more practice to get good at it). Family and witnesses may well be needed to work out what is going on if the patient is demented, confused or unconscious, or has had some sort of 'blackout'. 'No history available' written in the notes is a mark of very sloppy doctoring. There is always a history, even if you have to telephone someone to get it — relative, friend, ambulance driver, policeman. Moreover, the telephone can put you in touch with help and advice from a distant neurological or neurosurgical centre.

Nowadays you can also use your smartphone to send clinical photographs and scans to a distant expert, and get advice from websites. Doctors, just like patients (but hopefully in a more refined way), can Google symptoms to come up with diagnostic ideas they may not have already thought about.

For example, if you Google 'intermittent pins and needles and visual loss', the possibility of multiple sclerosis takes up most of your computer screen. And, as I found, Google can even help to solve a tricky clinicopathological conference (CPC) conundrum. In this exercise an 'expert' is sent a patient's story and examination findings a few weeks ahead of the meeting, and the results of relevant tests along with perhaps some brain scans, but not the diagnosis. In front of an audience eager to witness their failure and preferably humiliation too, the expert has to discuss the ins and outs of the case, how the diagnosis should be approached, and finally what it might be. The truth is finally revealed by a pathologist who shows slides of the brain inflammation, tumour, or whatever. The diagnosis usually turns out to be either something very rare, or a rare presentation of something quite common. This 'thinking out loud' is an incredibly useful educational experience for the audience, and indeed for the 'expert' who may have spent (as I did) several weeks worrying about the diagnosis, showing the scans to other experts, waking at night fearing the impending humiliation, and — Googling.

John Garfield had trained as a physician before turning to neurosurgery. If I had known that when a medical student I would not have been so astonished when he asked me to feel a neurosurgical patient's pulse and tell him if she was in atrial fibrillation (AF). Surgeons are supposed to ask questions about surgery, not cardiology. His teaching extended to photography too: 'make sure you get a really big sink for your darkroom,' he instructed me many years later. He always printed his own black and white photos taken with a trusty Leica, never getting into colour, and certainly not into digital photography. He was too old school for all of that. He retired early so that he could publish books of photographs, mainly of war cemeteries and musicians.

John became a friend, and when I was a young consultant in the 1980s we got together with various physician and surgical colleagues to put together two books: *Dilemmas in the Management of the Neurological Patient*, and *More Dilemmas in the Management of the Neurological Patient*.[2] We wanted experts to answer awkward questions, and to admit when they didn't know the answers. Until our lawyer friends intervened, we had later planned to ask friends and colleagues to write anonymously about what

---

2. Charles Warlow and John Garfield (eds), *Dilemmas in the Management of the Neurological Patient* (Edinburgh: Churchill Livingstone, 1984), and *More Dilemmas in the Management of the Neurological Patient* (Edinburgh: Churchill Livingstone, 1987).

they had learned from a mistake, with their names listed not against their own mistakes but at the front of the book — along with the names of those who had refused our invitation, a much more interesting list (like those who have turned down knighthoods and other baubles — not a list I have ever been on). Another plan to edit a book called *Recent Retreats in Clinical Neurology* never got off the ground, notwithstanding the very large number of books entitled recent *advances* in this, that and the other. John and I, sceptics both, wanted to reveal uncertainty. Without uncertainty we would all carry on doing just the same as usual; there would be no progress.

I had no recall of New Milton station. It looked as though it might have looked in the 1950s, old-fashioned. Did we walk to the school from there, or did we go by bus? Erased from my memory. A few years before this cruise I had crept into the school grounds to try and recall what the place had been like. And to find the tree at the top of which we used to sit and identify aeroplanes that were so much more frequent and varied in my school days (that tree must have long gone, or maybe it was by then unrecognisably high). And the curious hut where the chaplain used to live, he who exposed himself to the peri-pubescent boys staring out of their dormitory window from above — at least that's what we thought he was doing. The headmaster lived on site with his wife and, I seem to recall, another lady who taught us. She and the art teacher were the only female teachers; the rest were men, many of them not long emerged from the second world war. One I think had been a Spitfire pilot. 'Sir, sir, how many Germans did you shoot down?' He always refused to say. Maybe there weren't any.

I noticed there had been three rather inevitable changes since my time at the school. It was a day school, it took girls as well as boys, and executive housing and a care home had been built on some of the playing fields. But the smell was the same — the dry Hampshire air, hazy, warm, nostalgic. I wondered if the catch-all school rule is still 'A breach of common sense is a breach of the school rules'? The comic Tony Hancock was the most famous old boy. It is said that his father offered to teach the boys boxing instead of paying the school fees (currently over £15,000 per annum).

No longer do trains have corridors with sliding doors opening to compartments where we prep school boys sat opposite each other on long seats writing juvenile essays on what we did in our holidays, under the eyes of the headmaster who had come to Waterloo to collect us. Later, trains for me became places of uninterrupted calm, relaxation too, even in standard class if you aim for the quiet coach, for reading *BMJ*s and other medical journals. I developed this habit in the 1980s when constantly travelling around the country urging on the various neurology centres involved in our aspirin trial to reduce the risk of stroke. I got to know my country again, by train rather than hitchhiking but certainly not by the misery of driving anywhere south of Preston. To Sheffield, Newcastle, Leicester, Swansea, Smethwick, Plymouth, Aberdeen, Bristol and lots of other places. So now when I get on a train, I immediately start reading and can spend a whole morning just reading which never seems possible at home. It is almost a Pavlovian response, but I don't know what the reward was when I was being 'trained' (excuse the pun) — maybe just the peace and quiet. These days on trains, which I seek out when the reading pile gets too high, I read the newspapers and yachting magazines despite their doom and gloom (about the state of the world, and fog in the English Channel).

I am horribly addicted to newspapers, not a happy situation for an Englishman in Scotland. Unfortunately the so-called national (i.e. London-centric) papers do not have enough Scottish news (and certainly very few Scottish theatre reviews), and the Scottish papers do not have enough UK-wide or international news. So I have to read two papers every day, the *Guardian* and the *Herald* (as the latter is not found in the south of England, it was a relief on the train to Poole only to have to read the *Guardian*). I also get the weekly *Oban Times*, much to the constant surprise of the local young man who keeps it for me under the counter. He didn't know where Oban was. Now with a house in Orkney, I have to get the weekly *Orcadian* too, by post. More recently I have become a very late adopter of *Private Eye*, thankfully published only once a fortnight. Maybe I should read newspapers online, but somehow I can't bring myself to. Thankfully I am not addicted to cryptic crosswords. In fact I am hopeless at them, which is a bit odd for a neurologist who is meant to be good at them. An out-of-date stereotype, if ever it was true. The 'simple' *Guardian* crossword which requires general knowledge is much more interesting, but even together with Cathie it isn't always finished, at least not without a little help from Google (the capital of Uzbekistan is…?).

Like the train from Edinburgh to London, the train to Poole was packed. However, I was well able to bury myself in reading, and cut out the surrounding noise and mayhem. Somewhere near Winchester, I quickly solved the picture quiz in *Practical Boat Owner*, which was of Dartmouth — just been there, easy. However, I couldn't help noticing the noisy private-school girls, presumably on their way home from their day school. How crazy to waste parental money on private education if you can get more or less the same for free, which in most places you can. I don't want my children mixing with the children of parents I would not want to mix with myself, particularly in boarding schools — greedy bankers, over-paid CEOs, Russian oligarchs, so-called celebrities. How mad, and maddening, it is for free places to be available in private schools for a few clever children whose parents can't afford to send them there, crumbs from the master's table. This policy diminishes the state system. In general, children should mix with their local contemporaries, experience the socio-economic diversity of state schools, and avoid being corrupted by the elitism which still pervades many private schools, and from which I have not totally released myself 60 years later. I found myself wanting to get back to Scotland which is probably somewhat more communitarian and egalitarian than England, and surely more than London and the southeast.

Poole

For now it was back to Poole, to Pickle on the mooring. It's always such a relief to find she is still where I left her, whether on a mooring or at anchor, or even on a pontoon. David and Maureen Morgan came on board to guide me to the pontoon we had booked at Poole Quay Boat Haven. The marina may be right on the quayside in the centre of things with pubs and restaurants galore, but I wouldn't go back. It cost £89 for two nights (you could get almost four nights for that in Tobermory). It was full of ludicrously over-large and bling motorboats (one called Footsie, for goodness' sake) with fat over-fed men and tarted-up ladies grilling their bulging flesh on the sundecks. To get to the marina toilets you had to cross a quite busy road. And the staff did absolutely nothing to control the ridiculously noisy and smelly speedboats that arrived for a race. No wonder the younger generation can't afford to sail — a decent second-hand 26-foot sailing boat may not cost a lot, but it is about the same as you have to pay for just one year parked in a commercial south coast marina like this one.

What a different world it was compared with the Scilly Isles where those lovely pilot-gigs were raced by their lovely crews using oars, not environmentally unfriendly fossil-fuel engines. But then Poole is where so many of these motorboats are made. Without Sunseeker, the luxury motorboat builder which must employ hundreds of people, the town would go to the dogs, like those northern towns when their mines and heavy industry closed down. Sunseeker very nearly did go under in 2013 but was rescued by Chinese money, emblematic of the UK's standing in the global economy these days.

I was pleasantly surprised by how charming the old part of Poole is, just behind the quayside. Georgian houses, some older. Sadly the church was locked, with presumably too many thieves and vandals lurking in the town. In 1989 Libby Purves thought there was 'no chic nonsense about Poole Town Quay: girls in tarty short leather skirts shrieked at loafing boys, couples entwined purposefully in alleyways above the glimmer of the dock, the chip-shop blared old Beatles' tunes.'[3] In 2012 nothing much had changed. The evening was noisy, and got noisier as the quayside filled up with very thin girls, very fat girls, and very spotty boys. At least I was spared the bikers who gather on Tuesday evenings. It was very warm, very un-Scotland. I felt physically and socially uncomfortable.

I wanted to get away as soon as possible. But I had to stay put for the next day to await the new crew. Gradually they gathered (or mustered, as we sailors say). First came Peter Hatfield, but without his luggage which was still at Heathrow airport, or somewhere, but got to us eventually. Peter is a very outdoors type of New Zealander (so many are), and usually wears fetching red woollen tights when it's cold. He's a retired renal physician married to the ex-wife of an old neurologist friend of mine who now makes wine on Waiheke Island near Auckland. Then Steve Druitt arrived for another dose of sailing. And finally Klim McPherson, a statistician and epidemiologist, a very old friend, who had married Ann, one of my closest friends at medical school. Ann and I had been housemen (women) together immediately after qualifying as doctors, me to Tony Dornhorst, and she to the other professor of medicine who ran the obesity clinic. There he reduced overweight ladies to tears by telling them that if they ate less they would definitely lose weight, sometimes adding 'No fat person ever came out of Auschwitz'. He would never get away with that today. I didn't know at the time, but he was German and half-Jewish, his family having left Germany before the war.

Sadly Ann had died in 2011. Having survived breast cancer, she did not survive pancreatic cancer. She was a GP, an excellent one at that, and well able to stand up to the 'superior' Oxford consultants whose diagnoses she sometimes cheerfully — and successfully — challenged. She also found time to write best-selling medical books for laypeople. A great loss.

---

3. Libby Purves, *One Summer's Grace: A Family Voyage round Britain* (London: Grafton Books, 1989), 27.

It was too hot, far too hot. No clouds in the sky. But by evening it was tolerable. Other friends arrived: Nicky and Chris Brooker whom I had last met at the Naval Club just before starting the cruise. They had a family country cottage nearby, and had come to inspect us. Nicky had been at Cambridge with me, and I had taken her to a May Ball in 1965. But it was no good — she went to three May balls that year, on consecutive nights with three different men, such was her popularity. In those days there were seven of us undergraduate blokes to each woman at the university. Klim who was at Cambridge at the same time had surely been in love with Nicky (we all had been). Nicky became a teacher and Chris was the parish clerk for St Martin-in-the-Fields, the famous neoclassical 18th-century church in Trafalgar Square. Both are delightfully chatty, full of gossip, and satisfactorily left-wing.

Coincidentally, Nicky's father Bryan Brooke taught me at medical school, the professor of surgery, and a memorable man. As much a potter and artist as a surgeon, he developed the ileostomy whereby the gut can empty into a bag on the abdomen after the colon has had to be removed. And he was a great lecturer. He it was who proclaimed: 'Your medical education begins outside your medical school.' I had no idea what he meant then, but I do now. People who go to medical school, and who then work in the same hospital in the same town until they retire, never have the range of experience, and of life, as those who move about before settling down. For them it is much harder to realise there are more ways than just their local way of achieving the same result, in medicine and in everything else. Sadly, trainee doctors now get around much less than we did, tending to stay more or less in one place.

We all had a very jolly dinner in the Storm Fish Restaurant. Apropos nothing in particular, Nicky remarked that two of the new crew were on their second wives (me and Peter) and the other two were widowers (Klim and Steve). Maybe the way of the present world.

To the Solent

Sunday May 27th, off at last, goodbye to motorboats, and good riddance. We left at 8am and as the small amount of wind was against us from the southeast, we motored in the gradually warming day across Poole Harbour towards the entrance and out to sea. To port we noted but definitely did not admire the mishmash of ugly houses crushed together along the shore at Sandbanks. Here live millionaires, in the most expensive seaside houses in England, allegedly the fourth most expensive place to live in the world. It is favoured by Premier League football-managers and businessmen sporting Lamborghinis and progressively younger wives. Those houses lack taste, and personally I would prefer a bit of privacy and a far better view. (If you want the cheapest seaside house, look to the poor old north of England, Newbiggin-by-the-sea in Northumberland.[4]) The Condor ferry also lacked taste, its ugly bulk rumbling slowly past us on its way to the Channel Islands and France. With a top speed of something like 25 knots, it is not to be argued with.

To starboard was Brownsea Island, owned by the National Trust, where employees of John Lewis and Waitrose can take subsidised holidays — a nice touch from their bosses who, along with *all* the employees (or partners as they are called), get the same percentage bonus on their salaries at the end of the year. We should celebrate those successful businesses and businessmen and women who share their riches with their workers, like Julian Richer (an appropriate name) who in 2019 handed control of his hi-fi and TV retail chain to his 531 employees who had helped him generate those riches in the first place. Plus £1000 to everyone for each year they had worked with him.[5] If only more businesses treated their employees as generously, fostering a happier and more productive workforce. More and more money should not be going to the already over-paid bosses, but apparently that is what motivates them to work harder (while the low-paid are motivated by fearing for their jobs).

How could the CEO of Persimmon house builders possibly accept a £110 million bonus in 2017, after being 'asked to leave' (that euphemism for sacked)?[6] In the end he made do with a mere £75 million. What a rat. Pure unadulterated greed. It is utterly obscene. Even that was topped when the UK boss of an online gambling firm paid herself £265 million in 2017, and then £323 million in 2018 (£1.3 million per working day).[7] And what about the CEO of Vertex Pharmaceuticals who in 2019 was paid £14 million? This is the company that makes Orkambi, an unaffordable drug for cystic fibrosis, priced at £105,000 per patient per year.[8] (In 2019 the

---

4. *Mirror*, 23 June 2018.

5. *Guardian*, 14 May 2019.

6. *Guardian*, 9 January 2018.

7. *Guardian*, 18 December 2019.

8. J. Wise, 'NHS and Vertex Remain Deadlocked over Price of Cystic Fibrosis Drug', *BMJ*, 364 (2019), l1094.

company made a deal with the NHS and agreed a price for the drug, but astonishingly we taxpayers who pay for the NHS are not allowed to know that price due to 'commercial confidentiality'[9].) To add insult to injury Vertex destroyed 7880 packs of the drug after it went beyond its sell-by date: destroyed, not given away earlier. Welcome to the early 21st century — well, definitely in England, possibly not Scotland and Wales, or indeed the more peripheral parts of England like Northumberland and Cornwall. London in particular has more and more money. London rules. London is where so many people want to be despite the high house prices, the cost of commuting, and the difficulty getting your children into your chosen (state) school.

Once out at sea we got the sails up and headed slowly east. Gradually the coastline disappeared, not because of distance but because of fog. As a sailor on Scotland's west coast where we have little experience of fog, and given Pickle does not have radar, this was all a bit concerning, particularly as we approached the Hurst Channel, the narrow northern entrance to the Solent. I would never have attempted this in pre-GPS days, never ever. But now with a chartplotter it is easy to know exactly where I am, and with AIS to know where the big ships are too. But neither technology tells me about the smaller motorboats without AIS transmitters, powering through the fog at ludicrous speeds for the poor visibility. My father needn't have brought me up to hate motorboats. I hate them anyway, especially those that speed through fog. Luckily all went well. We never saw the Needles to the south, but there was a glimpse to the north of Hurst Castle on its point. Then, like the curtain rising to reveal a stage set, the fog lifted, the sun shone down, and we were in the Solent and soon approaching Yarmouth on the Isle of Wight, arriving at 12.30pm, 18 miles from Poole.

I have memories of Yarmouth, but vague ones because they were laid down a very long time ago. It is where we prep school boys were taken for special days out. It seemed such a big place then. It is really just a small attractive town, with lots of boats. But not too many in May when it was not difficult to find a space on the walk-ashore pontoons, a relatively new feature that had been objected to by many who preferred the old ones unconnected with the land. We were assisted by the highly friendly harbour staff who came out to meet us in their dory, no doubt worrying we would make a mess of tying up without their help.

---

9. Z. Kmietowicz, 'Cystic Fibrosis Drugs to be Available on NHS in England within 30 Days', *BMJ*, 367 (2019), l6206.

I didn't know the police had a marine branch, but they do. One of Hampshire's finest soon turned up on the pontoon for a 'friendly chat', possibly eying us up and down as (unlikely) drug smugglers. He handed us a leaflet on boat security, not something we worry much about in the Hebrides. What a pleasant job these aquatic policeman must have, at least on a sunny day, roaring around the Solent in their speedy RIB, stopping off to chat to boaties, and handing out security advice leaflets. This copper had a boat of his own, a Nicolson 35 indeed, so a man who knew about boats, a man with taste too.

Yarmouth was hot, really hot. And unusually crowded for the time of year because their Old Gaffers' Festival weekend was just finishing. Rather fun, with bands, food, booze, and dancing in marquees. And flags, lots and lots and lots of union jacks. This was during the build-up to the Queen's jubilee, 60 years after her coronation. The Isle of Wight is nothing but traditional, conservative and loyal. It is in fact rather urban too, not at all like an island, no abandoned and rusting cars in Hebridean ditches, rather more an ectopic bit of Hampshire which of course is exactly what it is.

Klim jumped on a ferry to the mainland to meet up with his three children, it was the anniversary of Ann's death the previous year. Steve, Peter and I boarded a double-decker bus to enjoy the child-like pleasure of sitting on the top deck in the open. It took us to Freshwater Bay where we got off for a bracing walk across Tennyson Down past the great man's monument, to the cliffs above the Needles. Tennyson lived on the island for a few years but was so pestered by fans that he moved away. He also has a waterfall named after him near Loch Aline on the Sound of Mull, but here on his Down is where he is better remembered.

The Needles are such a tremendously iconic feature of our coastline, and appear on so many calendars. They are a clear memory of my childhood because I used to gaze across to them from the beach near my prep school, in my school shorts and sunhat. The feel of the air on the cliffs was so familiar, the rather dry countryside of chalk down-land, and the light, too, slightly hazy in the heat. On some school 'treat days' we were taken to swim at Alum Bay on the north coast of the island just east of the Needles; here I nearly got carried away by the tide before that ex-Spitfire pilot rescued me. Alum Bay of the multi-coloured sand, available in bottles now as it presumably was then. I bought one from the tatty shopping arcade on the cliffs. That likely wasn't there in the 1950s nor I suspect the chairlift down to the beach, but it was impossible to retrieve such a distant memory. I certainly didn't recall being so amazed by the multi-coloured cliffs that produce the multi-coloured sand to fill the bottles. There were not nearly as many boats around when I was a boy, not like now — so many speedboats towing water skiers, the pestilence of jet skis, and a billionaire's superyacht anchored in the bay.

To the Beaulieu River

The next day Yarmouth was still hot. Notwithstanding the estuary accents, which I was surprised to hear as far west as here, it seemed quite a posh sort of a place. You could tell this because of the very expensive beer. And all those union jacks fluttering from lines strung up across every shop front, and pictures of the Queen in shop windows. Not that I am particularly against the Queen, as any alternative might be a lot worse. I couldn't bear the thought of President Tony-Iraq-War-Blair, for example. The Queen seems to do her job well, and besides she was very kind to my old friend Ian Campbell who died of mesothelioma in 2009.[10] He had been a GP in Snettisham in Norfolk where, after favourable references from medical colleagues and trial by cocktail party, it fell to him to be the Apothecary to the Royal Household (no less) when resident at their country retreat of Sandringham over Christmas, and at other times too. This duty regularly constrained Ian's Christmas (he did claim this duty 'saved his liver'). Not long before he died, Ian, by then retired, and his wife were summoned by the Queen to have a gin and tonic with her and the Duke, implicitly to thank him for his help over the years. Even the slightly eccentric Prince Charles called in to his home to wish him well a few weeks before he died. Nice, I thought. The Royal Family can't all be bad — the problem seems more the people who surround them and cling to their hereditary privileges. After all, Princess Anne had a Rustler 36 before trading up to the much larger Rustler 44. Unasked, she even once took my mooring ropes when I was tying up to a pontoon in Ardfern. No one else in the Royal Family seems interested in sailing.

It must be incredibly difficult to be a doctor to famous people, with all the normal pressure to get everything right compromised by extra nervousness. Luckily I was almost never called, probably because I didn't

---

10. Mesothelioma is a highly malignant tumour of the coverings of the lung, often caused by much earlier exposure to asbestos. Ian can remember using asbestos in the factory where he worked as a student. Because he had obsessively kept a diary he had the evidence to successfully claim for compensation.

do any commercial (aka private) practice. But once, long ago on a dark winter's evening, I was summoned to a grand Edinburgh hotel to see some long-past head of state of an Asian country. It may have been a transient ischaemic attack, a so-called mini-stroke (very like a stroke but lasting just minutes or hours before the patient recovers completely). It was difficult to tell. There were too many fawning hangers-on crowding round in his room to allow me to concentrate, the lighting was poor, his English was not that good, it was difficult to get the story of what had happened, he was soon returning home to see far more famous doctors, and was already on all possible stroke-prevention treatments … and more. I had no idea where to send my fee, so I didn't.

Back to the cruise. We left Yarmouth at 1pm and with a light westerly wind covered the ten miles to be off the Beaulieu River in a couple of hours. Despite its fame in sailing circles, the Solent seemed surprisingly dull to me, maybe because I am used to the scenic drama of the Scottish west coast. No such drama in the Solent. On offer was low-lying land, a very high chimney at the Fawley power station that you can see for miles (demolished in 2021), plus very big ships manoeuvring into Southampton. However, the Beaulieu River definitely did not disappoint. As we motored in between the green and red posts (no good asking Steve to identify them given his colour blindness) we gradually went from the salty sea and beaches, to the serene beauty of classic English countryside, oak woods, pastoral river banks. This really is historic — it is where many of Nelson's ships were built. Apparently you can pick up any vacant private mooring in the river. But we wanted to leave the boat to go for a walk so we pulled in to the marina at Buckler's Hard, at £34 for the night, not as much as Poole but a lot more than Tobermory at £25 (my local benchmark).

The hour or so wander beside the river up to Beaulieu was sheer delight, through lovely woods and by manicured fields. The very, very posh houses seemed to be on the other side of the river. One we had noticed for sale boasted a spiral track for cars to drive up to the garage on the roof. Maybe I dreamt that, as it sounds ridiculous. Beaulieu too was posh, and again festooned with union jacks. This jubilee business was getting wearing. As in many over-posh places we couldn't find a proper pub, just the Montagu Hotel, but no real ale. There was a gallery where I was tempted to buy an original painting, and succumbed. Not a town to return to, but the walk could certainly be repeated. Nor was Buckler's Hard itself much of a place for us, a bit dull and set in aspic. It still seemed 'a shamelessly picturesque and faintly twee tourist trap in the high season', as Libby Purves described it in 1988.[11] We meandered back to Pickle for our three-course supper, with the tablecloth and decanter of red wine. This posh business was catching.

Where does all this money round here come from? Maybe Lord Montagu who seems to own the vast estate, as well as the river. It would be nice if some of his riches trickled down, to places in real need like Maryport, as those ridiculous economists believed it would before it dawned on them how human nature worked. It is hard to believe that Maryport and Beaulieu are in the same country — England. But England is a divided country (Scotland thankfully less so). As ever we are all controlled from London. There is so much more money in London, notwithstanding the recession, and so little money-making capability outside London due to de-industrialisation. The divide continues to get worse and worse. The poor are really poor, the rich extraordinarily rich. In 2012 bankers were demanding salaries of £4 million a year, 40 times more than a consultant neurosurgeon who might remove their brain tumour, 160 times more than a teacher who might teach their children, and 340 times more than the lady who cleans their toilet. Not surprisingly the gap in life expectancy between the rich and poor is getting worse. In England, in 2015–17, males were expected to live nine years longer in the least-deprived compared with the most-deprived areas, females seven years. And for *healthy* life expectancy, 19 years for both genders.[12] A terrible indictment for a supposedly civilised country.

To Portsmouth

Tuesday May 29th, Klim reappeared and we were joined for the day by Alex, a local friend of Steve's. She was an engineering undergraduate in Edinburgh, unusual for such a male-dominated profession. But something has to compensate for speech and language therapy where somehow the women have put off all, or at least almost all, the men. Not much gender balance there.

At 7am it was a beautiful, still, warm and windless morning. Fish were rising in the river, mist rising off it. Pellucid must be the right adjective to describe the water that morning, pellucid. From the hated Latin — *per lucidus*. Quite fabulous, despite the distant sound of traffic reminding us we were in the overcrowded south of England, as we motored downriver to the

---

11. Purves, *One Summer's Grace*, 26.

12. Health state life expectancies by national deprivation deciles, England and Wales: 2015 to 2017. Office for National Statistics.

sea and back into the Solent, where there was no wind and no yachts either at that time of day. Later there would be all those speeding motorboats followed by their disruptive wakes, hundreds of yachts, ferries which have been known to mow down small boats, hovercraft, huge container ships and car carriers, and the occasional destroyer. Like smokers, motorboats should be confined to special places well away from me. The Solent is a hugely overrated sailing venue in my opinion, a 'yachting slum' according to Jonathan Raban in the 1980s.[13] One wonders what he would make of it 40 years later. Not a lot, I imagine. One friend avoids the Solent mêlée in August by bringing her boat ashore for antifouling and maintenance, and then goes sailing in the quiet of winter when everyone else is ashore.

We motored the 14 miles to Portsmouth, through the narrow harbour entrance, and turned immediately left into Haslar marina in Gosport where we were greeted by a couple of jolly and attractive young ladies perched on their electric marina buggy. One was Tunisian, on work experience, and to improve her English. The marina toilets and showers were in the converted 'Mary Mouse' lightship right next to where we tied up, an excellent facility. We could have drinks on the upper deck, but no real ale I'm afraid. What's gone wrong with England? So little proper beer, not even warm beer. A downside to this marina was the longish walk to get provisions, and Gosport is hardly the most attractive town in England.

Two childhood memories off Portsmouth. The first was a school outing on a tourist boat to see the British Fleet, about 300 ships lined up at Spithead between Portsmouth and the Isle of Wight, to celebrate the Queen's coronation in 1953. They included the aircraft carrier HMS Eagle, a reminder of that popular boys' magazine of the same name. And, as it happened, the last Royal Navy ship to bear the name 'Pickle', a minesweeper built in 1943. In those days Britannia didn't quite rule the waves, but she certainly did so more then than now. The navy is down to about 75 ships I believe, and by no means are all of them functional.

The second memory was when my parents hired a very modest car to motor down to see me at school, an almost unique occurrence. They wanted to take me around and about, and we picnicked on a beach overlooking the Solent. Here I gazed out to sea and remarked that the ships seemed a bit blurred, the first intimation of my short-sightedness, and the need for glasses. And the realisation that I could never become an RAF pilot, my

---

13. Jonathan Raban, *Coasting: A Private Journey* (orig. 1986; New York, First Vintage Departure Edition, 2003), 97.

first career aspiration. I had to change my plans, and a good thing too. I would have been a hopeless pilot — not nearly daring enough.

As we had sailed into Portsmouth, such an important naval base for hundreds of years, we just couldn't not do the naval heritage stuff. First up was the excellent Royal Navy Submarine Museum in Gosport, its highlight a 1945 submarine around which we were guided by a retired submariner. So cramped, such a complex cats-cradle of pipes and wires and switches and brass wheels and valves and dials … and torpedoes. In dimmed lighting we were subjected to an audio recording of depth charges being dropped around us; the real thing must be extraordinarily scary. A notice on a bulkhead read: 'There is no margin for mistakes in submarines, you are either alive or dead.'

Then onto the ferry across to Portsmouth itself, reminding me of the ferry from Devonport across the harbour to Auckland in New Zealand, where my first wife came from. Similar blue sparkling water and clear sky, not very attractive modern buildings in the downtown area, and the very strong naval connection. And so to the attractions of the Historic Dockyard, as it is billed. The centrepiece is HMS Victory, Nelson's already-ageing flagship by the time of the Battle of Trafalgar in 1805. It was surprisingly disappointing because somehow it was too sanitised and perfect, with very little if any explanation of what one was looking at. The small amount of signage was only in English as far as I could see, and there was nothing much for children. Surly and rather ignorant guides lounged about.

It was far too orchestrated in the sense that you had to walk round a fixed one-way route which I finished quickly so I could decide where to linger before going out on to the dockside and back in for a more focused and leisurely closer look. To my astonishment I was not allowed back, even though I had a ticket that had been sold to me for as many visits to the attractions in the dockyard as I wanted for a year. Ah yes, but the small print excluded the Victory. Rules is rules, irrespective of the fact that there were very few other tourists around, and it was nearly closing time. How cheated I felt, how irritated, and generally pissed off. Presumably this rule is a reflection of the pressure of tourism, but in my case destroying what I had come to see. I shall not be going back, and indeed I didn't in 2018 when I visited the truly marvellous Mary Rose exhibition. I had no idea there had been a Battle of the Solent, which is where in 1545 the Mary Rose turned turtle and sank into the mud that preserved her for nearly 500 years. Despite this loss, the French invasion of England was beaten off.

HMS Warrior, launched in 1860, the world's first iron-hulled, armoured warship, powered by steam as well as sail, was a much better deal than HMS Victory. It is an outstanding restoration of an abandoned hulk after decades of decline, and made for a much more relaxed visit. There were hardly any people, and you could wander around at will, with good signage explaining everything. We didn't feel inspired to explore the town any further in case Paul Theroux was right: 'Like most British sea-port towns, Portsmouth was its harbour. It was wrong to look behind the harbour for anything better.'[14]

That evening we met up with Peter Cardy, who lived in a modern flat overlooking the harbour in Gosport where he had been born. I first came across him when he ran the Motor Neurone Disease Association before going on to run the Multiple Sclerosis Society, then Macmillan Cancer Support, and after that he was chief executive of the Maritime and Coastguard Agency before winding down to run Sail Training International. He had been a tremendously effective leader of a medical charity — canny, hard-working, well-connected, and very able to mix with doctors without being intimidated. He it was who suggested to me that the Association of British Neurologists should have a mission statement, and meet up with the relevant neurology charities every year. We took his advice on both counts. Our first mission statement attempt started with something to do with supporting neurologists. That was quickly changed to supporting patients, I am glad to say. That evening his advice was for us all to have an al fresco meal at Pebbles, a restaurant on the beach with — as he warned us — poor portion control. He was right; I couldn't finish my enormous prawn salad.

To Sussex by the sea

Wednesday May 30th, fog, and ships' horns sounding eerily in the harbour. I was getting the hang of fog — chartplotter switched on telling me where I was, and AIS switched on telling me where most ships were, including the destroyer that loomed up out of the murk and passed us as we emerged from the marina at 10.15am. Not quite as dramatic, or indeed portentous, as Hilaire Belloc's encounter with the fleet when war was declared in 1914: 'Like ghosts, like things themselves made of mist, there passed between me and the newly risen sun, a procession of great forms, all in line, hastening

---

14. Paul Theroux, *The Kingdom by the Sea: A Journey around the Coast of Great Britain* (orig. 1983; London: Penguin, 1984), 79.

eastward. It was the Fleet recalled ... Then I knew that war would come, and my mind was changed.'[15]

We had to motor the five miles to the green Dean Elbow buoy (a strange name — who was Dean and why his elbow?) before there was enough wind to get the sails up. The fog cleared and, close-hauled, we sailed on to find our way through the shallow and narrow Looe channel off Selsey Bill at 1pm. Some people get very excited about this channel, which seemed a piece of cake to me. Just follow the buoys as you sail over what was not so long ago dry land. After that we bore away on a fine reach to arrive off Shoreham at 5.30pm, 32 miles in the day. Although there hadn't been much wind, we had had the tide with us (of course — see my passage-plan somewhere) and at times were gliding at 4–5 knots over the ground on a calm sea. It was a huge relief to get away from the over-crowded and scenically uninspiring Solent.

Shoreham may seem an odd choice for an overnight stop, a bit of a dump maybe. However, I didn't like the sound of Brighton Marina, no doubt full of a lot more of those horrible motorboats going nowhere, miles out of town too. I believe it is similar to corporate and soulless Sovereign Harbour near Eastbourne that Shane Spall thought, as she locked into the marina, was like entering 'a housing estate. It could have been anywhere. Manchester, Birmingham, Leeds or Limehouse. The same boring, generic architecture.'[16] Besides, I fancied another visit to Shoreham, having been there as a teenager on passage down the English Channel with Peter Gallichan when we had been gale-bound for a couple of days, tied up in what was then very much a working harbour. Now there is a marina, somewhat run-down, higgledy-piggledy with an eclectic mixture of boats, some a bit tatty, certainly no gleaming-white-in-your-face motorised monsters. It was somehow in tune with the whole place which was blessed with an excellent chandlery reminding me of old-fashioned ironmongers with their array of thousands of useful bits and pieces. And with friendly lock-keepers to let us into the river Adur from the sea. All for £20 a night, cheaper than Tobermory which was a bit of a first for us on the south coast.

Klim and Ann's oldest child — Sam — lived in Brighton with his wife Jane and two children, so obviously we planned to meet up with them. I think Klim also wanted to show his family that he was surviving the voyage, which for some reason they had predicted he wouldn't. He may

---

15. Hilaire Belloc, *The Cruise of the Nona* (London: Constable & Co. Ltd, 1925), 150.
16. Shane Spall, *The Voyages of the Princess Matilda* (London: Ebury Press, 2012), 128.

not be a sailor, and he was over 70, but he was pretty fit and up for some adventuring on the sea. This rendezvous was all very convenient as there didn't seem much to see and do around the marina that is a bit out of the town, which itself is of no great interest. Sam took us to a plain little restaurant on Shoreham Beach (*sic*), which was surprisingly in the middle of an unpromising housing development of high-rise flats. The 'Into the Blue' turned out to be an excellent fish restaurant, but maybe a more appropriate name would be 'Out of the Blue'.

Thursday May 31st, a mighty cock-up. Just how did we end up straddled across the lock after the gate was opened to let us out into the sea? Like a small child caught doing something naughty, at times of crisis like this I close my eyes which is why, when (occasionally) we go aground, I am never quite sure exactly what depth the echosounder was reading. I had probably taken the bow-line off prematurely while there was still enough water flow to catch our bows and swing us across the lock. Fortunately there was no one to see us, apart from the cheery lock-keeper who no doubt had witnessed this sort of hopeless seamanship a hundred times before. It wasn't too difficult to disentangle ourselves and head sheepishly out to sea.

Along this coast one has to get the tides right, and we needed to catch the rising east-going tide off Beachy Head at about 3pm. It all seemed very built-up, somewhat urban, as we sailed close inshore. Even a hundred years ago Hilaire Belloc thought the south coast here was 'turning into a sort of town',[17] notwithstanding his view that the south coast is a 'coast of good memories: may it stand for ever in spite of petrol and every other evil thing.'[18] I had pondered joining the on-going meeting in Brighton of the Association of British Neurologists, but quickly thought better of it with not a hint of guilt. On we sailed past Newhaven with its safe, friendly but slightly ramshackle harbour; the iconic and pristine Seven Sisters Cliffs much whiter than the 'white cliffs of Dover'; and the equally iconic lighthouse with its red stripes under Beachy Head. Then past Hastings in the distance, with its historic pier being restored. Hastings was where I had years ago performed in its mime festival with Michael Farthing, then a junior doctor but who eventually became vice-chancellor of Sussex University (which we had just passed). We arrived off Rye at 5.30pm, 43 miles from Shoreham.

---

17. Belloc, *Cruise of the Nona*, 345.
18. Belloc, *Cruise of the Nona*, 144.

Man-talk and other conversations

With a good breeze from the west and a bit of sun it was pleasant and relaxed sailing. There was a lot of talk in the cockpit. It is surprising how much men can gossip. Once again all the crew were anti-Tony-Iraq-War-Blair *Guardian* readers. I am not sure about Klim, but in her youth Ann had been a member of the Communist Party. They were both reassuringly well to the left of centre, and stayed that way, unlike many who drift to the right with age. And both were completely signed up to trying to change the law on assisted dying. Indeed Ann had helped found and then been the first chair of Health Professionals for Assisted Dying.[19] She had as ever put her own experiences to good use by writing movingly in the *BMJ* about her own dying weeks.[20] Very sadly, and despite palliative care, she had a very uncomfortable death which could so easily have been avoided if the law had allowed assisted dying.

Assisting a suicide in England is illegal, whereas in Scotland it isn't but it would be unwise to attempt it. Meanwhile I am sure that, under the radar, assisting the death of a terminally ill patient is not uncommon whether by the so-called double effect of a doctor prescribing more opiate than is strictly necessary to relieve pain and distress, or by a concerned friend or relative taking matters into their own hands. Maybe this prohibition will change, but in 2015 both the UK and Scottish parliaments debated — not for the first time — and failed to change their laws, albeit with an interesting difference between the two nations.

In England any change in the law would have been limited to mentally competent adults expected to die within six months, the so-called 'terminally ill'. However, although one can reasonably predict death within days or weeks in most patients who are clearly dying, six months is impossible to get right reliably. Moreover, many who now choose to go to Dignitas in Switzerland for an assisted death (at considerable expense, at least £7000) would be ineligible; they are not necessarily 'terminally ill' although in their own judgement their life is intolerable as a result perhaps of being paralysed in all four limbs after a spinal injury. And those who really are terminally ill may have to travel to Switzerland before they would have had

---

19. Healthcare Professionals for Assisted Dying is a campaigning organisation of doctors and other clinicians set up to change the UK law to allow assisted dying for terminally ill, mentally competent adults.

20. Ann McPherson, 'An Extremely Interesting Time to Die', *BMJ*, 339 (2009), 175.

an assisted death in England, simply because they have to be fit enough to get there. Once there, it is hardly a treat to die in an anonymous room in an anonymous house compared with in your own bed in your own home at a time of your own choosing surrounded by family and friends.

In contrast, in Scotland the proposed law would have included not just the terminally ill but also those who are unbearably suffering, despite the best possible care, with several built-in safeguards to avoid exploitation of the patient by unscrupulous relatives or others. Since then the Scottish law has moved on a little because terminal illness is defined in the 2018 Social Security Act as 'a progressive disease, which can reasonably be expected to cause an individual's death', *without* any qualifying period. It is unfortunate that the UK charity Dignity in Dying[21] have campaigned for an assisted death only for those expected to die within six months. In Scotland, however, Friends at the End[22] campaign to allow an assisted death under the new Scottish definition of terminally ill. Sooner or later this difference has to be resolved.

Survey after survey suggests that about 80% of the UK population would like to see a change in the law to allow assisted dying, or assisted suicide if you will. A change has got to come, despite the protestations of many but by no means all with religious convictions, and resistance from many doctors, particularly palliative care physicians, perhaps because they feel their professionalism has been overlooked or threatened. Nowhere in the UK is euthanasia being actively suggested, unlike in Holland where it has been legal since 2001 but subject to very strict conditions: the responsible doctor has to document the conditions, report to the state prosecutor, and some weeks later should receive notice that he or she will not be prosecuted.

Conversations on assisted dying seemed perhaps inappropriate as we passed Beachy Head, such a favoured place for suicides, but tragic ones, rather seldom the considered suicide of someone who is near to death or suffering unbearably.

None of us were too keen on the hype surrounding the Queen's jubilee celebrations, but tolerant enough of others wanting to flutter their Union Jacks, drink warm beer and generally have a good time. However, the last

---

21. Dignity in Dying (DiD) is a UK charity campaigning to change the law in England and Wales to allow assisted dying, as well as providing advice on end-of-life-care. These days it has a more prominent voice in Scotland.

22. The Scottish charity Friends at the End (FATE) more or less mirrors what Dignity in Dying does, although it campaigns to change the law only in Scotland.

thing I wanted was to tangle with the pageant of ships shortly due to sail through London, which was a pity because I had rather liked the idea of sailing up the Thames to St Katharine Docks marina under the shadow of Tower Bridge. But it would have been totally jammed with boats, with inevitable delays of one sort and another. As it turned out, heavy rain rather spoiled the whole event anyway.

Eventually, in 2015, I did sail up the Thames, but to Limehouse marina which is more interesting and far less touristic than St Katharine's, notwithstanding the surrounding uninspiring modern apartments and offices. There it was a good feeling to be tied up where so much cargo had once been transferred from sea-going ships to Thames lighters and then by canal boats to the Midlands and beyond — it was also a good feeling to be surrounded by liveaboards on various shapes and sizes of boats, no doubt many of whom commuted either to Canary Warf that could be seen from the marina, or to the City of London that is almost as close in the opposite direction. Indeed a lot of men in suits appeared first-thing in the morning, as well as lycra-encased cyclists speeding to work while checking their heart rates on various devices, scattering pedestrians, and overtaking determined joggers listening on headphones to their playlists. And how handy is the driverless Docklands Light Railway that rattles by just above the marina, and the well-known and historic Grapes pub that does excellent food. Ironically, one of the few places I have felt seasick is near Tower Bridge because of the chop from all the tourist boats speeding hither and thither (or maybe because of the anxiety of finding my way around in the busy river).

My desire to avoid anything whatsoever to do with the 2012 London Olympic games was not shared by the crew who discussed them at length. I am just not interested in sport. I was never any good at sport. I was so hopeless that I was awarded the best loser's cup for having my face pulverised in a boxing match at my prep school. I didn't enjoy kicking or hitting a ball around, and had felt uncomfortable about the ra-ra nature of team games at my prep and public schools where sporting prowess was valued as much as, if not more than, academic success, or indeed being a nice person. The sporty boys seemed to get all the favours, so it is easy to understand why unsporty me didn't get any favours then, and has unsporty views now. Only in my final year at Haileybury did we have, for the first time, a head boy who was not in one of the first cricket or rugby teams.

On the bright side, in that final year at school I had an inspirational teacher, Basil Edwards. He had I think been in the Guards, he was a

Cambridge hockey blue, and he taught English. He regularly invited groups of senior boys round to his house in the school grounds to discuss the books which he encouraged us to read, and even to have a smoke (for those inclined, not me). I still have his list of the 250 or so books he said we had to read to claim to be 'well read', categorised into novels, travel, autobiography, biography, plays, poetry, history, science, religion, art, short stories and science fiction. I am still working on that list, as well as on all the additional important books that have appeared in the last 60 years.

Are there still inspirational English teachers sticking their necks out, and not just cajoling their pupils to cram for exams, and teaching slavishly to the curriculum dictated by some far-off bureaucrat? In Scotland the marking scheme for English and some other school exams is unbelievably detailed to the extent that teachers teach their pupils how to maximise their marks by using the 'right' words and phrases, rather than understand the subject. I believe it is as bad in England. But, to be fair, all teachers teach tricks to pass exams. In vivas, medical students are often asked to list the causes of something, for example shortness of breath. The trick I passed on was 'Although you must start off with the most common causes and work down the list to the rarer ones, be sure to leave out the rarest one of all that you can remember. Because, when you get to the end of your list the chances are the bored examiner will ask if there any other causes you can think of. Rather than look blank, you can pull your metaphorical rabbit out of the hat.' As well as trickery one can strike lucky. In my finals viva, swot that I was, I mentioned a paper I had read in the *Lancet*. The examiner asked me who had written it. I hadn't a clue, but he knew: 'It was me,' he said. Job done.

And there was chat about women, at least about Steve's women, mostly initiated by Steve. Klim was astonished, claiming never before to have participated in what he called 'man-talk'. And there was chat about widowhood, an experience which Steve and Klim shared, although Steve was widowed far back in 1995. Nowadays 'man-talk' also includes discussing those cheap and cheerful drugs which so many men of a certain age are taking, as Klim and Steve were, but certainly not me, and not Peter either — statins. They reduce the blood cholesterol level and so the *relative* (or proportional) risk of a stroke or heart attack by *about* one third — irrespective of age, gender, or even the cholesterol level. The number of strokes and heart attacks in a population will certainly be reduced if lots of people take a statin. But are they worth it for an individual? Almost certainly yes for someone who has already had a stroke or heart attack because of their high risk of having another. But not necessarily for people who have *not* had a stroke or heart attack and who are at lower risk — people like me. My own risk, according to a reasonably well-validated risk scoring system (but imperfect as they all are) based on age, cholesterol, postal code (a surrogate for social deprivation level), smoking and such like, is now quite high at 27% over the next ten years. Not *exactly* 27% because this is an average for a group of people like me — it might be somewhat higher, or somewhat lower.

Taking a statin should reduce my 27% risk by about one third (the *relative* risk reduction) which sounds a lot, leaving me with a risk of having a stroke or heart attack of 18% over the next ten years. That is an *absolute* risk reduction of 9% (27% minus 18%) which doesn't sound so much. Therefore, of 100 people like me over the next 10 years, 27 might have a stroke or heart attack if none took a statin, while 18 might have a stroke or heart attack if all 100 took a statin every day. This means that nine (27 minus 18) avoid a stroke or heart attack for every 100 treated with a statin, while 91 would not have benefited, either because they were not going to have a stroke or heart attack anyway, or because the statin didn't work for them. However, each one of those 91 will have taken about 3600 pills (unnecessarily or ineffectively) because we can't predict exactly who will benefit and who won't. The number of people needed-to-treat to prevent one person having a stroke or heart attack is therefore 100/9 = 11.

Putting it another way, by taking a statin every day for ten years, I would have a 1 in 11 chance of benefiting. Presenting benefit like this, and so better informing patient choice, is not much written about, especially in national guidelines, or used. Is that 1 in 11 worth it? For me? Especially as so many people complain of leg muscle aches on statins as did Klim and Steve. Whether these minor symptoms are due to a structural or biochemical disorder of muscle, or — more likely — are in some way 'psychological' because people expect them, doesn't matter. They are still experienced as symptoms and need dealing with, perhaps by changing to a different statin, reducing the dose, or stopping it altogether (as eventually Steve did). What any *long-term* side effects of statins might be, or any unexpected benefits over and above reducing the risk of strokes and heart attacks, we simply don't know because the trials didn't go on for more than a few years. Known unknowns. For me if the benefit were, for example, only 1 in 100 then clearly I would not take a statin, but if it was 1 in 3, I would. 1 in 11 is a tricky in-between.

We ideally need to know who, out of the 11 people like me, is the one who *will* benefit and treat just him or her, without having to bother the other 10 who will not benefit. Everyone is struggling with this problem, hence the modern obsession with so-called 'personalised' medicine (not I fear in the old sense of taking time to understand and care for an individual, beyond mere prescribing). This has been rebadged as 'precision' medicine, to target those who *will* benefit from a particular treatment, not the much larger number who *might* benefit but in the end do not. Of course, from the public health perspective there would indeed be fewer strokes and heart attacks if all older people took a statin, but not only would that over-treat the individuals who do not benefit, it would cost far more than treating only those who will definitely benefit, if only we knew who they were.

This sort of calculation of risk is completely different to how we used to think. When I was a student a patient either had the disease called 'hypertension' (judged by the height of their blood pressure) or did not, and so was treated, or not. Very few doctors, if any, thought about gradation of risk as we do now — the higher the blood pressure, the greater the risk of stroke. Arguments raged about 'disease' versus 'no disease' when considering a continuous variable like blood pressure. Sir George Pickering succinctly lamented that 'Medicine in its present state can count up to two but not beyond'[23] because he realised that people can't be divided simply into either 'hypertensive' or 'not-hypertensive' based on an arbitrary blood pressure cut-off level that implies — incorrectly — that you must treat the former but not the latter. The decision to treat or not depends on the risk of future stroke or heart attack, and that depends not just on the level of blood pressure but on other factors too, particularly increasing age.

Irrespective of all this debate, no amount of statins will help the under-educated, poorly housed, obese, badly nourished, unfit, out of work, middle-aged man or woman whose problem is *not* a high cholesterol but poverty and the resulting lower life expectancy due to strokes and heart attacks, and a whole host of other diseases including Covid-19. For them, statins are mere sticking plaster. The solutions are political and social, not pharmaceutical.

For Steve it had probably been worth taking a statin as he had had a transient ischemic attack in 2009, rather memorably at Portavadie Marina on Loch Fyne. Because it was so remote, he was helicoptered to what the pilot referred to as the 'Govan Hilton', in other words the Southern General Hospital in Govan, a particularly deprived part of Glasgow. Such

---

23. George Pickering, *High Blood Pressure* (2nd edn, London: Churchill, 1968).

was the speed of the stroke service that Steve arrived there 55 minutes after the onset of his symptoms that had by then resolved. It might have been a stroke but in the end it wasn't, not quite but nearly. He was admitted anyway for a couple of days, quite unnecessarily in my view.

Rye

Rye is one of the ancient Cinque Ports, established in the 11th century to protect the coast from continental invaders, but long ago it gradually retreated inland, dragging behind it the muddy, winding, tidal and shallow river Rother which still just about connects it to the sea two miles away. I think I had picked Rye as a stopping-off place because I wanted to try taking the ground (as we mariners say), drying out, something I had never done in my life — leaning the boat against a harbour wall as the tide goes out.

From the fairway buoy we approached with extreme caution, under engine of course, an aid scorned by Hilaire Belloc who sailed in — although he could have used his sweep, or summoned a tow, especially as he remarked that 'Any man making Rye Haven must first resign himself to the will of God, and consider, especially if the boat is running and a little over-canvassed, that death is but a mighty transition.'[24] He was a devout Roman Catholic. In 1893, even the far better sailor Frank Cowper was daunted by the entrance and its inadequate buoyage. He was told, not very helpfully, that 'the harbour had altered a good deal since the time of Henry VIII'.[25] Indeed he recommended that 'no one attempt to enter Rye harbour without a pilot; in fact, we recommend no one to enter it with one'.[26] But then he generally sailed with no crew or engine, or perhaps just 'a boy' to help him. I had an engine, and crew.

There were three challenges. First we had to get over the bar at the mouth of the river that dries out completely at low tide. There was none of the reassuring blue colour on the chart (which signifies water — any water at all, even at low tide), but a widespread and daunting green right across the

---

24. Belloc, *Cruise of the Nona*, 295.

25. Frank Cowper, *Sailing Tours: The Yachtsman's Guide to the Cruising Waters of the English Coast*, part 1: *The Coasts of Essex and Suffolk* (London: Upcott Gill, 1892), ix.

26. Frank Cowper, *Sailing Tours: The Yachtsman's Guide to the Cruising Waters of the English Coast*, part 2: *The Coasts of Kent, Sussex, Hants, The Isle of Wight, Dorset, Devon, Cornwall and the Scilly Isles* (London: Upcott Gill, 1893), 35.

harbour mouth (signifying dry land at low tide). However, that was OK, as we were well up towards high tide.

Then, second, shortly after entering the river we had to perform a three-point turn to face the incoming tide and tie up to the harbour master's pontoon to port. In our case it was more like a seven-point turn, but I was getting better at this, with less caution and more welly on the throttle. In extremis (aka plan B) we would have flung the anchor over the bows bringing Pickle to a halt so that she would swing round to lie facing into the tide, provided the anchor held.

The final challenge was to creep up the river with the tide, but without going aground. Round a few bends, narrower and narrower with boats settled deep in the mud on either side, some dilapidated and others in good shape (presumably a few with liveaboards — it looked that sort of place). Right into the centre of the town, towards a bridge barring any further progress, with the harbour wall to starboard. There was one boat already there and their crew guided us to a spot where another boat had recently dried out at low tide, and might have left a helpful groove in the mud for us. We tied up, and to tilt Pickle towards the wall we carefully adjusted the tensioned spinnaker halyard to which we attached a rope (the recently purchased and expensive Ardfern snatch-block came in handy here) leading to a convenient bollard on the harbour wall. The harbour master had told us there was no need for such caution and he was right, naturally. With no fuss at all, as the tide receded, Pickle settled quietly into the mud, slightly tilted forwards but not a problem. We weren't even leaning on the harbour wall. But we were still afloat — in mud. The mud was so soft it almost came up to our normal waterline. There was no way I could have stood on the river-bed to scrub the weeds off our bottom, I would have sunk without trace. I triumphantly texted Greg with whom I had discussed the niceties of drying out:

'Lost my drying-out virginity in Rye.'

'I need to see photographic evidence,' he responded cheekily.

So I sent it, to which he replied:

'That's not really drying out ... that's more of a fumble than losing your virginity!'

Well it was a first for me, whatever it was. I have only once since summoned up the courage to do it properly again (dry out, that is). In Tenby, and it didn't go well. As the water receded, we tilted forwards at an increasingly alarming angle and looked so completely ridiculous that we escaped on the next high tide to anchor in the bay.

Klim had arranged a rendezvous with his new lady-friend. She had worked in the government's Office for National Statistics (ONS) so they spoke the same language. More importantly, after meeting us she had arranged dinner ashore *à deux*, and a night in a hotel. Such is love, even in the twilight years. Her ex-boss at ONS, a New Zealander who had returned home, was a close friend of Peter's, so they had a lot to chat about. After she and Klim left, the rest of us had to fend for ourselves, which of course was not a problem. My own Thai green curry all round.

How very odd to wake on the Friday morning to the sound of a lawnmower and the smell of cut grass. Of course, we were in the middle of a town, far from the sea. We had plenty of time to explore because we had already planned to stay until the next day. Rye is surely archetypal nostalgic England, perched on a small hill with its historic houses, and lovely church with a grand view of the surrounding countryside and distant sea from the bell-tower. Unbelievably, someone really was playing Rule Britannia on the church organ. Everything seemed set in aspic. Far more antique shops (can there really be 30, as claimed in the visitors' guide?) than food shops. Along with olde tea shoppes, ancient pubs (ah yes, 'taverns' in the visitors' guide), arty galleries, boutiques, union jacks everywhere, and no non-white faces. And very posh, at least in the centre if not around the station with its Budgens supermarket. So posh that all climbing roses around doorways and windows had been dead-headed, and a pint of beer cost £4.10 compared with £2.40 in poor old broken-down Maryport. We could have been in one of the 100-plus episodes of *Midsomer Murders*, a not dissimilar impression to that of Paul Theroux who thought Rye had 'the atmosphere of a china shop'[27] and of Jonathan Raban who saw it 'as a work of sentimental art' and 'nothing but services, with jobs for waiters, salesclerks, ticket sellers, P.R. men, holiday home leasers, hoteliers, coach drivers, tour guides'.[28]

That day was all very relaxed. I even had time to complete a UK Biobank online dietary survey, quite accurately on the food front as I had cooked the meal the night before, but maybe less accurately about my exercise (sex up) and alcohol consumption (play down). Like many of my friends as it turns out, I am a voluntary, indeed willing, participant in this vast prospective study of half a million people aged 40 to 60 at its inception. At the time it was by far the largest and most comprehensive study ever done of the personal and genetic predispositions — and predictors – of diseases in older

---

27. Theroux, *Kingdom by the Sea*, 54.
28. Raban, *Coasting*, 211–13.

age, such as Parkinson's disease, cancer and heart attacks. By its very nature it will take 20 or more years to come properly to fruition. Unfortunately I, like other participants, will not usefully contribute to the most important analyses until we have an event of some sort (a stroke perhaps), or die.

Coincidentally, Cathie spent six years as the UK Biobank chief scientist. Her main task seemed to me to be incredibly complicated. This was to sort out how all the participants' routinely collected electronic health service data could be corralled and then analysed to indicate when a participant has an event, and also its nature (e.g. heart attack, cancer, etc.). Even death certificates, which can accurately tell you the date of death, have issues with the accuracy of the recorded *cause* of death. Routine hospital discharge data may tell you something about patients who have been admitted, but nothing much about those seen only as an outpatient. GP records are even trickier to mine for information, but immensely valuable as they contain data about almost all illness contacts, including information from hospital outpatient visits and milder episodes not involving any hospital. Cathie has now moved on to try and make available for research the vast swathes of routinely collected data in the NHS, from the millions of health records across the whole UK population, but without compromising any privacy issues.[29]

Klim and his lady-friend knew all about this sort of stuff. Indeed she had been awarded an honour for her efforts. Even Steve had an OBE — for services to traffic lights or some such, in other words, transportation modelling.

'What exactly is transportation modelling?' enquired the Queen as she brandished a safety pin ready to plunge into Steve's chest.

'How long have you got, ma'am?' replied Steve.

'We have one-and-a-half minutes. Can you do it in one-and-a-half minutes?'

'Well, put it this way, it doesn't work,' he answered.

To Dover

Saturday June 2nd, overcast. We watched and waited as the sea very slowly dribbled back to surround and eventually float Pickle so we could escape the mud of Rye and head for Dover and then, turning left, back up north.

---

29. Health Data Research UK attempts to unite all the routinely collected health data in the UK and make it available for medical research — millions of health records from millions of people.

It was astonishing how fast the water did eventually rush in, but it was a surprisingly long time after low tide, and much nearer high tide. With the wind brisk from the northeast we were close-hauled along the Kent coast, with one reef in the mainsail. By the afternoon some sun was breaking through and the wind got stronger.

Steve got very over-excited at one point, not by the sailing but by a flypast of a second world war Lancaster, and then the modern Eurofighter, now called the Typhoon. Both of us had been keen aero-spotters in our youth and could recognise the characteristic sound of a Lancaster, the bomber that became so iconic after the Dam Busters raid made famous by the 1955 movie. The theme music brings a tear to the eye. Richard Todd played the fearless Wing Commander Guy Gibson with the clipped English accent one hears no more (nor his dog's most racially inappropriate name), and Michael Redgrave played Barnes Wallis who invented the bouncing bomb.

The Typhoon is not yet iconic, if it ever will be. What is it for? To attack Russian bombers? Unlikely. Hugely expensive to build, uses an unimaginable amount of fuel, turns on a sixpence, and so impressive flying vertically up into the clouds, engines roaring and trailing flames. Appallingly, we sell these planes and other armaments to Saudi Arabia that is now bombing the hell out of the Yemen. And as ever, we in the UK seem to be planning to fight tomorrow's wars, with yesterday's weapons. Why else would we build two enormous aircraft carriers that are sitting ducks to a determined air or sea attack? We should spend our defence budget on cyber protection, unmanned drones, and dealing with terrorists. Fight our wars deep underground, tucked up in front of a computer screen in Wiltshire.

Moreover, the nuclear deterrent which our ageing Trident submarines carry is dated and superfluous, and not as independent of the USA as our politicians would have us believe. Nuclear weapons are an abomination that should be scrapped, so say I as an alumnus of the Campaign for Nuclear Disarmament Aldermaston March in 1961. I had one of those 'woolly brains covered by woolly hats', a memorable quip by Michael Heseltine when he was defence secretary in the 1980s. 'We will overcome', as we used to sing on the marches … eventually we will. All this incontinent defence spending sucks money away from education, the care of children and the elderly, the NHS, and support for industry. As well as from our decaying infrastructure, the often late and ancient trains, and proliferating potholes. So embarrassing.

One easily forgets, living in Scotland, just how close England is to France, and to the German army in the second world war. The crew on this leg were all war or just post-war babies, a generation brought up to believe that 'we won the war' (even though it was won mostly by the Russians and Americans), and a few of whom still find it difficult to shake off suspicion of Germany. All that should be out-of-date now, and long past. (But not so out-of-date as some who still hate the French more than 200 years after the Battle of Waterloo; a passing motorboat named 'Agincourt' with a picture of two fingers held up was particularly tasteless.) The younger generation don't have anti-German feelings, they work together, they live in each other's countries, they inter-marry. They are untouched by the two world wars. These days we go to war with countries far away that can't bomb us into submission, or invade us — such as Iraq where Tony-Iraq-War-Blair insisted there were weapons of mass destruction which could wipe us all out, and which turned out not to exist.

It was a grand 28-mile sail in nine hours, except when towards Dover we had to start tacking along the coast (amazingly the first real tacking since we had left Ardfern). I don't mind being close-hauled as long as we are going in the right direction and the weather isn't too awful, but tacking backwards and forwards is very tedious. Eventually it got too much that afternoon. The tide turned against us, the waves got bigger, the wind blew stronger, and we were getting nowhere. So on with the engine for the last hour, to Dover Harbour where the waves really were quite impressive as they burst onto the western breakwater. Despite my misgivings, and how busy the harbour is with cross-channel ferries, the harbour master was very good over the VHF radio. Yet again I was impressed by just how helpful harbour masters are, almost without exception, and polite even to a small boat like Pickle. I'm sure they would be just as polite to even smaller boats, but not to a windsurfer crossing the harbour entrance just as a channel ferry is emerging. Maybe it was so early in the season that the pressure of visiting boats had not yet made them irritated and grumpy, or more likely they are so professional they are never irritated and grumpy.

Dover was grey, bleak, and messy. The white cliffs were not as white as you might imagine from the famous song of the forces' sweetheart, Vera Lynn. Indeed, film-makers tend to use the Seven Sisters by Beachy Head as a more authentic-looking substitute. Trucks heading for the continent were speeding along or stacked up on the dual carriageway to the harbour, cutting the marina off from the town. Once across that busy road there was a rather miserable convenience store by a garage, then a dull walk into the town. Not a place to linger, but we headed for The Allotment, a very pleasant and somewhat artisan restaurant. We even felt moved to try some English wine, Chapel Down Flint Dry from Tenterden in Kent. It was rather good, although I have never bought any since, and maybe I should. But I did give brother John a tour of the winery plus lunch for his 80th birthday.

Unfortunately there was one plus we did miss: Dover Castle, which has stood there for centuries, layer after layer of historical interest from the Saxon Church through Henry II's Great Tower to the underground hospital of the second world war. And it is remarkably un-crowded, maybe because it is so huge. In 2017 another plus appeared overnight, on a gable end, a large 'Banksy' painting, of the European flag and a workman up a ladder chipping away one of the 28 stars — our star, the UK's. What a potent image of the lunacy of Brexit right in front of all the traffic heading for the ferries, and on to Europe.

To Ramsgate (and Margate)

Sunday June 3rd, the day of the Queen's diamond jubilee pageant on the Thames. In Dover it was drizzling. In London it rained on the Queen, a lot. In Scotland, the sun was out in Edinburgh, and the midges in the Highlands. Pushed along by the tide and a bit of engine for a while, we had a brief close-hauled three-hour 15-mile sail to Ramsgate between the mainland and the notorious Goodwin Sands on which the ever-eccentric Lieutenant Middleton proposed building a harbour.[30] We did have to tack a few times, under the off-white cliffs of Dover (presumably whiter in sunshine). It was easy to imagine that we could just keep going on the port tack and end up in Calais, although the visibility was such that we couldn't see the French coastline. It was striking to those of us from the north to hear French chatter on the VHF radio, an awful lot of it too and surprisingly unchallenged by the coastguards on Channel 16 which is meant to be kept free for initial communications and emergencies.

We were very cheered by Ramsgate. The big harbour was almost full of a very mixed collection of boats on pontoons, more or less in the middle of the town, overlooked by grand Victorian buildings perched on the red sandstone cliff. Quirky 'kiss me quick' and Battle of Britain graffiti adorned some temporary hoardings. Much more fun, and lively, than Dover, more our sort of place, notwithstanding its United Kingdom Independence Party (UKIP) political tendencies. Those 'UKippers' were both underestimated and apparently derided by David Cameron as 'sort of a bunch of fruit cakes

---

30. E. Middleton, *The Cruise of 'the Kate'* (2nd edn, self-published, 1888).

and loonies and closet racists mostly', a moniker that could be appropriately transferred to the Brexit Party and to its successor — Reform UK. The scale of Ramsgate felt right for the so-called 'little ships', those boats that were sailed by their volunteer crews in their hundreds from here and other ports in Kent and Essex to rescue the remains of the defeated and demoralised British army pushed onto the beach at Dunkirk. This historic evacuation had been completed exactly 62 years ago to the day, in 1940. One or two 'little ships' survive and were still in the harbour.

Our afternoon was devoted to another piece of history, of a domestic nature. Steve persuaded me to accompany him by bus to Margate where he had spent his teenage years, sailing off the beach in dinghies, and wooing Marsha Brooks. The sailing club was still there with some old codgers who could reminisce with Steve about past and mostly dead commodores. Marsha wasn't, although we did view the house she had lived in ... twice. And the house Steve had lived in ... twice. And the remains of the open-air saltwater swimming pool where Marsha's towel had been whipped away from her otherwise naked body, not by a frenzied Steve full of raging teenage hormones but by a gale of wind. I suspect the attraction was not so much Marsha as her father who had been a Beaufort pilot in the war and her mother who apparently looked like Elizabeth Taylor (through Steve's rose-tinted spectacles).

Margate seemed a very run-down sort of a place; maybe it was ever thus. According to Paul Theroux, early 20th-century Margate had been described in Baedeker as 'one of the most popular, though not one of the most fashionable watering-places in England', but to Theroux in 1982 it was 'crummy and Cockneyfied'.[31] We viewed the dirty tower-block that had been stuffed with asylum seekers, and 'Dreamland', a broken-down and derelict rollercoaster which, being listed, could not be removed. (And luckily so, because it has now been restored to its former glory.) The new 'Turner Contemporary' right on the seafront by the harbour is an attempt to put Margate back on the map. It looked to me more like an electricity substation than an art gallery. Inside, as with so many modern buildings, it was much, much nicer. Rodin's 'The Kiss' (on loan from the Tate in London) held pride of place, framed by a view of the grey, grey sea behind it.

In the 1950s, according to Steve, Margate had been jammed with people and cafés. It is very different now. On the cold, grey, bleak, windy and almost deserted promenade we stopped to listen to a family rock-band

---

31. Theroux, *Kingdom by the Sea*, 26.

performing on a bandstand, rather well, but to almost nobody. On the beach we chatted to a pretty girl selling hot doughnuts, about the local schools that Steve remembered. He had been to the grammar school and his main memory seems to be of the V-bombers taking off over the school from Manston, the local RAF airfield, on their way to nuke Russia during the Cuban missile crisis in 1962. His Latin master sent his class home to await the nuclear holocaust while he said he would be going home to 'polish my boots'. That holocaust never came, luckily for us. How awful if your last memory had been of 'amo, amas amat'. We would not have bothered with Margate but for Steve. It is not a place even for anchoring as Henry Reynolds noted in 1921: 'To those who are anxious to marry, Mr Punch's advice is "Don't!". Let me impress, in the most emphatic terms, the same advice upon all who are minded to put into Margate. Matrimony, after all, has its points; Margate, so far as we could see, has none; at any rate, for the yachtsman who has the smallest regard for the safety of his yacht.'[32]

Later we found ourselves in the Royal Temple Yacht Club overlooking Ramsgate harbour. A very grand and imposing building, with extremely friendly people inside: 'Come in, have a drink, sit down and watch the end of the pageant on the TV out of the rain.' Which we did, with a large party of local members. At the end we felt compelled to join in with a rousing rendering of Rule Britannia, Land of Hope and Glory, and — standing up for goodness' sake like we did when I was a boy at the end of films — God Save the Queen. I couldn't see that happening in Scotland, at least not in the parts I inhabit. This was followed by dancing, all very jolly and English.

During his third UK circumnavigation, R. T. McMullen in 1887 celebrated an earlier Queen's jubilee: 'wine was placed on the companion at noon, and the toast "Long life and honour to the Queen" proposed and responded to in right royal fashion.'[33] But then he was a staunch royalist, conservative, and protestant. I bet he didn't read the *Guardian*. In the evening there were fireworks over the harbour — they were nice but it was so cold and drizzly that hardly anyone was out watching.

The next day the weather was even worse, so we stayed put and went to the brilliant and recently reopened, volunteer-run, Maritime Museum illustrating the story of Dunkirk and other bits of local history. The most interesting exhibit was a film by an American journalist who, because the

---

32. Henry Reynolds, *Coastwise—Cross-Seas: The Tribulations and Triumphs of a Casual Cruiser* (London: J. D. Potter, 1921), 32.

33. R. T. McMullen, *Down Channel* (orig. 1869; London: Grafton Books, 1986), 287.

USA was neutral at the time, was able to embed himself in the advancing German Army. The contrast between the laughing and relaxed Germans and the defeated, demoralised and depressed British troops was astonishing, if hardly surprising. Quite why Hitler stopped at the Channel and didn't invade Britain still divides historians, I believe. No wonder this part of England was so heavily defended, which still shows here and there, and no wonder the old TV comedy series *Dad's Army* was set not far from here too.

The museum had a model of *the* Pickle, the schooner that brought the news of Trafalgar to Falmouth. Despite being a New Zealander, Peter knew far more about Trafalgar and the rest of English history than any of us. Maybe because he *is* a New Zealander, and some would say they are still living in historical times out there. But that's a nonsense — I know, because I've been there a few times with my New Zealander first wife. It's where I would flee if Brexit turns out very badly, as would many others. My older three children all have New Zealand passports so it would be easy for them to abandon the sinking British ship.

The weather improved during the afternoon as we went by bus to the pleasant little town of Broadstairs, which is famously the birthplace of Ted Heath, unusually a prime minister into sailing. He found time for a lot of quite serious sailing in the 1960s, including the Sydney to Hobart race. Even a Tory is not necessarily all bad, at least not the old 'one nation' Tories. Conservatives in pre-Thatcher days were not nearly as awful as so many are today with their obsession with selling off almost all our public services, the 'family silver' as Harold Macmillan, an earlier conservative PM, put it.[34] Sadly, Labour became almost as bad under Tony-Iraq-War-Blair leaving me, and many others, wondering who represents our more communitarian views, socialist views I suppose. Perhaps the Green Party with their single Westminster MP in 2021, but with seven Members of the Scottish parliament thanks to partial proportional representation. The profoundly undemocratic Westminster first-past-the-post system results in small parties never having an MP, the UK government almost always being elected by a minority of voters, and there being no point in voting in safe seats with huge majorities for one particular party. In the 2019 general election the number of votes to win the Liberal Democrats a seat was 336,000, but only 38,300

---

34. 'It is very common with individuals or estates when they run into financial difficulties, to find that they have to sell some of their assets. First, the Georgian silver goes, then all that nice furniture that used to be in the saloon. Then the Canalettos go.' In Harold MacMillan's speech to the Tory Reform Group (8 November 1985).

for the Conservatives. The Greens have by far the fairest and most sensible left-wing policies, over and above their expected take on the environment, but it took 866,400 votes to win just their single seat.[35] Ridiculous.

From Broadstairs we walked along the cliffs round the North Foreland to Margate, again. Steve couldn't keep away from the place. I didn't realise that this part of Kent had been an island as recently as Roman times — hence the name the Isle of Thanet. Maybe that is why it seemed surprisingly remote for the Home Counties, feeling and somehow behaving still like an island. Klim, slightly chaotic as ever, left his wallet on the bus back to Ramsgate. Fortunately the bus was going round in a loop so an hour later he intercepted it, and there was his wallet under a seat. A couple of credit cards had gone. The bank told him that the thief must have been too dim to realise that without the PIN number he, or maybe she, would not get any money out of an ATM, and any attempt would merely alert the bank who would immediately inactivate the card. Nowadays, when a card can be conveniently swiped without using the PIN, it is far easier for a thief to drain quite a bit of money out of an account.

We liked Ramsgate. It was bustling, there were butchers and greengrocers and other proper shops, not just a high street of cafés, bars, estate agents, hairdressers, nail bars and charity shops (the last do at least provide a very good way of recycling). There was even a Waitrose for aspirational middle-class supermarket shoppers — rather surprisingly, it had been there for 40 years. The late 19th-century Sailors' Church by the harbour, below the zigs and zags of Jacob's Ladder up the cliff, was worth a look inside. Later that evening supper on board was a celebration of summer — asparagus, strawberries and cream, with something meaty in between, I forget what.

In spite of some very noisy French crews, I would go back to Ramsgate, and we did in 2015 when we circumnavigated clockwise and again in 2018. Perhaps we had been overly influenced by the lovely weather that eventually emerged. It is difficult getting the hang of somewhere after a short visit because one's views can so easily be confounded by what the weather is like. Comparing different towns and other places should ideally be in the same weather conditions, at the same time of day, at the same time of year maybe, with the same companions, and so on.

Confounding, particularly unrecognised confounding, is responsible for a lot of medical research nonsense. Take so-called case-control studies in which two groups of people are compared (this is one form of an

---

35. House of Commons Library, 10 January 2020.

observational study). For example, you might compare a group of fat people with a group of thin people, because you wonder if being overweight causes arthritis of the hip joint, certainly plausible given that more weight is put on the hip joints of overweight people. So you count the number of people with arthritis in each group and are delighted to find many more in the fat group, proving your point that being fat does indeed correlate with arthritis, and might even cause arthritis. But your two groups of people may be different in important and relevant ways. For example, if the fat people are on average older it would be hardly surprising to find they have more arthritis, because arthritis increases with age. This is confounding by age. You can avoid that problem by ensuring that the two groups of people are of about the same age or, failing that, by adjusting the analysis to account for any age difference between the fat and thin groups. That is relatively easy, but there may be other differences between the two groups that you don't know about. These too might affect the frequency of arthritis, but you can't account for them — the unknown unknowns.

There is nothing that you can do about unknown confounders, but at least you can try to avoid the trap of 'reverse causation'. Obesity's correlation with arthritis does not necessarily mean that being overweight *causes* arthritis. It might be the other way round. Arthritis might *cause* obesity, again plausible because arthritis might stop people exercising and as a result they gain weight. A way to get round this problem is to do a so-called observational *prospective* study, but that takes longer and is much more expensive. Collect a lot of people at baseline without arthritis, measure their weight, and then follow them for several years to see who develops arthritis. If the fat people at baseline develop more arthritis, then — provided there is no confounding by age or whatever — you can reasonably conclude that being fat makes it more likely you will *develop* arthritis, particularly if there is a dose-response relationship (the fatter you are, the more likely you get arthritis). You can be even more certain if several independent studies come up with the same result, provided there has been no suppression of the results of any 'negative' studies (a possibility if funded by the sugar industry).

But even observational prospective studies can get it wrong, especially for conditions like dementia that develop insidiously over many years. For example, the Million Women study collected information about a large number of cognitively normal people (including how much exercise they took) and followed them up to see who developed dementia and who did not. After a few years, those who exercised less at baseline were more likely to have a diagnosis of dementia. Conclusion: lack of exercise causes dementia, widely reported in the media. Wrong. Because, after waiting for several more years, this relationship between lack of exercise and the much later appearance of dementia disappeared. The most likely explanation is that people with early-onset dementia, not yet diagnosed but already present at the start of the prospective study, were already taking less exercise as they subtly started to lose their interest in life. The later diagnosed cases of dementia were those that truly arose well after the study started, and so level of exercise at baseline had no obvious effect[36].

To more reliably answer the question of whether exercise protects against dementia one would have to do an *experimental* study by randomising hundreds if not thousands of people to take exercise or not, and then see who gets demented several years later. That would be as difficult as it was to randomise smokers to continue to smoke versus to try to stop smoking to see if that prevented lung cancer,[37] and no one has even attempted to randomise women taking or not taking the contraceptive pill. This is why many regard case-control and even prospective observational studies as merely hypothesis-generating, not hypothesis-proving. While observational epidemiology is certainly not easy, randomised controlled trials may simply be impractical, unethical or impossible.

Unfortunately the media is full of the results of quick and easy-to-do observational studies claiming that x causes y. In practice, the conclusions of researchers who found a definite *correlation* between x and y might have been more modest — that x *might* cause y. But when their paper is published, their university press release easily morphs into x *probably* causes y, and is then followed by screeching headlines in the newspapers that x *definitively* causes y. Seldom is any thought given to the possibility of confounding, or of reverse causality that it is in fact y that causes x. Or even that both x and y are caused by something else. For example, a hypothetical case: eating ice cream is found to be correlated with children drowning while swimming in the sea. This of course is not because children eat ice cream while swimming and then drown. It is far more likely that both swimming *and* eating ice cream tend to occur in warm weather.

---

36. S Floud et al, Body mass index, diet, physical inactivity, and the incidence of dementia in 1 million UK women, *Neurology*, 94 (2020), e123-e132.

37. Geoffrey Rose and Linda Colwell, 'Randomised Controlled Trial of Anti-Smoking Advice: Final (20 Year) Results', *Journal of Epidemiology and Community Health*, 46 (1992), 75–7.

Across the Thames estuary to Essex

Thursday June 5th, the next bit needed a lot of thought — a proper passage-plan even. We had to catch the strong tide at the right time to sweep us round the North Foreland, and the sea was going to be far shallower than I was used to. I needn't have worried. It was a brilliant sail in a southerly wind, with sunshine, on a flat sea. We were off Margate in an hour, past the very spot where Steve as a teenager had been helicoptered ashore from his capsized dinghy. Three hours later we entered the Swale between the Isle of Sheppey and the mainland. Luckily we had been warned about the one place where we might have been confused. In Ramsgate a skipper who kept his lovely old Nicholson 36 on the River Orwell across the Thames estuary in Essex knew the area very well: 'Watch out for the green and red buoys taking you through the Copperas Channel off the north Kent coast,' he said. 'They have been moved and are not where your chart thinks they are.'

Too right. As we sailed between the two buoys with a few feet under our keel the chartplotter had us apparently aground. As ever, rely on the buoys in a place like this where the seabed shifts around from year to year, not on the chart or the chartplotter that can never be completely up-to-date. Chartplotters are certainly not works of the devil as some Luddites might think, although they can be beguiling and too easily relied on. Nonetheless, for this creeping around these muddy shallows, and being sure that you are where you think you are, the chartplotter is invaluable. It was not at all like that when I last sailed across the Thames Estuary as a teenager with Peter Gallichan. I remember peering through the mist with binoculars to identify the next buoy, getting close enough to check its name against the chart, and then heading for the next but unseen buoy on a compass bearing.

Originally I had planned to go through the Swale to the Medway, but as ever we were paying a lot of attention to xcweather which warned of gales and rubbish weather on the coming Friday. We clearly needed to be in shelter by Thursday evening, a day earlier than planned, so we stopped and anchored just inside the Swale for the night, at Harty Ferry, a 27-mile four-hour sail. This is an extremely well-known and rather remote (for the south of England) anchorage, but that evening it was a disappointment. Maybe because by then it was raining, it was bleak, the land was flat of course, and we had to anchor quite far from the shore because it was shallow. If we had not been meeting Klim's daughter Beth, we would have stayed firmly on the boat. She lived in London and had driven out to what must have seemed to her, a metropolitan employment lawyer, far more remote than it was even to us, at the very end of the road on the distant Isle of Sheppey, in the middle of nowhere.

However, there was a pub. Unfortunately, the Ferry Inn, despite its reputation, was a bit of a disappointment too. No Thames bargemen propping up the bar anymore, of course, and no local anyone really because there are few locals to speak of. Small cosy rooms must have been combined to make an open-plan bar and restaurant area, typical of so many 'restored' old pubs. Horrible. But at least the open fire cheered us.

As is so common with children, Beth revealed things about her father that I didn't know. Apparently he is always under-equipped for the occasion, which is why he had only brought a thin cagoule for the cruise. I did know, however, that in 1943 his father had been shot down in the war and killed when Klim was only one year old. He had been flying a Mustang over Brittany, attacking a train. There had been an amazing and very recent update.

In Toulouse there lived a Frenchman, one Gilles Collavari, whose obsession was finding and identifying crash sites of planes that had been shot down over France during the war. In 2008 he was alerted to a crash that had been witnessed by Jean Denouel, a retired teacher in the small village of Plouigneau. As a teenager, Jean had found Klim's father's body a few hundred yards from the wreckage. He was probably buried locally, before being moved to a Commonwealth War Grave in Guidel, Brittany — this last Klim knew. Jean also remembered that the Germans took away the remains of the plane quite quickly. More than 60 years later, guided by Jean, Gilles with his metal detector discovered various small fragments of the Mustang that had been long embedded in the ground and forgotten, including the cockpit clock. Investigating through the internet, Gilles discovered the name of the pilot, Tony Willcock, who was 25 at the time. And from Jean that the pilot had a son called Christopher, written on the back of a photograph Jean had found in the dead pilot's pocket. Gilles posted this information on an RAF website, hoping for but not really expecting a response.

Unbeknown to Gilles, Klim has a different surname to Willcock because his mother remarried. What is more, Klim doesn't use the name Christopher. By chance, some years after Gilles's posting, a cousin of Klim's who was researching their family history found the entry on the RAF website, realised Tony Willcock was Klim's father, and alerted Klim. Naturally a very excited Klim contacted Gilles and in the spring of 2012 he visited Plouigneau, along with his children and grandchildren to meet

Gilles and Jean, and to see the site of the crash. To add to the poignancy Gilles presented Klim with the cockpit clock, stopped probably at the very moment the plane crashed. The whole family were royally entertained in the village by the mayoress, who gave a speech, and unveiled a plaque to commemorate Klim's father. She was accompanied by an RAF officer as well as by an officer from the French Air Force.

Wednesday 6th June, Harty Ferry transformed. The sun was out, the sky was blue, the sea was calm. A few local boats bobbed on their moorings, a Thames barge was hauling its sails out. There are no longer any working barges, and those that survive are cherished and looked after, and mostly I think used for charters. It all looked rather different to the busy Solent from a few days earlier, serene even. We were off and away by 11.30am. Rather than heading for London along what mariners used to call 'The London River', but now more usually the Thames estuary, we were pointing north, 36 miles across that estuary to Brightlingsea in Essex. Another grand sail, the 15–20 knot southwest to west wind was just right, it was warm and sunny, we didn't even bother to hoist the mainsail. Under genoa alone we were doing 6 knots, which was plenty, as we passed one and then another wind farm, easily picking out the buoys, turning left and right to avoid the sandbanks. How, I wondered, can people sail around with so little depth of water under their keels, just 12 feet across the Buxey sand where at very low tide cricket is played? It is a completely different navigational problem to Scotland where there are few sandbanks, but rocks to worry the east coast sailors who venture up there. Personally I prefer the small chance of hitting a single rock along a mile of coastline to finding the one small gap in a sandbank along a mile of coastline.

As we were by now expecting, the Brightlingsea harbour master was helpfulness itself. He told us where to go (a good thing given that there was only a foot of water under our keel), which pontoon to approach, and he was there to take our mooring ropes. He put us among the classic boats — which was nice, there are a lot along this part of the coast — all for £11 for the night. By 6.30pm we were well secured. Because the pontoon was not connected to the land we got lazy, didn't bother to inflate the dinghy, and stayed aboard for dinner even though we were only a few yards from the land and the local pub — a mere 'biscuit toss'. Greg would not have allowed that pub opportunity to pass him by.

These days Brightlingsea is a backwater, and very quiet it was, too, on the Thursday morning out of the holiday season. There are still some typical Essex houses with weatherboarding, a few with thatched roofs. But mostly this is a town of brick terraces and a seafaring long past. It had been the sixth of the Cinque Ports (which doesn't make sense but it's true).

I had an ulterior motive in picking Brightlingsea as a stop-over. In my last year at school my parents moved from suburban Beckenham to rural Beaumont-cum-Moze in northeast Essex (originally two parishes, 'beautiful hill' and 'marsh' in translation). Ivan Pawle, one of my best friends at school, lived in Brightlingsea, just a few miles away, with his grandmother, in Raggs Cottage. He was, and still is, a very good musician, a founding member of the experimental Irish folk group 'Dr Strangely Strange' (Greg, who has a huge vinyl collection, knew all about this rather obscure band). Ivan has lived in Ireland for years while still seeking stardom maybe. I suppose it is not too late to *remain* a rock star (Mick Jagger comes to mind) but it is surely too late for Ivan to *become* a rock star.

Ivan's grandfather had been lost at sea off the Wash. His parents had split up, and his father was a bit of an itinerant and not much around, something of a man of mystery. Much later it transpired that he may have been 'in intelligence', as they say. In 1962, hitchhiking to what was then Yugoslavia, Ivan and I stayed with an American friend his father had lived with in Paris, an expert cryptologist, so the suspicion makes sense. Ivan was far more worldly than me. During that trip he introduced me to croissants and baguettes in France, and yoghurt in Austria. And, unlike me, he could speak French.

So in Brightlingsea I was revisiting my youth again, not that I recognised much if anything of the town. My main memory was that Ivan and I had arranged a New Year party in 1963, but we had picked one of the most severe winters in living memory. It snowed so much that hardly anyone could get to Raggs Cottage, but those who did — including Annette my then girlfriend — spent the night in sleeping bags on the floor in front of a wonderful open fire.

The next morning Klim was so anxious to escape for a walk ashore that he summoned a water taxi at 9am. I think he found the confinement of a smallish boat not to his liking, at least not for several days at a time. It is more difficult when older if not used to it, and after all he had not experienced the depredations of boarding school. (By coincidence he had been at the co-educational grammar school just down the road from Haileybury where I was at the same time. I think we referred to his lot as 'oiks'. I daren't think what they called us.) The rest of us went ashore later for a bit of a wander, and had coffee in a deserted café in some sort of old hut.

This reminded me — again — that getting the crew psychology right is just as important as getting the navigation right. But what to do when they don't clean the cooker after washing the dishes (often not very thoroughly), don't clear up the crumbs all over the seats, don't put their clothes away, don't secure the saloon table at sea, don't tie back the cockpit locker's open lid before it slams shut in a sudden swell, and don't clean the decks properly. I could go on. And on. But one must not be bossy. Maybe I should pin up this 1907 C. C. Lynam thought: 'For a schoolmaster, a parson, a writer of books, an undergraduate, or a businessman to have to get the grease off a plate covered with the cold gravy of the mutton-chop; to compound to the satisfaction of his friends the porridge or the soup; to keep the cabin decently tidy and clean — each of these humble employments is excellent for the understanding and the temper.'[38]

To Harwich

Thursday June 7th, once more we had to get the tide under us, so didn't leave until midday knowing full well that dirty weather was on the way. Leaving was exciting. When I asked — well, ordered — Klim to let go of the stern mooring rope, he promptly obeyed and dropped the end that was tied to the boat rather than the end tied to the pontoon. (Lack of clarity on my part. And never overestimate a crew's competence.) The tide swung us round on the bow rope to exactly where I didn't want to be pointing. Somehow we re-secured the stern mooring rope, dropped off the correct end from the pontoon, and made our escape without damage or further embarrassment.

It was soon raining, harder and harder as we sailed close-hauled along the coast in a 10–15-knot wind. Past Clacton-on-Sea with its funfair where I had ridden on the roller coaster. Past Frinton-on-sea looking bleak and cold where my parents had a beach hut and where I remembered the grocer, the old-fashioned teashop, and walking on the greensward. Past Walton-on-the-Naze where my parents had finally lived in a small flat that my mother hated, but she loved the walks out to the Naze. Then, bearing away north, we sailed round the Naze itself.

The sea was coloured dirty-brown by Essex mud, even in the sun — when it shone. I was getting used to sailing in 20ft or so of water many miles from the shore. I had hoped to tie up and change crew at the Walton

---

38. C. C. Lynam, *The Log of the 'Blue Dragon', 1892–1904* (London: A. H. Bullen, 1907), xii.

and Frinton Yacht Club on the Walton Backwaters from where I had once sailed with my father. But, looking at the chart, and given the difficulty of getting right up the shallow river to lock in at just the right stage of the tide, and the poor weather, I decided to head for Harwich instead. Titchmarsh Marina on the delightfully named River Twizzle in the Walton backwaters was an option but it would have been too far from shops, pubs and a railway station, so Harwich it was, 22 miles for the day. A good decision.

There is a pontoon at the Ha'penny Pier, a Victorian wooden structure near the middle of the town. We arrived at 4.30pm when the harbour master appeared with two huge fenders to keep us off the pokey-out bits, remarking: 'We like to see the yachts going out of here looking as good as when they came in.' Ever helpful, he charged us a mere £40 for two nights (no longer a ha'penny), provided loads of local information, and pointed us firmly towards the pub which was offering 25% off their food. So to The Alma we went, except for Klim who again escaped fairly quickly after we tied up, to catch the train back to civilisation. Nonetheless he had clearly enjoyed the trip (enough to come again too). However he never did master lighting the gas cooker with a match, and he left behind the instant coffee he had insisted on buying. Others have left watermelons (far too big to store, and a great disappointment to eat), cup-a-soup (revolting), textured vegetable protein or TVP (I'm not a vegetarian), Bovril (never in small enough jars to avoid wastage), and curry paste (I'm not sure how to use it).

The Alma, in a side street by the harbour, was terrific. Adnams ale from Southwold up the coast, and a whole lobster for £15, finished off — as recommended by the owner — with a heart-warming Adnams brandy-like spirit, which in that chilly damp weather was just the job. Steve practised his embryonic Polish on one of the bar ladies. He surely wasn't learning Polish just to chat up the increasing number of young Polish women coming to work in the UK. But maybe he was. We talked to other diners, in English. That night the wind howled but we were snug. Such a good decision to get shelter a day early. Thank you xcweather — so much more accurate than an amateur like me could possibly be, however long I gazed at synoptic weather charts of the North Atlantic.

In the morning there were no trippers about; Harwich is not that sort of place, or maybe the horrible weather was keeping everyone indoors. It was all very quiet, hardly anyone to be seen, a few old people sitting on benches with or without dogs. The place had a dead feeling, and was clearly a bit of a backwater, a ferry port at the end of a railway line. Despite living not far from Harwich with my parents during university vacations, I had never been there except once as a small boy when I vaguely recall getting off the ferry from the Hook of Holland. There were no food shops we could find apart from a few boarded up, and just a couple of small convenience stores along with a surprising number of pubs, and a couple of junk shops. It seemed like a suburb of somewhere bigger. You have to go up the road towards Dovercourt for provisions, we were told. That is where my mother regularly went to the dentist to rescue her teeth which were falling apart, as mine are now. But I have the advantage of modern technology, implants at about £2000 a pop, three so far (with permission from my children to eat into their inheritance). That's geriatric dentistry for you.

However, Harwich has not always been a backwater, peripheral, and a bit down-at-heel. The master of the Mayflower came from Harwich, and the Mayflower may have been built here. The Pilgrim Fathers story has long been captured by Plymouth (the Mayflower steps, etc.), but the Mayflower had only called at Plymouth to pick up the pilgrims from another ship that had sprung a leak. Samuel Pepys had been the local MP, and Harwich was a port of importance. You do almost feel this in the town centre which is small, historic, and charming. Clearly a group of locals in the Harwich Society are keen to keep it that way.

There is an excellent maritime heritage trail past the cramped and crowded lifeboat museum looked after by a couple of elderly volunteers; old weatherboarded houses, one going back to 1450; the rare 17th-century Treadwheel Crane which never had a brake and so unsurprisingly the unfortunate men running around like rats inside the wheel had lots of accidents; the firmly locked St Nicholas church; and the restored Electric Palace Cinema harking back to the age of silent movies — one shilling for admission. The old leading lights were built in 1818, with the lower one on the shore, now a small museum. The higher one is further inland and looks like a lighthouse. You can clamber to the top, passing a series of small round rooms with fireplaces. It was once used as a council house complete with an Aga, a surprising badge of bourgeois aspiration.

Another reminder of the past was the restored 'LV18' tied up to the harbour wall, the last surviving manned lightship, built in 1958. Long ago it had hosted various pirate radio stations, and still contains memorabilia from that period — wirelesses and record players. As well as transmitting Radio Mi Amigo, it now boasts a garden on the foredeck. One can wander around to admire the original fixtures and fittings, and imagine what it must have been like tethered to the seabed, the crew tossed about in a gale, seasick, with no means of escape for days.

Peter left by train, back to New Zealand via France to visit friends, and then to Turkey to sail in warmer waters. He had become hooked on Bovril, that evil-smelling, black, sticky stuff which someone had insisted on bringing. But he is one of those strange people who never drink tea or coffee. I was pleased that as a renal physician he agreed with me that the modern cult of carrying a water bottle everywhere is completely mad. We are not all at imminent risk of dehydration and too many of those bottles are made of plastic.

Back on the pontoons Pickle was being battered by what turned into a force 9 gale. However, we had several mooring lines out and all was well. Other boats had come in for shelter including a 75-year-old Baltic Trader, the Queen Galadriel, looking a bit like a Thames barge. And the 1926 Spider T, a so-called Humber Super Sloop, which had been on the pageant. The skipper certainly looked the part as he slowly and skilfully edged his unwieldy vessel alongside the pontoon, a big man all the way round. He had been her skipper for 20 years, and clearly knew his stuff.

Pickle was fine, except that the instrument in the cockpit which electronically displays the wind direction and speed from the top of the mast was all over the place, and stayed that way for the rest of the trip. No matter, as a long-retired dinghy sailor I could still look up, not at a fluttering burgee but at the simple mechanical wind-direction indicator, even though this did still sometimes make me dizzy. I phoned home which seemed more than two weeks away, and was still standing. Cathie had just come back from the USA, and almost immediately spent a day in London, all too much I reckoned.

Brother John with Sally, his wife, turned up for another trip down memory lane, an older person's tendency. But first to The Alma again, for lunch where John entertained us with stories of his National Service in the navy, which interestingly had been partly spent making charts around Colonsay and the west side of Jura. And then off he drove us to Frinton to see Mary Barton, a very old friend of our parents who had also once lived in Beaumont. She lived alone in a flat overlooking by then a very rough sea. She must have been well into her 80s, but going strong, and absolutely on the ball. When I had been a medical student at St George's, she had come in to have most of her inflamed colon removed by Bryan Brooke, father of Nicky whom we had met in Poole. I, the soon-to-be-doctor, had felt very important visiting her, and I imagine it was reassuring for her to see a familiar face. Frinton had changed, but not by much over the years. It acquired its first pub in 2000, and in 2009 the railway level-crossing gates were replaced with lights, the man in the hut to operate them gone. But no amusement arcades yet, God forbid! The place was still douce, and rather up itself.

We drove on to Beaumont to see Bob Cole who was once married to Mary. He had been a farmer and had lived in the same house for 60 years. Bob was in his 90th year and, like Mary, still right on the ball. I had forgotten, or never knew, that he had been in the second world war, flying seaplanes. He and Mary had befriended my parents when they arrived in Beaumont in 1960, a connection made through the church he still took a hand in looking after, a church standing since the middle ages but much restored in the 19th and 20th centuries. The tattered banner of Viscount Byng of Vimy hung in the nave as it always had, just more tattered. The organ on which I used to surreptitiously play the blues sequence (my entire repertoire) was still there. And the familiar smell. But of what exactly? Damp? Hymn books? Naturally the trees in the churchyard were higher. Three had been planted in memory of my parents, with a plaque recording they had worshipped here. Their ashes are scattered under the trees. It was genuinely very touching.

It had been impossible for me, the church-going business, much to my parent's annoyance, changing gradually to disappointment and finally acceptance. The trouble was I couldn't sing and I didn't believe in God, the two rather crucial essentials for church-going. One attribute might have done, but I had neither. Nonetheless, I do love church architecture, and like Samuel Johnson I too 'look with reverence upon every place that has been set apart for religion'.[39] As an undergraduate I was always searching out monumental church brasses to rub; there were plenty in East Anglia. Churches are usually open but less often than they were, they are free to enter, and they provide shelter, and even sanctuary in times of unrest or personal turmoil. No other public spaces can claim so much. I still go into churches to admire them, for peace and calm, and for that ever-so-familiar smell. Their churchyards too are often a haven of peace and contemplation. Apart from castles and cathedrals, the humble parish churches are often the only physical remains of another age.

As I have already mentioned, my scientific scepticism must surely have come from, or at least been accentuated by, rows with my father. It couldn't have come from the very appropriate and long-standing Royal Society's

---

39. James Boswell, *The Journal of a Tour to the Hebrides with Samuel Johnson, LL.D.*, ed. R. W. Chapman (orig. 1785; Oxford: Oxford University Press, 1970), 270.

motto which I have only recently stumbled on: 'Nullius in verba' (take nobody's word for it). Have faith in God, my father told me, as did the school chaplain, and the local vicar. But where is the evidence? Of course, lack of evidence does not necessarily mean that something isn't true. I have no doubt the Church does good works, and its loss can blast a hole in a community's cohesion (along with closure of the local pub, shop, library and primary school). Where else can we all come together in a shared space? The vicar often has to act as a social worker, supporting the community in entirely admirable ways, particularly since the age of Thatcher and so-called neo-liberalism which has destroyed so much of our post-war welfare state, and hollowed out our local government services. On the other hand, competing religions can be the source of endless trouble. Protestant Christian versus Catholic Christian in Northern Ireland, Shia Muslim versus Sunni Muslim in the Middle East, Hindu versus Muslim in India. Maybe all this religious conflict is just what one must expect from the human condition. Even without religion conflict might — probably would — still exist.

Much to my surprise, I recently discovered that my father's father, Charles Ord Baumgarten, who changed his name back to his father's original name of Warlow in 1915, took part in a bit of history (my great-grandfather Warlow had changed his name after being adopted by a Reverend Baumgarten in about 1835). I knew my grandfather had been rector of St George's Church in Bloomsbury, an impressive and recently restored 1730 Hawksmoor building. Like any central London church it now seems to have little in the way of a congregation left to fill it, or look after it. My grandfather died long before I was born, and I had always imagined him as a very austere and conservative Victorian. What I didn't know was that in the early part of the 20th century St George's was regarded as the suffragettes' church. Indeed it was where my grandfather helped conduct Emily Davison's memorial service in 1913 after she had been run down by the King's horse at the Derby. Maybe his church was also chosen because he was a member of the Church League for Women's Suffrage and had once said that 'women's influence might enrich the nation'. He had even been in a deputation to 10 Downing Street to protest against forcible feeding of the suffragettes. For Londoners that memorial service was the funeral, with a crowd of 50,000 following the coffin from Victoria Station, although the real funeral took place the following day at Morpeth in Northumberland.

Godly people can certainly do good work. Perhaps my grandfather is where my rebellious streak comes from, bypassing my father who, to be fair, had a difficult life. Both his parents had died when he was young, the family ran out of money so he had to leave Haileybury before having a chance to get to university, and his career in insurance was interrupted by serving in the war. He was undoubtedly a good man, but to my regret I never told him that, or thanked him and my mother for their unstinting love and support.

Our old house in Beaumont looked much the same. The strung-out and scrappy village looked much the same too — still with no centre. The pub had gone, there was never a shop that I can remember, no local football or cricket team. John and Sally's old house had once been a pub in the neighbouring village, and it too looked the same. It even had the same owners to whom they had sold the house many decades ago. Ilona and I were married in the garden in 1976. This whole rather dull area of England, at least the interior bit, was so very familiar — the terrain, the feel of the air, the old weatherboarded houses surrounded, indeed swamped, by very dull 20th-century brick houses, and the views over the Walton backwaters made famous by Arthur Ransome in *Secret Water*. I am far too easily afflicted by nostalgia. Flat, muddy, Essex. Not a bad county really, and as Frank Cowper put it: 'Everyone hears of the gardens of Kent, the downs of Sussex, the heaths and forests of Hampshire, the combes of Dorsetshire, the lanes of Devon, and the tors of Cornwall; but Essex is only known for its marshes.' And yet 'Few counties have finer manor houses, more magnificent monumental tombs, timber work of nobler architectural character, than Essex.'[40]

Time to stop wallowing in the past, and move on — up north.

---

40. Cowper, *Sailing Tours*, part 1, p. 33.

Chapter 8

From Harwich to Edinburgh

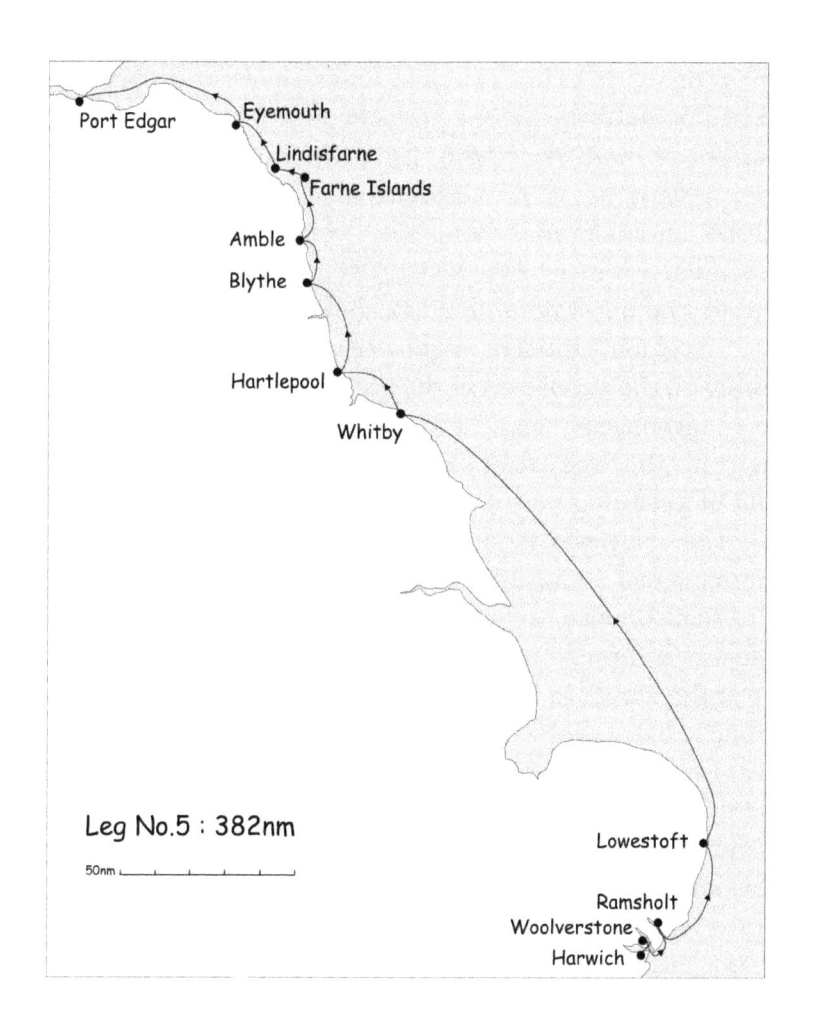

Leg No.5 : 382nm

Saturday June 9th, Steve left, and Stu Fisher, my old friend from university, arrived. He is from a many-generation colonial family in Zambia where he had been brought up before arriving in Cambridge to read medicine. He later worked in Zambia for a few years, but then he and his family left for a safer and easier life in England. Having been out of the UK health system for a long time, he was lucky to land a consultant respiratory and general physician post in Milton Keynes. Stu had sailed with me for years, but not regularly enough to pick up many of the essentials. And he does tend to fall asleep while steering. Nonetheless, he is terrific company, full of crazed yarns about Africa, and something of an amateur naturalist, once having discovered a new African butterfly. In the past he had been a very strong crew, well able to pull up stuck anchors and the like. He had been quite a climber too, but was now increasingly disabled, gradually more unsteady, going up steps one at a time, and he had rather clumsy and weak hands. I had no idea whether the problem or problems were 'neurological', 'orthopaedic', or more likely both. It was impossible to get a proper story from him because he would keep changing the subject, casting out red herrings like an ankle injury long ago (which certainly wouldn't explain clumsy hands). Stu being Stu, he was avoiding going to a doctor of any sort, even to find out if nothing much could be done — which is what he believed. That gloomy thought might well apply to a neurological condition like pressure on the spinal cord in the neck from a form of arthritis, but less likely to an orthopaedic one that might be fixable with surgery.

A few years after this cruise Stu did have his arthritic ankle fused, but with a lot of persisting postoperative pain and serious disability requiring crutches. The ankle was in the wrong position and had to be re-fused. Sadly he remained unsteady, but at least with his foot pointing in the right direction. Problem definitely not solved. In 2020 he eventually saw a neurologist. It turned out he has a rare slowly progressive inflammatory disorder of the nerves in his arms and legs. Sometimes it is treatable, but the treatment hasn't worked for him, probably because the disease is too advanced. Even back in 2012 he was becoming a liability on the boat, but he enjoyed himself, took time to do lots of maths for an Open University degree, and he was — as I said — excellent company. We made sure to look after him, but sadly he is now too disabled to crew again.

These days consultants are so specialised in 'their own thing' that a patient like Stu can easily land up with a consultant who does not see the whole picture, or with completely the wrong specialist — fragmented medicine. A neurologist might well not recognise any orthopaedic problem, while

Stu's orthopaedic surgeon clearly didn't recognise his neurological problem. Furthermore, fragmented medicine can lead to the same 'disease' being divided up between different specialists. For example, a patient with giant cell arteritis (an inflammatory disorder of blood vessels) who has gone blind in one eye would be seen by an ophthalmologist. But the same disease could cause a stroke so a neurologist might be involved; muscle pains so a rheumatologist; depression so a psychiatrist; weight loss a gastroenterologist. Not one of the specialists sees the whole picture of the disease, or can manage its ramifications in a single patient who may be 'looked after' by several specialists who are not necessarily good at communicating with each other. They may even work in different hospitals with different sets of hospital records for the same patient.

As well as fragmentation, over-specialisation leads to specialists, including neurologists, tending to over-diagnose their 'own disease'. 'Give a man a hammer and he will see every problem as a nail' is only too true. As a neurologist I often had to remove the diagnosis of stroke made by a stroke specialist, and reassure the patient the problem was only migraine, or possibly functional. Detaching patients from the wrong stroke diagnosis (not always easy) not only reduces their anxiety but means they don't have to take statins, aspirin and blood pressure-lowering drugs for ever, or have their car and travel insurance compromised.

A related problem is trying to find out who is in overall charge of a particular patient, if anyone. Someone must surely put their hand up for the task, and this doctor may well need input from several specialists. Leaving it to the GP to gather all the medical strands together is hardly appropriate for a relatively rare disease like giant cell arteritis, while having several different specialists, each tinkering with the same treatment (corticosteroids in this case), can lead to disaster. Maybe we should go back to the days when there were far more general physicians, before specialists emerged. They dealt with everything that was thrown at them — but sometimes not very well, partly because it was so difficult for the generalist to keep up-to-date across the whole spectrum of fast-evolving medicine. And maybe because, as the neurologist Henry Miller waspishly observed: 'The specialist is more likely to appreciate his limitations and less reluctant to seek specialized help for a patient outside his field than the optimistic generalist.'[1]

So we are stuck unless the various specialists are easily able to talk to each other. This means putting them in the same, necessarily large hospital,

---

1. Henry Miller, *Medicine and Society* (Oxford: Oxford University Press, 1973), 29.

large enough to contain all the specialist departments. And making sure there is plenty of opportunity for them to chat — corridors rather than lifts to prolong the chance encounter, well-organised and attractive medical meetings, and enough time to have lunch in a congenial space. It is ludicrous for example to put neurology in a separate hospital. During my consultant career I never worked in a proper hospital with all the relevant specialist departments on one site, or even an A&E department. Not in Oxford or Edinburgh. Oxford and Edinburgh have at last seen the errors of their ways, but not the National Hospital for Neurology and Neurosurgery in London. It remains isolated, a mile from University College London Hospital where all the other specialities are clustered. To get between them you have to put on your hat and coat, and walk for 20 minutes. A pleasant walk, but madness for patient care.

It is not easy to see a colleague as a patient, let alone one who is a friend like Stu. There is always an added tension, perhaps because of feeling unable to delve into a proper history, and presuming the doctor-as-patient knows more about his or her medical problem than is the case. But I knew exactly the consultant Stu should see — Kevin Talbot, a neurologist in Oxford with a good general medical background, and who would not tolerate any bullshit. He was in his early fifties, the best age for a doctor who by then is highly experienced after more than ten years as a consultant, but not so old as to be bored and burnt-out. But in 2019 even he was nearly defeated by trying to disentangle Stu's history, and emailed me after their meeting: 'It was a lively encounter. Most doctors are poor historians but he is in his own league. Such that one of my more "hard-wired" colleagues thought he was frontal [doctor slang, lesions of the frontal lobe causing disinhibition]. I agreed with Stu that he was cognitively normal, but dilatory, circumlocutory and tangential in his responses. He said, "I'll take that as a compliment!"'

It may be wise to avoid seeing very newly appointed consultants who these days have had their training attenuated by over-compliance with the European Working Time Directive. They have had far less hands-on experience than my generation. Sometimes they have a clock-watching mentality as well as a 'not-my-job' attitude, along with over-rigid adherence to guidelines and algorithms un-tempered by clinical judgement, and perhaps a rather weak commitment to persevere with a problem until it is solved. Through no fault of their own they are hampered by 'job-plans' and paid 'sessions' which allow and even encourage the view that it is OK to knock off before a job is done, with 'I am not doing more sessions than

I am paid for'. Treat professionals like employees for long enough and they will surely behave like employees. Having said all that, the surgeon who removed half my colon had only been a consultant for 18 months, but he had been carefully chosen by the older and experienced physician who knew how skilled he was.

When I felt very ill and developed a high temperature and a painful calf, I went to hospital where (just about reasonably) I was put through the deep vein thrombosis (DVT) leg ultrasound scanning protocol. Not surprisingly it came back negative because my temperature was much higher and I was more ill than would be expected with a DVT, and my blood tests screamed 'infection'. So I didn't have a DVT (which I knew, as did Cathie who was keeping a sharp eye on my medical attendants), but what did I have? This was not really revealed even though the radiographer wielding the ultrasound machine told me that he could see gas bubbles in my calf muscle. I had no blood culture to test for infection and was discharged, albeit on antibiotics, and I got better. Presumably I had had a bacterial infection in my calf, and probably in my blood too, a very rare condition but unproven in my case. This wasn't so much fragmented medicine as blinkered medicine driven by too many protocols.

By contrast with Stu, the other crew, my second son Oli, was young, at 27 years old, strong, and very familiar with sailing from childhood when Scottish west coast family sailing was compulsory. He had plans later in the year to climb El Cap, the 3000-foot vertical cliff in the Yosemite National park, which he did, solo, taking a week. Bonkers in my view, sleeping in a hammock thing attached to the cliff face, carrying all his food and water, as well as his climbing gear, and his own poos. This needs the right psychology as well as climbing ability. Apparently, almost no one comes to grief on those huge cliffs, either because they have to be very competent climbers to even contemplate the climbs, or because the protection on the face is so good. Oli is certainly a very good climber, a skill much honed as an undergraduate and then PhD student at Newcastle University. Quite how all this climbing fitted in with a career as a mechanical engineer was difficult for Ilona and me to fathom, but he has turned out fine, nowadays doing complicated sums on computers to make wind turbines more efficient. Thankfully he was never tempted to use his mathematical skills to earn his fortune in the City of London.

Oli and Stu had plenty to talk about, climbing chit-chat which rather left me out — but that was OK, as I was brooding about the sailing along the east coast.

A short hop, to the Butt and Oyster at Pin Mill

That afternoon our plan was to meander five miles up the River Orwell, past the huge cranes of the Felixstowe container port, to Pin Mill. The wind had died down but was still strong so we used a partially unfurled genoa for the two-hour sail, gently tacking up the river under a warming sun. I have tended to use just the genoa more and more often. The boat sails very well without the mainsail, even close-hauled. Using the mainsail is altogether more stressful, particularly if the wind is up your back with the risk of a mainsail gybe and a crack on the head from a wildly swinging boom. It is far easier to control just the genoa rather than both sails when single-handed, or with young children. And people learning to sail can more easily see the genoa tell-tales, small strands of wool or other light material, fluttering in the wind; this helps them understand the laminar, or not-so-laminar, flow across what is essentially an aerofoil. If those small bits of wool attached to the front of the sail are not flying back horizontally then something is wrong. If the one on the side of the sail on to which the wind is blowing flicks up, the boat is heading too close to the wind. Although you may think you are approaching your target better you are in fact travelling slower and being pushed away from your course by the wind, in effect sliding sideways. If the tell-tales on the other side flick up, you are sailing too far away from the wind, away from your target and you need to head more towards the wind to get the tell-tales flying horizontally, and so your destination. Simple. But it requires concentration uninterrupted by distracting chit-chat in the cockpit.

From a previous trip crewing up the east coast I knew how difficult it would be to find an unoccupied mooring, or enough room to anchor, within easy reach of the Pin Mill slipway. And that the slipway doesn't extend far enough to make for a mud-free dinghy arrival, or departure, at low tide. So we motored a little further upriver to tie up in the marina where there were rather a lot of glitzy yachts and a few over-large motorboats. But not so much further that we couldn't take a lovely evening stroll through beautiful woods and fields of waving barley back to Pin Mill for a pint and supper. The Essex-Suffolk border really is a lovely part of the country, at least the coastal part.

It is real Arthur Ransome country. The children in *We Didn't Mean to Go to Sea* (from the *Swallows and Amazons* series) inexpertly anchored the Goblin off where the Felixstowe cranes are now, but drifted away on the tide to end up improbably in Holland where even more improbably Daddy on his way home on leave from his destroyer in the China Seas just happened to be there to find them. Ransome was good at picking the very best watery locations for his children's books — the Lake District, the Norfolk Broads, the Hebrides, the Walton Backwaters, as well as the rivers Orwell and Stour (and the Caribbean for *Peter Duck*).

The Butt and Oyster at Pin Mill is a fabulous and justly well-known pub, fulfilling everything a pub should be. Right on the waterside, real ale, cosy public rooms, animated, historic, decent pub grub, and outside seating for when the sun shines, which it was that evening. A real pub on a real river, with various types of boats — ancient and modern — bobbing on moorings, Thames barges resting in the mud, and the occasional quite big ship going up to Ipswich.

We were joined by Martin Rossor, and his wife Eve. Martin is another neurologist friend, well known in his field of dementia. More to the point, he had kept a boat on the River Deben for years and the next day he was to be our pilot to Woodbridge where we were due to meet my oldest daughter Margaret off the train from London. We had to make a proper passage-plan to get there at the top of the tide, pick her up, and then quickly escape back down the river before the water disappeared from under us.

To the River Deben across the bar

Sunday June 10th, sunshine. We left the marina at 11.15am with the wind in the south. Because we had to get the timing exactly right for the 17 miles to Woodbridge, we soon abandoned tacking to motor down the Orwell to the open sea where we could turn to port and set sail. We got to the tricky entrance to the Deben at 3.30pm, switched the engine on, took down the sails, and crossed the bar. I had been there before, albeit as crew, so was not too daunted by how close one has to get to the shore before turning sharpish to starboard, with the sound of waves breaking on the shallows over your right shoulder and the land uncomfortably close to port. And then having to avoid that notorious sandbank just inside the entrance, right in the middle of the river.

Martin was a cautious pilot; he didn't want to damage someone else's boat. He shouldn't have worried. Although Pickle is quite a bit bigger than his own boat, and draws more water, he knew the river so well with all its twists and turns that he could guide me along, often between rows of moored boats, with no problem. He is a real east coast sailor. I mentioned how nervous I had been with less than 15ft of water under my keel in the Thames Estuary, to which he replied, 'I get nervous with more than 15ft!'

How well we did. We arrived at Woodbridge exactly an hour before high tide and there was Margaret just arrived, sitting on the harbour wall. We only went aground — gently — at the very last moment, and for mere seconds before we motored free, such is the softness of Suffolk mud. Oli was off in the dinghy in a flash to collect Margaret and deposit Martin back on Suffolk soil (he was working in London the next day). Then a quick motor back down the river on the ebbing tide, following the earlier track we had taken, to Ramsholt where we picked up Martin's mooring. After wintering ashore he had not yet got his boat in the water. Sadly the tide was really too strong, and we were too far away, to get to another lovely pub, the Ramsholt Arms, right on the river. Besides, it was raining. So it was spaghetti bolognese followed by rhubarb pie on board, and a viewing of an episode of *Miranda* on Margaret's laptop — such wonderful TV comedy.

The two grown-up children and Stu were a very different sort of crew to the last lot. They were not so obsessed with the news on the radio. The days were no longer punctuated by the Today Programme from 6 to 9am, the World at One, PM at 5pm, more news at 6pm and again at 10pm. I was even beginning to wean myself off my addiction to newspapers (soon to relapse). There was climbing talk between Stu and Oli, and much yarning about Africa from Stu. Maybe a bit too much, but this was not inappropriate because Margaret was in between being the doctor for a party of tourists trekking to Everest Base Camp and for another group to Mount Kilimanjaro (as well as to India and Guyana later that year). After passing (first time) the exam for membership of the Royal College of Physicians (MRCP), she had taken a year out from the grind of hospital medicine during which she also collected the Diploma of Tropical Medicine at The London School of Hygiene and Tropical Medicine.

After her medical studies in Sheffield Margaret worked there as a junior hospital doctor for two years, before moving to Newcastle upon Tyne for another couple of years as a slightly less junior hospital doctor. Now there was this year out, and after that off for GP training. Thankfully she had abandoned the idea of becoming a cardiologist. I can't imagine anything more boring than sticking catheters up coronary arteries morning, noon and night, working shifts too. And what happens when their main disease — of the coronary arteries — disappears, which it may do in the next 50 years or so? Even the kidneys are more interesting than the heart, such a boring lump of muscle. Nor was Margaret having any truck with the modern and boring medical training sausage-machine in which young doctors pass seamlessly from one pre-ordained post to another, sometimes in the same part of the country, even occasionally in the same hospital, to become a consultant or GP — so-called 'run-through training'. Far better to get around and about, see the world. But this strategy does depend on having the right rebellious attitude, and on not being 'attached' to anyone who might not be able or willing to follow your zigs and zags. During the first three years after qualification I did five six-month jobs, in four hospitals, so what was I doing for the other six months? Some locum neurosurgery, a bit of locum general practice, a little travelling, some lazing about.

My generation had to move from place to place to train, and quite right too, although it could be stressful. Before eventually settling in Edinburgh I worked in Birmingham (where I re-learned to glide), in London (where I learned some mime skills), in Aberdeen (where I learned to ski), and in Oxford (where I started married life and where my three oldest children were born). In one way I was lucky. Until Oxford I had not been 'encumbered' with a wife who might well have had her own ideas of where she wanted to work and live. I did not have to compromise on where I wanted to work in those days when it was still just about acceptable for a wife to follow her husband and put his career before hers. Besides, doctors were then mostly men, and wives were often nurses so they could quite easily get jobs wherever their husbands picked up training. This is now much harder because so many more doctors are women and marry doctors or other professionals, and couples naturally want to pursue their careers in the same place. This may not work out which leads to weekend commuting, sometimes over large distances, hardly ideal in the short term and definitely not in the long term.

In my medical school year a couple of students got married to each other and were lucky enough to both land their first job in the same hospital. They were on call alternate nights but unfortunately not on the same nights. To make matters worse, the hospital declined to provide them with a double instead of the customary single bed (we lived in the hospital in those days). So the couple bought their own double bed and sometimes got to sleep in it together. My advice to Margaret has always been to find a portable partner, maybe a plumber or a poet.

There are rather few GPs like Margaret who have the MRCP. Too many medical graduates go too early into GP training after medical school and lack experience of both hospital medicine, and life in general. Unfortunately there is a workforce crisis in general practice. Fewer medical students want to do it, and many that become GPs leave prematurely for other medical jobs, emigrate temporarily or permanently, or take early retirement. To compound matters, the huge increase in consultant numbers in the last decades has not been even nearly matched by an equivalent rise in GP numbers (their numbers fell from a peak of 67 per 100,000 population in 2009 to 60 in 2018), while the UK population increased.[2] Part of the problem may be that medical schools don't always encourage a career in general practice, particularly those like Edinburgh which seem to want all their graduates to be scientists as well as doctors. Why otherwise has Edinburgh insisted that all their medical students take an extra year to do a BSc? Of course there is no reason why GPs should not be scientists as well as doctors. John Fry was one, in his epidemiological way, but not in the Edinburgh Medical School way of working in a lab with rats and molecules. And his job as a 'mere' GP in California didn't stop Lawrence Craven in the early 1950s being the first to suggest aspirin might prevent heart attacks and strokes. His mistake was to publish in the *Mississippi Valley Medical Journal*, which was hardly of any great impact (and is now defunct), so no one noticed at the time.[3]

We need both sorts of research — laboratory-based so-called basic science, and patient-based so-called clinical science. Each has their different traditions and methodologies, and for that reason alone they can learn from each other. But first of all basic and clinical scientists have to communicate, and to do that they have to mix together in the same buildings, cafés and pubs. Very few people are able to be excellent, or even very good, at both basic and clinical research. The world has got too complicated. Personally I think clinicians are wasted in basic science, but they should work *with* basic scientists. We clinicians have the advantage of access to patients because we look after them; basic scientists only have access through us (and even then maybe just to a blood sample). This is very relevant in neurosurgery where only the neurosurgeons have direct access to the human brain. It is this that should be exploited in their research — not experimenting on rats.

Other problems for general practice are far too much time-wasting bureaucracy, box-ticking imposed by distant mangers doing politicians' bidding, tedious algorithms purporting to be care pathways but inhibiting thought, an over-abundance of guidelines also inhibiting thought,

---

2. W. Palmer, 'Is the Number of GPs Falling across the UK?', Nuffield Trust blog, 8 May 2019.

3. Lawrence L. Craven, 'Experiences with Aspirin (Acetylsalicylic Acid) in the Nonspecific Prophylaxis of Coronary Thrombosis', *Mississippi Valley Medical Journal*, 75 (1953), 38–44.

responding to top-down incentives which increase the practice income but not necessarily patient health, not having the time to meet with colleagues over coffee or lunch, increasing numbers of patient complaints (which became particularly unreasonable during the Covid-19 pandemic), exposure to litigation, and the fear of making a mistake during a career in that most difficult of specialities. But they have one enormous advantage over hospital consultants — a privilege too — in being able to visit people at home, in the context of their family circumstances, as do vicars and social workers. People who live in damp, overcrowded and crumbling rented properties have rather different health needs than those living in gilded mansions behind locked gates. Unfortunately GP home visits are less often achieved in these time-pressured days.

To Lowestoft, the most easterly town in the UK

We dropped the mooring at the ungodly hour of 4.15am. We had to get out of the Deben at high water when our chances of going aground were least, and we wanted to catch as much of the ebb tide as possible up the 39 miles of coast to Lowestoft. It was overcast, grey, drizzling, and the colour of the water was somewhere between shit-yellow and shit-brown. Not encouraging as under motor we slipped over the bar with 10ft under the keel. Unfortunately the wind was not only from the northeast which is where we wanted to go, but at 20 knots we needed two reefs in the mainsail which we hoisted at 5.30am. The wind got stronger, and the sea got rougher, as we put in long tacks up the coast and shorter tacks out again until we could hardly see any land at all.

The trouble with having Margaret on board is that she seems to bring bad weather with her. This is doubly distressing because, of my older children, she is the one who gets most seasick. Not surprisingly she was soon sick, and cold, and sick again. Stu stayed down below most of the time, tucked up in his bunk doing some maths interspersed with trips to the heads. He had a typically male prostate problem, which again he wouldn't have fixed. We did have urinary catheters on board, just in case anyone's prostate blocked the flow of urine, which leads to extremely painful over-filling of the bladder. So far so good, they are all still in their packets, possibly beyond their 'best-before-dates'.

Oli was brilliant, helming most of the way. He had of course sailed with me for as long as he could remember, so he was a great person to have on board. He is not a man of many words but is strong and very reliable, quick to act when the spinnaker boom suddenly fell off its clip on the mast and crashed to the foredeck. He rushed forward to sort it out, covered in waves breaking over the bows. Again it was a lost split-pin problem, as with the kicker earlier. (Must be more careful to check every split-pin there is.)

Do I like sailing in this sort of weather? No, not really, but needs must. You can't stay in port for too long if you have new crew to pick up further along the coast, and anyway it gets boring. Cabin fever can be very debilitating. But I do often curse myself for subjecting the crew to discomfort they are not used to, and seasickness, like poor Margaret. Years ago sailing off Greece in the middle of the night, one of the women in the crew asked me, 'Do you really enjoy this?' Yes, I did; it was warm and dry. But she didn't come sailing again, and she certainly would not have enjoyed the North Sea on that miserable day.

I had wanted to get into Orford and take a look at the castle, but with a very shallow and tricky entrance that I had never attempted, no Martin Rossor as pilot, and with the wind at least partially onshore, that was not going to be sensible. In fact it would have been crazy. And with Southwold a few miles further on almost as tricky as Orford, it had to be to Lowestoft or Great Yarmouth — even though neither was that easy with narrow harbour entrances, and by then quite an onshore swell to think about. By midday the tide was against us and we were still four miles from Lowestoft. The wind was against us too, so much so that we could see on the chartplotter the hopelessness of our tacks in getting us further north, at an angle between them of about 60° instead of 90°. So, on with the engine for a bit of assistance.

I was nervous about getting in to Lowestoft with an onshore wind and swell, but at least with the chartplotter there would be no worries about finding the buoys and dodging the offshore sandbanks. Margaret was desperate to stop and not have to suffer pressing on to Great Yarmouth, which anyway is not an attractive place to visit, even though the entrance is easier I believe. I even considered running back to the shelter of Harwich but rejected that, in part because we had a date in Whitby on the Friday to pick up new crew. It is so much easier finding shelter on the west coast of Scotland, where there are far more options — plan B, C, D, E and more.

Having got the sails down and the engine on, and rolling badly, we contacted Lowestoft Harbour Control who were not altogether helpful, saying it was my decision whether we tried to enter, or not. These 'do we don't we?' decisions are rightly up to the skipper, but it would have helped to be told about the sea conditions at the harbour entrance. Nothing daunted, we decided to give it a go. Oli was on the helm as we lined up with the entrance at 2pm (just 39 miles had taken a long time). I had drawn a line to follow on the chartplotter that I was watching down below. Off we crabbed at a 45° angle to the coastline to allow for the strength of the flood tide pushing us to port. Typically the waves got bigger as we approached the harbour entrance, and more confused as they reflected off the harbour walls. And the sea got shallower. To complicate matters, a small ship was coming up behind us which I thought was going to go past as we went in, bringing with it even more difficulty. But no, we heard them talking on the VHF radio to Harbour Control — their plan was to get close behind us to give us some shelter from the wind and swell, and, as they put it, 'allow the small boat to shoogle in through the entrance'. How very helpful. So shoogle we did, straightening up at the very last moment between the harbour walls. All very sporting and not quite as difficult as the Sailing Directions made out, at least in retrospect. Nonetheless, we were mightily relieved to find ourselves on the flat water of the outer harbour, out of the wind, and with plenty of space to consider where to go next.

There was a choice of three places. After some thought we opted for the Royal Norfolk and Suffolk Yacht Club pontoons as being nearest the centre of town. However, with the wind straight up our stern we did not do well. There was no space on the long pontoon to port, and before we hit the wall at the end we had somehow to do a hand-break turn to port and stop. As ever it was a mess — but somehow we got close enough to a pontoon where three men who happened to be there caught our ropes and hauled Pickle to safety without us hitting anything, right under the very attractive clubhouse. How I hate marinas. Give me a spot to anchor anytime and I am happy; there's nothing to scrape or bump into. Mind you, it was worse in Lowestoft before it had pontoons. When Hilaire Belloc sailed into what he referred to as 'the unpleasant harbour of Lowestoft' he had to tie up 'criss-cross' to an 'entanglement' of buoys, far too close together.[4] No wonder he and other sailors at the time often preferred to anchor out in a roadstead, even if swell and wind made it uncomfortable. They didn't then have to jostle with other boats in harbours, or get in and out of harbours with no engines to help.

I didn't know what I expected of Lowestoft. It didn't look too encouraging,

---

4. Hilaire Belloc, 'The North Sea', in *The Hills and the Sea* (London: Methuen and Co., 1906), 1.

and the peeling sign ' owes oft Station' did not inspire much hope. It ought to make something of being the UK's most easterly town, attract more tourists, and then maybe it would not feel such a broken-down sort of a place. As Oli pointed out to me, it could be the start of a roughly 650-mile east-west cycle route to the most westerly point of the UK mainland, Ardnamurchan Point, a much more inspiring destination than either Land's End or John o' Groats at each end of the popular north-south cycle route of 870 miles.

There weren't many people in the centre of town, but there were a remarkable number of electric mobility scooters, some aggressively storming along the pavements scattering pedestrians as they went. Somewhere I read that lots of mobility scooters are correlated with poverty. The town was badly damaged in the war, hence the uninspiring post-war buildings in the main street. There seemed to be very little left of historic Lowestoft, and no obvious preservation society as there was in Harwich. It was all very scrappy and down-at-heel. Unfortunately I managed to miss the Maritime Museum (a reason to return one day, perhaps). However, there were the shops we needed, in particular a chemist so Margaret could get some antibiotics to take in her medical bag to Kilimanjaro.

The yacht club was more or less empty, but the staff were friendly, the showers good, and the meals not bad. I wonder how they keep such a magnificent 1902 Grade 2-listed building going. One member told me that he kept his boat in Lowestoft because it was cheap, even though, 'Let's face it, there is nowhere to cruise to!' Indeed not. Turn left out of the harbour and there is just Great Yarmouth up the coast, turn right and there are those tricky river entrances and nothing safe until you get to Harwich. Across the North Sea to Holland is far too far for a weekend jaunt. However, that didn't bother one Dutch boat coming the other way, overnight. The late middle-aged but clearly horribly fit couple leapt on to the pontoon, unfolded their bicycles and headed off to Norwich to do some tourism and shopping, more than 60 miles there and back. Makes me feel breathless just thinking about it.

I was getting used to the harbourside chat from onlookers gazing at Pickle, along the lines of:

'Why do you call your boat Pickle?'

'Because of the Trafalgar story, and the dead cat.'

'Why is she green?'

'Far nicer colour than white, but does show up the scratches.'

'Why do you have a tiller and not a wheel on a boat that size?'
'Because I prefer it, gives a better feel for the wind and sea.'
'Have you got a spinnaker?'
'Yes, but we don't use it a lot, too much of a hassle.'
'Do you sail alone?'
'Sometimes because I'm beginning to run out of crew as they age with me, but only in familiar waters where I can anchor and avoid the traumas of tying up to pontoons like here.'

We took a day out on the Tuesday, partly because Margaret had to leave the next day by which time we could not have dropped her off at our next stop of Whitby (where we didn't need to be until the Friday evening in any case). For old times' sake, I wanted to see the Norfolk Broads so we jumped on a little train for Oulton Broad a couple of miles away. Just £4 return for the four of us from that rather clapped-out 'owes oft Station'.

Was it around here or Great Yarmouth when as a teenager I was sailing on the Broads just with my father and he was hit by something, maybe the boom, which cut his forehead badly enough to require a visit to the local hospital casualty department? I remember being left alone on the boat while he got himself patched up, coming back with stitches. A more definite Broads memory was 'shooting' the exceedingly low and narrow medieval Potter Heigham road bridge. At the last moment we lowered the mast with the sails still up, and with our remaining momentum we could also get through the adjacent railway bridge (now gone) before hauling up the mast again and sailing smugly on. I believe you now have to hire a pilot, which must be no fun at all.

How well I remembered the typical Broads scenery as we walked along from Oulton station. So much wide-open sky, the flat, flat landscape, miles of reeds, distant sails apparently drifting slowly across the fields. The place was empty of people, too early in the season I suppose. Empty pub for lunch, empty café for tea, a small museum — also empty.

That evening David Dick turned up in a suit and tie fresh from his neurology clinic in Norwich. He drove us the 22 miles to his home in Kirstead next to the beautiful old church, for dinner. He would be joining us later on Pickle. His wife Roz, who had been a secretary in the hospital where David and I trained as neurologists, cooked us an excellent meal, very seasonal – the starter was asparagus, Parma ham and Parmesan. Then David drove us all the way back to Pickle where we indulged ourselves with another episode of *Miranda* on Margaret's laptop before bed.

To Yorkshire, skipping Lincolnshire

Wednesday June 13th, goodbye to Margaret at 7am and off we went in the sunshine on a calm sea. It was to be a long sail to Whitby, 150 miles away. I had decided against stopping along the north Norfolk coast because most harbours or their entrances are too shallow for a keel-boat like Pickle to get in and out, particularly as we were at neap tides. Wells-next-the-Sea would have been lovely to visit, but too shallow even though boats are now monitored on CCTV cameras and guided by the harbour master on the VHF radio up the winding river between the red and green buoys ('you are too far to starboard, a little bit to port now', etc.). Nor did I fancy the detour up the Humber because it is a long way to Hull, and even to Grimsby.

The wind was predicted to shift from northwest to north to northeast to east during the day — not too bad if it really was going to do that. We started on the port tack, with the tide just beginning to ebb under us, sailing beside the flat Norfolk coastline inshore of yet another of the wind farms springing up all round the coast. Irritatingly, at 3pm off the north Norfolk coast the wind faded and we had to start the engine. At least it wasn't smelly like Calypso's. On we motored northwards, checking we had plenty of fuel, until we could put the sails up again at 9pm. But the wind didn't last and we ended up motoring through the night, past gas- or maybe oilrigs, lit up like Christmas trees. There were not many ships to dodge off the Humber, and seeing their AIS signals on the chartplotter made it no problem anyway. Oli and I shared the watches, mostly motoring over a flat sea, which was tedious until we could get the sails up again at about 6am.

The Wash was more difficult in 2018 when Oli and I crossed it again, this time further west aiming for the Humber, and so of necessity between the proliferating wind farms where all the other boats were clustered too. This required serious concentration in the dark, close-hauled, trying to figure out the tides, but thankfully by then with our own AIS transmitter to alert us to passing ships, as well as the receiver.

But in June 2012 on we went leaving all those sandbanks in the Wash behind, eventually flying the cruising chute, close past Flamborough Head in a light and by then northeast wind. I began to feel almost at home — while it wasn't even nearly Scotland, it was very definitely not the south of England. The French chatter on the VHF had disappeared, the sea was blue again, the evenings were lighter, and at last there were many more seabirds. Not just aggressive seagulls but puffins, guillemots, gannets and fulmars.

Also off the Yorkshire coast on an empty sea there was plenty of space, no big white plastic motorboats, no yachts, and no coastal shipping to speak of. It was very different in the 19th century, McMullen complaining, 'The greatest drawback to sailing on the east coast of England is, that it is cursed with unmanageable screw steamers, far beyond any other coast in the world.'[5]

As the afternoon wore on it got warmer, the coastal scenery improved with lovely cliffs stretching on past Filey and Scarborough — places I had never been to by either land or sea. Off Robin Hood's Bay we were able to bear away for Whitby but couldn't keep the cruising chute full so down it came (successfully). At least there was some wind. Whitby beckoned as it has for several centuries. Greenvile Collins again: 'To the northward of Robinhood-Bay lieth Whitby, where Ships enter at high-water into a River, where you lie dry at Low water… There is a Rock lieth off, the Mark to sail clear of it is Whitby Church Steeple open to the Northward of the South Point of the Harbour.'[6]

What an attractive place Whitby is for the cruising sailor, easy to enter (except for some issues with depth at low water springs and no doubt in an easterly gale) — and what a fabulous place to wander around, and to hang out in. We arrived shortly after the 100-year-old swing bridge closed so couldn't get into the marina immediately, but we could tie up to the holding pontoon. The whole place was buzzing with pubs, chippies, and chatter. It was a lovely evening to explore the town, on both sides of the harbour, past the statue of James Cook overlooking the huge sandy beach, the kiss-me-quick English seaside attractions, and a 40% scale reproduction of the Endeavour for trips round the bay (the 'Captain Cook Experience'). Now there is a really awful Disneyfied, full-scale, steel Endeavour reproduction tied up in the harbour, minimal rigging and no visible sails, looking bare and inappropriately shiny. Popular with tourists apparently. In the summer holidays Whitby gets even more jammed with tourists than it was that June, until the evenings when they seem to vanish.

Whitby majors on *Dracula*, largely because Bram Stoker holidayed there in 1890 and got to know the place so well that in his famous book he accurately described the harbour into which the mysterious foreign schooner with all sails set was driven by an unexpected August storm. The observers on the shore were horrified that 'lashed to the helm was a corpse,

---

5. R. T. McMullen, *Down Channel* (orig. 1869; London: Grafton Books, 1986), 99.
6. Greenvile Collins, *Great-Britain's Coasting Pilot* (London: 1693).

with drooping head, which swung horribly to and fro at each motion of the ship'. No one else was on board, but an 'immense dog sprang up on deck from below' and leapt for the shore and disappeared —Dracula himself, on his way to terrorise England. This is one of the spookiest passages in the book, which has since inspired hundreds of Gothic horror stories and films.

Whitby had also been famous for shipbuilding. Three of Captain Cook's ships were built here, including the Endeavour. Amazingly, some small-scale shipbuilding survives. And there is a nostalgic steam train running on the North Yorkshire Moors Railway, hooting and puffing streams of smoke. Lots of atmospheric pubs, too. For us it was to the Duke of York for supper, at the bottom of the 199 originally wooden, but now stone, steps. I didn't on this occasion climb those steps to the ruined and very atmospheric 13th-century Benedictine abbey, and St Mary's church with its weathered gravestones tumbling over the cliffs (just as in *Dracula*), but Oli and Stu did. The church has enclosed pews, some of them named for particular families (including one kitted out with ear trumpets for deaf Mrs Andrews, a long-dead vicar's wife wishing to hear her husband's sermons).

When we returned to Pickle, a couple of 4-oar coastal rowing-gigs were in the outer harbour evening sunshine, practising for some regatta. Getting friends together to build their own gig, and then rowing and racing it, was becoming something of a craze all around the coast, and very congenial it must be too. At about 10pm the swing bridge opened, and we puttered into the marina in the dark.

Friday June 15th, a late rise for breakfast, very late at 10am. There was plenty of time for boat-cleaning, oneself-cleaning, and stocking-up in the very convenient Co-op by the marina. There was no hurry; we were not planning on going anywhere, and besides it was rather grey and wet in the morning, and by the afternoon we had thunder and lightning. The summer was turning out to be one of the worst on record, but it didn't bother us too much. It meant we had more than the average amount of wind and therefore less motoring than many others who have sailed around Britain. For example, in 2015/16 Mike Goodwin and Roger Colmer had to use their engine for three-quarters of their time at sea, and even managed to completely avoid anchoring which must have limited their options[7].

Yet again I brooded on just how stressful it can be keeping the crew happy. Maybe because the last time I had been to Whitby I had been crewing

---

7. Goodwin M. and Colmer R., *Blue Star Adventure: a Circumnavigation of Britain* (Independent Publishing Network, 2021).

myself, completely free from worrying about the weather, the wind, the tides, pilotage, passage-plans … and the crew. I was just doing what I was told, and reading far more books than I was able to on this trip. As well as the routine boat tasks, the skipper has to be sure the crew all get on together, a bit like hosting a dinner party, but lasting not just a few hours but several days, at close quarters too. It was ever thus, in the late 19th century Archibald Young rather sensibly writing, 'On board a yacht there are no conveniences for being separate and sulky in the event of a quarrel, and gloomy faces and sour looks are intolerable, where all must constantly meet on the same deck at the same table.'[8] How to get the balance right between being unbearably bossy versus tolerating second best whether it be washing up, cleaning the decks, or steering in a straight line?

Might some topics of conversation on a small boat be off limits? Politics and religion are the usual ones. Grammatical pedants can be a problem, particularly when it comes to apostrophes. Commas and hyphens are less controversial but no less necessary — 'Students get first hand job experience' needs a hyphen somewhere.[9] And 'Next stop Brexit' has two completely different meanings depending on where the comma is placed.

We had been early in Whitby — irrespective of adverse weather it didn't do to be late because crew were being picked up in the middle of this leg. As a result we skipped some places I would have enjoyed seeing, like Scarborough. However, Whitby is a good spot to linger in, as it was that Friday. We spent quite a bit of it in the Captain Cook Memorial Museum dedicated to the great navigator's life. Although he was born in Cleveland, Whitby claims him as their own, largely because he did much of his seaman's apprenticeship in the very house, much altered, that the museum is in. It is right on the edge of the water, with a grand view from the attic where the apprentices, including the young James, once slept. Libby Purves was on to this Yorkshire sleight of hand: 'Whitby, having long ago joyfully annexed the entire life and work of Captain Cook on the grounds that he served his apprenticeship as a Whitby collier, and having milked dry the picturesque potential of its old whaling industry, has lately taken over Dracula as well.'[10]

---

8. Archibald Young, *Summer Sailings by an Old Yachtsman* (Edinburgh: David Douglas, 1898), 50.

9. Gyles Brandreth, *Have You Eaten Grandma?* (London: Penguin Random House, 2018), 43.

10. Libby Purves, *One Summer's Grace: A Family Voyage round Britain* (London: Grafton Books, 1989), 214.

David Dick, the Norfolk neurologist, turned up in the afternoon, luckily before the shops shut as he had forgotten to bring his deck shoes (boots not shoes are what we wear in Scotland to keep our feet warm and dry). In the evening in the Station Inn, tucked away with no views, a more local, more friendly and less touristy pub than many in Whitby, we were joined by Will Whiteley. He is a young Edinburgh neurologist, who was then burdened with three little children. His wife is not too keen on sailing so he often jumps at the chance of a bit of crewing, but not for too long, his domestic responsibilities being never far away. He is a great enthusiast, and something of an amateur biologist, so not surprisingly he hit it off with Stu. Later we were all back on the boat for a posh supper to celebrate the arrival of the new crew — tablecloth, decanter, dips, homemade burgers, strawberries and cream. No need to stint just because we were on a boat. There was more climbing chit-chat over whisky.

To Hartlepool and the Trincomalee

Hartlepool is 24 miles from Whitby, it has a marina, and I was curious to see the place although it is often regarded as something of a joke. Maybe because hardly anyone has ever been there including me, perhaps because it is well-known for having been hard hit by the collapse of the coal industry, and because of the incongruity that Peter Mandelson, that arch New Labour and money-loving mate of Tony-Iraq-War-Blair, had once been the local MP (he claimed as untrue his widely reported confusion between mushy peas served with fish and chips and the more upmarket guacamole he was familiar with). And then there is the monkey legend. During the Napoleonic Wars a French ship was wrecked off the coast and it is said that a bedraggled pet monkey, dressed in military uniform, was washed up on the shore. The Hartlepool fishermen, not having ever seen a Frenchman, and imagining the monkey's chattering was in French, assumed the bedraggled beast was a French spy and hanged him. This rather unlikely story has echoes in other ports.

The Whitby swing bridge opened to let us through at 9.30am. We then had to wait a while at the holding pontoon for the tide to turn north, and for plenty of depth of water to allow us to get out of the outer harbour without bumping the bottom. This gave us time for coffee and doughnuts while I briefed the new crew on all the safety stuff — gas safety, flares, EPIRB, fire extinguishers, grab bag, and so on. While doing this we listened in to an amusing incident on the VHF radio. Someone had spotted a crude raft made of planks of wood, with an outboard engine clamped on the back and two youths on board, heading out to sea. The gruff Yorkshire harbour master clearly thought they were crazy, told them so in no uncertain terms, and sent a boat out to fetch them back.

We left at 11am, out onto a blue and sparkling sea, and a welcome southerly breeze to fill our sails. With five of us on board there was little for me to do, particularly as Oli was leaping about doing useful things in his usual enthusiastic way. As a child during family walks he used to run off to the side and then back again to return to the rest of us, consuming excess energy, rather like a playful dog. He hadn't changed.

At 7 knots it didn't take long to get to Hartlepool, a mere four hours, past Redcar with its still smoking steelworks (now closed), and the mouth of the Tees. Not quite as it was in its industrial and polluting heyday. In 1908 Claud Worth, sailing by, found that 'The whole coast of Durham from the Tees to the Tyne, seen from the sea, has the appearance of one vast manufacturing town, with innumerable factory chimneys and blast furnaces pouring out clouds of black smoke.'[11] We only spotted two other sails despite it being a Saturday, and good weather.

Hartlepool marina turned out to be a real treat, and a surprise. Motoring into the lock we were met by the lock-keeper who took our ropes. When I jumped nimbly onto the pontoon he greeted me with 'Good afternoon, how d'ye do, I'm Ray, welcome to 'artlepool' and shook my hand. Beyond the lock, and the statue of the wretched monkey, the harbour opened out into several huge basins, for which there was no longer any need as most of the industry had gone. In one we found the marina. Like so many post-industrial coastal towns, Hartlepool has attempted to regenerate its empty docks for the leisure industry. It was all however a bit down-at-heel, the pontoons showing their age or lack of funding, needing some tender loving care. As usual for this sort of marina development, there were surrounding newish apartment blocks, rather soulless, and I suspected not all sold. £150,000 seemed rather a lot for a two-bedroom flat in Hartlepool.

It was ominously quiet, with hardly anyone about even though there were around 500 berths which seemed mostly occupied. Down one side of the dock was a row of unpromising restaurants and pubs, designed to attract people to what was billed as a 'modern waterside development'. Given we were in the middle of the worst recession since the 1930s, not surprisingly they didn't seem to be doing very well. The Italian restaurant

---

11. Claud Worth, *Yacht Cruising* (3rd edn, London: J. D. Potter, 1926), 164.

we selected for dinner was ... well, better unsaid. There were some rather overweight girls around, showing a lot of abdominal flesh, and the men all looked like bouncers. But, everyone, just everyone, was good-natured and friendly. Welcome to the north of England.

In the morning we didn't walk into the middle of the town, so-called West Hartlepool. Instead, we were delightfully and comprehensively waylaid by the beautifully restored early 19th-century warship, the Trincomalee — built in Bombay. There she was, her three masts towering over everything else in sight, afloat next to a reproduction 18th-century dockside with an excellent museum that featured a first-rate audio show illustrating life aboard a fighting ship. Along with reproduction small shops demonstrating what they must have been like a couple of hundred years ago — cooper, gunsmith, naval tailor, and so on. This was all so very much better than the rip-off Victory in Portsmouth. Far less crowded, too, not a honeypot tourist destination. Here was a ship properly showing off how naval life was once like, with manikins of officers going about their business, the ship's surgeon, powder monkeys, a sailor asleep in his hammock, the cat-o'-nine-tails in action, the sailmaker and others.

I had hoped to completely avoid the Olympics, being of such an unsporting nature and fed up with all the hype. But here, in Hartlepool of all places, I was trapped. The Olympic torch was about to arrive outside the museum, crowds of people were waiting, loud music, cheerleaders, trucks bearing garish advertisements for the Olympics sponsors. Ghastly. A quick retreat to Pickle and off and away by midday.

We hadn't given ourselves enough time to look at West Hartlepool and the chance to wonder, as Paul Theroux did, 'how people could stand to live in such a place'.[12] However, some years later I did sail into Hartlepool again, and that time I had a good wander round the town. Theroux was right. It seemed the most dystopian and most miserable town in England. Despite the attractive modern brick civic centre, there were so many empty shops, a dispiriting shopping mall, and decaying Victorian-era buildings with broken windows. Mobility scooters cruised the land. The art gallery was making an effort, and served coffee and a scone for a mere £3.50.

West Hartlepool is relatively young. It was developed in the mid-19th century, with a railway to connect the coalfields with the newly built docks enabling coal exporting far and wide. Fishing boomed, businesses moved

---

12. Paul Theroux, *The Kingdom by the Sea: A Journey around the Coast of Great Britain* (orig. 1983; London: Penguin, 1984), 317.

in, those were good times. But now, with coalfields closed and the fish long gone, the town seems redundant and apparently unloved; it is perhaps financially broke, with one in three households jobless in 2020, and food banks proliferating. Maybe the solution is to knock it all down, move the population to somewhere else, and return the whole place to grass. Businesses and jobs are what places like this need, decent well-paid jobs to boost the local economy; their high streets will otherwise continue to wither, and their civic pride will vanish. A coat of paint is not enough, nor a marina. The latest wheeze is to attract inward investment by Hartlepool becoming part of the proposed Teesside 'free port', a controversial idea as it may facilitate tax evasion and lax regulation.

The smaller and older town of East Hartlepool sounds nicer, but is a quite long and rather boring walk from the marina which we didn't have time for. At least the sea is in a much better state since Theroux's journey when 'Even the sea was grim here – not rough but motionless and oily, a sort of offshore soup made of sewage and poison.'[13] Presumably an improvement as a result of the decline of coal mining and heavy industry.

A maritime museum and the Trincomalee are all very well, but these alone will not restore even partial former glory to West Hartlepool (any more than the Turner Contemporary by itself is likely to in Margate). Something more is needed. These places don't have the option of devolution and possibly future independence that we have in Scotland, one way of being able to disentangle oneself from the priorities of London. If politicians were serious about the north they would build a high-speed rail network to connect the major cities between Hull and Liverpool, before the High-Speed-2 Birmingham-London line that will just suck even more people into the capital.

What about locating large medical research laboratories up north, like the Crick Institute which in 2016 instead descended next to St Pancras Station? The 1200 or so scientists are mostly not well-paid and so cannot afford to live near central London — some have to commute for miles. In a northern city they could buy a much cheaper house, bike to work, and get easily to the countryside. They would need a local university to interact with, and definitely would need superlative broadband, video conferencing and excellent transport links to the rest of the UK, and the world. Leeds would do very well, or Liverpool, or Newcastle. But maybe not poor old West Hartlepool. An infusion of scientists would make such

---

13. Theroux, *Kingdom by the Sea*, 316.

a big difference to the North. They would have a far better quality of life than in London. What's not to like? In 2017 Google started building a campus for 7000 workers round the corner from the Crick. Crazy. Put them in Swansea, or Truro, where new blood is needed. Take a tip from Hull that has redeveloped its docks area without losing a sense of history, pedestrianised its centre, built a modern aquarium, and generally spruced itself up. And in Hull marina you will find the full-sized seaworthy replica of HMS Pickle tended by Mal Nicholson, who also owns the adjacent Spider T we had seen in Harwich.

No wonder people in post-industrial towns like Hartlepool, marginalised and ignored by the London-centric elite, mostly voted for Brexit in 2016. It was surely a well-justified scream of pain rather than a thoughtful decision. Back then we didn't have even half the facts we needed to make a rational decision. I had no idea what a customs union was, even though I would regard myself as well-educated and reasonably abreast of current affairs. I voted remain because those who supported remain looked a better and more intelligent bunch than those who supported leave. And besides, I had worked with and was good friends with many Europeans, a deliberate strategy on my part back in the 1980s to encourage scientific cooperation, collegiality and friendships among European nations, after so many wars over so many centuries. For the same reason, in 1988, I had organised a meeting between British and Soviet neurologists in what was then Leningrad.

Working with, talking to, and making friends across countries seems a much better idea than the Brexiteers' vacuous slogan of 'taking back control', whatever that means. As a result of leaving the European Union we are likely to lose I don't know how many workers from the NHS, the hospitality industry, and agriculture. Scientists too are leaving. And many UK businesses are relocating to Europe. I am now even more of a remainer than before, as well as ever more convinced that we have to do something to rejuvenate our left-behind towns and cities. Compare Maryport and Hartlepool with Rye and Yarmouth (Isle of Wight) to appreciate that we live in a very divided (by wealth) country.

To Blyth and the friendly Royal Northumberland Yacht Club

Sunday June 17th, we locked out of the harbour at 12.30pm. There was no wind but at least it wasn't raining as we motored north over a slight swell. By 2pm we could get the sails up and with a light wind from the west were soon doing a steady 4 knots up the coast to Blyth 28 miles away, on a flat sea in five-and-a-half hours (if only Margaret could have experienced this rather than the East Anglian horrors).

I had pondered on Newcastle, but decided against. I had crewed there a couple of years earlier, and it is a long motor up the Tyne, past decaying post-industrial areas, as well as some glimmers of hope with offshore wind developments. However, despite the loss of shipbuilding and coal, the city has a buzz about it, is very friendly too, and the Geordie accent appeals. These days there is a pontoon right in the centre, and to get to it you duck under that interesting tilt of the millennium bridge. The pontoon is well-placed near the station for changing crew, and for all the pubs and other activities on the waterfront (Friday nights are a carnival of exposed flesh and bravado). Later, during each of my two stays on that pontoon the staff gave us a bottle of Prosecco, and on the second a box of chocolates too (for Mother's Day).

As we approached the mouth of the Tyne, Oli pointed out the landmarks and proclaimed with his local knowledge: 'The Amsterdam ferry comes out about now.' And there it was, behind the high harbour wall; a funnel moving down the Tyne was all we could see of it to begin with, plus a good signal on the AIS. At one point the AIS told us we were going to be only 6 feet away, but the ferry soon accelerated and passed well ahead of us. Hardly how the Reverend Hughes described the exact same place in the mid-19th century: 'As we approached the mouth of the Tyne we were astonished at the dense smoke and the buzzing of innumerable steam engines distinctly heard at sea, trains passing and repassing, tugs bustling about, light colliers discharging ballast, heavy portly grandfatherly brigs, slowly and surely crushing through the sea to the southward.'[14] How the north of England has changed — in some ways better, in other ways worse.

Blyth was brilliant. Not just because the sun had come out, but because of the legendary friendliness of the Royal Northumberland Yacht Club based in a converted 19th-century wooden lightship, with their own pontoons. 'Come in, welcome, have a drink, what would you like to eat?' What a lovely place to stop. Nautical pictures on the walls, a bar with real ale, cosy. I got the impression they didn't have many visiting boats, although clearly there were some from Holland. Most of the English sail on the south coast, or around Essex and Suffolk, not along the somewhat more hostile northeastern coastline. They very seriously miss out on the friendly people. For this pleasure we only had to pay £16 for the night.

---

14. Robert Edgar Hughes, *Hunt's Yachting Magazine*, 1 (1852), 315.

A climbing friend of Oli's pitched up from Newcastle to drive him back where, having just passed his PhD, he could carry on marking undergraduate exam papers. It had been good to have him with us, and he had been very chatty, probably because he and Stu exchanged so many climbing stories. Will went with them too so he could catch his train home to Edinburgh, and no doubt a Monday outpatient clinic. In the meantime Sophie Hambleton arrived, also from Newcastle, an old friend of Cathie's from medical school, a paediatrician, formidably intelligent, quick to spot the most miniscule anti-feminist remark, and heavily into paediatric immunology basic research, in which she is the national or maybe the world expert. It was rather nice, this coastal hopping from place to place meeting up with friends, who no doubt were curious to see how we were getting on even if, like Sophie, they had no interest in, and certainly no intention of, going to sea themselves.

The docks at Blyth are, like Hartlepool, huge. In the 20th century it was one of the biggest coal-exporting ports in Europe. Shipbuilding had been a major industry too. But almost everything had gone, all was quiet, mouldering except for one small coaster being loaded up. Mostly the docks were closed, ruined buildings here and there, windswept, the wooden boards of the piers rotting away. Just a couple of teenage girls, and a man with a dog, to be seen. Did Thatcher have any idea what deindustrialisation would lead to in places like Blyth, without help from the state to introduce new types of work? Perhaps it is a bit more cleaned-up than when Paul Theroux passed through in 1982: 'The real nightmare of northern England today was not the blackened factory chimneys and the smoke and the slag-heaps and the racket of machines; it was the empty chimneys and the clear air and the grass growing on the slag heaps, and the great silence.'[15] Blythe docks were still silent.

One big plus for Blyth is the stunning sandy beach with tiny particles of coal mixed in. The small town itself, a short walk from the docks, seemed a neat sort of a place, with its ectopically located and now unused 1788 lighthouse. There did seem to be some light industry around, but very little. It would have been nice to meet more people to get a better feel for it. This would have been easier if I had been single-handed — then again that would have been lonely, not to mention stressful, particularly given my incompetence with marina pontoons.

Again I found myself wondering what can be done about the declining

---

15. Theroux, *Kingdom by the Sea*, 209.

north of England. And parts of Wales for that matter, and Cornwall, all peripheral and ignored by London. It would surely be a mistake to regenerate them with just one major industry because if it goes down, the town that relies on it goes down with it. As has happened before — fishing in Lowestoft, my ancestors' shipping line in Maryport, very nearly the RAF in Lossiemouth. Perhaps even one day the financial industry in London on which we are told the UK economy depends, Brexit already starting the rot.

It is all very well extolling our booming financial sector, but the banks lend to people who can't pay the money back, the investment bankers gamble our money in the international markets, cheating on interest rates, mis-selling financial products, strutting and boasting, hiding their money in tax havens tolerated if not encouraged by our Westminster government. But what is all this about? These people don't *make* anything tangible. They don't grow anything. They are not a service industry, like the NHS or our universities. They don't entertain or educate us. What on earth do they actually do in all those shiny, new, and mostly extraordinarily ugly, high-rise buildings in the City of London and Canary Warf? Look after someone else's money, I suppose, money that is said to partly come from corruption in distant countries. A mystery to me.

To be fair, doctors are not immune to bad behaviour. Ian Paterson the breast surgeon talked hundreds of women into inappropriate and damaging surgery, and there was Harold Shipman of course. Nor are other professions — bent accountants siphoning off money from old ladies, solicitors doing much the same, teachers abusing children, and even vicars with their hands in the collection plate and down the choirboys' trousers.

To Amble, and upmarket Warkworth

Monday June 18th, to Amble, planning to be over the bar and marina cill within three hours of high water. We left Blyth at midday in sunshine, on a flat sea, in a 10-knot wind from the west. Brilliant. A perfect sail, three-and-half hours for the mere 16 miles up the coast. Round the small and uninhabited Coquet Island with its 1841 lighthouse, yet another part of the kingdom of the RSPB reserved for seabirds rather than humans. Now knowing where that island is, I realise it is easily visible from the east coast mainline train between Edinburgh and London, and from the air as planes from Edinburgh turn east to head towards Europe. It was good to see hills again, almost mountains even, the distant Cheviots bordering

Scotland and England. And it was hot, very hot in the sun, at least by my Scottish standards.

Amble is another of the old coal-exporting ports, much smaller than Blyth, but like Blyth all washed up, and literally silting up. The marina makes a brave effort to restore the seagoing past, a family-run affair as it turned out. The man on the boat on the pontoon next to us had set it up, and his son is now the boss. Earlier we wondered how he had so impressively backed out of his berth with panache, spun round, gone out for a solo sail, before coming back a couple of hours later, all without hitting anything. I envied his parking skills, but his boat could be steered in reverse, unlike Pickle. He didn't half talk, which was fine for a while. David slipped away when it all got a bit too much about the history of the marina, the local population, the Duke of Northumberland who seemed to own most of the county, and on and on. He had been chief engineer to British Coal, but everything there and everywhere else he said was rubbish — the bloody miners, their unions, the harbour authority, the local authority, the Duke's minions, the management of other marinas. He was one of those people more interested in what they have to say than what other people have to say. Quite the opposite of doctors who need to get patients to talk while not revealing anything of themselves. How well he told us the marina was managed, how they were not greedy, how they had spent thousands of pounds putting electricity sockets on to the pontoons, and on dredging. One plus point was that the marina had a real bath for the ladies (almost unique around the coast), but it apparently could be used by men as well. And at least he gave us useful local information.

By the time we extracted ourselves from the two-hour and rather one-sided conversation it was time to stroll into Amble. It was very quiet, rather down-at-heel, and we found an indifferent Italian restaurant for supper. When we got back, what a surprise! Despite those thousands of pounds, the electricity had packed up. It was impossible to restrain Stu from trying to open up the power socket on the pontoon and poke around with a screwdriver. Fortunately he didn't electrocute himself because there was no power — perhaps a circuit breaker somewhere had tripped. Next morning we politely told the man in the marina office that we had worked out it was with them not us that the problem lay. 'No, there is no way you could have reset the circuit breaker at the pontoon,' he replied. 'Electricity, water and the general public don't mix.' He blamed us for overloading the circuit: 'you must have been using an electric kettle or toaster.' Some chance, we had neither. Thankfully he didn't hear Stu say he had shoved a voltmeter up his power socket the night before. Not good customer relations, and in fact the only cross word we had from anyone in any marina or harbour all around the coast. Someone must surely have been having a bad day. Later visits restored my faith in the marina, when it was all smiles and friendliness, a place to return to.

That morning Amble was much more animated, and was rather good too because it had lots of small shops for bread, meat, groceries, infiltrated by just one Tesco Express. But not many promising-looking pubs. Scottish accents were beginning to appear. There was a chemist for David who needed some Rennie's antacid to relieve the effects of the whisky the night before. He was younger than me, still working, and a canny Scot from Aberdeen who had been the treasurer of the Association of British Neurologists, the main qualification for which was, and presumably still is, someone with a successful private practice. I always puzzle at the large number of Scots who move to England and get stuck there, presumably because they have jobs to sustain them, children at school, an increasing number of local friends and — as in David's case — an English wife. While I, having decided to move to Scotland in 1987 to escape the ravages of Thatcherism and the hopelessly overcrowded roads, would never move back to England. Lucky me. I had had a wife who was happy to move from Oxford, at the time only one child in the school system, and a terrific job to go to. Perhaps cross-border migration will gradually make Scotland more 'English', and England more 'Scottish'.

In the sunshine we walked the mile or so along the pretty River Coquet to Warkworth with its ruined but grand castle set on a hill within a loop of the river, and which gave me free entrance with my Historic Scotland membership card. The town is very different to Amble. Upmarket with several hotels and tea rooms, lots of little shops but only one which offered what we might have needed — food supplies. But perhaps, with apologies to the witches, 'by the pricking of my thumbs maybe a Waitrose this way comes'? It's that sort of a place. Wrong, it's far too small; the nearest Waitrose is actually 28 miles away by Range Rover, and is not surprisingly in Ponteland, that well-heeled suburb of Newcastle. I rather doubt if the residents of Warkworth go to Amble for their shopping, or maybe they do. Libby Purves had a similar feeling to mine 30 years earlier: 'We grew used to Amble and its strange contradictory views: looking upriver, cobles and smooth river and the eminence of Warkworth Castle make it a place of timeless English beauty fit for the guidebooks; downriver lies the ugly sprawl of bad modern housing, the chaos of the old docks, the air of rusty deprivation which make it part of the modern North-East, where one man in eight has no hope of work. Britain: the beauty and the beastliness.'[16]

Amble has seen a few changes in more recent years, some rather colourful apartment blocks appearing by the marina. Apparently they are all or nearly all holiday homes — expensive, too — so it is unclear how they will benefit the town. And there now seem to be more eating places round the harbour. Overall, not a bad place to stop off, not bad at all.

To the Farne Islands for the birds

Tuesday June 19th, another lovely sail for 18 miles up the coast, sunshine, westerly wind off the land, flat sea, close-up views of ruined Dunstanburgh castle standing above a small cliff, hills, small harbours, past Boulmer and Craster, to anchor in the strangely named Newbiggin Bush which is an east-facing bay in the Farne Islands. With just my eyes, I found it difficult to orientate myself approaching these very low-lying islands, but there was no problem using the chartplotter (this will of course deskill my piloting skills and make it even more difficult to cope without one). If we had had more time I would have stopped at Craster for the pub, and some kippers. There are a lot of small anchorages along this coast to explore in the right weather. The mainland looked and felt almost like Scotland — indeed, it almost was Scotland with the border only about 15 miles away. I felt much more at home than in Poole, or many other places in England.

At last we were in an anchorage, not on a pontoon. Hilaire Belloc puts it perfectly: 'The best noise in all the world is the rattle of the anchor chain when one comes into harbour at last and lets it go over the bows.'[17] However, we were back with the problem of the anchor chain getting stuck when we ran it out — our own rattle abruptly stopped before the anchor hit the seabed. I never experienced this on other boats, it seems to be a Rustler 36 problem, but an intermittent one. When the anchor is winched up, its chain makes a neat cone-like heap in the anchor locker under the foredeck. Later, in a rough sea, the heap may collapse with the chain becoming tangled up and later getting stuck when you come to let it out for anchoring. The emergency solution is to dash to the forecabin, fling yourself prone onto

---

16. Purves, *One Summer's Grace*, 212.

17. Hilaire Belloc, 'On Dropping Anchor', in *On Sailing the Sea: A Collection of the Seagoing Writings of Hilaire Belloc*, ed. W. N. Roughead (London: Rupert Hart-Davis, 1951), 152.

the bunk, open the hatch to the anchor locker, pull out the chain onto something that can get wet and muddy until it is untangled (not the bunk cushions), and hope in the meantime that the crew haven't put you aground. Because this snag doesn't always happen, when it does I am usually caught by surprise. It is not frequent enough to go to the bother of laying out the chain on the foredeck before anchoring. No permanent solution has come to mind, although some recommend a traffic cone in the anchor locker so that the chain falls around the cone and not on top of itself. An alternative is a nice, smooth, slippery — and very expensive — chain of stainless steel.

We were the only boat in the Farnes on that calm and sunny evening. With all around us seabirds, loads and loads of them, almost the full cast — puffins, gannets, guillemots, razorbills, shags, fulmars, eider ducks, terns, gulls. Seals, too. A fabulous evening with a fabulous sunset over the mainland, Bamburgh castle in silhouette. What a coast Northumberland is for castles. Dinner was cooked by David, eaten al fresco in the cockpit for the first time on this cruise, and in broad daylight because we were definitely back north again.

Wednesday morning was just as good. Sunny, warm, lazing in the cockpit in pyjamas with breakfast, terns chirruping and diving around us, puffins splashing about, shags cruising low over the water. This was the life — cruising in north Britain. At last I managed to finish Lieutenant Middleton's book about sailing round Britain, *The Cruise of the Kate*. At the time all I had was the second edition, self-published in about 1888, which contains far too much rambling about his crazed ideas. The first edition published by Longmans in 1870 is the one to read. It was with relief that I turned to *Racundra's First Cruise* by Arthur Ransome, a real writer, about his escape from revolutionary Russia to sail on the Baltic with his paramour who had been Trotsky's personal secretary. This was published in 1923, some years before his success with *Swallows and Amazons*.

We didn't land, not because of laziness but because the islands immediately surrounding us were owned by the National Trust with highly protected seabird nesting sites. Tourist boats came and went, full of people peering through binoculars and snapping with their cameras, but quietly, without disrupting the peace.

To Eyemouth and Scotland, via Holy Island

As there was no wind we motored the six miles to Lindisfarne, or Holy Island, such an obvious landmark from the east coast mainline train because of the characteristic outline of the castle perched on top. The two tall towers for the leading line into the anchorage are also easy to see from the train, but I had never known what they were; now I do. As ever, the pilotage was more straightforward than expected from the Sailing Directions. I had aimed to have 10ft under the keel over the bar, being a cautious sort of sailor unused to shallow waters, and of course it was more than enough. A creek-crawling east coast sailor would have done it in far less. Now I probably would too, having more experience of shallow waters.

We had to have this visit well planned to get into the anchorage on a rising tide and out again before the tide fell too far to allow us to escape. In the event we managed to have two-and-a-half hours ashore, enough time to walk up to the castle and look round what for me is one of the best National Trust properties. (No doubt there was confounding by the weather — which was perfect.) It had been a defensive 16th-century castle before being converted by Edwin Lutyens in the early 20th century into an Arts and Crafts family home for Edward Hudson, the founder of *Country Life* magazine. There must have been money in glossy magazines in those days. The small and homely rooms were lovely, beautifully furnished in period, plus wee passageways, and wonderful views in all directions. There were also a lot of tourists, mostly elderly at that time of year (like us), hobbling up and down the steep cobbled path to the castle entrance. Neither they nor the local people were particularly friendly. No one said hello as we passed them, as is the nature of tourist honeypots.

It was odd how this felt like an island as soon as we stepped ashore, even though it isn't really. It's connected to the mainland by a causeway that is covered at high water. Inevitably some people get stuck there in their cars, as famously did Dickey the American gangster and his companion Albie at the start of *Cul-de-sac*, the 1966 Polanski film. Rather surprisingly, Libby Purves was less taken by the castle than by the 'practical and pleasant sheds made by the lobster and crab fishermen on the beach: these were the black humped shapes of old herring-boats, upended, tarred and canvassed.'[18] Apparently those cut-in-half boats are what inspired Enric Miralles's design of the Scottish parliament building in Edinburgh.

The castle was all we had time for, and we only dashed past the sheds. We upped anchor at 3pm, motored out to sea, and in a light westerly wind sailed, or rather drifted, nonchalantly 20 miles up the coast, past Berwick-upon-Tweed into Scottish waters at 6.30pm. An hour later we were off Eyemouth, which reasonably badges itself as 'Scotland's first port of call'.

---

18. Purves, *One Summer's Grace*, 204.

The entry is very dangerous in bad north to easterly weather given that you have to approach quite close to rocks before turning sharp to port and into the narrow entrance between very high harbour walls known appropriately as 'the canyon'. Indeed it was not just dangerous but fatal in 1881. Ignoring the rapidly falling pressure on the public barometer, the local fishermen headed out to sea but were caught in a severe gale. They tried to get back but 189 men drowned in front of their distraught families watching from the harbour wall, leaving 93 widows and 267 fatherless children. (Eyemouth is the only harbour I have been refused entry, in 2019; waves were breaking over the harbour walls, so I had to find shelter in the Forth.)

But for us that evening, apart from a fishing boat that came charging out just as we were approaching, it was a dead-easy entrance. And there was Steve Druitt standing on the pontoon, waiting to catch our ropes as we rafted up against another boat. He had come down from Edinburgh to experience sailing up the Forth with us the following day.

Eyemouth looked unpromising under what was by then a grey overcast sky. It was and still is very much an active fishing harbour, with huge refrigerated trucks drawn up on the dockside. There seemed to be quite a few proper shops, by which I mean a butcher and a baker. Sadly the Co-op didn't do their usual doughnuts. If the houses were painted white it would look like Cornwall without the trippers. As it is, it is all very grey, dour like the Scots are supposed to be, but are not, at least no more so than the English. As ever I can't beat Libby Purves's description: 'Eyemouth is a fishing town, with only a light, dignified gloss of tourism.'[19]

We found a rather dull-looking pub for a meal. While it lacked real ale, its food was terrific, lamb kebabs and a seafood platter — really excellent. The place was decked out with Italian flags that we initially thought was because England was playing Italy at something. (Many Scots will support any team playing against England, other than their own — it is much the same between New Zealand and Australia.) In fact, the flags were in honour of the several Italian staff.

And who could forget the tall and beautiful Polish waitress? Steve, spotting her Polish name on her badge, and ever eager to practise his Polish, started off boldly as she approached with the menu: 'Dzień dobry.' Steve has tried this greeting before and, as before, the Polish recipient looked astonished because very few Brits speak their language. 'O bardzo mi miło. Ty mówisz po polsku?' she replied, so quickly that Steve looked completely

---

19. Purves, *One Summer's Grace*, 201.

lost. In the inevitable pause she added: 'Never mind, I can speak English!' Steve deflated. Six years later we found her still there, as the manager of the pub, but not of Steve to his regret.

To Edinburgh, Athens of the North (or Reykjavík of the south)

Thursday 21st June, bad weather was coming and we needed to get well into the Forth before it arrived. I was sorry we hadn't had time for a proper look round Eyemouth, particularly at the local museum and Gunsgreen House overlooking the harbour and famous for its subterranean smuggling facilities. David went to find someone to pay for our berth for the night.

'I've come to pay our harbour dues,' he started off, once he had found the harbour master.

'What's the name of your boat?'

'Pickle.'

'Ah, yon wee green thing. How long is she?'

'11 metres.'

'Surely that wee thing doesn't measure 11 metres, she must be under 10.' A pause while the harbour master thought some more. 'Aye, just under 10.'

He undercharged us accordingly, and off we went at 8.30am in an easterly wind. Sadly the sun didn't appear that morning; indeed, it became gloomier and gloomier as we sailed north close to the coast but were hardly able to see anything of it, certainly nothing of Fife across the Forth. We turned more to the west past St Abb's Head packed with seabirds, and then one-by-one past the familiar landmarks from the east coast mainline train, and weekend walks — Torness nuclear power station (one of the two in Scotland), the Dunbar cement works, Tantallon Castle and North Berwick Law. The wind stayed easterly so at least we were sailing fast on a surprisingly flattish sea.

Because of the very poor visibility, Steve didn't get his views up the Forth that he wanted, but at midday we all got a fabulous close-up view of the Bass Rock off North Berwick absolutely plastered with gannets, about 150,000 of them. I have never seen so many in the air and on their nests, and so close up, even out at St Kilda. From a distance in the summer the rock looks white, as though covered in guano, but actually it is covered with white gannets packed together on their nests. We didn't dawdle; by this time it was raining, so we were not tempted to sail right round the rock, just close past the south side.

My plan had been to anchor for the night off the west side of Fidra, the small island by Yellowcraig Beach, a favourite spot for our New Year Day walks. But it was hardly comfortable at anchor, it was raining harder, the cloud base was somewhere near sea level, and the thought of being stuck down below for the rest of the day did not appeal. So we had lunch, piled into our waterproofs, weighed anchor at 2.30pm, and continued up the Forth with the wind behind us. On past Edinburgh, under the iconic railway bridge opened in 1890 (now a UNESCO world heritage site), which is a good reason to sail up the Forth, and then under the less iconic 1964 road bridge over which I understand more vehicles head north than south (suggesting there must be hundreds of abandoned cars piled up somewhere near Wick). The third bridge was not then under construction. It had been a grand 50-mile sail from Eyemouth, despite the weather. At 6.30pm it was a quick tie-up to a Port Edgar pontoon at South Queensferry, and a taxi home to the family and a bath.

Home for a week

How lovely to see everyone again. It had been Father's Day so Lucy produced a self-portrait for me. William was as bouncy as ever, and had made a chocolate cake, under supervision. Cathie was pleased to have adult company again. Margaret was there too, tired but very pleased with herself at having got all her party up and down Kilimanjaro without medical mishap, or death. And back to the news too. Tony-Iraq-War-Blair had announced he would be happy to be prime minister again. God forbid! More banking scandals too — Barclays fined £290 million for fiddling interbank interest rates (whatever they are). When will these awful people be jailed? Never, as far I can make out. Later I removed my accounts from the disastrously over-ambitious Royal Bank of Scotland, a paltry gesture but at least it made me feel better. I joined the more socially acceptable Co-op bank, but then it too had its own scandal with their cocaine-snorting Methodist lay-minister CEO. I moved again, to the Nationwide, the last mutual bank in the UK — but for how long?

The next day I was back to Pickle. However willing the crew may be, I still prefer to be on the boat by myself to clean up and sort everything out. It is quicker that way. I don't have to worry about skimpy cleaning, or stuff stowed away in the wrong place. Port Edgar seemed rather run-down as a marina, and it was definitely silting up. The City of Edinburgh Council who owned it was trying to sell. A shame, really — here was a publicly owned facility, albeit with staff incongruously in dark suits, which could have been so much better if there had been more public money to support it. In 2013 it was sold to some private outfit that may or may not make a success of it. I hope they do. Or will they just sell off the land for 'waterside apartments' and destroy the rather charming remains of all those second and even some first world war sheds that are still in use for various boatie activities? Mind you, it is not a convenient place for a visiting boat. It is too far from any shops, restaurants and pubs, although two restaurants have sprung up by the marina itself. And the bus journey into Edinburgh is quite long.

Granton would be much more convenient, but then visitors would miss out on the Forth bridges, and there are few facilities in the way of pontoons and mooring buoys. That may change if the proposed 250-or-more-berth Granton marina eventually gets built, only about three miles north of Edinburgh Castle. In the 19th century visiting yachts like the Reverend Hughes's 'Pet' headed for Leith with easy access to Edinburgh itself, which he remarked was 'A city placed on the banks of an estuary, compared to which the Thames is a ditch, and the Seine a sewer; a city presenting from its very streets views of mountain and sea, rock and island, palace and ruin, bright flowery gardens, stern castellated crags, wide modern streets and squares, architectural splendour, and alas! squalid filth; — such is Edinburgh, the most beautiful and the dirtiest capital in Europe.'[20] It is still the former, but thankfully not quite the latter. Leith still has docks, but no longer any facilities for sailing boats.

While messing about on the boat it was a good time to plot and plan the next leg of the trip, and reflect. Was it time to completely give up all my medical activities? After all, my policy had always been not doing anything unless I could be right on top of it, rather similar to my schoolboy policy of not going in for prizes unless I expected to win them. My mind was eventually made up by the GMC wanting to revalidate me, definitely time to hand in my cards. Only later did I discover that part of the GMC subscription is used to fund private health insurance for their staff, truly shocking. And worse, they pay for staff to be medically screened which is mostly unnecessary, and a rip-off. But what should I do instead? Art classes (these happened). More photography, certainly. Child-coming-on-teenager care, of course. More involvement with the local community, yes. Write articles for sailing magazines, OK. Write a book … here it is.

This was also a good time for catching up at home, and taking friends for

---

20. Hughes, *Hunt's Yachting Magazine*, 1 (1852), 350.

day-sails on the Forth. If the west coast of Scotland didn't exist hundreds of boats would be out on the Forth, even though it is not a great cruising area. The anchorages and harbours are too shallow for keel-boats, the tide is quite strong, and there are not that many places to go, either in the Forth for weekends or further afield up or down the coast. However, there is little to beat the thrill of sailing under the two — now three — bridges, marvelling at the over-engineered Victorian railway bridge in particular.

Margaret and her old medical school friend Josie came sailing for what turned out to be a sunny day. Josie was off to Christchurch, New Zealand, where her electrician husband could get plenty of work helping to restore the city after the devastating earthquake, and she could get a less sclerotic training than in the UK. So many junior doctors were and are escaping abroad, taking their expensive medical training with them. We had two excellent ones just before I retired. Because specialist training was in such a mess at the time with all sorts of restrictions on where you could train, and how you got selected, I encouraged them to train for a year or so abroad until the UK system had shaken down. Big mistake. One stayed in New Zealand, the other stayed in Australia.

Steve and I took our old friend Richard Broadhurst for a sail. Poor Richard had been suffering the rigours of myeloma and its treatment for some years. He was very stooped and in a lot of pain, but delighted to be on the water again. He died the following year and had a surprisingly Christian funeral in Roslyn Chapel. I didn't take to one of the two ministers officiating, who listed three completely bogus but which he thought were compelling reasons for the existence of God (which I have forgotten). I prefer what Richard Holloway, a former Bishop of Edinburgh, once said or wrote — something like 'even if you don't believe in God's existence, it is as well to behave as though he does exist'. I can buy that.

We also took the Stone family for a trip. They had never been on a sailing boat before, and as usual I forgot to warn visitors about heeling. Jon Stone has become the national expert on functional neurological disorders, indeed an international expert. All achieved from a busy NHS consultant position, not a university chair — which says something about my blinkered university not recognising his huge scientific contribution (eventually they did in 2018). Maybe not enough rats, molecules and genes for their priorities. Jon's research is with people, clinical research in which you shake hands with your subject. He had discovered a good if rather challenging niche that was mostly unoccupied until he took it on and ran with it so successfully.

A good general principle when starting off in clinical research, or indeed as an NHS consultant, is to find a niche that is unoccupied, preferably of public health importance although very rare diseases need attention too. Then set up a clinical service to meet the need, and start trying to answer all the interesting questions that will undoubtedly arise. Exploit the situation you find yourself in, concentrate on what you do best, and don't attempt the impossible. For example, following up patients over years through their medical records is possible in the NHS where almost everyone is registered with a GP, but largely impossible in the USA. You need that sort of edge over any competition.

I had found stroke research more or less unoccupied in the late 1970s. However, I had to concentrate on patients with transient ischaemic attacks (the so-called mini-strokes) because these patients were generally referred to neurologists as outpatients. Stroke itself was at the time ignored by neurologists and left to the geriatricians. Only later in Edinburgh did we start research into stroke, and that was simply because Martin Dennis had joined us and set up a city-wide and properly organised stroke service. You can't do clinical research with patients unless you are seriously involved in looking after them, and so competently that they are referred to your service. These days stroke research is too crowded. If I had my time again I would join Jon with functional disorders.

Chapter 9

From Edinburgh to Orkney

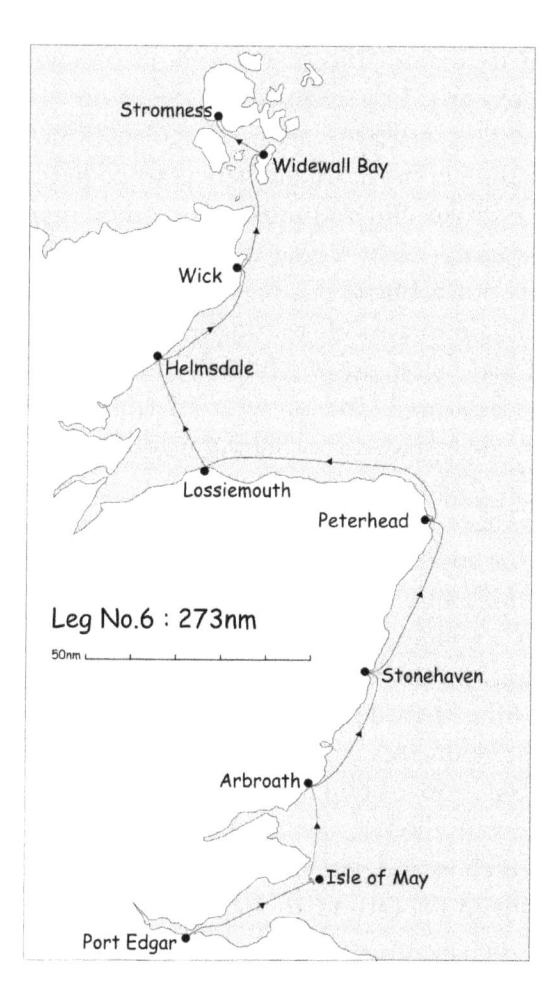

Tuesday July 3rd, well rested, caught up with emails, mowed the grass, re-victualled Pickle, and now ready for the off. Sunshine too, something of a change from the previous week. It had been the wettest June on record in the UK, but out at sea it hadn't felt too bad; at least there had been plenty of wind so we hadn't needed much motoring to keep to our schedule. Those 19th- and early 20th-century sailors with no engines had to wait for the wind — and wait — as they drifted backwards and forwards with the tide.

Again I was nervous, about restarting the trip as well as the unfamiliar coastline ahead. And sad to leave the family again, albeit for less than a fortnight. Maybe it was a mistake to take breaks, and maybe I should have kept going and not disrupted the rhythm of the voyage. At least I had no concerns about the crew for this leg. My 31-year-old son Ben certainly knew what he was doing, as he like his brother Oli had sailed with me since he was a small boy. After a degree in physics and philosophy at Bristol, where he has lived ever since, he worked as an events manager for a small company in Chepstow, even managing it when the boss went off to New Zealand for a year. But events management, however interesting and fun it can be, is for younger people who don't mind the strange hours. So Ben retrained as a physics teacher and at the time of the cruise had just finished his first year of teaching for real, in a large comprehensive school, which had all been pretty stressful.

Neil MacLennan was the other crew, a retired GP friend from medical school, who just happened to be the very doctor who had brought Ben into the world (with a skilful and atraumatic forceps delivery). He too was an experienced sailor, albeit not recently. Like so many people of my age he was in atrial fibrillation and taking warfarin, an anticoagulant which reduces the risk of blood clots forming in the heart and being carried in the circulation to the brain to cause a stroke. But you must get the dose right — not too much to cause bleeding, not so little that it is ineffective. The trouble is that anything that cuts down blood clotting also increases the risk of bleeding, and so far it has not been possible to completely dissociate these two opposing effects. Neil had better not cut himself and bleed all over my sails, or worse bang his head and land up with a haemorrhage between his skull and his brain, an extradural or subdural haematoma. As a neurologist I could make the diagnosis as he slumped into a coma, but also as a neurologist I would have no treatment to offer. The nearest neurosurgeon who could actually do anything useful would be in Aberdeen.

Surgeons certainly can cure people, while we neurologists have relatively few cures on offer. Unfortunately so many of 'our' diseases often go from bad to worse — multiple sclerosis, motor neurone disease, dementia. A reasonable hope is prevention rather than outright cure. Which is what I had concentrated on. While many doctors worked on the genetics and causes of Parkinson's and other degenerative brain diseases, often in animals and in laboratories, I and colleagues in the UK and Europe managed, over a couple of decades and with a few thousand patients in randomised trials, to show that aspirin and operating on the carotid artery in the neck could reduce the risk of stroke, but by no means prevent it completely. Others showed that reducing blood pressure and blood cholesterol also reduced the risk. Between us all, we must have been doing something right because strokes are becoming less common in every age group except — curiously — young adults.[1] However, even now, there are more strokes in the UK than in the past simply because there are so many more older people in whom strokes are much more frequent than in the young.

To Arbroath for a Smokie, via the Isle of May

We left Port Edgar at 12.45pm to catch the ebb tide out of the Forth, under engine for the first hour because of the modest easterly wind against us and the need to get a move on if we were to reach the Isle of May before dark, 31 miles away. By 3.30pm the wind had got up and we were close-hauled on a very long port tack, the sun was out, and we were making about 4 knots over the ground. It always surprises me just how much wildlife there is in the Forth, so close to quite large centres of population as well as to the oil refinery and chemical works at Grangemouth not far upstream, and tankers moving backwards and forwards with — so far — no oil spills. As you sail east there are more and more puffins, hundreds if not thousands of gannets flying to and from the Bass Rock, gulls nesting on the islands, and a lot of seals, one of which had taken up residence on a large navigational buoy. The wind eventually died so we motored the last bit, arriving off the Isle of May at 8.30pm. In the easterly wind the obvious anchorage was at West Tarbert, under the cliffs on the west side of the island.

The Isle of May is one of those very special seabird places like the Farne islands, Skomer, St Kilda, Noss in Shetland, and the Treshnish Islands off Mull. It is no surprise that it's a National Nature Reserve. There seemed to be thousands of birds whirling around us, mostly puffins — apparently 46,000 pairs nest on the island, up from only a handful in the 1950s (not everywhere has a declining seabird population). Plus fulmars, kittiwakes, shags, razorbills and guillemots, making a lot of noise, and smell. No other boats anywhere in sight. Ben is vegetarian and an excellent cook, far better than me, so he took over the galley and served up delicious vegetarian pasta bolognese. We bedded down after admiring a lovely sunset.

The next morning started dull and misty, but by 10am the sun was out. Going ashore was a must, to see the hundreds and hundreds of nesting puffins almost under our feet. Access was not easy. There may be a helpful

---

1. Catherine Scott, Linxin Li and Peter Rothwell, 'Diverging Temporal Trends in 21st Century Stroke Incidence in Younger versus Older People: Population Based Study and Systematic Review', *Stroke*, 51 (2020), 1372–80.

ladder up the cliff, but the bottom rung no longer reaches the ground at low tide, if it ever did. But once on and up the ladder we had the place to ourselves, as the tourists who come by boat from Anstruther on the Fife coast had not arrived yet. A magical spot to generally wander around, trying not to disturb the birds.

We inspected the outside of the 1816 lighthouse building which although a 'Stevenson' does not look much like their usually more elegant structures. It isn't even white but a grey, stone-built castle-like affair, more domestic than marine. There is also a much earlier structure, built in 1636, said to be the first 'lighthouse' in Scotland but originally a coal-fired beacon described by Greenvile Collins: 'The Isle of May… on which standeth a Light-House, that Ships may know the Frith in the Night; this Light may be seen 6 Leagues off.'[2] Yes so it might have been, provided the wind hadn't blown out the fire. The bottom part still stands, thanks to Walter Scott's insistence in 1814 of 'ruining' it 'à la picturesque' rather than destroying it completely which had been Robert Stevenson's plan.[3]

We left at 11.15am. The sea was flat, the wind was light from the southeast, there was some sun, and we were all alone on the ocean sailing at 5 knots over the ground. How different this must have been even just 50 years ago when there was still a large Fife fishing fleet. This is almost all gone now, the fishermen's houses taken over as second homes by the well-off from Edinburgh, including Scotland's Chief Medical Officer. When we were all expected to stay at home to counter the start of the Covid-19 pandemic in 2020, she unwisely broke her own rule and drove from Edinburgh to Fife, not just once but twice.[4] She resigned because the rules clearly applied to her as much as to everyone else, but not, it seems, to the UK's narcissistic and hypocritical Prime Minister Boris Johnson who partied in Downing Street.

It was a lovely gentle broad reach northwards, until the wind ran out and we had to motor for the last hour to find Arbroath at 4.30pm in the increasingly dense mist and, by evening, fog. It had been an easy 23 miles. Not surprisingly, given the visibility, we never saw the Bell Rock lighthouse standing six miles east of our track; it is the oldest surviving sea-washed rock lighthouse in the world, one of the first of the many Stevenson lighthouses.

---

2. Greenvile Collins, *Great-Britain's Coasting Pilot* (London: 1693).

3. Walter Scott, *The Voyage of the Pharos: Walter Scott's Cruise around Scotland in 1814* (Hamilton: Scottish Library Association, 1998), 8.

4. *Guardian*, 6 April 2020.

The small marina is in the old harbour, protected by lock gates. This is a typical pattern now that fishing, ship building, the coal industry and coastal traffic have disappeared from so many towns with harbours, which have had to reinvent themselves for the leisure industry. The marina staff were friendly, the surrounding houses a bit dull, and presumably because of the foggy evening there was no one around, even though it was the school holidays. A part of the smart new building by the harbour turned out to be a very acceptable restaurant for dinner, with excellent scallops. The other part proclaimed itself as something to do with wealth management, a surprise in a small town with very little visible wealth. A lot of the pubs were shut down, and those that remained didn't look all that tempting, but outward appearances can deceive. We could have done with Greg to nose out the best one, but instead we all went to bed.

Thursday July 5th, morning, Arbroath still seemed empty, and rather depressing. A soulless Abbeygate shopping centre had inserted itself into the middle of the winding main road where there were a lot of vacant spaces for shops. The town is larger than Maryport maybe, smaller than Lowestoft, but it has the same down-at-heel, seen-better-times atmosphere. We may live in a 'United' Kingdom but there doesn't seem a lot to unite these depressed coastal towns with the over-paid, over-bonussed and sometimes corrupt bankers, the moneyed classes including bosses paid several hundred times more than their workers, and the swanky modern skyscrapers springing up in such unplanned and higgledy-piggledy profusion all over London (for the results of apparent complete lack of town planning just visit Canary Wharf).

I doubt that very many of the politicians at Westminster, several of whom have never had a proper job, have a clue about what it is like to live in a small post-industrial coastal town with generally very poor health outcomes. They should care, but mostly they don't seem to, particularly the Tories whose MPs were more or less wiped out in Scotland and the north of England after the ravages of Thatcherism. By 2012 there were more pandas in Scotland (the two in Edinburgh zoo) than Tory MPs (one). Since then there has been some Tory recovery, but for how long we shall see. Mind you, the once dominant Scottish Labour party has collapsed too. Only one Labour MP was elected to the 2015 Westminster parliament, increasing to seven in 2017, but collapsing again in 2019 to the same one (who happens to be my MP). The SNP has taken over.

It is easy to understand the emotional pull of Scottish independence in places like Arbroath. Edinburgh is only down the road and hopefully would not be so remote a capital city for Scotland as London currently is, and so seemingly uncaring, as London is. But maybe it would. After all, this was my own first visit to Arbroath even though I had lived in Edinburgh for 25 years. Proximity clearly doesn't necessarily lead to familiarity. It was here in Arbroath in 1320 that the famous declaration of Scottish independence from the Norman kings of England was written, probably by monks in the abbey that is now an impressive red sandstone ruin. It took the form of a letter to the Pope seeking his support. Naturally, the stirring and bold sentiment, variously translated from the Latin, has been taken up and amplified over the centuries by Scottish nationalists — 'For so long as there shall but one hundred of us remain alive, we will never consent to subject ourselves to the dominion of the English.' Maybe we need a new declaration to energise another Scottish referendum, as the one in 2014 didn't produce the required majority for Scottish independence.

One bright spot in Arbroath is the Signal Tower museum, a short stroll from the harbour. It is part of a serene complex of buildings designed by Robert Stevenson in 1811 as the shore station, and lighthouse family accommodation, for the Bell Rock lighthouse. Walter Scott rightly described it as 'a handsome tower, with two wings'.[5] The museum is small (therefore easy to digest) and covers not just the story of the lighthouse but other bits of Arbroath history like the fishing (now gone apart from a few creelers in the harbour). The museum is owned by a Trust and — astonishingly — is open in the depths of winter.

That morning brought the aroma of Smokies, haddocks being smoked on sticks right by the harbour. A few smokeries survive, dark and atmospheric, with blue smoke wafting out of their chimneys. Of course we bought some, from Ian Spink's. 'Eat them cold,' we were told, but that didn't feel quite right. Google suggested opening them up, removing the bone, and grilling them with knobs of butter. Which is what we did. Delicious. As were the ice creams on the quayside. Arbroath was not so bad after all, so much better when the sun shone.

To Stonehaven, the town of the deep-fried mars bar

Unfortunately, given the tidal constraints, we couldn't lock out until midday by which time the tide was going to be against us for five hours. Irritatingly, we had the wind against us too, but at least the sea was flat, and it was sunny and warm. We manfully tacked north, backwards and

---

5. Scott, *Voyage of the Pharos*, 9.

forwards at depressingly narrow angles over the ground, well under 90°, each of us taking an hour on the helm. Despite a boat speed of around 5 knots, we were still only off Montrose when the tide turned north and the wind dropped, but at least we could then make 6 knots over the ground. On we went, getting colder as the sun set, arriving off Stonehaven at 11.30pm having covered only 30 miles in 12 hours.

The unfamiliar harbour made me anxious, particularly as it was by then dark. However, the entry seemed simple enough. But would we have to raft up to another yacht, or a fishing boat that might leave in the early hours of the morning? The plan was to motor straight for the end of the outer harbour wall with its white, red and green sectored light to guide us, turn sharply to starboard, hope for some illumination from harbour lights, and tie up as far as possible along the wall before the water became too shallow, hopefully far enough to be out of any swell. Just how far involved calculating tidal heights and ranges in my slightly tired brain. I should have done the calculations before we set off, as part of a proper passage-plan. But hey ho, I'm not perfect.

In the event, the entry was easier, but also shallower, than I expected. We had to tie up rather close to the outer end of the harbour wall; even there I estimated only 6 feet of water at low tide (we draw 5.5 feet). Tired, we scuttled below and shut the hatch, eager for Ben's mushroom risotto, and bed.

Talking of feet, I am hopelessly stuck between eras. I think in feet because of the age I am, so our echosounder is set in feet. But modern chart depths are of course in metres, while my anchor chain is still nostalgically marked in fathoms as the depths were on charts when I started sailing. Despite Steve's forebodings over the years he has sailed with me, this has not caused a muddle. Eventually, in 2020, to be sure of no confusion, I reluctantly changed the echosounder to read in metres (although it has a curious tendency to spontaneously revert to feet).

Friday July 6th, we were woken by shouting. Not at us, thankfully. A sailing boat tied up further along the harbour wall had, while trying to leave and turning round in the harbour, gone aground. On a falling tide. And there it tilted and tilted until the water returned and it refloated upright. Just the sort of thing I fear doing but never have. So far. I went back to sleep until someone was thoughtful enough to go out and buy those Aberdeen morning rolls (aka butteries, or rowies) that you can only really find north of Edinburgh. They are rather like squashed croissants. Their smell and taste took me straight back to my days working in the Aberdeen Royal Infirmary in the early 1970s when the nurses dished up warm butteries and toast at coffee time. The butteries now are not so full of salt (bad for the blood pressure), sugar (bad for the teeth), and calories (bad for the weight). I doubt if congenial coffee breaks allowing doctors and nurses to exchange information about patients on their ward exist in many hospitals these days. Everyone is too busy and pressurised to be even busier — and toasters are banned anyway (health and safety, don't you know).

In my first week as a doctor, the kind and very good registrar urged me to make sure I always took coffee and tea breaks. And so I mostly have ever since. Good advice. Mind you, he was later jailed for paedophilia. He was by then a professor of paediatrics of all things. Sadly, today's young hospital doctors running from patient to patient, many of whom they have never seen before, may simply be too rushed off their feet to stop for a glass of water, let alone a proper tea break. Clutching a bottle of water is hardly a good substitute for a canteen which may or may not be open.

The small town of Stonehaven looked highly appealing in the warm sunshine. An attractive inner harbour which dries, pubs on the inner harbour wall, a wide beach, seaside sculptures of dolphins made of wire, an open-air 1930s lido (usually filled with heated seawater, but closed unfortunately), ice cream, trippers, school kids, shops, and lovely views out to sea. Somewhat surprisingly it is where the deep-fried mars bar was invented, a Scottish 'delicacy' which is not entirely responsible for the low life expectancy in many parts of Scotland. All in all Stonehaven is a good place (although Ben preferred Arbroath, he said, because it had more charity shops). Harbours like this are delightful to visit, and are so unlike the soulless marinas built too far from anywhere like Brighton and Eastbourne. The only problem is having to tie up alongside a possibly rough harbour wall with the correct length of mooring ropes to allow for the rise and fall of the tide. This dying art in these days of marinas is what everyone had to do not so long ago. Sailors then were happy to dry out, their boats leaning picturesquely against a wall at low tide. With far more leisure boats today, it is a good compromise to have pontoons that float up and down with the tide, but which are conveniently attached to a harbour wall in the midst of harbour activities, as in Weymouth and Harwich. Maybe one day in Stonehaven too.

As usual we bought the *Guardian*, but it was so depressing. The banks cheating us all yet again, the Royal Bank of Scotland software cock-up, ridiculous bonuses for their staff, and the huge cost of the Private Finance Initiative (PFI) to build new hospitals going through the roof. PFI seemed such a clever wheeze to move the cost of the very-much-needed hospital building programme away from the public sector borrowing figures and on to private companies, supposedly more efficient than the state sector. Unfortunately, the whole package is far, far more expensive than if the government had borrowed the money to build the hospitals. Instead, the NHS has to rent and pay enormous annual interest for their hospitals which are now owned by banks and hedge funds, and will be for decades to come — an astonishing waste of public money.

Worse still, this cunning PFI plan siphons off government money from the NHS to shareholders and directors, a problem clearly seen very early on by Allyson Pollock, a public health physician with a serious campaigning streak (which sometimes overwhelms her science). Unfortunately she was largely ignored, but in retrospect she has been proved dead right. The Tony-Iraq-War-Blair Labour government didn't start the PFI bandwagon, but sadly with Gordon Brown as treasurer they took up the Tory idea with great enthusiasm. This has pitched our hospitals into being pawns in a great corporate gravy-train where it can be difficult to change a light bulb, let alone close an un-needed hospital, without the permission of the owners, whoever they may be.

From my Aberdeen days, I knew Dunnottar Castle was the place to see near Stonehaven. The crew had never been there, and I last had been 40 years ago just after it was opened to the public. We set off, not by the short cliff-path which was still closed following a landslip three years earlier, but by a long way round on a tedious road. However, we were rewarded by the sight of the spectacular ruin perched on its steep rock over the sea, almost cut off from the land. What had changed in 40 years? Loads more people, a lot of Italians for some reason, and an entry charge. It was still privately owned, and still rather spooky and more overgrown than the standard Historic Scotland offerings (now Historic *Environment* Scotland, a difficult mouthful, and a totally unnecessary change for no discernible reason). Back in Stonehaven the local folk festival was getting into its stride, and as it was a Friday evening it was difficult to find somewhere to sit for our pub supper. The Ship Inn and the Marine Hotel both looked good, chairs and tables outside (very un-Scottish). I can't remember which one we picked.

The next morning was horrible. The wind was force 6 from the north (from exactly where we were going), it was drizzling, and proper rain was forecast. I hadn't planned to stay another night but under the circumstances that is exactly what we did. I tucked myself up with the *Guardian*, the *Oban Times* to keep me up-to-date with the west coast, more butteries (not as good as those in Arbroath), and a splicing lesson from Ben. A few days later I had yet again forgotten how to splice and was back at square one.

The ageing brain. Ben had learned to splice from reading a knots book as a teenager, I certainly hadn't taught him. Personally I find diagrams in books hard to follow, I much prefer to be shown. Maybe YouTube will come to my rescue, although I do now have an app on my phone with a video demonstrating just how splicing is done (knots too), speeded-up or sloweddown and with a pause function to suit my confused brain.

Maybe I don't have the right sort of brain, which could be why I always found learning and indeed teaching clinical medicine was better done on the job, showing and doing. As a student I will never forget being *shown* during a postmortem how spontaneous bleeding into an atheromatous plaque in a coronary artery had lifted it up to block the artery and kill the patient. I can still see that plaque in my visual memory and can even remember the pathologist's name, Mike Davies.

Unfortunately, postmortems are now almost relics of the past. Partly because properly dissecting a body — or sometimes just the relevant part of a body indicated by the clinical history — is labour-intensive and expensive. Partly because many pathologists seem to have lost interest which is exacerbated if the clinicians are not prepared to attend or even discuss a postmortem (maybe they don't want any clinical mistakes revealed). And partly because doctors are more diffident about — and certainly less experienced in — asking the next-of-kin's permission for a postmortem. Furthermore, so confident have we become with our scans and genetic tests that postmortems are often regarded as superfluous for that final diagnosis, the cause of death. Over-confident, I would say, although in many cases the cause of death is indeed so obvious that postmortem confirmation is quite unnecessary. It may nonetheless be very educational for students and doctors (a justification which obviously has to be explained to the next-of-kin).

It was the combination of routine postmortems, along with clinical skill and long-term prospective epidemiological surveillance of the very rare condition of Creutzfeldt-Jakob disease (CJD) across the UK, which in 1996 led to the remarkably early realisation, after only ten cases, that a completely new type of CJD had emerged. This became known as variant CJD, a uniformly fatal brain disease usually acquired by eating meat products from animals infected with BSE (bovine spongiform encephalopathy). My neurologist colleague Bob Will was the clinician responsible for this discovery, along with the neuropathologist James Ironside, in the context of the prospective UK-wide CJD surveillance programme set up by Bryan Matthews 17 years earlier.

I had realised something was up when getting our boat ready for the sailing season and Bob phoned to ask me to cover for him because he had to go to London for 'something important'. He wouldn't say what. The next day it was all over the media. 'What's going on?' I asked my veggie son Ben when I got home. 'Bad news for you meat eaters,' he replied, with just a slight sense of superiority in his voice.

Without postmortems we might still be none the wiser about variant CJD, or it would have taken much longer to appreciate that a new disease had emerged. Notwithstanding the modern educational claptrap (sorry, methods), clinical medicine is still best learned as an apprenticeship, round a real patient's bed or at a postmortem, no more than five students at a time. Absolutely not just in a large lecture theatre, or by poking fingers into the orifices of manikins.

Our Oxfordshire Community Stroke Project (OCSP), which we started in 1981, was a much less dramatic example of the usefulness of a prospective study of a disease where patients were seen by experienced clinicians, studied as well as is practically and ethically possible, and followed up to find out what happens to them over years, not just for weeks or months, sometimes to postmortem. It later became the Oxford Vascular Study (OXVASC) under Peter Rothwell, and still continues (as indeed does surveillance of CJD). When I was writing the first grant application I bumped into the Professor of Epidemiology, Martin Vessey, in Oxford's Keeble Road. He asked what the point of the study was. I had no clear idea but remember saying 'I am sure something interesting will come out if it'. And something has — more than 200 scientific papers so far. When Bryan Matthews started CJD surveillance he surely had no idea how useful it was going to be. Contrary to what some scientists believe, you don't need to have a hypothesis before starting a research project.

Back to the present in Stonehaven. We were advised by the harbour master to move a bit further along the harbour wall, but that was a mistake. By low tide we were bumping the seabed in the swell, fortunately not for so long that we had to move again. In fact the tide was even lower than I had expected, and the short rope holding us in to the harbour wall ladder became so tight we had to cut it. A classic blunder. The longer bow and stern ropes were fine. All in all, rather a dull day, best forgotten.

Sailing by Aberdeen

Sunday July 8th was better, with no rain, light wind from the northwest rather than the less favourable north as had been forecast, flat sea. It all felt good as we headed out of the harbour at 6.30am while eating butteries and croissants. Off Aberdeen the chartplotter was full of Ben's 'triangles of doom' on the AIS, mostly ships going nowhere, at anchor waiting for work I suppose. I would have stopped off for old times' sake and to revisit one of the best maritime museums in the country. It doesn't just celebrate the past (fishing and oil) but looks to the future too (marine renewables). Unfortunately, because the harbour was bursting with commercial traffic to do with the off-shore oil and gas industry, yachts were strongly discouraged, which is a pity. This is nothing new — back in the late 19th century, Frank Cowper was so disgusted at the way he was treated when he sailed in to the harbour that he complained to the local newspaper.[6]

How different the harbour is now compared to when I arrived as a young lecturer in medicine in 1971. North Sea oil was a very recent discovery back then. Aberdeen was still a big fishing port, with an amazing early morning fish market. For me as a southerner it was impossible to follow what the auctioneers were shouting. Even at the best of times the Aberdeen accent was not easy to follow. Rather to my disappointment, patients used to clean up their accent when they realised they were talking to an English doctor. But not always, so I got used to simultaneously translating expressive words such as fushionless, oxter, peely-wally and many others.

As I liked to do at the time, I was keen for us junior doctors to see what the local population — our potential patients — did at work. In Birmingham we had arranged a tour round the Cadbury chocolate factory. After eating two free Easter Eggs you never want another one ever again. Later in Oxford we organised a trip round the Cowley car-works, impressive production lines in those pre-robot days. In Aberdeen it was the fishing. Ashley Mowat, a local medical colleague had two uncles. One was professor of something, I forget what, in Dundee, and the other the skipper of a local fishing boat — a fraternal combination that I don't think you would have found much in England. It seemed to me something very Scottish. Nothing wrong with being a fisherman with an academic brother, or for an academic to have a brother as a fisherman. Why not?

The skipper took me to sea for a couple of nights on his trawler, and my-oh-my was I impressed, so very impressed. I don't think he slept or left the bridge from when we got to the fishing grounds off Peterhead to getting back to Aberdeen (he had a toilet put in by the bridge so he didn't need to leave it, particularly important for him as his colon had been removed to sort out his ulcerative colitis). Naturally, we all ate fried fish on board, dabs

---

6. F. Cowper, *The Vagaries of Lady Harvey* (Kirkwall: W. R. Mackintosh, 1930), 76.

being the favourite among the crew, flat fish like small flounders. Nowadays a workplace visit in many places might have to be to a call centre, or an Amazon warehouse — what a depressing thought.

By the time I left Aberdeen in 1974 everything was changing. Fishing was in decline and eventually moved away to Peterhead and Fraserburgh up the coast. Oil was about to flow in, and property prices were rocketing including the value of my small one-bedroom flat that I had surprisingly wisely bought with a deposit from cashing in all three years of my NHS pension, because by then I had moved over to the university pension scheme.

Friends in the south thought I was quite mad to step out of the London medical scene. I might never get back, they said. Shock horror. A typical London-centric prejudice, which if anything may be worse now than it was then, although nepotism may be less, too. And what about the social scene, they wondered? And frequent visits to the theatre? Before I moved north I had seen the mime artist Lindsay Kemp camping it up with the young and unknown David Bowie playing his guitar in the corner of the stage in a tiny Notting Hill theatre. And there were the jazz clubs, Chinese restaurants up rickety stairs on the Isle of Dogs, pubs in the East End with hilarious drag entertainers, my mime classes, the amateur dramatics with friends who went on to be proper actors, and the Portobello road market. London, the centre of the universe. Maybe it was back then, maybe it is again, but for me Aberdeen was a career master-stroke for four almost accidental reasons.

First, as well as the teaching and research expected of a lecturer, I did the equivalent of the year of general medicine that was required before specialising in neurology. Although not a feature of training in most other European countries, in the UK we think this general experience is crucial for an aspiring specialist who otherwise can become dangerously blinkered as their specialist career advances into middle age. As a neurologist I didn't need to know how to treat a slow heart rate if it rather than epilepsy was causing sudden loss of consciousness, or if an underactive thyroid gland rather than a muscle disease was causing cramps. But I did have to be able to recognise the non-neurological problem, and refer on to the appropriate specialist (cardiologist and endocrinologist respectively). This may be apocryphal, but apparently at Atkinson Morley's Hospital when I was a medical student, before any CT scanners, a patient had his head opened by a neurosurgeon when the problem with his brain was not a tumour at all, but that it was bathed in blood overfull of glucose — he had diabetes. No one had thought to measure his blood glucose before surgery.

Second, it turned out I could not only do a postgraduate degree (more or less compulsory then if you wanted to be a neurologist), but had landed up in a department which actively encouraged me to do research. But what research to do? I hadn't a clue, having never done any. I didn't know which questions needed answering, and which could be answered in a couple of years. 'Let's see,' said the shy, kind and understated Professor of Medicine, Stuart Douglas, when he called me into his office. 'You want to be a neurologist,' he said. 'We do research into thrombosis. So I suggest you look into deep vein thrombosis (DVT) in stroke patients; it might be a problem in their paralysed leg.' So I did, just like that. It turned out that about half our stroke patients had a DVT, usually just in their paralysed leg, but mostly of no clinical consequence. For me the consequence was a career in stroke research.

Professor Douglas had tempted me to consider that lecturer's job over dinner at the Royal Society of Medicine in London, and then flew me up to Aberdeen in a Vickers Viscount on one of those early spring days when every stone in the granite city sparkled in the sunshine. He showed me an office that would be all mine, an extraordinary luxury after three years running round wards as a junior doctor with not even my own chair to sit on. He told another young lecturer, Graeme Catto, to show me round, instructing him to reveal everything, bad as well as good. Graeme was as amused and amusing as he still is, even though he has somehow survived being President of the GMC while heading King's College Medical School at the same time. Encountering him by chance in London, I asked him how he was managing to do both jobs simultaneously. 'Badly,' he replied, laughing.

I was helped enormously by Derek Ogston, a senior lecturer in medicine who was making a name for himself in thrombosis research. He showed me how to use the recently developed technique to detect blood clots in leg veins by injecting radioactive fibrinogen into the bloodstream (since abandoned for involving too much irradiation). In addition it was extraordinary to have such an excellent medical library down the corridor from my office. There were antiquarian books on open shelves, and reading them I made two discoveries. The first was that although DVT as a complication in the paralysed leg of a stroke patient was not mentioned in my contemporary textbooks, it had been described by John Ferriar, a Scottish physician way back in the early 19th century.[7] Delighted, I decided to use my favourite quotation to head up my thesis, not 'there is nothing new under the sun' from the Book of Ecclesiastes, but the more ambiguous version from the first

---

7. John Ferriar, 'An Affection of the Lymphatic Vessels hitherto Misunderstood', in *Medical Histories and Reflections*, vol. 3 (London: Cadell and Davies, 1810).

line of Samuel Beckett's 'Murphy', 'The sun shone, having no alternative, on the nothing new.'[8] I eventually thought better of it.

I was also delighted to discover that the well-known 'triad' of the causes of thrombosis — damage to the blood vessel wall, changes in the blood, and in blood flow — attributed to but never succinctly stated by the great German pathologist, Rudolf Virchow, had been implied, if not stated, a century earlier by John Hunter, the famous Scottish surgeon.[9] So much in medicine enters the lexicon under false pretences; attribution is misplaced, perhaps through ignorance but sometimes through prejudice. My two 'discoveries' probably helped to cement my view that it is a very good idea to know the history of a subject before starting to do research, and my determination that future research fellows of mine must devote the first chapter of their theses to the history of their topic. To finish my research degree I stayed more or less happily in Aberdeen for three years, not the originally anticipated one.

Third, I started to be properly taught neurology, by doing clinics with Allan Downie, a kind man with five children and an ex-nurse wife from London, the first and only consultant neurologist in Aberdeen at the time. As was common in the 1950s and 60s, he had been unable to land a consultant job in the UK and emigrated to the USA, thinking he would never return. Luckily the call came from Aberdeen where he had qualified in medicine. Back then, there were very few consultant neurologists in the UK, and far too many training to become a neurologist. These days there are vacant consultant positions all over the country and not enough trainees. As a result, many consultants have been recruited from Europe and further afield, at least until they were made to feel unwelcome by the nonsense of Brexit.

While I was in Aberdeen, Allan was joined by John Hern, perhaps like others banished from London by Roger Gilliatt, the Professor of Neurology at the National Hospital for Nervous Diseases who controlled so many appointments in those nepotistic days (he himself was the son of the Royal Household's gynaecologist). Contrary to expectations, John thrived in Aberdeen, as do so many incomers from England despite their early misgivings, and he even became a part-time sheep farmer. Once I heard him shout at the medical students from behind a patient's screen, 'You should feel breathless if you have properly assessed a patient's muscle

---

8. Samuel Beckett, *Murphy* (London: G. Routledge & Co., 1938).

9. John Hunter, 'A Treatise on the Blood, Inflammation and Gunshot Wounds', in *The Works of John Hunter*, ed. J. F. Palmer (London: Longman et al., 1794).

strength.' Good advice which I have not forgotten, and have passed on to my own students (but not I hope by shouting).

And finally — the hidden agenda — I learned to ski, although I was too old to learn to ski well. The drive early on a Sunday morning up Deeside to Glenshee with the rising sun lighting up the frosty landscape in front of me, and illuminating the white trunks of the bare birch trees, was a constant delight. As was driving around the Cairngorms to Aviemore in my convertible two-seat Triumph TR3A in my eager-young-man stage, which is long past — along with fancy cars as I next moved down to a slow and clunky Deux Chevaux. But what fun that TR was, my foreskin extension as a rude friend remarked. Well, it did have a long bonnet. Sadly, there is not nearly so much snow for Scottish skiing now.

On the downside it was not easy to make local friends. I never got as far as an Aberdonian's kitchen, although I did get inside a few Aberdonian houses. An English friend in Aberdeen, in desperation, even enquired at his local newsagents who else bought the *Guardian* in the hope that he might gain another friend or two. The stereotype of the rather reserved and joyless Aberdonian still lingered, as James Clark Maxwell, the very young and newly appointed Professor of Natural Philosophy in 1856, moaned, 'No jokes of any kind are understood here. I have not made one for two months, and if I feel one coming I shall bite my tongue.'[10]

A big plus was that no one of importance to my chosen neurology career down south had a clue what I was actually doing; indeed, they mostly didn't know whether Aberdeen was north or south of Dundee. I could hype up one or other aspect of my activities as required for the occasion. After some thought I decided not to be sidetracked by my research interest in thrombosis into becoming a haematologist, and still to make neurology my career, even at the risk of not finding a UK consultant job and having to emigrate. So I headed south for some informal 'chats' at the National Hospital for Nervous Diseases in London. So specialised (blinkered?) was a neurologist there that when I told him I had been researching venous thrombosis he assumed I meant thrombosis in the veins in the brain, considerably rarer than thrombosis in the veins of the leg.

That Aberdeen diversion probably stood me in good stead years later when I applied for the neurology chair in Edinburgh, because I had worked in Scotland and by then knew the country well. It was even preordained,

---

10. Lewis Campbell and William Garnett, *The Life of James Clarke Maxwell* (London: Macmillan and Co., 1882), 297.

sort of. When I was a junior doctor in London, a patient's husband told me that his wife was a bit of a witch — she could tell people's fortunes. Later I asked her about this talent, if that is what it was, to which she replied by telling my fortune:

'You will be a professor in a northern country.'

'Do you mean somewhere like Norway, or would Scotland do?' I asked, probably beginning to nurture the idea of a move to Scotland.

'Scotland certainly would do,' she replied. And so it came to pass.

Academics were, and still are, very prejudiced against moving away from the 'golden triangle' of London, Oxford and Cambridge. A neurologist friend in London, hearing I was going to Aberdeen, looked very puzzled and said, 'Well at least it's in Scotland, not the north of England.' That antinorthern prejudice — smoking chimneys, flat caps and funny accents. In contrast to 'Scotland the brand' with misty mountains, lochs, grouse moors, bagpipes, tartan and that ridiculous Loch Ness monster. Southerners tend to stick with old stereotypes like the 'dour Scot' (generally untrue) and 'The schools are so much better up there' (maybe true, I am not sure).

Certainly, in the past, education was the route out of poverty for many Scottish children. And today, our pupils are largely spared the disruption of constant testing, and the league tables plaguing the English schools so that they can be graded from outstanding (encouraging complacency and inhibiting innovation) to inadequate (depressing morale, and losing staff and funding). Unfortunately, it is all too easy to game a school's position in the league tables by discouraging pupils from taking exams if they are not expected to do well in the subject, even forcing them to leave and go to another school — so-called 'off-rolling'. Sadly, England's teachers are hounded with metrics and an overwhelming box-ticking bureaucracy. They have become mere employees, not the professionals they were trained to be. No wonder one in three quit within five years of starting teaching.[11]

But Scotland is not completely spared. A previous headteacher of our local high school wisely quipped that league tables, which we do sort-of have, were more useful for estate agents than parents, such is the difference in house prices between a 'good' and a 'poor' school's catchment area. Happily, Scottish unlike English children usually take five or more, rather than three, subjects in their final two school years. They can keep studying at least one of the creative subjects of art, music or drama — along with,

---

11. School Workforce in England: November 2018. Chart 2. Department for Education, June 2019.

say science or the humanities — until the end of their school days. I wish I had had that opportunity.

But I fear we do share with England that awful modern trend to teach to the curriculum and no more, and to strive come what may for the best possible exam mark. As ever, what is easily measurable (an exam result) does not necessarily reflect how good schools are at educating their pupils. Far more important, but next to impossible to measure reliably on a large scale, is the ability to learn (eventually unsupervised), critical thinking, preparation for the world as an adult, team work, tolerance, openness, curiosity, and good citizenship.

Enough of all this. Back to Pickle, we were sailing on.

To Peterhead

The wind was gradually veering to east of north so we had to tack backwards and forwards as we headed north, but at least we were going through the water at 5–6 knots. In the afternoon the cloud-base lifted but there was still no sun. On we tacked, past the Sands of Forvie where I first heard eider ducks cooing; past creepy Slains Castle standing ruined and gaunt on its cliff, apparently the inspiration for Bram Stoker to write *Dracula* (although Whitby has claimed him as their own); past Cruden Bay where there had been so much fuss when the oilmen wanted to land their pipelines there in the 1970s; and past the Bullers of Buchan, the cliffs where I first saw seabirds nesting in their thousands.

It was Wimbledon fortnight, that annual English tennis bonanza, and we were listening to the British hopeful Andy Murray once again trying to win the men's final, and avoid being known as the second Tim Henman who tried and tried but never did. Radio Scotland was inviting texts in support, so we sent 'Battle on Andy as we are battling against wind and tide off Peterhead, from sailing yacht Pickle'. This was broadcast, no doubt because it came from out at sea. But he still lost, to Federer, again. How boring tennis would be for me if I was one of those stars (such an unlikely scenario). Same game, every time five sets, same-sized court, same opponents, living out of a suitcase in international hotels. And so stressful because you are all alone on the court, with no team camaraderie once out there. But the money is good for the stars, and I presume others play tennis because they enjoy it (and want to become stars too).

Annoyingly the wind died away and by 3.30pm the tide was against us. We switched on the motor for the last few miles to Peterhead, arriving at the marina in the far corner of the vast harbour an hour later, 36 miles from Stonehaven. The huge south breakwater was constructed at the end of the 19th century by inmates of the somewhat notorious local prison, originally designed to hold Scottish convicts instead of sending them off to be incarcerated in England.

The marina manager was friendliness itself — handshakes all round, local information, for a mere £17 for the night. Three years later, during my second circumnavigation, I entered Peterhead harbour in a heavy snow shower with very poor visibility. Tying up at the marina I was surprised to be called up on the VHF radio by the harbour master to ask if we were alright:

'Yes, fine,' I replied. 'Why do you ask?'

'We have a CCTV camera over the marina and we couldn't see you because it is covered in snow!'

Now *there* is helpfulness for you, even in a large harbour with very big working ships. All a bit different in the late 17th century when Greenvile Collins wrote: 'Peter-Head lieth to the N.ward of Buchannais, and lieth within Calk-Inch. Here are two little dry Piers only fit for small Vessels to enter in at High-water.'[12] And in the early 19th century when the inveterate traveller, the Hon. Sarah Murray, opined in what was probably the first travel guide to Scotland: 'Most people know that Peterhead is a place for sea bathing. There is also a well of mineral water for drinking, which I believe is good for the scurvy. Peterhead is a neat, and almost newly built town. The inn is not a very good one to sleep at.'[13]

Notwithstanding the friendliness, I cannot love Peterhead and nor do many other people judging by the fact that it features on one of the three least popular Ordnance Survey maps of Britain.[14] Maybe it was the poor weather and a Sunday, but I found the whole place very depressing. We walked the mile or so into the town, which was dead and silent and grey. The pubs looked not just unfriendly but positively threatening. There was nowhere to eat other than a chipper. Everywhere else was closed. The main street looked awful. Huge sheds blocked the views from the houses by the docks. Why did it seem so depressed? There was surely plenty of money around with the fishing and the fish market, work on the oilrigs, and ship

---

12. Collins, *Great-Britain's Coasting Pilot*.

13. Sarah Murray, *A Companion and Useful Guide to the Beauties of Scotland, and the Hebrides*, vol. 2 (3rd edn, London: 1810) [p. 74 in the version printed and bound by Pranava Books, India].

14. *Guardian*, 9 September 2018.

repair. We scurried back to the boat, tucked ourselves up down below, closed the hatch, and ate a delicious aubergine curry, cooked as ever by Ben.

On Pickle we have almost as good cooking facilities as at home — two gas rings, a grill, a not great oven, and a double sink. There is no excuse for baked beans on toast, or pasta with sauce out of a bottle. We do eat well, and so we should. If C. C. Lynam managed on his very small yawl at the end of the 19th century, so can we in the 21st: 'The skipper cooked a magnificent stew of hare-soup, curried fowl, rice and onions, which with strawberry jam to taste, was highly appreciated.'[15] In contrast, Hilaire Belloc didn't believe in cooking anything at sea, especially meat — probably because he made such a mess when attempting to cook even on land, according to Dermod MacCarthy, the medical student who was one of the young crew who helped sail his boat for him when he was in his 60s.[16]

To Lossiemouth and the RAF

Monday July 9th, another dull and grey day. And an extremely bouncy exit from Peterhead harbour at 8.30am. It remained bouncy until we got well round Rattray Head even though we kept four miles off to avoid the worst of the overfalls. The northwesterly wind was 20–25 knots so with two reefs in the mainsail we were working quite hard, taking four tacks north before we could head west along the Moray Firth coast in a wind that fortunately by then had veered to more or less northerly. We batted along on a fine reach, our mood improved by the sky brightening although the sun never appeared, and it was far from warm. At least it wasn't raining, as it was over most of the rest of Scotland. Just a bit of spray in the cockpit, far less than we would have had in our Contessa 32.

The crew were very good. Despite feeling a bit sick, Ben did most of the helming. Neil didn't do much because he managed to lose his balance and fall rather heavily on his ribs. Fortunately just bruising, not bleeding given his anticoagulants. As we age, our balance is just not as good as it once was. On this cruise alone, I had fallen and hurt my back, brother John had fallen, and now Neil. Note to self: do not rush about so much, and hold on more. If only.

Some crew (but not this one) never seem to learn. How to steer the

---

15. C. C. Lynam, *The Log of the 'Blue Dragon', 1892–1904* (London: A. H. Bullen, 1907), 15.

16. Dermod MacCarthy, *Sailing with Mr Belloc* (London: Collins Harvill, 1986).

boat in a straight line, and how to wash the dishes without wasting fresh water. Worse, some sit about while I do everything. Is this laziness? Lack of interest? Anxiety? Under-confidence? Not realising what jobs have to be done? Not knowing how to do them? As most of my friends are now of the age, a sign of early dementia perhaps? Surely not mere wilfulness. Whatever the cause, this must be partly my fault for not engaging the crew enough, and not showing them what to do, but I hesitate to repeat myself again and again. And I certainly shouldn't shout at the crew; after all, we have to live together for several days in a very small space with no escape (my shouting is generally reserved for arriving at and departing from marinas).

By 3pm we were off Banff and going at 5–6 knots. Gradually we could sail more freely and were approaching Lossiemouth by 8pm, not too bad for the 59 miles from Peterhead. We had seen no other yachts all day. Fortunately we didn't have to worry about arriving late, as it was not properly dark until at least 11pm. Of the few possible places to stop along this coast I thought Lossiemouth would be the best, given the wind direction. I had wanted to go to Whitehills but with the wind from the northwest the entrance to the harbour would not have been sensible. Since then I have sailed to Whitehills, and it is one of the friendliest and best-appointed marinas on the planet, albeit with a scary entrance requiring a sharp hand-break turn to port before mounting the old lifeboat slipway straight ahead. Once into the harbour there is not much room, so turns of three points or more are needed to get on to a pontoon. But it's well worth the effort. The harbour master photographs the entrance, competent or not, of nearly every boat, and later presents you with the images on a memory stick.

Entering Lossiemouth was not at all easy, even coming in from the east. The harbour entrance is narrow (shades of Lowestoft) and quite large waves were breaking on the shore. My nerves were not helped by Ben on the foredeck shouting back to me that surfers were having a great time off the beach just outside the harbour. With rocks to starboard, the beach to port, and the swell twisting us this way and that, I got even more anxious. The dodgy entrance remains Ben's main memory of this leg. But all went well, and it was the usual remarkable relief to feel the sea flatten between the harbour walls, the peace and quiet out of the wind, to unclench jaw and buttock muscles, and look for the pontoons and an accessible space for us.

Lossiemouth was grey and mostly closed, even though we were into the school holidays. The Steamboat Inn on the harbour wall had no real ale, and no food. The Lossie Hotel looked grim and had stopped serving food. Eventually we found a café with hardly any customers, so ate there. The next morning was still grey. The town is laid out on a grid pattern, with small houses down each side of the wide streets. Despite some shops for sale, there were still at least two butchers, and a baker. In the end we found a really nice little café, the Harbour Lights, in a converted warehouse right on the harbour wall. Very cosy, good coffee and buns.

There is an RAF base just outside the town. According to the retired fishermen in the local museum on the quayside (who I think ran it), the base had saved Lossiemouth from going completely downhill after the fishing industry collapsed. The museum was very good with its display and explanation of the town's seafaring past. A sobering DVD showed waves crashing over the harbour wall. It was sad, too, because the displays could only celebrate the glorious fishing past with seemingly little hope for the future (thousands if not millions of herrings, all gone now). One interesting titbit was the reconstruction of the study of Ramsay MacDonald, the first Labour Prime Minister. He was born and brought up in Lossie (by then I had cottoned on to the shortened name), the illegitimate son of a farm labourer and a housemaid. Clearly a lad o' pairts.

When all the old fishermen have died who will be left to illuminate this little museum, reliant like so many others on enthusiastic and knowledgeable volunteers? What hope is there when a town's single industry disappears with nothing to replace it? The marina in the old harbour won't bring in much income. An RAF base is hardly a stable alternative. Indeed, in 2013 the government announced its closure, but have since relented. But we surely won't need fast jets for much longer, more likely drones controlled from Melton Mowbray, and cyber-warfare conducted from Cheltenham.

We struck Lossie at a bad time. Not only was the weather dreich, but only a few days earlier two of the local RAF Tornado fighter-bombers had collided over the Moray Firth 25 miles south of Wick, killing three of their crew and leaving the other badly injured. The navy had been out searching for them, and the remains of their planes. Young men (and now young women) in their flying machines — too many are killed in accidents during low-flying exercises over Scotland where their planes are much in evidence. Some of the wreckage had already been brought in to the harbour, a very emotional blow to this little town, especially poignant as Tornados were still taking off right over our heads. The show clearly had to go on.

To Helmsdale

Tuesday July 10th, we left at 2pm, but in slight chaos. We had carefully looped a mooring rope around a cleat on the pontoon and by bringing the two ends back to the boat we could hold ourselves in and slip the rope when we were ready to leave (by releasing one end and pulling on the other to get the whole lot back onto the boat, carefully avoiding winding it around the propeller). Unfortunately the rope had an unexpected knot in the end that naturally got jammed in the cleat. With the result that Pickle was left hanging off the end of the pontoon with none of the crew ashore to release the rope. Embarrassing, as we hauled ourselves back to the pontoon to sort out the problem, and start all over again.

Outside the harbour the swell was almost as bad as the previous evening, and there was no wind. We had to motor 26 miles across the Moray Firth, plodding along at about 5 knots, feeling slightly seasick in a long slow swell under a continuing grey sky with light rain. To pass the time I tried another splice, but Ben still had to help me get started (my problem being exactly where the third strand goes). In the distance we spotted a naval ship, still searching or perhaps guarding the crash site.

Helmsdale is shallow so we aimed to be there near high water. At 7.30pm, two hours after high water, we found a depth of 8 feet, enough to allow us to tie up to the pontoon. No other visiting boats, just one or two local boats, creelers I think. Difficult to imagine that this had once been a major herring port, now all gone. No harbour master was to be found, and indeed the post was advertised on the harbour wall. So no help, no berthing fee (even though as instructed we tried to pay at the Post Office who knew nothing about it), and no one to tell us the code for the toilets. Neil Gunn, who came from this area, based his novels on the communities along this coast in the days of fishing, poverty — and education as the way out for the bright Scottish lad (not so often for the bright Scottish lassie).

The next morning we looked at Helmsdale, a neat little town, in a lovely setting with a serene 1809 Telford bridge that once carried the main road high over the river just upstream from the pontoons. Under the bridge we found Timespan, a terrific local museum with good displays, a geology garden (all the rocks neatly labelled), and gallery (its art too modern for my taste). Astonishingly, we discovered an artist in residence, two months into the job, from London (I wonder how long he lasted). There must have been money around to pay this guy, and a lot of enthusiasm, without which no amount of money would keep the place going. Clearly a number of local (perhaps amateur) historians and archaeologists were involved.

Among the sprinkling of shops, and a remarkable number of pubs and hotels for the size of the place, we found a little gem selling 20th-century memorabilia. The owner was so laid-back he didn't even know he was mentioned in *Scotland the Best*, my preferred guide to Scotland. For a fiver I bought a small leather handbag shaped like a woman's breasts, a jokey gift for someone — well, for daughter Margaret as it turned out. She had just texted on her return from Guyana where she and her expedition had avoided any dreaded tropical disease, or snakebites.

It was odd how Helmsdale seemed so much more together than Lossie, but my impressions may have been very superficial, and weather-dependent. The sun had come out a bit, always good for the mood. But since then I have often stopped in Helmsdale when driving to and from Thurso, and am still impressed with how attractive the place is. The village shop is a hive of activity, and gossip. Sadly, the memorabilia shop is no more, nor is there any artist in residence.

To Wick

Wednesday July 11th. Being addicted to newspapers (as well as trains, and biscuits), and seeking both UK and Scottish news, I indulged in much *Guardian* and *Scotsman* reading while waiting for the tide to turn in our favour. Why oh why do I do this? I really am hopelessly addicted, it's just as bad as Lucy and William's addiction to their phones. It takes at least an hour of my day, 363 hours a year, so more than two weeks out of the 52. The news was yet again of the appalling behaviour of bankers; the Olympic games in London brewing up in a couple of weeks (of no interest to me); Michael Gove the Tory education secretary aided by his Svengali-like assistant Dominic Cummings laying waste to the English schools; not enough money for mental illness and even if there were it is unclear where all the staff were going to come from; Andrew Lansley — the Tory Health Secretary — destroying the English NHS; and as always failure to reform the House of Lords. I got caned at Haileybury after having had the temerity to tell a more senior boy that he was a total dimwit (which was true). He became and still is one of the 92 remaining hereditary peers, and was once minister for defence procurement in a Tory government. No wonder we have such old-fashioned weapons like our two new aircraft carriers without any planes, and that nothing comes in at anything like the originally estimated cost.

How on earth do we tolerate a second legislative chamber full to bursting with not just the residual hereditaries, but mates of previous prime ministers — 374 life peerages dished out as patronage by Tony-

Iraq-War-Blair, another 245 by David Cameron?[17] An incontinence of peers. Plus wealthy donors to political parties, superannuated MPs, editors of supportive newspapers, mediocre celebrities, Boris Johnson's brother. All unelected. For life. A good way of keeping people sweet and on your side, at least in public. And 'The Lords Spiritual', 26 Church of England bishops in their cassocks, a purple-shirted affront to democracy, and indeed to our many other religious communities. Over eight hundred peers in total, paid £305 a day if they turn up, sit on the red benches before falling asleep, have arcane debates which can do almost nothing to change the legislation brought forward by the House of Commons, and fiddle with their phones — before having a good (subsidised) lunch. No record is kept of how long the peers stay for debates, or who has lunch. In 2018 one peer claimed nearly £50,000 for travel and attendance, yet never spoke or put down a written question.[18] Furthermore, one in five peers is a consultant or advisor, some to very dodgy organisations, including foreign governments with appalling human rights records.

Apparently this load of chancers is the largest parliamentary chamber in any 'democracy'. Largest is clearly not necessarily best, and democracy is an odd word to use for a bloated chamber that is unelected and still contains those hereditary peers because their forebears were long ago rewarded by the monarch for something, possibly reprehensible. Reforms are hopeless; they have been tried and frustrated for 500 years. Abolition is the only answer. We wouldn't have such nonsense as the Lords in an independent Scotland, but that is not a good enough argument for independence, at least not by itself. At the time of the cruise the 2014 Scottish independence referendum was still two years away. When it did come it certainly energised almost the entire Scottish population to a previously unheard-of extent. I even found myself discussing the pros and cons with the lady selling me shoes in an Edinburgh shop.

During 2014 my own independence views changed every day. To me the question was not '*Could* Scotland become independent?'. Of course it could, just look, for example, at how we perform in an area I know well: Scottish medical research is the second most cited per 1000 population, after Sweden, and well ahead of England and the USA.[19] Despite what

---

17. House of Lords, Library Note. Peerage creations since 1997.

18. *Guardian*, 31 May 2019.

19. Allen Coppen and John Bailey, '20 Most-Cited Countries in Clinical Medicine Ranked by Population Size', *Lancet*, 363 (2004), 250.

may be another suspect metric, I am sure our medical science really is right up there with the best, and I am sure other things are, too. The correct question is '*Should* Scotland become independent?'. Yes, if that means no more House of Lords, no more Trident on the Clyde, a closer relationship between the government and the governed. No, if that means years of expensive chaos sorting out the dis-union and an appalling and divisive mess like Brexit is proving to be. I woke at 5am on the morning of the independence referendum worrying about my final but still shaky decision to vote yes. In the end I did. Perhaps luckily, the referendum result was a no.

One option, not on the ballot paper but which many Scots might have supported, would have been far more devolution from Westminster, perhaps leading to a federal UK. Now, as we destroy ourselves with the consequences of Brexit, Scottish independence is back in the news. But how would we cope with a hard border spanning Berwick to Carlisle if Scotland was back in the EU single market and England was not? Tariffs on whisky, and customs checks too? But if an independent Scotland could not return to the EU that would surely be a disaster. The independence problem is very far from straightforward.

We left for Wick at 3.15pm. Although it wasn't raining, it was cold, overcast and — far worse — the wind was only 10 knots as well as being from the northeast. So it was slow tacks northwards along the coast. And what a formidable coast it is, all those small east-facing harbours with narrow entrances, silting up after being abandoned by the fishermen who now have no fish to catch, impossible to get in or out of in an easterly blow or swell, and mostly too shallow for us too. As Libby Purves remarked: 'There is something indescribably gallant about an East Coast harbour: few natural features assist its safety, as they do in the rocky west; nature throws up sandbanks, treacherous longshore currents, anything to cause trouble. But the harbours creep seawards, not always with the arrogance of the great industrial shipyards but more often with persistent, under-financed, local determination to catch fish, to take trade, to give small, insignificant towns a maritime backdoor. I saluted it all.'[20] We saw very few boats of any sort along this part of the coast, not surprisingly.

Unusually for me, I didn't have a plan B anywhere in my head, my excuse being that there was no bad weather brewing. I have no idea what we would have done if we couldn't make Wick for some reason. Into Lybster perhaps,

---

20. Libby Purves, *One Summer's Grace: A Family Voyage round Britain* (London: Grafton Books, 1989), 216.

but tricky with a very narrow entrance and hardly room to turn. Or press on across the Pentland Firth into the shelter of Scapa Flow. Fortunately by 5pm the wind shifted to sufficiently east of north that we could make one long port tack towards Wick, in light rain. Who cares about a bit of rain? Wind direction is far more important, as well as tide direction and speed. Tacking backwards and forwards against the wind as well as the tide is far, far more debilitating than standing in the rain but travelling in the right direction, albeit close-hauled.

Again I found myself marvelling at the technology we now have to take the stress out of navigation, if not pilotage into harbours and anchorages for which one's eyes are still more important than the chartplotter. Before chartplotters and AIS we did have GPS from which we could at least mark our position on a paper chart — in pencil, with a rubber to hand. I can't remember when I last used a pencil and rubber, but I do write down our position (from the GPS) in the logbook every hour when we are on passage out of sight of land. Nor can I remember when I last used a hand-bearing compass. I still have one on board in case the GPS packs in, most likely because the boat batteries have gone flat. But even then we have a handheld GPS with its own batteries. And an emergency jump-starter power-pack to resurrect a dead battery, not yet used in earnest.

Before GPS we did have the Decca system, but that was far less convenient and reliable, and before that nothing. Well, there were radio direction finders. Sodding great earphones connected to a big chunky thing which you pointed at the shore and turned until the beeps from a distant radio beacon sounded equally loud in both ears, which gave its bearing coming maybe from a lighthouse — but no information about its distance away. Lots of sailors now have radar which has got smaller and cheaper, although we don't, partly because I don't want even more electronics to flatten our batteries. My older three children, being brought up sailing in the late 20th century, can just about navigate with pencil, compass and chart if they have to, but I fear for the two younger ones. What will they do if all their boat electrics pack up? Or if the GPS signal is switched off or maliciously jammed? Even I am getting deskilled for lack of practice. Could I still work out my position by 'doubling the angle on the bow'? Probably not, unless I had my dog-eared navigation class notes on board to remind me how to do it.

And before mobile phones allowed us to talk to family and friends, we were at the mercy of contacting a coastal radio station through the VHF radio (I don't think they still exist), and from there were connected to the telephone system. Disconcertingly, anyone with a VHF radio within range could listen to your conversation. When I started cruising in the 1970s there was not even VHF radio for leisure sailors. On land we had to find a red telephone box.

We were able to make Wick in daylight, arriving in the bay at 10pm, a run of 29 miles. Sails down, motor on, three fenders tied up on port as well as starboard for whichever side turns out to be appropriate and to allow for any of my last-minute foul-ups. Mooring ropes each side front and back for the same reason, another rope for a midships spring, again each side, and the sprayhood down for maximum forward visibility. Identify the entrance to the harbour, beware fishing boats shooting out from behind high harbour walls, and watch out for lobster-pot buoys waiting to entangle the propeller. Finally, negotiate the unfamiliar pontoons and find a Pickle-sized gap which would also be possible to get out of.

In the event, the entrance to Wick harbour was easy and there was plenty of space between the pontoons, lots of empty berths in a remarkably sheltered marina that had only opened three years earlier. Indeed, it all went uncharacteristically well, although the 'fixed red light' we had to aim for beyond the end of the harbour wall suddenly moved off. The rear light of a car. Having tied up, it was down below out of the cold, shut the hatch, boots off, slippers on, gin and tonic to hand with lemon but no ice (no freezer on Pickle), nuts and crisps, dinner courtesy of Ben again. And wine. Maybe a single malt whisky, for night sedation.

Unfortunately there was very bad news from Holland, an email on my phone telling me that Maarten van Gijn had been killed. He had ridden his mountain bike off a narrow cliff path in the Alps. His father Jan, my age, had also been a professor of neurology (in Utrecht), he too had had cancer of the colon, and we shared many of the same interests and obsessions in medicine. He was a close friend and colleague. What a disaster. How can one bear the loss of a child? Not so long ago this was commonplace, through illness or war, but nowadays we are just not ready for it.

Other friends have lost children too, usually through accidents, or sometimes cancer. Like Neil, right next to me on the boat, whose daughter Alice had died of bone cancer while still at university. And Stu, from the previous leg — one of his three sons had frozen to death when caught by bad weather near the top of Mont Blanc; his climbing companion survived but lost both hands and both feet from frostbite. I can recall other young friends and acquaintances who died young. One from testicular cancer; a school friend who didn't turn up at Cambridge because he had been killed in a motorbike accident; a young mother wiped out by a truck when she had stopped on the hard shoulder of a motorway; a young woman who had slipped on top of the Cobbler mountain; a young man while running for a train in Oxford who fell under the wheels; a young woman who tumbled over a landing; and another just found dead. Strange that we had been thinking about those young airmen who had died that same week so close to here. And I was worrying about Ben and Oli who were planning to climb the Old Man of Hoy on Orkney the very next week.

Thursday July 12th was explore Wick day while waiting for the right moment to cross the Pentland Firth to Orkney. I didn't have high hopes for Wick, which is one of those very distant places that one jokes about. That said, two friends had been junior doctors here, one being John Rawles whom we had met in Penzance. Libby Purves was not too encouraging: 'But Wick is a comely, decent, grey-stone Scottish town, with manicured lawns on its clifftop, a neat lifeboathouse, and the remains of old kippering sheds standing rather forlornly around the harbour walls.'[21] Like other coastal towns hereabouts it had a glorious but brief few years in the sun, as the biggest herring landing port in the late 19th century, absolutely stuffed with boats — over 1000 had been based there. Apparently 50 million fish were once landed over a two-day period. Those 'silver darlings' are long gone but some remnants of the past remained, in particular Old Pultney Town above the harbour with its splendid early 19th-century stone buildings, solid and imposing, and the large harbour designed by Telford (that man never stopped working, from humble Scottish stonemason to the first president of the Institution of Civil Engineers).

The town itself was reasonably bustling with a good feel. It even had an attractive bookshop combined with a café (sadly no more). But there were also many closed pubs and shops, almost no decent food shops, with just one butcher hanging on (the supermarkets had done for the rest). Around the harbour there was quite a bit of dereliction, but maybe Wick, and other depressed east coast towns in Scotland and England, will be rescued by the huge recent developments in offshore wind farms. Indeed, by 2019 rescue was in progress for Wick because the support boats for the recently built offshore Beatrice wind farm are based in the harbour, and their office is in a nicely converted historic building. Among some quotes fixed to old walls near the harbour I liked the sly wisdom of 'A new broom can sweep clean … but 'e owld broom kens aal 'e corners'.

A real plus was the local heritage museum, a remarkable wonder, maybe

---

21. Purves, *One Summer's Grace*, 185.

the best museum around our entire coastline. It had taken over several adjacent properties (Telford's designs yet again) into which it spread like Dr Who's tardis. Manned — no, womanned — by incredibly helpful and enthusiastic volunteers who showed us quickly into each of the 25 rooms in case we got lost when going round by ourselves. And what a wonderful collection of stuff. Lighthouse memorabilia; hundreds of old photographs by a local family of photographers; paintings; domestic rooms furnished in various styles and periods; collections from the local printing industry; war medals; fishing bric-a-brac; model yachts; and with a lovely garden spreading up the hill in terraces at the back, full of flowers where ladies weeded.

As Pete Irvine wrote in *Scotland the Best*, these ladies should have MBEs. Indeed they should if one had faith in our honours system, which I don't. Some totally undeserving people I know have CBEs for doing nothing discernible to me, while many far more deserving do not. As for knighthoods, don't get me started. What is so irritating is the common reaction of 'oh, I am only accepting this on behalf of all the people who have worked so hard in my team'. Phooey. They are accepting the honour to improve their chances with the next grant application, and to get a better restaurant table. They may even have been given the honour to persuade them to keep their mouths shut. Some say honours can be bought, too. The best reasons to accept an honour are that it makes you feel appreciated, and for your parents to be even prouder of you, which was their reaction when Cathie was awarded an OBE in 2020, for services to medical research (and I am proud of her too!). Of course, although everyone feels that need of appreciation, not everyone gets an OBE. And as Cato the Elder wryly observed, 'I would much rather have men ask why I have no statue, than why I have one.'

Our final task in Wick was to inspect the footbridge over the river on the edge of the town. Sally, Neil's wife, had a great-grandfather from Wick who provided the money to build that bridge in 1893. It still stands. I met Sally and Neil when we arrived as clinical students at St George's Hospital Medical School in 1965, they from King's College London, me from Cambridge. I remember them as always being a pair, which they demonstrated in spades by Sally falling pregnant. Hardly anyone was taking the contraceptive pill in those days, partly because of the deep vein thrombosis scare stories at the time. Undeterred, they both carried on as medical students, married, had the baby, did junior hospital doctor jobs, had two more children, and eventually moved out of London, Neil to train as a GP and Sally as a medical ophthalmologist. We were all reunited when I moved to Oxford in 1976, by which time Neil was in one of the best practices in Oxford, later joined by Ann McPherson. Friends from university, and particularly medical school friends, are so often for life, certainly in my case, even when I now live a few hundred miles from them.

To Orkney

The Wick harbour master was friendly, amusing and helpful. He even complimented us on our entry the previous evening, a sure way to make me like someone. His advice was to leave at 4pm while the tide was still flooding south, to keep close to the shore in Sinclair's Bay to catch the north-going eddy, and then be off Duncansby Head as the ebb built west into the Pentland Firth. We left at 4.15pm in a northwest wind of 15–20 knots, not too bad a direction. And no rain, just overcast. Irritatingly the wind quickly shifted more to the north so we had to put in several tacks that took us out of Sinclair's Bay and that helpful eddy.

There seemed to be a lot more seabirds around than on the west coast. Off Duncansby Head we came across bonxies (great skuas) for the first time, those rather nasty aggressive birds which dive-bomb you if you get anywhere near their nests, as well as the more elegant and slimmer Arctic skuas attacking gulls. We were definitely up north, not in Yorkshire, which is what Londoners mean by up north, but really north, approaching the Northern Isles of dark winter nights but fabulously light summer evenings.

In truth the dreaded Pentland Firth was no big deal. The sea was flat, the tide was not that fast because it was neaps, and there were no tide races and overfalls to bounce through. A good thing really, as we had to put in a number of tacks across to Orkney until we were carried by the tide through the gap between the islands of Swona and South Ronaldsay into Scapa Flow to arrive in Widewall Bay at 11.15pm, 25 miles from Wick. No tangling with marina pontoons — it was so much easier to creep into the wide-open and gently shelving bay, with not a single rock to be avoided, and then anchor at a suitable depth, even in the dark. It was so peaceful in Orkney, at least it was after we had sorted out the jammed anchor chain, that Rustler 36 irritation again.

Friday July 13th, off at 10.15am. The wind was still in the north, light at 10 knots, which meant tacking across the amazing — and flat — Scapa Flow, past the oil terminal on Flotta, in sunshine and cloud, light and shade drifting over the pastoral scenery of Orkney with scattered farms and houses. There wasn't anywhere which looked remotely like where Mary Shelley sent Frankenstein to make his second 'creature', an Orcadian island which was 'hardly more than a rock ... the soil was barren, scarcely affording pasture for a few miserable cows, and oatmeal for its inhabitants, which consisted of five persons.'[22]

Like Libby Purves I too found it odd 'to be among such fertile, arable flatlands again, gentle green hills with barely one rock per field'.[23] Compared with the wild emptiness of Caithness on the north Scottish mainland, Orkney is another world. There may be few trees to speak of, but the hills are gentle (with the exception of Hoy), so many shades of green, sheep lazing, cattle knee-deep in meadows, hay fields, and wide-open sky. There was not a single other yacht, or any other sort of boat, to be seen on the Flow, despite the good weather and holiday season.

Scapa Flow is a magnificent inland sea, about ten miles by five, a huge natural harbour, which provided the ideal base for the British Grand Fleet during the first world war when the enemy was no longer France and Spain in the south. From here the fleet could control the entrance to the North Atlantic across to Norway and keep the German fleet bottled up in harbour the other side of what was then known as 'The German Sea', now the North Sea. Nowadays, Scapa Flow has only three relatively narrow entrances. To keep out German U-boats during the second world war, the four other entrances were obstructed with huge concrete blocks — the Churchill barriers — and laid mostly by Italian prisoners of war, and along which a road was built, connecting the main Orkney island with the smaller islands to the south.

The last view of Britain had by my mother's father, John Hine, must have been of Orkney, because he was part of that Grand Fleet, on HMS Invincible, one of the battle-cruisers built for speed but at the expense of inadequate armoured hull protection.[24] He had originally joined the army but as the navy was short of engineers he switched to become Engineer Lieutenant Hine at the rather advanced age of 42. The Invincible was one of 250 Allied and German ships involved in the Battle of Jutland on May 31st 1916, the biggest full-scale naval clash in the war. Both sides claimed victory, but it was probably a stalemate, and certainly not another Trafalgar as many in Britain had anticipated, and hoped for.

Early in the battle, a German shell scored a direct hit on one of the

---

22. Mary Shelley, *The New Annotated Frankenstein*, ed. Leslie S. Klinger (New York: Liveright Publishing Corporation, 2017).

23. Purves, *One Summer's Grace*, 176.

24. Angus Konstan, *Jutland 1916: Twelve Hours to Win the War* (London: Aurum Press, 2016).

Invincible's gun turrets. The flash ignited the magazine far below because the hatches had been left open to allow faster shell-loading. The ship blew up and sank within minutes. All but six of the 1032 officers and men were killed, including my grandfather. Unlike senior army officers in Flanders who were often well behind the forward lines, senior naval officers died with their men as their ships sunk under them. After all, the naval tradition was always that the captain is the last person to leave his sinking ship. It is somewhat irritating that the Royal Navy's role in keeping the sea supply lines to Britain open during that war has been rather eclipsed by the horror stories of the trenches, the subject of countless books and films.

The family story told to me as a child was that the explosion was so big that my grandfather would have known nothing about it. Far more likely is that he and hundreds of others were trapped below decks as the ship sank, a terrifying experience for so many sailors in wartime. Deep down in the engine room he would not have had a clue what was going on until it was far too late to get out. My grandmother, whom I remember as quite a severe lady, wore black for the rest of her life. She was left with four children to bring up, and never remarried. How she managed financially I have no idea, but she did come from a well-off Suffolk family. She and her children lived in quite a nice house in Nottingham. My uncle Alfred went to university, while the three girls instead left school to find work, which was typical for those times. Also typically, after they married they never worked again (outside the home).

My mother was a secretary before getting married in 1931. She never forgot her father. Even late in life she visited the 'new' and final HMS Invincible, a 'through-deck cruiser' (looking more like an aircraft carrier to me) that took part in the 1982 Falklands War. She was also in occasional correspondence with the captain as 'a friend of the ship'.

We arrived in Stromness 14 miles from Widewall Bay at 1.15pm. It is a wonderfully salty place, the narrow winding main street a constant delight, with no pavement but laid with stone slabs and a central cobbled strip to prevent the horses slipping in the old days. In those old days Stromness would have been dirty, crowded, chaotic and smelly, which is how Walter Scott, arriving on the Lighthouse yacht, the 'Pharos', found it in 1814: 'a little dirty straggling town, which cannot be traversed by a cart, or even by a horse, for there are stairs up and down, even in the principal streets'.[25] Nowadays, what is locally known as 'The Street' is a good example of how

---

25. Scott, *Voyage of the Pharos*, 60.

mixing pedestrians, cyclists, buggies, mobility scooters and motorists forces everyone to slow down and take more care (apart from one local wild young man on his mobility scooter). I had first come here in the early 1970s while working in Aberdeen and watched anxiously as my car was craned off the ferry at Stromness. Now the ferry is a more convenient roll-on roll-off affair.

Stromness is where the great whaling fleets gathered in the 19th century, where the Hudson's Bay company recruited, where Franklin and Cook's ships called in for water, where John Rae who discovered the fate of Franklin's expedition came from, and where thousands of servicemen in both world wars were stationed and became mightily bored, cold and fed up. It is said to be Captain Hamish Blair of the Royal Navy in world war two who wrote that poem about bloody Orkney which I remember as a teenager in the Faber paperback *Verse and Worse*, long before I knew where Orkney was. It ends:

'Best bloody place is bloody bed,
With bloody ice on bloody head,
You might as well be bloody dead,
In bloody Orkney.'

These days there is an excellent marina, right by the ferry from where Oli emerged to meet us, in the centre of town, handy for pubs and shops. It is probably my favourite marina, although with one small problem: no cleats on the pontoons, just hoops to which it is much more difficult to attach a mooring rope in a hurry. (But still better than the hoops at Tórshavn in the Faeroes which are flush with the pontoons and have to be found and then pulled up to be useful.) The marina was looked after (just before his retirement) by Bobby who carried a shiny black briefcase stuffed with harbour documents which he opened up while kneeling on the pontoons, and telling Orcadian stories. It is difficult not to stop for a chat in Orkney, usually a rather long chat.

Silly of me to have once regretted that marina's arrival at Stromness. I was too nostalgic for earlier times when I had tied up to a buoy in the harbour and rowed my inflatable dinghy ashore. It was during an early sailing trip that Ben, right here, aged ten at the time, astonished his parents. We were standing on the quayside, by the pens for the cattle ready for shipping south (no longer there now). He asked if this was where they were herded before being taken to the mainland, to be killed. Yes, we said, at which point he announced he was going to be a vegetarian when we got home. And so he has remained, apart from now eating fish. Very admirable, but for me a lamb chop is the killer, and the occasional steak.

Despite what many still regard as a peculiar diet, Ben grew up to be tall and strong, as did meat-eating Oli although he too is now mostly vegetarian. Both were off on the small ferry across to Hoy that very evening, with serious designs on the Old Man of Hoy, the 449-foot sea stack off the west side of the island. They bought a return ticket, which was a vote of confidence. Meanwhile Neil and I repaired to the Stromness Hotel for the first of several very good meals there. That hotel was requisitioned by the military during the second world war. Vera Lynn had sung from the first-floor balcony for the troops gathered below.

Saturday July 14th, at last some sun, good for boat cleaning and bunk-cushion airing. Good for climbing too. Needless to say I was anxious all day. The boys had not even told their mother what they were up to — she would have been far more anxious than me. My worries were relieved in part when Oli phoned from on top of the Old Man, and then completely relieved when I heard they were back on the ground. It had been tougher than they expected, but it is an important stamp on every serious climber's CV. I felt rather pleased with myself, vicariously. I had never progressed past leading the 'very difficult' category of rock climbing, and even that had scared me enough. The Old Man was first climbed in 1966, and I can remember the BBC TV programme which filmed the second climb by three pairs of climbers. Little did I anticipate then that I would have children who could and would climb this iconic structure. One day it will no doubt fall into the sea. After all, there was originally an arch, clearly drawn by William Daniell in the early 19th century. It later collapsed, so leaving just the 'Old Man'.[26]

It had taken the boys five hours to get up the climb, and two to abseil down, by which time they had missed the last ferry back to Stromness. But no problem — as it was a lovely evening, Neil and I could sail Pickle under genoa alone the four miles across to the pier at Moaness on Hoy. The boys arrived by taxi from Rackwick Bay where there was a bothy they had stayed the previous night. They were very pleased with themselves, and I was very pleased with them. It was a calm sunny evening for the return sail to Stromness. To celebrate we all piled into the very handy Stromness Hotel for dinner; it's a pleasant place to hang out for a pint of real ale from either of the two local Orkney breweries, and a pretty good meal.[27] Again thanks

---

26. William Daniell, *A Voyage round Great Britain Undertaken in the Summer of the Year 1813*, vol. 5 (London: Longman et al., 1821), 8.

27. In 2021 the hotel was sold and is now alcohol free, much to the consternation of most Stromnessians.

to mobile phones we were able to book ahead and warn the hotel we were going to be a few minutes late.

Poor Oli — he had left his camera somewhere on Hoy, with precious photos of his climb. More mobile phone calls, to the taxi driver. The phone wasn't in the taxi, but the driver drove several miles to check Oli hadn't left it on Moaness pier. He hadn't. Might it be in the bothy? The taxi driver phoned the warden, and yes it had been found on the wall by the public toilet. The next day Oli caught the ferry back to Hoy. The taxi driver had picked up the camera and handed it to him on the pier in return for a big thank-you card and a handsome tip. To add to his pleasure, Oli met a passenger on the ferry back to Stromness who happened to have been on the cliffs watching his climb the previous day, and had taken photos that he later sent to him. A silver lining indeed, and an illustration of just how friendly Orkney is. No need to lock your house, bicycle or car. No absentee landlords of large estates. No malign influence of the more extreme corners of the Presbyterian church. No private schools. The last place for water and supplies for ships sailing from Europe to the Americas in days gone by. No wonder strangers feel welcome. A grand place to be.

Back to the Saturday evening. It started to rain, but who cared? Cathie, Lucy and William arrived by car from Kirkwall, having successfully found their way from Edinburgh to Aberdeen and on to the ferry to Orkney. Holidays beckoned.

An Orkney Yole in Scapa Flow.

Chapter 10

Round Shetland and back to Orkney

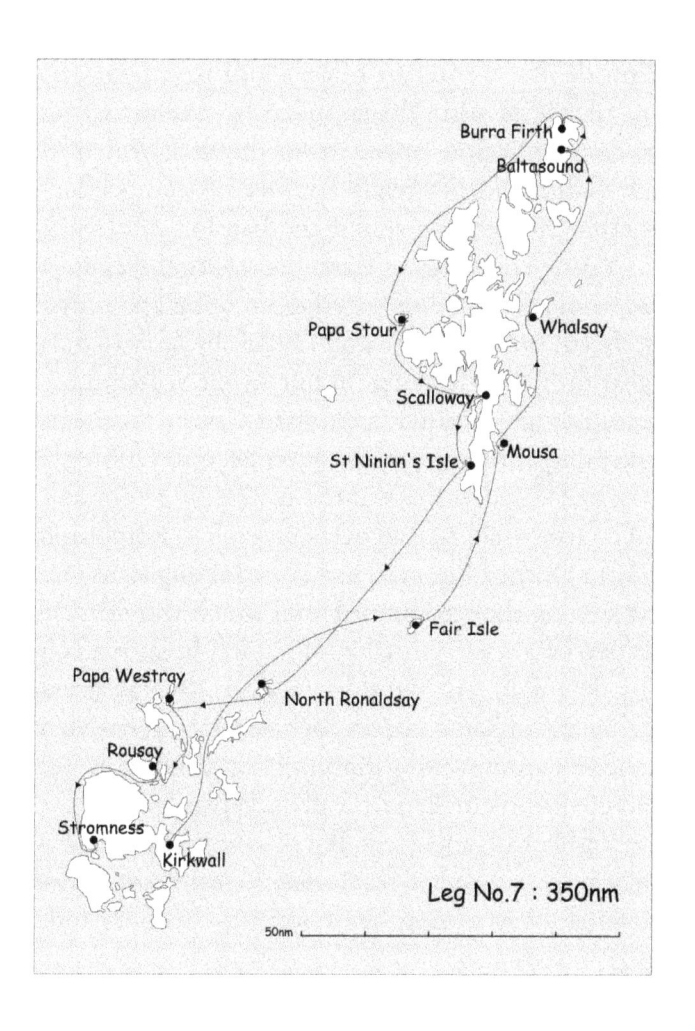

The next fortnight made a very welcome break from having to deal with new crew. Just an easy family holiday, with the car for trips round the Orkney mainland, called 'Pomona' on older maps. But that comes from a blunder by the 16th-century Scottish historian George Buchanan who mistranslated Solinus, a third-century Roman author. Solinus had used 'Pomona' not in reference to Orkney, as Buchanan believed, but to Thyle (Thule), a much more distant island which he described as being fruitful and abundant (Pomona being the Roman goddess of fruit and plenty).

With the boat for some waterborne exploration here and there, mostly based in Stromness, what a relaxing time it was. Even the weather was kind which made a change for that 2012 summer. By chance it was the annual knees-up in Stromness, the quaintly named 'Shopping Week'. Nothing to do with shopping, more a community summer fair including bouncy castles; loads of live music; horse and cart rides; a kids pavement-art competition; an evening cavalcade of witty floats pulled by tractors ('FlyMaybe', etc.); a yard of ale competition; a 'queen' from the final year of the local high school, which Cathie did not really approve of (too gender-stereotyped); and a memorable lifeboat trip round the bay for children (some parents sneaked on, too). Such a shame Margaret wasn't there, as my four other children were having such a time together — tying knots, tying each other up, laughing. It was sad when Ben and Oli left by ferry to Scrabster, loaded down with gear for more climbing, in northwest Scotland.

Libby Purves thought Orkney 'a dangerous place for dreamers'.[1] Indeed it is. Cathie certainly dreamt. She had never been to Orkney but by the end of the holiday had decided she wanted to live in Stromness. Completely unrealistic, of course — she had an over-busy job in Edinburgh which could not be done from Orkney. She even had crazed thoughts about retiring from medicine and buying the Stromness Hotel which was for sale (in 2021 the hotel with its two bars was eventually sold, but it became alcohol free which may prove its downfall). As one does in these dreamy holiday states, we looked at the details of some houses for sale (not expensive by Edinburgh standards) and air routes to Edinburgh and London (extraordinarily expensive and environmentally not really acceptable).

We discovered Hamish and Freda Bayne whose Rustler 36 was right next to us in the marina. Hamish had built a fixed 'sprayhood' because the canvas one kept blowing away during his many trips to Shetland, and he had

---

1. Libby Purves, *One Summer's Grace: A Family Voyage round Britain* (London: Grafton Books, 1989), 178.

electric winches as he was often single-handed. Owning one of these lovely boats is clearly a way to meet likeminded people. Like dog owners, we too stop to compare our proud possessions, exchanging the names not of each other but of our boats. I can imagine the same effect with Contessa 32s and 26s, Nicholsons too, but not with mass-produced boats like Bavarias, Hanses, Beneteaus and Jeanneaus. Hamish had been a founding member of the well-known (but not to me) McCalmans folk group, and was the only concertina maker left in Scotland. Freda weaves North Ronaldsay wool into rugs and lengths of fabric, and made the handbag I later bought for Cathie.

Hamish and Freda live on 'The Street' in one of the characteristic stone houses with gable ends to the sea, which often have a slipway to one side as well as their own pier poking out into the harbour (and sometimes a small crane for loading into and from ships in times past). As does Anne Tait, a retired friend from work, whose surname reveals her Orkney origins — indeed she seems to have cousins everywhere. She it was who heard from her friend Inga Williamson, a marine biologist, who had heard from her friends Elaine and Mike Henderson, potter and musician, that their Stromness house was for sale. And that is the house we bought in 2015, with wonderful views over Scapa Flow. For Cathie's retirement, maybe. And holidays for family and friends in the meantime. Although now in these days of Zoom video conferencing Cathie works as well from Orkney as from Edinburgh.

Up the hill lived yet another old friend, David Simpson, who used to run ASH (Action on Smoking and Health). He lived part-time in London, still lecturing at the London School of Hygiene and Tropical Medicine, but was so integrated into Orkney society that he seemed to know everyone worth knowing. At the time he was heavily involved with the Stromness Drama Club, the Stromness Museum, and the Pier Arts Centre. As a campaigning charity director, and despite early life as an accountant, he must already have been incredibly good at networking or became incredibly good at it. He still can't help himself, and was constantly introducing us to local people.

Although David has no children of his own, he is delightful with ours — there is always a ready supply of interesting toys in his house (as well as original art for the adults to enjoy). Visiting Pickle one day, he exclaimed at the cleanliness of our heads. No surprise there. Cathie is a great cleaner, as I've said, much more obsessional than me, and so very triumphant when she finds some speck of mildew — or worse — that I have (deliberately?) missed. It is as well to leave a little dirt so she is not disappointed. It's not a bad idea in medicine, either, when you ask a colleague for a second opinion, to maybe leave at least one test undone or one diagnosis not thought of. Equally, when asked to give a second opinion you must find at least one thing to suggest. That way, everyone is happy, hopefully including the patient. The memorable but irascible Tony Dornhorst taught me this strategy, half-jokingly of course. He had been asked to see someone with a rash, and I tagged along. To my surprise all he did was recommend that instead of hydrocortisone cream (a mild steroid), the patient be tried on Betnovate cream (another steroid, albeit stronger):

'But that's more or less the same stuff, just a different name and dose,' I said.

'I know,' he replied. 'But it's important I do just one thing, then everyone is happy.'

Again half-jokingly, he told me that the treatment for heart attacks was to tell the patient they had indigestion and put them to bed, which at the time was the same advice for real indigestion from a duodenal ulcer. In the 1960s there was no other treatment for heart attacks anyway. He also pointed out to me that 'enough of anything will block everything', in other words, all effective drugs are poisonous. And so they are if given to the wrong patient, at the wrong time, in the wrong dose, and for too long. But all this knowledge transfer took time — his ward rounds usually lasted the whole afternoon, attended by his registrar and houseman, and a gaggle of students. He always taught on the first patient on the left for over an hour (irrespective of their diagnosis). Then the second patient on the left for a little under an hour, after which we slowly went round all the other patients for another few hours. As his houseman, I usually went round the patients again to explain what he had said to them, which was not always very obvious even to me. Later, when I told him I wanted to be a neurologist, he sniffed, 'Well, someone has to be one.' He never had much time for neurologists, regarding them as far too specialised and arrogant, and often wrong. He once muttered that Sir Charles Symonds, a very famous London neurologist, was 'second only to the Archangel Gabriel'. Not meant as a compliment.

Professor Dornhorst always urged me to read all the notes of a patient if the diagnosis was obscure. One day we went to see a woman who was jaundiced for no discernible reason. While I impatiently waited, he read every page in her bulky notes, eventually coming to the record of the blood transfusions she had received for some recent but unrelated problem. 'There we have it!' he exclaimed, pointing to the fact that she had been given — by mistake — incompatible blood. The transfused red blood cells had broken down and she had become jaundiced as a result.

Years later I passed on this titbit of wisdom to my Edinburgh colleague Bob Will. He had a patient with Wilson's disease, a very rare disorder of copper metabolism that requires taking a daily drug for life. He couldn't understand why the patient kept relapsing even though she said she was definitely taking the tablets. Rather than disbelieve her, an all too easy reaction, Bob read through the entirety of her voluminous notes. There he chanced on the drug data sheet, reading that the drug should be stored in the fridge. When he asked the patient where she kept her drug, she said in a Welsh dresser — which happened to be right next to a radiator. The heat had deactivated the drug, rendering it ineffective. Job done. I suspect that trying to read through the morass of today's electronic records would be more tiresome.

There was another David in Stromness, David Bowdler, who had greeted our arrival at the marina with all the local information we needed — where the three pubs were. He owned a very sporty sailing boat and had just raced around Ireland (bonkers, but at least he had earlier owned a Contessa 32, so not completely bonkers). He was super fit with sailing, running, climbing and motor biking. Having retired early from IBM in the south of England, he was clearly enjoying himself. A good tip of his was to employ a diver, of which there were many around, to scrub the bottom of Pickle and so remove quite a collection of beasties and green stuff. Cheaper than being hauled out, and more convenient than drying out.

Despite envying Kirkwall the capital, a much older and bigger town, for capturing more resources, upstart Stromness seemed to be doing OK. Although there were a number of empty shops, the smattering of proper shops included Tam's wonderful little bookshop. He had migrated from California decades earlier. I once overheard a tourist ask him if he had any second-hand books. 'No,' he said. 'But some have been here 30 years.' None of our visitors to Orkney are allowed to escape before buying at least one book from the shop (now run by Sheena, following Tam's death). And Flett's the butcher, and a shop for wool with a sign 'Sorry — closed today due to very bored kids', various galleries, Julia's café by the ferry terminal for coffee and buns, the lovely museum, the swimming pool, the harbour activity generated by the ferry from Scrabster on the north coast of Scotland and by the tourist dive boats in Scapa Flow, and the Pier Arts Centre. This last is a world-class gallery with its Barbara Hepworths and Ben Nicholsons displayed in the 18th-century house (and strikingly attractive modern extension) where the agent for the Hudson's Bay Company once lived. There was a wooden boat builder too, Ian Richardson, the last on Orkney. No one then was working with him to carry on the tradition, but he is now assisted by Jeff Mackie who may eventually take over. Of course the longer we lingered around the marina the more biased towards Stromness we became, lapping up the friendliness of the local people. Always in the background behind the town is that view of the looming lump of Hoy, the only island of any height in Orkney. Naturally we did the Orkney mainland sights too — the Ring of Brodgar, the Italian Chapel, St Magnus Cathedral, Skara Brae, Maeshowe.

Given its key position on the old North Atlantic trade routes, and during the two world wars, it is perhaps no surprise that the sailing world still seems to congregate in Stromness — alongside us were Norwegian boats, French boats, Dutch boats and one round-the-world American boat. Indeed there were more foreign than UK visiting boats, four of them from Norway. 'Why so many?' I asked a Norwegian skipper. 'Because the weather is better here,' he replied. Tell that to sailors on the south coast, I thought. I suspect the real reason is the extraordinarily high price of alcohol in Norway compared with the UK. Also, of course, Norway is closer to Orkney than even the Clyde is, let alone the Solent. Orkney was always far away. Way back in 1906 Henry Reynolds, who had sailed from the Deben, remarked that 'it would be the paradise of small cruisers, were it not so far removed from busy centres'.[2]

One day we sailed across Scapa Flow to Lyness on Hoy to visit the naval museum, housed in the old pump room and one of the last remaining huge metal drums that once held fuel for the Royal Navy. It was to Scapa Flow that the defeated German High Seas Fleet was brought at the end of the first world war. After considerable delays and misunderstandings, the demoralised and bored Germans, fearing their ships would all fall into Allied hands after the muddle of the Treaty of Versailles, finally lost patience. On 21st June 1919, on a secret order from their commander Rear-Admiral von Reuter, all the ships hoisted their flags, opened and disabled their seacocks, hatches and torpedo tubes, and their skeleton crews took to the lifeboats. In the chaos that followed, 42 ships sank while 22 others stayed afloat or were eventually beached by the Royal Navy who came racing back into the Flow having for some reason gone out for an exercise on that very

---

2. Henry Reynolds, *Coastwise—Cross-Seas: The Tribulations and Triumphs of a Casual Cruiser* (London: J. D. Potter, 1921), 209.

day. This left a lot of lucrative salvage work for the several years, and the few remaining wrecks now provide a paradise for sports divers and serious benefits for Orkney tourism.

Towards the end of the holiday we sailed to Pierowall on Westray, round the west side of the Orkney mainland, out into the ocean swell but with very little wind — a bad combination. All the family apart from me were seasick. Lucy ten times, William nine times, Cathie three times. 'A total of twenty-two sicks,' Lucy proudly announced (still a Pickle record). Not too surprisingly she added: 'I am not going sailing again.' But the next day when I was taking a photograph of her looking very charming as she helped tidy up the sails I said: 'This will be the last photograph of you on Pickle.' 'Why?' she asked. 'Because you said you are not coming sailing with me again.' 'Oh,' she replied. 'I suppose I'll have to!' And she has.

Pierowall has a small marina where we found French, Norwegian and a couple of British visiting boats, and a friendly and very chatty harbour master who directed us to the excellent bakery by the harbour where there are croissants, butteries, rolls and bread if you manage to get there for 8.30am.

The next day we had a sunny sail 18 miles south to the small island of Egilsay, where we played hide and seek round the ruined medieval St Magnus church with its round tower. I got the tides all wrong and we nearly went backwards, probably because we started off too late. Easy to do among the Orkney islands, even after consulting the Sailing Directions. Greenvile Collins got the right idea: 'The Tydes run very strong amongst them.' Indeed they do, and his chart made a stab at their direction with arrows which 'shew that the Tyde of the Flood setteth the same way the Arrows Point'.[3] Years later Walter Scott remarked that 'no boatman or sailor in Orkney thinks of the wind in comparison of the tides and currents'.[4] And so we still do.

Later that day we sailed the ten miles south to Kirkwall where we stopped for a few nights. The marina is not so central to the town as in Stromness, but it is bigger. 'You go shopping while we do your washing,' commanded the lady in the launderette, so we did, and then we looked at the sights. Kirkwall is full of surprises, not least the very large and impressive St Magnus cathedral built in the 12th to 15th centuries. It is the most northerly cathedral in the UK, does not have a bishop, and is owned

---

3. Greenvile Collins, *Great-Britain's Coasting Pilot* (London: 1693).

4. Walter Scott, *The Voyage of the Pharos: Walter Scott's Cruise around Scotland in 1814* (Hamilton: Scottish Library Association, 1998), 56.

not by the church but by the local council. A gravestone records the death of one John Mainland on a curious date — 30th February 1867.

The second Kirkwall surprise was the charming but eccentric wireless museum which, among many ancient radios, has the translated log of U-Boat captain Günther Prien. On the night of October 14th 1939, he managed to sneak into Scapa Flow on the surface through a narrow gap between two islands, and torpedoed and sunk the Royal Oak battleship with the loss of 835 men. This astonishingly bold feat of seamanship was acknowledged even by the British Navy. Prien and his submarine were lost at sea some months later, presumably sunk by that same British Navy. R. F. Nichols, who was commander on the Royal Oak, survived and, by an extraordinary coincidence, as a midshipman he had also survived the sinking of HMS Vanguard that had blown up in Scapa Flow in 1917.[5]

Orkney is well-ordered, prosperous, and potentially self-sufficient. It is said you can get anything done in Orkney, excluding brain surgery of course. Unlike so many parts of Scotland it is not overwhelmed with holiday and second homes, and certainly not by absentee landlords sitting on vast sporting estates. For better or (many think) worse, Kirkwall is the most visited cruise-ship port in the UK; hundreds of passengers are taken off in coaches to trample over the archaeological sites almost every day in the summer. Unfortunately there is no tourist tax to fund better visitor facilities, but there should be despite the protests of some local businesses. Orkney is also astonishingly beautiful, particularly in the low northern light with endless varieties of green on the gentle hills, and rainbows.

Maybe Orkney could even be 'independent'. Plenty of well-tended farmland; good education (almost everyone goes to the same state schools, with next to no one exiled across the Pentland Firth to board); although Orkney does not have its own university, Heriot-Watt has a campus in Stromness, and the University of the Highlands and Islands has colleges in Kirkwall and Stromness; a busy arts and crafts scene; lots of fresh water; and a remarkable array of different forms of energy from oil landed at Flotta (before it runs out, or is banned) to wind turbines to the future possibilities of wave and tide. Marine energy is a sector on the up in the UK, particularly in Orkney with the strong tides and waves. There was even a new pier being built in Stromness to service the marine energy support-vessels. How pleased I am that Oli has put his engineering skills to good

---

5. Patricia Meehan and Malcolm Brown, *Scapa Flow: The Story of Britain's Greatest Naval Anchorage in Two World Wars* (London: Pan Books, 2002), 144.

use, first by working on tidal energy, an emerging and still very young technology, and now on wind turbines.

Curiously I got one of my very infrequent attacks of migraine on Orkney. The gradual awareness that something was wrong with my vision, then a realisation that it was a migrainous aura starting gradually with flickering white lights in the lower right part of my visual field. Over minutes they changed to zig-zag lines (so-called fortification spectra because of their similarity to the aerial view of a medieval castle) that slowly moved across my vision to the centre and finally to the top right, intensifying and fading away in about 10 minutes. Absolutely typical. I never really get a headache, sometimes a little nausea. No need for any test to make the diagnosis. The story says it all. An examination of the patient tells you nothing more because it will be normal, but as mentioned before patients appreciate and expect the 'laying on of hands', which has a reassuring effect not to be denigrated. Many obviously migrainous patients like having a brain scan, largely because our society is obsessed with technology, while the media worship it. This is shown very clearly in commercial (aka private) medical practice where the charge in Edinburgh for a visit to a neurologist is about £250, while the charge for an MR brain scan is twice as much even though it is not nearly as diagnostically valuable as a consultation with someone who knows what they are doing.

Unsurprisingly, private practitioners tend to over-investigate, therefore lining their colleague's pockets in radiology, as well as their own. One argument for commercial practice is that doctors in the NHS can easily become idle because they don't have to compete for patients, and are paid more or less the same irrespective of how hard they work. However, like Samuel Johnson who remarked about a thresher that he would 'rather trust his idleness than his fraud',[6] I too find it is easier to deal with idleness than greed which so easily leads on to fraud.

Unfortunately, the younger generation of doctors live in fear of retribution if they don't order yet another unnecessary, and costly, test — so-called defensive medicine, defending the doctor against litigation, not the patient. More and more tests get done. More and more incidental findings are discovered, most of no consequence, and everyone becomes increasingly anxious. Unnecessary treatments are offered and enthusiastically accepted, so increasing costs at the expense of more important things. What a waste.

---

6. James Boswell, *The Journal of a Tour to the Hebrides with Samuel Johnson, LL.D.*, ed. R. W. Chapman (orig. 1785; Oxford: Oxford University Press, 1970), 337.

Waste is a huge problem in the NHS but is seldom mentioned in the media, even when ambulances queue outside hospitals, sick patients are lined up on trolleys waiting to be admitted from A&E, and routine operations are cancelled. Almost everyone I know who has had medical treatment in recent years has had unnecessary tests, or been admitted to hospital for no good reason, and kept in too long despite perfectly good home circumstances (like Steve after his transient ischaemic attack). One friend lost his memory for a few hours before it returned to normal — transient global amnesia. This is entirely benign, although alarming for any witness who cannot understand why the patient repeatedly asks the same question despite being given the same answer. If the attack is typical there is no need for any brain scanning although often a CT or MR scan is done. But my friend had an MR *and* a CT scan, which is ridiculous. To compound the nonsense he later was surprised by a home visit from a consultant old-age psychiatrist who administered a memory test. This is both expensive in consultant time, and unnecessary because his memory had returned to normal and he was perfectly capable of going to an outpatient appointment.

Unnecessary operations waste even more money, as well as potentially causing harm. I had a general anaesthetic and a nail pushed down my fractured tibia in 1993 even though the fracture was undisplaced and there was no deformity. A plaster would have done just as well but I was persuaded by the surgeon who said I would get going quicker with a nail. Who was I to argue while stretched out in pain on a trolley in the A&E department? In fact I didn't 'get going' all that quickly, and have been left with a permanently numb knee which I was not warned about. Years later I had another operation to remove the nail as it may have been partly the cause of my temporarily infected calf muscle. How much did all that cost, I wonder, compared with a simple plaster?

Thankfully the plague of tonsillectomies for recurrent sore throats has more or less disappeared, but not before I had my tonsils out, providing a traumatic early memory of post-operative vomiting blood. As have grommets for glue ears, but not before daughter Margaret had them inserted. There must be contemporary equivalents — perhaps too many stents in the coronary arteries of patients who don't need them. Good for commercial practice, not so good for the NHS. Finally, there is the futility of striving to keep patients alive who are clearly dying. Surely they should be made comfortable in their own homes, not admitted to an anonymous hospital where they get to know none of the rapidly rotating doctors who come to see them, and who in their turn don't know the patients or their wishes. More money wasted.

Unnecessary health checks (aka screening), unnecessary polypharmacy, unnecessary operations, unnecessary admission to hospital, unnecessary tests, and unnecessary outpatient appointments — all costing money, money wasted which could be used for something useful. And damaging the environment by increasing carbon emissions, and single-use plastic. The Covid-19 pandemic might provide a research opportunity to study over-testing, over-diagnosing, and over-treating because almost all non-Covid healthcare services declined sharply for several months after the pandemic began. What effect did this have on health? Probably a rise in mortality for some conditions like heart attacks, but possibly a decline in mortality for others because some things should be left well alone.

On Thursday July 26th, we drove across to Stromness where Cathie and the children left for home on the ferry. It was sad to see them go after a particularly good summer holiday. Of course at times the children get me down — I am after all an old dad for my younger children, which is some sort of excuse. Once again they had been plagued by head lice that required major dousing with potions. However, it was good to be alone for a while, wandering around Stromness and ordering a book from Tam's bookshop, popping into a gallery or two, taking a few photos, inspecting the houses for sale board in the local solicitor's.

Back on Pickle in Kirkwall that evening there were little reminders — some loving messages from Lucy to her mum and dad, model robot evidence of Will. Once again I found myself reflecting on how awful it must be to lose a child. And I brooded on how I would have to again ensure that all the new crew bonded. After all, the two couples had never met each other before. I needn't have worried, as they were all to get on brilliantly. During the night it seemed that Pickle was on a river being driven under a bridge, possibly that very low arch of Potter Heigham bridge on the Norfolk Broads. But we didn't have a hinged mast to lower, even though my son Ben assured me it would fold down. Somehow Ilona was there too, getting into a wetsuit. And William was in the Tinker inflatable dinghy that was full of water. I woke up with relief — only a dream.

The new crew arrive, and to Fair Isle

Friday July 27th, Steve returned for another leg, this time accompanied by his current paramour Eileen who hails from Paisley, a primary school teacher well able to stand up for herself in any arguments. Once a manager of restaurants, she certainly knows a thing or two about cooking. She has sailed with me before, and generally takes over provisioning the boat and doing the cooking, which is fine by me — up to a point. David Lea, whom we had last met in North Wales, turned up with Sylvia in tow. They had been having a few days as tourists on Orkney. Sylvia, a librarian in the Cardiff University architecture department, is a marvellous Indian lady whose father, a jazz musician during the Raj, had taken his family to Singapore when India became independent. He reckoned there would not be much future for jazz once the British left. Sylvia has an uncanny musical ability to recognise almost any song, and it is very difficult to catch her out. I think we were all concerned how she would cope on the boat, not being at all used to sailing, and wanting to be very well turned-out — which she always was (Eileen thought she came out of the heads every morning looking like an Asian princess). While she did take a while to emerge for breakfast, all was forgiven because she was so much fun, always laughing (well, almost always).

Saturday July 28th, off again, at 9am after a hearty breakfast. This was more a porridge-eating crew, so there was no need to lay on cornflakes, and Eileen appreciated my homemade marmalade. It was also a sugar crew, with some taking it in their tea. Having sugar is just horrible on a yacht, at least it was until I realised lump sugar is far easier to clear up after a spillage than granulated sugar. However, even kept in a tightly sealed airtight jar, lump sugar still absorbs moisture and soon ends up as an unpleasant crystalline mess. Best to avoid sugar altogether.

I felt almost on home territory, familiar views while gently motoring between the north Orkney isles. There was no wind, it was sunny and hot, calm, and the sea was flat. At least it was flat until we got to Lashy Sound between Eday and Sanday where, despite the flat sea, there was an incredibly bouncy tide race. No wonder so many companies test their tidal energy kit around these islands.

By lunchtime the wind had got up, then died, but by 4pm we could start sailing properly. The wind from the southeast gave us a steady reach across a completely empty ocean towards Fair Isle, the ideal halfway stop-off to Shetland or indeed to Europe as it has been for many centuries. Greenvile Collins again: 'The Dutch East-India Ships, as they go and come from India, sail between the Islands of Orkney and Shetland; and homeward bound they send ashore at this Faire Island for Letters of Advice; but commonly the Dutch East India Company send a Ship to meet them here.'[7]

---

7. Collins, *Great-Britain's Coasting Pilot*.

It was a lovely evening, wonderful light, puffins on the water, gannets diving, fulmars nesting on and whirring around the dark and daunting cliffs on the north end of Fair Isle presided over by the Skroo Lighthouse, which we rounded at about 8pm, the sun sinking in the west. Half an hour later, and 58 miles from Kirkwall, we tied up to the harbour wall in North Haven behind a French boat. There was enough room because The Good Shepherd, the aptly named ferry to Shetland, was away to Lerwick. We were lucky because in summer the small harbour can get surprisingly crowded.

It was a good introductory day for Sylvia although the smooth swell had made her feel slightly sick. Steve, being the same way inclined, didn't want to risk going below where it is always worse unless lying down with your eyes shut. No worries about Eileen, who in fact had spent the last part of that day in the galley making our dinner — scallops starter, crab pasta, and nectarines to follow. Impressive. It is rather extraordinary that you can put two couples on a boat at very close quarters, who have never met each other before, and yet they can all get on so well, as clearly was the case here. Even older couples like this lot, more likely to be set in their ways. However, somebody was putting used matches back in the matchbox, illogical and very irritating. Years later Eileen fessed up, explaining she always replaced them, but back to front, to avoid throwing them into a waste bin and causing a fire, and to have them available for relighting from a candle or gas flame. The female brain at work.

Sunday July 29th dawned cloudless, ideal for a stroll. We didn't have time to see everything so we skirted the birdie north end with its mostly English RSPB staff in their Bird Observatory (now being rebuilt after a disastrous fire in 2019) and headed south to where the small population of about 60 permanent residents live. There are a lot of incomers as well as indigenous Fair Isle people (Marie Bruhat, a French woman is now helping to revive the Fair Isle knitting tradition). Past the airfield with just a hut for its terminal. Past increasingly organised fields. And yes, the chair-maker was still there. Back in 2003 I had sailed here and ordered a Fair Isle chair from Stewart Thomson, a former lighthouse keeper. It is very like an Orkney chair, made of wood with a high straw back to keep the draughts away when you pull it up to the fire.

The experience was rather like being put on the waiting list for a hip replacement in those days when you had to wait years, before the 1997 Labour government put more resources into the NHS. I waited five years before the chair arrived in Edinburgh. Stewart had refused any payment until I had actually got the chair, wanting to first ensure I was satisfied with it. Of course I was! How could I not be after the hours of work he had put into it. He had learned the craft from his father, but the skill will die out as he has no one to pass it on to. Sadly his fingers had become badly affected by rheumatoid arthritis so he was packing it in, making just eight more chairs for family and friends. We were delighted when he invited us into his workshop to show us how he weaved the chair backs. Not surprisingly David and Sylvia were fascinated, as any architecturally aware people would be. IKEA this was not.

To Mousa and the broch

Monday July 30th, at 12.30pm we left quietly to head north again. Unlike Walter Scott, who clearly rather fancied himself when he left Fair Isle on the Pharos 'amid the cheers of the inhabitants, whose minds, subdued by our splendour, had been secured by our munificence, which consisted in a moderate benefaction of whisky and tobacco, and a few shillings laid out on their staple commodities'.[8] Sunshine, light wind, warm even, a slight swell, cruising chute up, 4 knots over the ground, all pretty good. Until the wind died off Sumburgh Head, the southern tip of Shetland. We had to motor on towards the now uninhabited island of Mousa with its famous broch, a modest 30-mile day trip. There was too much swell in the anchorage on the east side of the island so we moved across to the mainland to anchor in the curiously named Wick of Sandsayre at about 8pm (not so curious really as 'wick' is Norse for 'bay'). A huge moon rose to complement the northern sunset as we settled down for another excellent dinner.

Tuesday July 31st, William's 5th birthday, and I could speak to him thanks again to mobile phones. Thanks too for the continuing sunny weather, as we paddled the dinghy over to tie up to the Stevenson-constructed slipway, sniffed the smell of burning peat in the air, and went ashore to inspect Sand Lodge, a peaceful ensemble of manor house, walled garden and outhouses, early 17th century. The ancestral home of the Bruce family, Shetland bigshots. Again our architect crew were in their element.

After that little treat, and wearing shorts and T-shirts, we motored Pickle across to Mousa. Just up from the anchorage we found a bothy, a tent, and a family. The man, English, who worked for the RSPB, had been coming here for 20 summers to study the UK's largest storm petrel colony, and had actually lived on the island with his wife for three years (shades of the life

---

8. Scott, *Voyage of the Pharos*, 40.

depicted by Fraser Darling in his 1940 book *Island Years*). There are said to be 7000 breeding pairs on Mousa, but we were very unlikely to see a storm petrel in daylight. Nor did we, but we could hear a few chirruping away hidden deep in the dry-stone walls. To see them one needs to be around at dusk.

The 2000-year-old Iron Age broch is a short walk from the anchorage, a fabulous relic. It is the most complete broch in Scotland, a typical circular structure found in no other country, with its walls still standing to their full height — 13 metres. We climbed the narrow steps spiralling up between the double walls, right to the top and gazed down into the hollow interior, and admired the extensive view out to sea. The dry-stone masonry was perfect, which is presumably why it has lasted so long with very little stabilisation needed to keep it standing. Walter Scott was equally impressed, although damning too: 'to give a vulgar comparison, it resembles an old ruinous pigeonhouse'.[9] Again our architects had a field-day, full of admiration for their ancient forebears.

At lunchtime a boatload of tourists arrived, reminding me just how fortunate and privileged I am to be able to sail to these beautiful places without relying on anyone else, and away from any crowds. To me this is the whole point of sailing, getting to places. Very definitely a means to an end. Back on board, there was lunch courtesy of Eileen, always willing to give anything culinary a go.

To Whalsay, and the millionaires

We upped (aka weighed) anchor at 2pm and continued north, light wind from the northwest so we were close-hauled along the coast, flat sea, delightful sailing at about 5 knots. Apart from one Drascombe and a small Westerly we saw no other sailing boats all day. We rounded close under the huge cliff on Noss with its masses and masses of seabirds, gannets everywhere in the air and on the water. Then on past a few above-water rocks to keep us on our toes, to arrive at Symbister, the main settlement on the small island of Whalsay (just five miles by two), still in sunshine at 7.30pm. We had to motor for the last hour-and-a-half for lack of wind. An easy 26 miles. There were pontoons for various local boats, no other visiting boats as far as we could see, and space for us.

Whalsay is where we were told the Shetland millionaires live. I could well

---

9. Scott, *Voyage of the Pharos*, 32.

believe it, looking at the two vast oceanic fishing ships (hardly mere boats) tied up in the harbour. These enormous machines hoover up goodness knows how many tons of fish at a time, they must cost millions to build, and make millions for their owners. As well as being rich, Whalsay is also historic. In the 13th to 17th centuries it was part of the Hanseatic league when Germans came to buy fish in exchange for seeds, cloth, iron tools, salt and spirits. They built the small and now restored trading booth or warehouse at the edge of the harbour, with its museum. There was no one to collect any entrance fee, and no honesty box either; maybe this place is so rich they don't need our paltry pennies. It is I fear a very Brexity place — Whalsay voted 81% to get out of the EU in 2016, compared with 44% in Shetland overall and 38% in Scotland. Presumably under the illusion that out of the EU and the Common Fisheries Policy they could make even more millions from fishing. They may be disappointed.

In the morning we went for a walk, discovering the large and magnificent 1991 leisure centre with its indoor sports-hall, swimming pool and — for us — showers. This facility must reflect either Shetland oil money, or local fishing money, for Whalsay's population is only just over 1000. Shetland seemed geographically rather like the Highlands, much more severe than Orkney, the light not so interesting. Not so friendly either, in Whalsay at least, with no cheery waves from the expensive cars. But the shop was brilliant, seeming to sell everything from butter to screwdrivers, toothpaste to blankets, lemons to engine oil (as well as olive oil). Of course it has to; otherwise it's a ferry ride across to the mainland of Shetland and then a drive down to Lerwick the capital. Mind you, internet shopping must have made a huge difference to remote islands like this, no doubt with an added delivery charge. Island living has costs as well as benefits.

Whalsay must have been the sort of place from where patients travelled to Lerwick to see me and my consultant boss when we did clinics there every month or so in the early 1970s. We certainly didn't expect the patients to travel even further — to Aberdeen where we were based. For many Shetlanders it was time-consuming and, from some parts of Shetland, difficult enough getting even to Lerwick. I remember one man with ridiculously high blood pressure who had to take two ferries, several buses, and spend a night away from home. And then make the return journey. It is surely better for consultants to see patients near where they live, if possible. As well as learning more of the patients' home and social background the consultant can communicate much more easily with the local GPs, and get to know them, as we certainly did — over pleasant dinners in a Lerwick hotel. This is so important for what managers like to call 'joined-up care', while at the same time they have almost destroyed the close contact between GPs and consultants. Except in commercial practice, GPs can seldom refer a patient to a consultant of their own choice whose strengths and weaknesses they know; instead they have to write to a whole department ('Dear neurologist …'). Letters are then intercepted and vetted for referral suitability, not necessarily by a doctor but by some clerk — an insult to our medical professionalism.

In Shetland I had learned about distributed rather than centralised healthcare long before it became fashionable among reforming politicians and managers. Sadly, however, this idea of consultants providing decent medical care near to where people live is still not widely implemented. The same in general practice where needs are not always well matched to resources. Julian Tudor Hart may have been 'only' a GP in a Welsh mining community, but his 1971 inverse care law[10] remains as valid as ever: 'The availability of good medical care tends to vary inversely with the need for it in the population served.' He went on: 'This inverse care law operates more completely where medical care is most exposed to market forces, and less so where such exposure is reduced.' To nail his socialist colours to the mast he later paraphrased his law: 'To the extent that health care becomes a commodity it becomes distributed just like champagne. That is rich people get lots of it. Poor people don't get any of it.'[11]

Bryan Matthews understood. When he became professor of neurology in Oxford in 1970 he didn't just sit in the Radcliffe Infirmary, he started an outpatient clinic 30 miles north of Oxford, in the Horton Hospital, Banbury, of ride-a-cock-horse fame. Today's professors would be far too obsessed with their research prestige to dirty their hands in a district general hospital clinic. They lurk in their ivory towers (and in airport departure lounges). I joined Bryan in 1976 and, inspired by him, started a neurology clinic in Newbury Hospital, 30 miles south of Oxford.

Not just better clinical care but, with enthusiasm and determination, major medical advances can emerge from quite ordinary hospitals, driven by far from ordinary people. Patrick Steptoe developed IVF in Oldham General and District Hospital, and John Charnley invented hip replacement surgery in Wrightington Hospital, Wigan, both bog-standard hospitals, to coin a phrase. Both procedures are now bog-standard too.

---

10. Julian Tudor Hart, 'The Inverse Care Law', *Lancet*, 297 (1971), 405–12.
11. Nuffield Trust, press release, 24 December 2018.

To Baltasound on Unst, the very far north

Wednesday August 1st, sunshine and clouds, and a brilliant 28-mile four-and-a-half-hour fine reach in an easterly wind towards Baltasound, the main community on Unst, the most northerly inhabited island of the British Isles. Eileen and Sylvia were getting on famously, both trying their hand at the tiller, and giggling like schoolgirls in their united bond of womanhood (among the boorish men maybe). En route we could see the Out Skerries in the distance, a very remote group of small islands, surprisingly with a secondary school of only three pupils (now closed, not so surprisingly). It's tough living in that sort of place, and tough to be a weekly boarder on the mainland too, but such a small secondary school is crazily expensive and can hardly provide a decent education, at least of a conventional sort.

Then on we sailed past the island of Fetlar to port. By 5pm we were bearing away into Balta Sound. We arrived at the very beaten-up temporary pontoon attached to the harbour wall (the 'permanent' one had blown away in the winter), to be greeted by a very jolly Geordie harbour master who charged us all of £9 for the night. Mind you, there was no electricity, and the water from a distant standpipe didn't taste too good.

The harbour master produced a sketchy map of the local attractions, along with a piece of crucial local information. There was a tea dance in the village hall, just a mile away. That of course is where we headed, and where we sat at trestle tables, drank tea, and ate homemade cakes, scones and sandwiches. The band consisted of a variable number of up to four fiddle players sawing on their instruments, an accordionist, and a keyboard. The music was the genuine local stuff, more enthusiastic than technically brilliant, but certainly good enough for everyone there — family groups, children and grannies sitting round the tables, and our crew — to be up on their feet doing reels. Some of our more enthusiastic crew, led of course by Eileen, were taught a dance local to Unst.

Next to me was a woman in a wheelchair who turned out to have a neurological problem. As far as I could tell she had not seen the neurologists in Aberdeen, which she should have done because they provide the Shetland neurology service, albeit only by video link. (This is not good enough for most new patients although it certainly can be for follow-up appointments once the doctor and patient have met face-to-face.) The local consultant general physician had told her there was no diagnosis, and possibly used the dreaded phrase 'it's all in your mind'. Although you can never completely believe what a patient reports a doctor to have said, I imagine he thought her neurological problem was functional. I would never trust a general physician to make that diagnosis, it is tricky enough as a neurologist.

Then on we walked through the developing mist to the most northerly pub in the British Isles, the Baltasound Hotel, there to drink the most northerly beer from the local Valhalla brewery, but from bottles only I'm afraid. Not many people propped up the bar, and it was getting distinctly bleak outside as we walked back to Pickle. By the harbour we were directed to a box of crabs caught by a local fisherman. Missing some legs, they were no use to him and he told us to help ourselves, which we did. By the time we got back on board it was 8.30pm, still light of course, and the ever-resourceful Eileen had already prepared our dinner.

Thursday August 2nd, rubbish weather, mist and rain, but this was well predicted. We got a taxi the couple of miles to Haroldswick to view the Unst Boat Haven, a large shed with a fine collection of traditional wooden Shetland boats. Wood from Norway, only 165 miles away, because there was none on Shetland (still the case). The Heritage Museum was not quite so impressive, but the bistro, run by an ex-truck driver from southeast England, certainly was. Excellent scallops for lunch. Just up the road we inspected the Skidbladner, a full-size replica Viking longship that was longer and broader in the beam than I imagined it would be. And a reconstructed Viking long-house. All very interesting, this very close connection between Shetland and Norway, of which more later.

Round the top to Papa Stour

We motored out of Balta Sound at 4pm in thick fog, visibility about a quarter-of-a-mile. I would never ever have attempted this before I had a chartplotter. Even with one it was a bit nerve-racking as we crept past the rocks each side of the 100 metre-wide northern entrance, Eileen on the bows watching for buoys marking lobster pots ready to ensnare our propeller. I am told that I kept yelling 'go to port, go to port' on the basis of what I could see on the chartplotter to which I was glued down below, while Steve on the helm did his Nelson act by disobeying orders and so avoided crashing into the very visible rocks — er yes, to port. Irritatingly, the wind was from the northeast, not east as forecast, so we motored on into it until we could turn west outside the tide rip — with the strange name of Skaw roost — off Lamba Ness and get the sails up at 6pm (up here, a 'roost', from the Norse, is a tide race, usually with overfalls, not a place where birds sleep). Then it was a good reach with the west-going tide in quite a swell before turning in to the Burra Firth, still in fog and seeing nothing of the land.

However, that fog was nowhere near as stressful as the fog off Hurst Point at the entrance to the Solent had been, not because I was getting used to fog but simply because the chance of meeting any speeding motorboats was about zero. It was as it must have been before ships had engines to allow them to charge around in fog when the sea becomes, as Hilaire Belloc put it, 'in one moment a field of terrors'.[12] That evening there were no terrors and we anchored off a hardly visible beach at the head of the firth at 8pm.

It was all very damp and dank as we dumped our waterproofs under the sprayhood and scrambled down below for a splendid crab salad prepared by Sylvia and Eileen. They had been beating the hell out of crab shells with the boat hammer more or less all evening (to my too-obvious relief they did at least clear up their considerable mess). That mere nine-mile hop had us well positioned to get round the northernmost outpost of the UK in the morning.

Friday August 3rd, the fog had cleared, but it was raining. After getting up we were all ready to go in one hour flat, a record for this crew. They were all bonding, holding up, and generally cheerful and tolerant of each other. By the time we motored out of the Burra Firth at 8am, it had stopped raining and we were off, sailing in a 15-knot northeast wind. Perfect. There was even some blue in the sky, the tide was with us (my good passage planning, of course), the waves were rolling along, Muckle Flugga was not far away. It's not strictly true that it is the most northerly tip of the British Isles. There is a rocky spike — Out Stack — one-third-of-a-mile further north, which has been landed on occasionally. However, rather than round that we wanted to get in close to Muckle Flugga where we got a terrific view of the lighthouse. This is a remarkable Stevenson-family construction again, by David and Thomas, built under difficult conditions in 1854 and then rebuilt under equally difficult conditions in 1857 after the original living quarters had been inundated by a huge wave. The birds whirred around us, the tide swirled under us, the sea was unsettled and unsettling. There was much excitement as we crashed around in the waves, and many photographs were taken. A real turning-point this place, iconic even (such a cliché, that word).

Turning left and to the south we went, pointing back towards home, and it was still only 10am. Then a splendid run all the way down the west

---

12. Hilaire Belloc, 'Channel Fog', in *On Sailing the Sea: A Collection of the Seagoing Writings of Hilaire Belloc*, ed. W. N. Roughead (London: Rupert Hart-Davis, 1951), 231.

side of Shetland on a smooth sea, no other boat in sight all day, travelling at 4–5 knots over the ground. There was a whale in the distance, the only one of the whole voyage. In 1869 the 18-year-old Robert Louis Stevenson accompanied his father on an inspection tour of the Orkney and Shetland lighthouses. No one can beat his description of the coast south of Muckle Flugga: 'the western seaboard of Unst, is wild and rugged, dark cliffs riven with inky voes and caverns, white with sea birds, marked here and there by natural arches, and crowned with round hills of sere sun-burnt grass.'[13] It really is exactly like that.

The cliffs and stacks of Papa Stour were particularly impressive, and at 7pm we turned in to Hamna Voe, old Norse for harbour bay. Which is just what it is, a large and almost landlocked bay on the southwest side of the island. There had been no sun, no rain, and no fog all day, and we had sailed nearly 50 miles. We anchored in plenty of space, no other boats of course, no visible people either. The south coast of England this is not — a very different sort of cruising experience up here.

However, even so far from London I still couldn't get away from the Olympics because Steve was glued to the radio. Do single people switch on the radio more often than couples who (should) have to take more notice of each other? I am overly curmudgeonly, not liking sport at all, at least not organised sport. Maybe because my rebellious teenage self reacted against the over-emphasis on sport at school. Being good at rugby didn't seem to me to be a valid reason to be a school prefect and have a fag polish my shoes. I was hopeless at ball games, unable to emulate my sporty older brother, and saw no point in playing sport unless you were going to win. None of this nonsense of it being more important to compete than to win. Winning is what it is all about, is it not? Well, maybe not entirely, as social interaction with like-minded people must be important too, and keeping fit (cycling to work, walking everywhere and running up stairs has kept me fit enough).

Awful in high-level sport is the corruption, ball-tampering in cricket, performance-enhancing drugs, hyped-up advertising, national and international politics, squabbling over what female athletes should wear, and the excessive cost (time and money) of training from sometimes a very young age. Added to which is the physical and even sexual abuse of athletes by their trainers. So few among the thousands who train will ever 'make

---

13. Robert Louis Stevenson, 'Letters to His Mother from the Lighthouse Steamer, 18–22 June, 1869', in *Stevenson's Scotland*, ed. Tom Hubbard and Duncan Glen (Edinburgh: Mercat Press, 2003).

it'. It is so very disappointing when sporting 'heroes' like Lewis Hamilton move to Monaco to avoid UK tax, and Chris Frome overdoses on his asthma inhaler to help him cycle faster. And when paralympic sportsmen and women accuse each other of being in the wrong category of disability (although how you categorise the myriad of possible disabilities is quite beyond me). Now we have complaints that transgender females are too 'male' and thus too advantaged to be allowed to compete against 'real' women, as well as the extraordinary business of eligibility — or not — being determined by male hormone levels in women's blood. What next? People of particular races excluded from some sports because they are at some 'natural' advantage? Even running shoes are controversial. To apparently make you run faster (although as ever one wonders about a placebo effect), Nike Vaporfly shoes at £240 a pop were permitted in 2020,[14] ushering in an arms race between trainer manufacturers. The same problem with high-tech swimsuits. Maybe runners shouldn't be allowed to wear shoes at all, Zola Budd did pretty well barefoot ... but swimmers without swimsuits?

Also unattractive is the extraordinary amount of money that successful sportsmen and women get paid through prizes and sponsorship. And the bungs, and the international gambling with the potential for matches to be thrown. There is far too much money floating around bringing with it the temptation towards criminality. It was not ever thus. In 1954 Roger Bannister ran that quick four-minute mile while still a medical student, with far less training than a modern athlete, certainly on no drugs, and for no money. Many modern athletes are so obsessed with their sport that when they have to retire at a relatively young age they don't know what to do other than have a ghost-writer write their autobiography, or become a TV pundit. Roger Bannister left running behind him in his 20s and was lucky (and sensible) enough to be able to continue his career as a doctor. Good for him.

Of course doctors are not immune to cheating any more than sportsmen. Too often they accept 'hospitality' from industry (aka bribes) and then unsurprisingly favour the industry's drugs, devices or equipment. And so-called medical 'leaders' can be paid such enormous fees to speak on behalf of industry that they become essentially a 'respectable' mouthpiece. Landing huge grants from industry to conduct trials of their new treatments is another difficulty (gratitude easily morphs into grovelling subservience). Amazingly, there is still no mandatory and public register of doctors'

---

14. *Guardian*, 1 February 2020.

interests in the UK; there should be. We all need to know who is paying how much to whom, and for what.

This cheating applies not just to doctors, but to other healthcare professionals who can get sucked in to the system, for example specialist nurses lavishly entertained by the makers of drugs for epilepsy or makers of stoma bags. Nor are yachting magazines immune. In an article on places to visit around the UK, I was asked to substitute one of my favourite places for Lymington, where I have never been, in order that advertising revenue be maximised. Pathetically, I agreed. At least I am now far more circumspect about the reviews in those magazines extolling the virtues and wonders of new — and expensive — boats, marinas, and equipment. In the absence of an independent consumer organisation like *Which?*, it is far preferable to read sailing publications with no advertising at all, like the incomparable *Marine Quarterly* where you will find the best writing laid out on the nicest paper and with the most attractive drawings. 'The thinking sailor's sea journal' is the appropriate strapline penned by Tom Cunliffe, that inveterate marine scribbler.

But back to sport. Is it right to send young kids out before their school-day to train for competitive swimming when the vast, vast majority will never get anywhere near a professional career, let alone elite status? Rowing requires just as much commitment but at least the rowers are generally older and able to make their own decisions. For two years Oli's social life at Newcastle University was compromised (he said) by the demands of training, but at least he got to row in the first eight which must have been fun, as well as a helpful line on his CV. Sport in excess is almost like a religion, and we the unconverted are ripe for conversion, so the converters think. Well I'm not. I can't bear the celebrity nonsense with constant tweeting to the fans, numbered in thousands, and the selfies. And what about the extraordinary cost of hosting the London Olympic Games in 2012 without serious hope of the much-trumpeted 'Olympic legacy' as more state-school playing fields are flogged off to developers? On a later cruise of mine the harbour master at Weymouth certainly hadn't noticed any legacy from their hosting the Olympic sailing. But on this cruise the only way I could escape the Olympics was by going up on deck, or down below, depending on where the radio was not.

In the back of my mind was the memory of Roger Bannister, who became a neurologist. When I was his registrar in 1975 he was the last of the consultants who insisted his team meet him at the front door of the hospital. I am told that years before, at an Association of British

Neurologists' meeting, a cat was being demonstrated on a treadmill, but with the thinking part of its brain removed. It was de-cerebrate. And yet as the treadmill speeded up the cat 'ran' faster and faster. Roger Bannister — yet to be knighted — had left during the presentation. Afterwards a well-known neurologist stood up to say how sorry he was that Dr Bannister had not been able to see how fast one could run 'with no brain at all'. This witty neurologist was never knighted, despite ministering to the Royal Family and other very important people in his Harley Street practice. He was far too indiscreet. During his last ward round in 1975 before retiring he demonstrated to us juniors his rather suspect skills at water divining with a bent coat hanger outside the back of the hospital. He claimed to have located the water main. He also claimed he knew where in the brain a patient's tumour was, using just his clinical skills. On CT brain scanning (very new then) it turned out to be in a completely different part of the brain. 'Time to retire,' he muttered — probably back to his farm where he told me how much he enjoyed having a pee in the open air. Which I imagine most men do.

I worked for some quite strange people in British neurology, and maybe there still are some. Nonetheless, most were excellent clinicians. One in his spare time wrote embarrassingly trashy novels. When I was his junior, during a tea break during a ward round he told me, apropos nothing in particular, that he really enjoyed porn. Honest at least. Another consultant devoted almost all his ward rounds to discussing ceramics. During weekends on call, there was no point in phoning his home in London, as he was in his other home in the country, with his other wife.

By this stage in the cruise I realised even more what should have been blindingly obvious before I had even started. That dealing with a succession of different crew is actually more challenging than the sailing. Which got me thinking about what makes the perfect crew. Certainly keeping the boat clean and tidy is important, preferably spontaneously. Eileen was particularly good at this. After noting the men's inaccurate aim in the heads, she left cloths soaked in lemongrass oil to conquer the unpleasant odours. Having to show the crew again and again how to do something is tedious, particularly flushing the heads properly, and not wasting freshwater, gas, and electricity. However, a more important criterion for a perfect crew must be enthusiasm, and this Shetland crew certainly had that. Empathy is pretty important too, and not footering about keeping everyone else waiting. But one cannot go on and on at recalcitrant crew; after all, they are often on holiday. The skipper just has to accept second best and live with it, and enjoy the fun times, which are most of them. Shouting is no good, neither is going all grumpy, although I am quite good at both.

Saturday August 4th, a bleak landscape out there, treeless smooth hills, even bleaker with no sun to illuminate them. Made bleaker still by the abandoned and ruined cottages dotted around, and the call of curlews. We clearly had to take a closer look so we inflated the Tinker dinghy, rowed to the shore, landed, and plodded to the top of the island where we found the airstrip, deserted, no terminal not even a hut. Then over to the main settlement surrounding Housa Voe, which faces the Shetland mainland. There were about 12 houses (not all of which looked inhabited), surrounded by land that had been only somewhat tamed. After various bust-ups a few years earlier many of the residents had left, and the population was down to something like 10–15. Hanging on the edge. Among the houses we found a partial reconstruction of a medieval log-timbered Viking Stofa House (logs courtesy of Norway). Otherwise there seemed little to keep us so we set off back to wander around Hamna Voe. There were a couple of broken-down horizontal watermills, various ruined cottages, and a fairly substantial ruined farmhouse at the entrance to the voe. A lot of ruins, and a lot of birds, arctic skuas and terns in particular. It remained grey and sunless. I don't think we saw a living human soul on the island. Papa Stour didn't seem at its best, but maybe our views were confounded by the dreary weather.

To Scalloway

We weighed anchor at 1pm and puttered out of the voe to get the sails up on an astonishingly flat sea under an overcast but brightening sky. The wind was light from the northeast which gave us a relaxed reach south under the crazily fractured cliffs, past dark and beckoning caves, only 20 miles or so to our next destination — Scalloway. Those cliffs must surely be good for climbing, all those fascinating curved and bent rock strata, spikes and pinnacles. Again there were hundreds and hundreds of birds all around us — gannets, fulmars, shags, bonxies, kittiwakes, guillemots, puffins.

Not surprisingly the wind died as we got among the islands protecting Scalloway so it was on with the engine at 5.30pm, and we were off the town an hour later with a bit of sun at last, peeping through the clouds. It all looked a bit Scandinavian, with more colour to the houses than the usual Scottish grey. After trying and failing to find a free spot in the marina we were advised to tie up to the pontoon off the Scalloway Boating

Club; a much better choice it was, too, even though there was no water or electricity. We pulled up ahead of the only other boat, a Dutch yacht with its designer living on board, and his wife. They had been to the Antarctic, which made us feel a bit out-classed.

So we crept off to the Scalloway Hotel for excellent bar food, but no real ale, and more Olympics on the TV, on not just one but two TV sets. The locals weren't looking at them, only we foreigners were (well, not me of course — I have had to be reminded that we won two or three gold medals that evening). However, I do like a spectacle, like an international rugby match. I have only been to one, when to everyone's amazement Scotland beat Australia. The experience of premier league football is very different, but just as interesting.

On the way back to Pickle we came across a chatty man with a trailer-load of fish hitched to the back of his car. He insisted on giving us a large ling, something for Sylvia to deal with the next day. There was a very flamboyant hen-party going on in the boating club bar, a lot of noise, so clearly not for us. Too old.

Sunday August 5th, a somewhat brighter day, but still rather grey. As ever, Eileen did an excellent cleaning job, so excellent that she blocked the jets on the gas-stove rings. The crew wanted to see Lerwick so set off by taxi. I preferred to stay on the boat. I needed some space to think, plot and plan, and tidy up. I was getting far more bother from my hernia. It was ridiculous to have to keep pushing it in with my hand in my trouser pocket to stop it hurting. I must be falling to bits. Again that slight hand-shake doing my teeth. Was my hand slower too? That sore bit on the side of my nose — skin cancer perhaps?

I rang home, to find the family ebullient, getting out and about for the Edinburgh Festival. I felt rather envious, and lonely. The thought of introducing yet another new crew to Pickle was daunting, but it would be for the last time. At least Pickle was going really well, with nothing broken for ages, except those gas jets which only needed drying out and a scrub with an old toothbrush. As ever with mechanical things I was at first daunted, imagining I was never going to fix them, but I did. Did anything *not* daunt me?

I went for a wander round Scalloway. The very evident Norwegian connection was not surprising. I had read David Howarth's *The Shetland Bus* (1951) on a previous visit. It was here in Scalloway that fishing boats with concealed guns had been based, taking spies and supplies to occupied Norway in the second world war, and bringing on-the-run Norwegians to the UK. The memorial to those who lost their lives during such high-risk activity is on the waterfront. The museum was excellent, telling this story and others about the community. The ruined 16th-century castle — more a fortified house — was a surprise so far north. It was built in the early 17th century by the notorious and brutal Patrick Stewart, Earl of Orkney, who eventually had his head chopped off.

I had lunch back in the hotel, chatting to the proprietor, a big man of strong opinions. Clearly he was ambitious for his hotel, which he had only owned for four years. But it must be a tough call. I didn't know about Shetland, but on Orkney at the time there were at least seven hotels for sale.

Bearing provisions, the crew were back after lunch and off we went again at 4.30pm under a grey sky, occasional drizzle, for just a three-hour gentle sail in the favourable northeast breeze for the 13 miles down to St Ninian's Island. This is connected to the mainland by a double beach, 500 metres long, the largest active tombolo in the UK. It also happens to be the closest anchorage on the Shetland west coast for getting back to Orkney, and well protected too because you can anchor either side of the tombolo depending on wind direction. It is often used for weddings and sure enough a marquee had been erected on the mainland end of the beach. However, we were more interested in walking over to the island.

The sun was out at last, low in the sky giving a wonderful light. We found the remains of the 12th-century St Ninian's chapel where in 1958 a Shetland schoolboy, Douglas Coutts, helping on an archaeological dig, stumbled — literally — on buried treasure. A big stash of eighth-century Pictish silver jewellery, bowls and weapons in a wooden box under a graveslab. It's now in the National Museum of Scotland in Edinburgh, although it would surely be more appropriately housed in the Lerwick Museum.

According to Eileen's memory, on our way back to the boat we met a beautiful young woman out for a run. She had been an international model but gave it all up to live in Shetland and clean the horrible insides of oil industry vats. How did I forget her? By the time we got to Pickle we were in shadow, time to cook the fish and have an early night. All in all, a very beautiful and faraway spot.

Back to Orkney

Monday August 6th, up at 6am for the 48-mile sail south to North Ronaldsay. The wind was still light from the northeast, perfect. The sea was calm, the sun soon came out; it was even warm. The west coast of Shetland was spectacular, shafts of bright sunlight piercing the dark clouds still clinging to the cliffs, painting moving silver patches on the dark sea. We got the spinnaker up first time, where it stayed for several hours until 4pm when the wind became too light and the swell too much to keep it full. By the time we were off the island of North Ronaldsay the tide had turned west and was flowing very fast, at about 4–5 knots. I had misjudged where we should have been at that point, much further east. As a result we had a struggle under engine to get round the east side of the island to anchor in Linklet Bay at 9.30pm. Lights illuminated the small windows along the spiral stairs of the lighthouse, the main light flashing at the top every 10 seconds.

The next day we had a very leisurely start— we were, after all, only about 50 miles from Stromness for the final crew change at the weekend. After some boat cleaning it was off in the Tinker inflatable to view this rather extraordinary island. It is only three miles long with a population of about 70, and has the highest land-based lighthouse in the UK, which is what we wanted to see. It was yet another Stevenson structure; this Edinburgh family clearly had the 19th-century Scottish lighthouse business completely sewn up. Built in 1853, it had of course been automated for several years but the last keeper, Billy Muir, was on hand to show visitors around (he it was who the previous evening had turned on all the lights up the spiral stairs, possibly just for us).

Up the 176 steps he led us, 130 feet to the top. He was an engaging guide, although not I think a very official one, who clearly loved 'his' lighthouse. He was full of stories about the island where he had lived all his life (his family had been on the island for generations). He took us right into the huge multi-mirrored lens with its many reflections that trick the mere 400-watt light bulb to shine out brightly for 24 miles. The views were of course fabulous, both to far down below where sheep were being collected for shearing and the tide was swirling round the north end of the island, and to way out over an empty sea to the horizon. Back on the ground Billy was clearly keen to demonstrate the foghorn — now never used in anger. What a magnificent noise, and deafening to us standing only a few yards away. So he sounded it again, just to show off. We found him later, hand-shearing sheep with his daughter, near the older 1789 lighthouse covered in scaffolding for restoration.

The island seemed incredibly stony, making it relatively easy I suppose to collect the material for the Grade-A listed 13-mile dry-stone wall right round the shore-line. It was built to keep the sheep on the beach where their diet is more seaweed than grass, and away from the arable land. These sheep are prized for their wool, and their meat that is more mutton than lamb in taste (served up in high-end London restaurants and Edinburgh's George Hotel). The small stone enclosures were apparently not for animals but for growing crops out of the wind, which says something about that wind.

There was an excellent small shop, café and display in the old lighthouse keepers' cottages where we ate tasty lamb pies, a local speciality, and where I bought the Freda Bayne handbag for Cathie, and some books for William. Unfortunately, North Ronaldsay is another island on the edge. Part of the problem is the lack of a proper harbour, but no one is going to build one now. The resident population continues to decline and may soon be lost entirely if nothing is done to help (the primary school closed in 2017 for lack of any children to teach, but reopened in 2021).

Back on the boat the excitable Eileen rather excelled herself by loudly hailing some fishermen, asking, no demanding, that they come closer. 'Ha' yee got any lobsters?' she screeched. 'Aye, how many d'you want?' came the reply. How did Eileen know they had some? Our collapsible lobster pot was not nearly so successful: in four hours it had entangled just two small crabs … and a dogfish.

To Papa Westray

It is only 17 miles to Papa Westray so there was no hurry, and I wanted to get the tides right, a task that was giving me a headache. The Sailing Directions seemed inaccurate in their tidal predictions, and Reeds Almanac was not detailed enough to be helpful. However, we managed OK, catching the west-going tide off the south end of North Ronaldsay to hurry us close-hauled to the south-facing Bay of Moclett on Papa Westray, another small Orkney Island with a similar-sized population to North Ronaldsay. Although a chilly evening, the sea was flat, and the roost in the North Ronaldsay Firth comfortably quiescent. After a four-hour sail and motor, we arrived at 8.15pm, the only boat anchored off the pier, perfect timing for Eileen and Sylvia's very fresh lobster salad.

Wednesday August 8th, David, Sylvia and I set off to explore the island, specifically to check out the Knap of Howar, a Stone Age house even older than the more famous houses at Skara Brae. Better too, because unlike Skara Brae it is open to wander around at will. It was not a disappointment. We were the only people there, free to poke at the old stones, admire the curved stone walls with their stone 'cupboards', lie on the grass in the sunshine listening to the sea. Definitely worth a detour. David and Sylvia with their architectural sensibilities were thrilled.

Not so many tourists get to Papa Westray, perhaps most have had more than their fill of archaeology and other delights on the Orkney mainland. But some do want to tick off the shortest commercial flight in the world — depending on wind strength and direction, Papa Westray is about two minutes' flying time from Westray. What an attractive island Papa is, especially with the sun shining. 360° views of fields of varying green, old houses (some restored), views of the sea from more or less everywhere, an old windmill, cows, sheep. Ideal for wandering, dawdling.

To increase our delight, we bumped into Neil Rendall who, tipped off by David Simpson, was looking for us. He owns the Farm of Holland with its lovely buildings, including a circular one with the beautiful timber roof where horses were used to pull round a horizontal grinding millstone. And the amazingly long barn where they hold parties, as well as animals, and where they dry grain. He and his wife Jocelyn, an author of some repute, had set up a small museum showing how people lived about 100 years ago, charming and very realistic. Neil is a lovely man. Driving us back to the anchorage, he asked:

'How many do you have on board?'

'Five,' I said.

'Oh,' he said. 'You must be good friends.'

'We will be in two weeks,' replied David.

And I think we really were, despite some ups and downs.

Neil's sister Anne was well-known as the 'flying banker'. From 1988 until she retired in 2019, she flew on nearly 12,000 inter-island flights to provide Royal Bank of Scotland services to the remoter Orkney islands. Before her and her predecessor, a ship — the 'Otter Bank' otherwise known as the 'floating bank', now preserved at the Lyness museum — provided the same service. Whether such personal service will survive the age of internet banking, and the commercial 'bottom line', remains to be seen.

Eileen and Steve missed all this because they had gone for a swim at the anchorage. Eileen tended to be more enthusiastic about her own enthusiasms, which included wild swimming rather than old stones. Having two very chatty women on board was quite hard work, but then without them where would we have been? No lobster or crab salad. And much less fun. The perfect crew should certainly be enthusiastic like Sylvia and Eileen, but not take over the whole show. The skipper of a charter boat, or a sailing instructor, presumably has more control, and is better able to boss people around, because they are not friends or family. Nonetheless, it must be tough having to introduce a new crew to each other every week, look after them, feed them, sail them around, teach them, without knowing them at all, or indeed their sailing abilities. But if it's your livelihood, that's how it has to be. Cathie's sister Jane managed pretty well as a sailing instructor in the Canaries, and even married one of her clients.

What makes the perfect skipper? Or indeed a perfect leader of any sort? The naval officer Jack Aubrey in Patrick O'Brian's novels set during the Napoleonic Wars seems a pretty good role model. He knew his crew well, and they knew him. He didn't bully although he was not averse to wielding the occasional cat-o'-nine-tails (this I have not done, yet). He took advice, listened, had a think and then did the necessary — boldly. He was better in command of one ship rather than of many when he tended to lose control. Most of his crew always wanted to return to his ship, which must be a good sign (some of mine do, but not all). A rapid turnover of crew on a boat, like staff in a medical department, is always a bad sign. Aubrey avoided the loneliness of command by his friendship with a totally different kind of person, the ship's surgeon and Irish-Catalan Stephen Maturin. The combination of their very different skills, knowledge and character is what made them such a good team.

To the island of Rousay

I got the tides right this time. In the afternoon, with the wind from the west it was an easy reach flying the great green cruising chute, down the east side of Westray, through the small gap between the south end of Faray and Eday, hauling more into the wind towards the south end of Egilsay, and then turning west. There were just two other sails, otherwise no boats to be seen. The anchorages between Wyre and Rousay were too exposed in the westerly wind so we opted for Ham Bay on Rousay, facing south, 18 miles in four-and-a-half hours. It was too far to walk to the many, many archaeological wonders of Rousay. We didn't have folding bikes, which rust and take up too much space; in any case we could never carry enough for a crew of four or five to go exploring. As the shore itself didn't look terribly enticing, we stayed on board and just admired the fields of varying greens in the special Orkney evening sunlight, colours intensified after the brisk rain showers. We finished the day with a posh dinner, tablecloth and marine decanter included.

I found myself wondering again why so few UK boats visit Orkney. Presumably it is because of its distance from where most people live. And there is only one local sailing boat to charter. Maybe people are put off by the weather which while not as warm as the south coast is not that bad. Besides, the flat-water sailing between the islands surely makes up for this, notwithstanding sorting out the tides. As do the long summer evenings, the beautiful skies, all the wild life … particularly the birds. There is also so much of interest to see on the land from the Stone Age through the Viking period to the detritus left by the two world wars. However, much of what there is to see is accessible from the land, quite unlike the Hebrides where most of the interesting places are by the sea, with many only accessible by boat. And in truth the sailing in the Hebrides and the Scottish west coast is more intricate and interesting, the scenery grander too. Orkney is more for land-based creatures, with occasional boat trips — the Hebrides for marine creatures who enjoy exploring ashore.

Nonetheless, there are definite advantages for adults and kids who sail in Orkney. As well as beaches to play on and sea to swim in (with wetsuits), the sails can be short and therefore child-friendly. You don't have to worry about getting caught out in the dark in the summer. You have anchorages all to yourself, and they are far easier to get into than in the Hebrides. There are three marinas if you don't want to anchor. The weather forecasts are excellent. Provisions are easily available. Added to all that, the local real ale is good and the whisky too. There is lots of art and music. The natives are friendly. What's not to like?

That evening there was the sad news by email that Peter Harvey had died. Not much older than me, Peter was a rumbustious, pinstripe-suited, larger than life, overweight and sweating, but highly amusing and intelligent London neurologist. Given his size, he should have been dead years ago. Reassuringly there are still a few characters like him in UK medicine. Unlike the somewhat similar-looking Sir Lancelot Spratt in *Doctor in the House* (1954) Peter was a very good doctor. I was sad that there would be no more phone calls asking me about some finer point of stroke medicine to help him in a medico-legal case, no more loud interventions at rather too serious medical meetings, no more well-aimed jokes. Rising to ask a question of a speaker at an Association of British Neurologists meeting, he once started off with 'Although I have heard this same talk for the seventh time, could you please tell me …'. We need more Peter Harveys in life as well as in medicine.

And back to Stromness

Thursday August 9th, the last sailing day of this leg, up early at 6.30am. The wind was westerly, about 10 knots, so in long tacks on the outgoing tide we sailed through Eynhallow Sound, which was not as tricky as I anticipated. There may not be much room between the Orkney mainland and Eynhallow Island, but the roost across the gap is short and no problem, at least not that day. We were soon off Birsay Head in a modest Atlantic swell, some sunshine and showers, then close-hauled south past Marwick Head. Perched on top is the memorial cairn to Lord 'Your Country Needs You' Kitchener who drowned off here along with most of the crew of HMS Hampshire after it hit a German mine in 1916. David, Sylvia, Steve and I are all of the generation that was born during or just after the second world war, and grew up in its rather austere aftermath. We know all about battleships and Spitfires, rationing, the Dam Busters, and the last gasps of Imperial Britain. It meant less to Eileen who is about 20 years younger.

It was a grand sail, and lots of fun, everyone taking a turn on the tiller. Why are we so attracted to the sea? Because we are an island race? Or is there a special something which appeals to everyone, even someone who has been brought up in the middle of the USA, or land-locked Switzerland? Probably both, but the aesthetic appeal is surely very great. The constant movement of the sea, even on a calm day, the changing colours, the rise and fall of the tide, the catenary curves of ropes attaching boats to harbour walls, and boats bobbing on moorings or at anchor, reflected in the water. Bobbing boats are ridiculously charming — well, almost all of them, as some are ugly even when bobbing. The most charming are of course the traditional boats, so there's nostalgia for you.

We got the timing perfect to arrive off Hoy Sound just as the tide was turning east. By 2pm we were tied up again at Stromness marina, the crew well-bonded and in good shape. There were no visiting UK boats, just a Dutchman doing a round-Britain in 10 one-week legs, a speed that wouldn't allow him to see as much as I did.

Steve and Eileen had to leave rather quickly to catch the ferry to Scrabster and the train south, right in the middle of David's birthday tea and cake (courtesy of Sylvia). No boat cleaning for them. But in truth I mostly prefer to do it myself, as at least it gets done properly, and in peace and quiet, which I rather like. It is strange how clean one keeps a boat (brass polished, wood polished too) compared with a house, or at least I do. Certainly compared with my car. If only the crew kept the boat as clean. There were bits of discarded food all over the place, including a rotting watermelon, all for the bin. 'Shipshape and Bristol fashion' kept coming into my head. Shipshape of course means everything is in its right place, clean and tidy. You know where it all is — not in the wrong place where an eager crew has put it where you can't find it. Why Bristol I know not. The most plausible explanation seems to be that before the Floating Harbour was constructed in Bristol, the water disappeared completely at low tide, ships heeled over as they dried out, and anything loose slid about before crashing to the floor

On the other hand, if alone for too long I become demotivated, a bit sad and lonely, and start worrying — on this occasion about Oli who was about to climb those ridiculously steep and high cliffs in the Yosemite national park. Recently one climber had been killed, but he wasn't even climbing, and was on the ground when hit by a rock-fall. Too many friends' children have been killed in mountain accidents. Jamie Fisher frozen to death on Mont Blanc, Maarten van Gijn falling with his mountain bike off an alpine path. With these gloomy thoughts, I squirted a bit of WD40 here and there, that little 20th-century miracle which frees up everything which should move but doesn't. I squirted some more, over the electrical contacts of the Torqeedo engine; astonishingly it came to life again. To fix something loose, which shouldn't be loose, there is that other little 20th-century miracle — gaffer tape.

It was good to be back in Stromness. David Simpson turned up for a drink, and we all had a very pleasant dinner. On board, with the tablecloth and the decanter full of wine, after which we trooped up to David's house above the town for coffee. The next morning David Lea and Sylvia went off sightseeing, leaving me in peace and quiet to get on with sorting out the boat, taking a few trips to the local Co-op for provisions, and to Flett's the excellent butcher, and to generally enjoy being by myself. No stress. True to form, Tam at the bookshop had located the book I wanted (he is said to have been able to source any book you could possibly want). His portrait now hangs in the Stromness library — not bad for a laconic west-coast American who washed up in Orkney and came to love and be loved in Stromness.

That evening we had our final dinner in the Stromness Hotel, and then enjoyed a dram on board Pickle while discussing the philosophy of architecture, and David's buildings. Interestingly, if you want to be an architect, David reckons philosophy is as important to study as art and maths at school. There were plans for a book about his work, which was published in 2016.[15] The book's best part is the long conversation between him and the author; the saddest part is the drawings of all the buildings that he designed but which never got built.

---

15. Adam Voelcker, *David Lea: An Architect of Principle* (London: Artifice Press, 2015).

Only recently did David Lea tell me the three underpinning principles of architecture — commodity, firmness and delight. 'Commodity' of course refers to the function of a building, which has to do what the client wants it to do. 'Firmness' simply means it has to stand up to whatever the environment throws at it in terms of flood, earthquake or frost. 'Delight' is the real surprise and the final test — the building must be delightful. Not dreary, drab, and dull … but delightful. The same must apply to boats, which are in a sense buildings that float. But not to caravans, of which I have never seen a delightful example, other than the old-fashioned gypsy ones. Pickle is certainly delightful, has been firm so far, and does what sailing boats are supposed to do — sails well, and accommodates in comfort. Architecture and boat design are clearly very similar in their intentions.

On Sunday David Simpson drove us all to Kirkwall so that David Lea and Sylvia could catch their plane south, and for me and him to go to the Kirkwall Agricultural Show, the big Orkney event of the year. In warm sunshine hundreds of people were there (almost the whole of Orkney it seemed) with their animals: bulls with huge balls, sheep with shampooed fleeces. And Orkney ice cream, Orkney beer, Orkney whisky, huge agricultural machines which do the jobs of a hundred men, young women doing (is that the right verb?) dressage — trot trot trot, bumpity bumpity bumpity on their pert bottoms, up and down, up and down, up and down. Very sexy. Of course David knew everyone. Later that evening we had a pint in the Stromness Hotel. This was becoming a habit, a rather nice one. I would miss it. It had felt weird being out of doors almost all summer. A completely new feeling, and rather good. Neurology was very far away. But home beckoned.

THE BROCH OF MOUSA

Chapter 11

The final leg, to Dunstaffnage (and Ardfern)

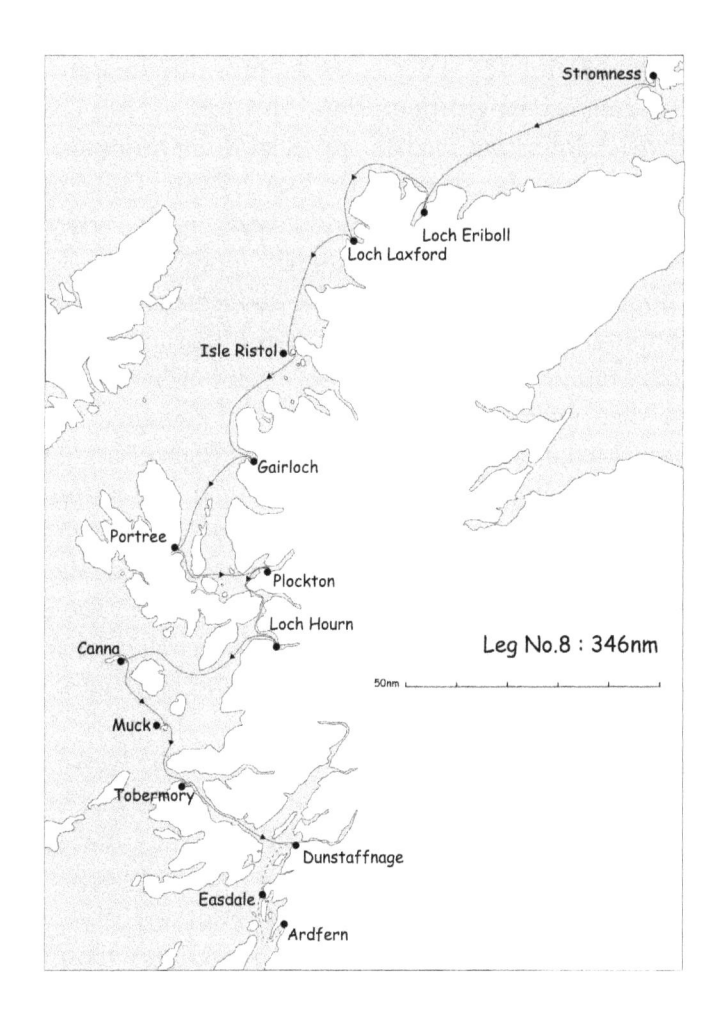

Orkney was starting to feel like home. Not too surprising as I had been there off and on for four weeks. It was going to be difficult to leave, but I was missing my real home in Edinburgh, and the family. Lucy had just got her first mobile phone, and sounded so sophisticated when I spoke to her. William the opposite. 'Hello. Goodbye' was all I could get out of him. Apparently Lucy and William had been at loggerheads again, driving Cathie mad — again.

Dear William had been so keen to be the one to use the fob to open the gate to the marina. And so keen to watch the ferry dock and then open its huge bow-doors to release the cars and trucks to drive down the ramp, but he delayed too long that urinary urge, with the inevitable result. These and other new memories of Orkney could be added to the old ones. Sewing up the gash on six-year-old Oli's head in Kirkwall harbour after he unwisely tried to climb the shrouds. Further back, my introduction by Heather Dawson — a long ago ex-girlfriend from Aberdeen — not just to Orkney but to Dr Derrick Johnstone, a character of a GP in Stromness with whom she had studied. And to Jo Grimond, the local MP and leader of the Liberal Party at the time, who was also rector of Aberdeen University and whom she knew through its Students' Association.

Sunday August 12th, preparing for the last leg on a lovely sunny day. Shower, shopping, emails, deck cleaning, polishing the brass, polishing the interior joinery too, reorganising the galley back to where everything ought to be rather than where the previous crew had thought it should be. It would be a relief to have company because of my demotivation when alone, tending to take too many breaks sitting about doing nothing, reaching for the biscuit tin. But it would not be so good to have to go through all that safety stuff again, and sort out the personal interactions — again. Would everyone get on with each other? We would see. The crew arrived at teatime, off two flights that had landed at Kirkwall at nearly the same time. Somehow they realised they were all in the same crew, introduced themselves, and shared a taxi to Stromness.

David Thrush, whom we had had dinner with in Newton Ferrers, I was very confident about. He was a bit older than me but had done lots of sailing, chartering here and there; ever ready with a dreadful joke and far too many silly stories, but always cheerful. He had been a neurologist toiling at the NHS coalface in Plymouth without any time for research. I had first met him when we were both at St George's Hospital Medical School. I am sure he had been a terrific doctor (Cathie agrees, and she should know having once been his registrar).

Catherine Royce was about my age. I hadn't seen her for years, and not really since she had come on some of our early sailing trips in the 1970s. She had worked in the pharmaceutical industry but then returned to her early speciality as a surgeon, working part-time in Ethiopia. She was almost retired, a single mother, and ever so confident as surgeons generally are — and have to be or they would be paralysed by doubt and wouldn't dare cut people open. Luckily they are more often right than wrong. Anyway, who am I to complain when surgeons have saved my life more than once.

Irene was slightly younger than Catherine, and a very experienced medical statistician in Oxford I had worked with but didn't know well. Her husband had died of a brain tumour in 1999, a missed diagnosis for some time, a fact she unsurprisingly was unable to forget. Like many medical statisticians she tended to be critical of doctors, who generally know little of statistics — 'the last thing you want is a medic wrangling your data,' as she put it. This can't have helped when she had to interact with doctors as a patient's wife. She had sailed with me a couple of times when she was with Konrad Jamrozik, a tall, rather brusque Polish-origin Australian epidemiologist. He wore shorts through the Oxford winters and often came sailing, referring to me as 'The Admiral'.

The completely unknown was Irene's daughter Thea, a first-year Cambridge engineering undergraduate. She worked as a part-time model, merited by her sultry and beautiful looks, and extraordinarily long legs, not a bad way to fund your university fees. How could she have been a rower at school? She seemed too frail. Deceptive. Irene assured me that although Thea was quiet she was keen to come, and had done a lot of dinghy sailing.

So there we were, three women and two men. That would have been almost inconceivable 100 years ago when most sailing was a male-only buddy or solo affair, wives left at home to crochet and look after the children. But Frank Cowper saw the light, sort of, in a rather misogynistic kind of way: 'It adds greatly to the enjoyment of the party if one of them brings his wife with him. A lady who is a good sailor and ready to put up with little discomforts is a great blessing. She is the softening, refining influence which puts everything straight, and, of course, her domestic virtues are of the greatest assistance.'[1] I have almost always sailed with women in the crew; indeed, Catherine was on our very first charter on the Clyde in 1974.

I have always worked with women, too, from being a junior doctor

---

1. Frank Cowper, *Sailing Tours: The Yachtsman's Guide to the Cruising Waters of the English Coast*, part 1: *The Coasts of Essex and Suffolk* (London: Upcott Gill, 1892), 167.

alongside Ann McPherson through working with Pam Hinton in Birmingham and the flamboyant sari-wearing Indian anaesthetist with her mask slung round her chin whose name I forget, to doing research with Joanna Wardlaw, a neuroradiologist, in Edinburgh, and indeed with Cathie. It makes more sense for men and women to work together, more productive, less macho-posturing than in men-only groups, perhaps less gossiping than in women-only groups (but how would I know?).

I have also become more aware — by proxy — of what it is like to be the only woman in a group of men because this is where Cathie often finds herself (less so in recent years). And, for myself, how uncomfortable it can be to be the only man in a group of women, for example in our primary school playground (one other dad confided to me that he sometimes felt he had a contagious disease); in our high-school school parent council; and to a lesser extent in my art class. I have never dared join book groups, which are almost all women-only. This all reflects the gradual, post-second world war decline of the male-dominated society which had existed for centuries, but maybe it can go a bit too far (at times).

In the evening, as all the crew were keen to explore Stromness before we left, we walked along 'The Street' through the lovely old town. Past the house that Cathie and I later bought with its blue plaque celebrating Ma Humphrey who opened the house in 1836 as a temporary hospital for sailors returning from the whaling with scurvy. On past the campsite where in 1973 Heather and I had pitched our tent. Out to the golf course with the splendid views over the Sound of Hoy to the dark hills of Hoy. And back to the Stromness Hotel for another excellent dinner. And then that safety briefing.

To Loch Eriboll

Monday August 13th, it was our own 'Farewell to Stromness', the title of the haunting music by Peter Maxwell Davies who lived on Orkney for many years. His 'farewell' was a protest against the proposal for a nearby uranium mine (which luckily never happened). Unfortunately my own farewell was seriously hampered by a 20-knot southeast wind pinning us to the pontoon. However, this time I did get it right. We motored forwards against a spring to get the stern out, then quickly motored backwards into clear water — neatly. I impressed both myself, and hopefully the new crew too.

Timing is everything for getting out of the Sound of Hoy, needing to avoid a strong ebb tide with you and a big swell rolling in from the west against you. Greenvile Collins got it right again, more than four centuries ago: 'The tides run in and out very strong between the West end of Hoy and Pomona, where you will have great Riplings and Breaches, as though there was shoal-water, yet the Channel is bold and deep, and no danger.'[2] That morning at 8am we had the tide on the turn, the wind behind us, and a flat sea — no 'riplings'. Unlike Archibald Young in the late 19th century, we were not 'astonished' to find ourselves 'all at once in the midst of a tremendous sea, pitching bowsprit under, and the spray flying over our deck'.[3]

I needn't have warned Thea about big waves, at least not until we emerged from behind the shelter of Hoy — definitely a two-reefs-in-the-mainsail day with a 20-knot wind on our port quarter, and then three reefs as the wind got up to 25 knots, gusting 30. It all got extremely bouncy but it was a grand sail on a beautiful day, making about 7 knots all the way across the 54 miles to Loch Eriboll. But, oh dear, despite the sunshine there was a lot of sickness. First Thea who retired below into her sleeping bag, then Irene, and finally David. Thea was not helped by having only thin dinghy-sailor waterproofs. Luckily Cathie's proper waterproofs were still on board (my pre-boarding instructions to the crew had clearly not been emphatic enough about the need for serious waterproofs in the north of Scotland, as much for wind resistance and warmth as to keep the wet out).

By 3pm we were off the entrance to Loch Eriboll. Once in the loch the water was smooth, and the crew cheered up, as did I. But we still had a hard beat backwards and forwards halfway towards the head of the loch where we found a comfortable anchorage on the east shore in a north-facing bay formed by Ard Neakie, which is almost an island. Perfect shelter. The old house still standing on the island is from where the ferry to the west side of the loch ran before any roads were built.

It had not been the most comfortable of introductory sails for the new crew, but we had to get a move on and leave Stromness when we did. Otherwise, with a forecast of a near-gale force 7 later that day, and the next, we might have been stuck in Orkney for two or three days. Ideally, of course, I should not have taken a new and relatively untested crew for such a long sail on their first day, but it was a penalty for our deadline (most of the crew had to be back home in a couple of weeks). But for me and Catherine, and Pickle of course, there was no penalty — we had had an excellent sail.

---

2. Greenvile Collins, *Great-Britain's Coasting Pilot* (London: 1693).

3. Archibald Young, *Summer Sailings by an Old Yachtsman* (Edinburgh: David Douglas, 1898), 15.

In the old days Catherine always wanted to sail on and on, further than the rest of us. Very pushy. Typical surgeon. She hadn't changed.

For some reason it took three attempts to get the anchor to hold, which made me uneasy enough to set the anchor alarm on the chartplotter for the first time. A radius of 0.01 miles was too sensitive because the alarm kept going off, but 0.02 was better and no alarm was bleeping to keep me awake that night. Catherine cooked us an excellent vegetarian curry (Thea is a veggie). Then it was early to bed, a bit shattered really. I was worried Irene and Thea were not going to enjoy themselves; so far, not so very good.

To Loch Laxford

Tuesday August 14th, a lighter but still southeast wind, off at 9.15am for a fast flat-water sail back down the loch at 5–6 knots in some sunshine (contrary to our expectations from the weather forecast). Scottish sailing at its best. But not appreciated by Irene who fell asleep in the cockpit as we turned to port, between some small islands, and then off on a run to Cape Wrath. There is a firing range off this coast, but the Ministry of Defence official was clueless on the telephone when we rang to find out if we were going to be shot at or not. 'Where is Cape Wrath?' he asked, presumably answering a phone in a bunker somewhere on Salisbury Plain. 'Would you spell that?' Then he gave us another number which didn't answer, and nor did Stornoway Coastguard, so we sailed on. In any event, live firing is usually accompanied by a patrol boat to chase you away. That morning there were no boats of any sort anywhere to be seen.

What a magnificent and dramatic headland Cape Wrath is. The name is nothing to do with wrathful but is derived from the Old Norse 'hvarf' meaning turning point, which is just what it is. The Vikings turning from heading west to heading south on their way to plunder North Britain if you take the traditional view of them as aggressive invaders, which may not be entirely correct. For us the weather was brilliant, the tide was under us, and we could sail close in under the cliffs well away from the Duslic Rock to starboard. The lighthouse was just visible, which means you are not too close. The seabirds were wonderful, the ocean was blue, as were the mountains in the distance. Irene slept on while David took photographs. At midday a single Typhoon Eurofighter swept low over us, much noisier than a Tornado. Tornados are usually in pairs.

We were down to just one reef in the mainsail, on a fine reach heading south. Off Sandwood Bay we could shake out that last reef, sailing on in the sunshine until we were off Loch Laxford by 3pm, according to Murdoch Mackenzie a 'capacious very fine harbour, there is nothing to fear coming in'.[4] Forty-five minutes later we had motored in past the Ridgeway family's adventure school, in and out between little islands. Among innumerable anchoring possibilities we chose to anchor all alone in Loch A'Chadh-Fi which could have been a freshwater loch so sheltered was it from the open sea. The perfect Scottish sea-loch.

Thirty-five miles of sailing under our belts. Sunshine, and warm in the cockpit. But very soon we had thunder and lightning, and rain bouncing off the sea, so didn't go ashore that evening. Instead we enjoyed Irene and Thea's spaghetti bolognese. They were both so much more cheerful out of the waves, but I was uneasy that they were not coping with the sometimes chilly weather.

Again I found myself thinking what a wonderful boat Pickle is, and how lucky I had been to find John and Miranda Myers on board their Rustler 36 in Ardfern just after we had ordered our build but before it was too late to get their advice. 'Bring a notebook and pencil,' John ordered when he heard we were buying a Rustler, 'and I will tell you what you need to add to the basic specification.' John speaks in orders, Yorkshire orders, although he prefers to call them 'recommendations in the light of experience'. He ordered us (recommended us) to get chunkier genoa-sheet winches, grab-rails on the saloon ceiling, down-lighters in the galley, a double rather than a single sink, an extra cleat amidships on each side-deck, a nice brass hook by the chart table to hang my waterproof jacket, 70 metres of anchor chain, and more that I can't remember. All turned out to be useful although 70 metres of chain has felt excessive. My own additions were the seats each side of the pushpit from where one can admire the whole length of the lovely boat plunging through the waves. What a change from Calypso. Cruising in a Contessa 32 is generally likened to camping. Pickle is much more comfortable with its hot and cold running water, efficient heater, fridge, wonderful interior joinery, and shore-power when on pontoons. Unlike many modern boats, Pickle has a proper-sized chart table, not so much for paper charts these days, more a good place to put stuff (well, my stuff, certainly not the crew's stuff).

By the time it was dark the weather had cleared; stars glittered in a cloudless sky and were reflected in the completely still water. No light pollution to

---

4. Murdoch Mackenzie, *Nautical Descriptions of the West Coast of Great Britain from Bristol Channel to Cape-Wrath* (London: 1776), 57.

spoil the effect. What a difference to the Solent, and that Poole marina. What a privilege to be here on one's own boat, sharing it with friends.

To Isle Ristol

Wednesday August 15th, a cloudless morning, and enough time for a brief stroll ashore. It was good to be back wading through the highland bracken, seeing all the familiar Hebridean wild flowers — tormentil, bog asphodel, common orchids — and the sweet-smelling bog myrtle. There were a couple of houses on the shore, holiday homes I imagine. No one around, and no other boats.

I don't think I had a very clear idea of where we were going next, just to get south. There would be plenty of choice of anchorage. We were off by mid-morning, for an absolutely brilliant sail in a light southeast wind, with the big green sail (aka the cruising chute) pulling well. By the time we were off Handa Island the wind had strengthened and we were bowling across Eddrachillis Bay at 6 knots. By Stoer Head the wind was 25 knots, gusting 30, and we were up to 7 knots, reaching with one reef in the main. The Old Man of Stoer is not quite so iconic as the Old Man of Hoy, perhaps because it has not been featured on TV as far as I know, but as another sea stack it is still a magnet for climbers. Ben and Oli had climbed it on their way back south after Orkney. It was a shame to streak past all those wonderful places on the mainland but we had to be back home on time. The characteristic mountain shapes of Suilven and Stac Polly appeared, one after the other, behind the foreground of the dark blue sea.

We needed to anchor somewhere sheltered from the strong easterly wind which was forecast, indeed had been forecast for the previous five days — that impressively accurate xcweather again. Escaping up Loch Broom to Ullapool would be too far out of our way, and the anchorage on Tannara Mòr, one of the Summer Isles, would be too open to the east. Instead, I picked the small gap between Isle Ristol and the mainland. So, rounding Rubha Mòr into Loch Broom and getting the southeast wind on the nose we switched on the engine for a rather vigorous half-hour motor to the anchorage, 32 miles from our starting point that day, arriving at 4pm.

There was not a lot of room. One French visiting yacht left as we were circling round looking for a good anchoring spot in very gusty conditions. Although there were quite a few local moorings, not all with boats on them, I wasn't going to pick one up. I had no idea how much rust might be eating through their shackles and chains. Eventually we found a place to anchor very close to the east shore, and assumed (hoped) the wind wouldn't shift round 180° and drive us aground.

It was far too windy to get ashore so we stayed put for an early supper and a good read of our books. I was reading *We who Adventure: Cruises in British Waters* by a Dr Winter, recommended by the author's nephew whom I had discovered running the Stromness dive shop. What tough guys those sailors were in the 1930s, my parent's generation, not so very long ago. Unreliable petrol engines, no echosounders, buckets instead of heads, heaving-to in the Thames Estuary surrounded by ships steaming up and down, nights at sea spent lost and meandering in the shallows of the Wash. All calling each other by their surnames, as indeed we did when I was at school in the 1950s. That 'Winter' must have been well-off to have had a boat built for him when he was only in his 30s. I imagine he was 'manly' too.

Four is definitely the right number for this sort of long-distance but still mostly daytime cruising on Pickle. Three means too much hard work steering, at least it was until we got the rather neat Neptune windvane. Five is a bit too crowded unless the crew are experienced so they don't get in each other's way in the cockpit and down below where even six can be OK. It should go without saying that any crew has at least to be enthusiastic about the sailing, and we were struggling with enthusiasm on this leg given the strong winds and generally rather unpleasant sea conditions. The door to the forecabin was off its hook and banging in the swell. No one did anything. A good crew knows what to do — hook it back!

I was nervous about our anchorage, as the wind was gusting up to 30 knots making us swing about wildly. Having once got two anchor chains wrapped around each other, I am not one for putting out two anchors from the bows in a blow. The alternative is to put out more anchor chain, but the boats behind us were too close for comfort. Fortunately the anchor alarm seemed to be working rather well now that its sensitivity was sorted out. We watched with interest the wiggly line of our 'course' on the chartplotter, which seemed to be over a rather larger area than I had anticipated.

It was wonderful to phone home on the mobile. Cathie was coping OK, it had been Will's first day at school, and she had texted a great photo of him — eager, ready to go, the perfect wee school boy, which he still is … most of the time, but not so wee now. One primary school teacher called him impeccably well-behaved. Mistaken identity perhaps.

Eight more sailing days to go, and what could go wrong I wondered. The scab on my nose had disappeared so not cancer, but I still felt my right hand was not quite right for teeth brushing. The Parkinson's disease I'd earlier thought of was still a possibility (but hasn't materialised ten years later). Doctors do worry about themselves, however much we may pretend not to, of course we do — a little knowledge is indeed a dangerous thing, or at least disquieting. As a junior doctor I convinced myself that I had Hodgkin's disease that had affected one of my friends. A bit later it was motor neurone disease when I first noticed the (still) flickering muscle on the back of my hand, and more recently cancer of the palate after a good friend developed cancer of his gum. At least Pickle seemed fine.

Yes, it would definitely be good to get home. No more worrying whether the crew were enjoying themselves, were warm enough, and not too seasick. Or fretting about hair blocking the sink, stuff put away in the wrong place, non-stick pans attacked with abrasive pads, poor cleaning, hot pans put down on varnished wood, and so on. And on, until I fell asleep.

To Gairloch

Thursday August 16th, much less wind, a sunny day, warm too. We were motoring out to sea by 10am, and then had the sails up for a slow reach south, with grand views of the Torridon mountains in the distance and the familiar triangular-shaped mountain on Skye at the end of the Inner Sound, Beinn na Caillich I think. By midday the wind had veered more into the southwest so we were tacking backwards and forwards, 5 knots over the ground. It was very slow progress, but sunny, and calm enough for me to make that salade niçoise for lunch. Cruising can be like giving anaesthetics — 95% boredom and 5% panic. But not boring if you enjoy staring at the sea and thinking and reading, which I do. Racing is rather different (which I don't do).

What is it I wondered about crew who can easily steer a straight course until they start talking when it all goes pear-shaped? 'Can you walk and talk?' is one of those questions we ask during a geriatric assessment. As you age it becomes increasingly difficult to combine a motor task like walking — or maybe steering — with a cognitive task like talking. But my crew were not that old. Mind you, I was beginning to understand what I had been taught at St George's Hospital by the first professor of geriatrics. 'Ears, eyes, teeth and feet,' he proclaimed. 'That is all you need to remember.' How right he was. Check the older person's hearing and that any hearing aid is switched on (I now have a hearing aid, though have lost it, twice so far). Check that the spectacles are the right prescription and make sure they are within reach, or on the nose (I must get my cataract done soon). Check that the false teeth fit (ah, these days I have three implants, the modern and costly alternative). And check that a chiropodist has fixed any unruly toenails and sore bunions (I still have a touch of metatarsalgia, that pain in the ball of the foot when walking).

However, I would add, do also beware the elderly male and carry a urinary catheter on board just in case his enlarging prostate obstructs urinary flow while his kidneys go on making urine. Unlike some skippers, I do allow male crew to pee off the back of the boat as long as they hold on (to the boat) with one hand. Maybe that is what the disgraced press baron Robert Maxwell failed to do the night in 1991 when he disappeared from his motor yacht off the Canary Islands, or perhaps he jumped — or was pushed. Once, while relieving myself off the stern, I spotted a long fishing net trailing from our fortunately static propeller, and so saved us from entanglement.

It dawned on me that Irene was the only one of the crew who was actually working. Most of us were too old. David and I had retired, and Catherine was more or less retired. Thea was too young. It's an odd feeling, not working after so many years of going to work. In the geriatric age group, but not yet 'geriatric' — hopefully.

There seemed to be very few porpoises and dolphins around. Not many other boats either, but that is not unusual, just two sails all day, both heading like us for Gairloch. By the time we entered the loch after the 30-mile sail the wind had dropped so we had a 45-minute motor into Badachro Bay, the best anchorage, arriving at 6.30pm. Given the large number of private moorings, we had to anchor quite a long way from the harbour wall, and the pub. I found myself wondering whether the electric outboard motor was such a good idea after all. It may be environmentally attractive, and can drive the dinghy very well, but the battery charge has to be watched rather carefully — what electric car drivers are now calling 'range anxiety'. We used 20% for the two return trips to the pub.

Badachro is a bit touristy, not worth a detour if you want the true Hebridean experience, and there is no shop for supplies. The pub grub was certainly not cheap, nor was the wine, and nor were the showers at £4.50 per person. Personally I prefer showering on the boat, which may be cramped but it is a luxury we hadn't had on the Contessa 32. Mind you, Pickle's hot water does depend on us either being connected to shore-power, or having had the engine running for half an hour or so.

For some reason Thea seemed a bit upset when she came back from the showers with Irene, but soon perked up again. Unfortunately Irene was really properly upset when she tripped on the slipway and got a serious soaking. As we got ourselves into the dinghy post-pub for the journey back to Pickle the midges were impressive, but as ever they didn't get far out to sea, a big plus for anchoring. Midges are not marine animals (how often do I have to say that?).

To Portree

Friday August 17th, dull, damp and raining, so a slow and somewhat unwilling start after a late breakfast during which Catherine tried to persuade us that the Liberal Democrats were the future. Some hope. She was even going to try and be selected as a candidate in the next general election. Good thing she didn't. They were almost completely wiped out in 2015, largely because in 2010 they had very unwisely hitched their wagon to the Tories in a coalition government, such was their lust for power. Had they rejected a formal coalition, and turned their backs on the red boxes and limos, they could still have usefully influenced government policy but avoided their own comeuppance. They have not been forgiven; even in the 2019 general election they did badly and lost their leader.

Our first task that morning was to motor further up the loch to the pontoons in Flowerdale Bay, top up with fresh water, and dump some rubbish. Easier said than done. The pontoons were mostly occupied by local boats, four visiting boats were already rafted up, and the one free finger-berth we thought we could use was soon claimed by a returning tourist boat that thought it appropriate to shout at us to get out. I can't remember if I shouted back. Probably did. This was not the best of places, particularly in the rain. We would never have gone there but for our need for more fresh water. All those sweet-smelling lady crew must have been washing more than us grubby men.

We left as quickly as we could at 11.30am, in a slightly bad mood. This was not a place I would return to, as no point really. No pub, no handy shop, nothing much at all. There are far nicer alternatives within easy reach. The sea was flat and the wind light, still from the southeast, so it was a slow reach out of the loch, then hardening up the sails as we turned south past the north end of South Rona. Then it was long tacks down the Sound of Raasay as the wind shifted against us, with occasional spells of motoring when the wind died altogether. Much to the crew's irritation, I tend to keep sailing until we are down to about 1 knot before resorting to the engine, my father's anti-engine influence I suspect. But I am getting better, maybe it's as much as 2 knots now. Some people switch on at below 4 knots. They should be done with it and buy a motorboat.

The views all around were lovely, mist over Skye, steep cliffs, grey, rather daunting. Memories came flooding back. Sailing through this area during wonderful summer holidays I had with friends, chartering from Ardvasar on Skye. New Year when Ilona and I and the children stayed at Staffin Bay and there had been clear blue skies, and spectacular views of the mainland from the Quiraing. My very first night-sail as skipper, from Gairloch past the north end of Skye to Rodel on Harris, in a chartered Rival 34. Diabaig on Loch Torridon where I had recuperated with the family after my colon cancer surgery, and Oli and I climbed Liathach as part of my rehabilitation. Teenage Ben being hauled to the top of the mast to collect an errant jib halyard when we were anchored in Staffin Bay. The autumnal storm in Acarsaid Mòr on South Rona with Stu and others, two anchors down and motoring up to them all night to try and ease the strain on the chain.

I don't know what the crew were thinking. The ladies spent most of the day reading down below, it was that calm. I was worried that Thea and Irene were not very involved in the sailing. Perhaps my fault for not delegating enough of the sailing tasks. I did try, but probably not hard enough. I should have taken more notice of John Inglis's advice from more than 100 years ago: 'In small craft every one must make himself useful in some capacity, and the necessary work is just sufficient to occupy mind or body, without being harassing.'[5] Of course, compared with dinghy sailing there really isn't much to do on a cruising yacht except when leaving or approaching an anchorage. It can be as boring as it must be for a long-haul pilot dozing at the controls as his jumbo jet wings across the Pacific.

How strange it was, I thought, to have been through almost all the seasons from the bird-nesting time in April to now being surrounded by young guillemots floating on the sea and scuttling out of our way before diving to avoid us, and signs of early autumn. Tacking on flat water down the Sound of Raasay looking at the wonderful scenery was all a bit different to tacking along the east coast of England on that chilly North Sea. One similarity, however, was the lack of almost any other boats — only two sails all day, and one fishing boat.

I spent some time deleting rubbish emails from my phone (no more the huge task of the old days, deleting 2–3 weeks of emails when getting

---

5. John Inglis, *A Yachtsman's Holidays or Cruising in the West Highlands* (London: Pickering and Co., 1879), 7.

back to my computer at work). But one was important: brother John had at last gone to the doctor and it turned out that he too had colon cancer. These things are in part inherited. My remarks in Wales might well have spurred him into action. I spoke to him on the phone when we were off the north end of South Rona. The plan was for radiotherapy, surgery, and possibly chemotherapy.

Thankfully I had not had to suffer the dreadful rigours of chemotherapy, but John did. Rather to my embarrassment, I turned down being entered into a randomised trial of four types of chemotherapy for colon cancer. One of the four sounded just too scary and not worth it for me with a good prognosis (which nearly 30 years later has been proved to be correct). I suppose the treatment was all worth it for poor John, who thankfully has remained cured. I had been so much younger and fitter when going through my surgery. It is very hard to work out the 'worth it' business when there are only probabilities of what *might* happen with treatment versus without it, and no one knows what *will* happen. But that is what patients have to do. As doctors we try to explain these probabilities as clearly as we can, without assuming patients would want the same as us under similar circumstances, notwithstanding the commonly asked question, 'Doctor, what would you do if it was you?'

By 6.30pm we had at last covered the mere 25 miles to Skye's capital Portree, discovering it surprisingly well tucked-away, agreeing with Libby Purves: 'It seemed utterly impossible that out of this desolate landscape could come a town, let alone Portree.'[6] We found a visitor's mooring, but no one to pay, and it was a bit too exposed to the south from where quite a strong wind had got up, but not for long. Surprisingly, I had never sailed in to Portree before. The place was looking good in the evening sunshine, from the cockpit, in shirtsleeves, with a gin and tonic at hand. It was a calm and lovely evening. Irene and Thea cooked up spaghetti bolognese, meaty for the meat eaters, not meaty for the vegetarians.

Flicking through the pictures on my camera I found myself remembering earlier crews. Klim who had never been able to light the rings on the gas cooker with a match, just as Thea couldn't light the grill with a match. Catherine couldn't light matches at all — as a surgeon, you'd have thought she would have been better with her hands.

---

6. Libby Purves, *One Summer's Grace: A Family Voyage round Britain* (London: Grafton Books, 1989), 149.

To Plockton

Like so many visitor moorings on the west coast of Scotland, those in Portree are uncomfortably far from the shore, at least for people like me who prefer to row our dinghies and not faff about with motors. Even my electric one takes time to assemble and mount, but it is so much lighter, less smelly and less mucky than a 4-stroke petrol engine, and doesn't mind being tipped on either side, or upended. So that morning it was out with the Torqeedo motor to get us ashore, but it really struggled in the windy conditions. Only later did I discover the prop was slipping on its shaft, and there was nothing inherently wrong with the (surprisingly good) power of the motor. There seemed to be nowhere to pay any mooring dues, and no one came to collect them.

Portree was very touristy indeed, a lot of people aimlessly milling about. Skye is such a magnet for tourists, along with Loch Ness. Strange, really, for I think Mull is a much nicer island, and there are hundreds of lochs more beautiful, more stark, and more dramatic than the really rather dull Loch Ness (particularly if the wind is against you and you have to tack for all of its 22 miles, or motor for that matter). That Loch Ness Monster is an astoundingly successful tourist confidence trick. Scotland undoubtedly has a brand which it exploits for all its worth, profitably too as the tourists flood in, at least in the summer. Nowadays there are too many tourists for places like Skye, at least until there is better infrastructure (more public toilets for one thing) — bring on tourist taxes I say.

Portree seemed a scrappy sort of a place. The main part is above the harbour which itself does not have any waterside cafés or pubs that we could see. However, the town does have a lot of useful shops for stocking up, attractive buildings, and we discovered a good café — Arriba, with views across the bay. Guided by the Sailing Directions we found the restaurant on the hill where showers should have been available, but that turned out to have been in the days of the previous owner. The current owner had never bothered to get the directions amended, but didn't seem to mind David and me having showers (very laid-back he was).

We left after lunch in squally rain, the mountains lit up by intermittent sunshine, very spectacular. I was not particularly keen to stop on Raasay, unusual in being a Wee Free island in the Inner Hebrides, closing its play park on Sundays as do so many places in the Outer Hebrides. Besides, we had a date at Plockton 22 miles away. Thea and Irene again stayed down below, tucked up under sleeping bags, reading the papers about all those bloody investment bankers again, and another scandal — manipulating the LIBOR (whatever that is).

Thankfully the Olympics were over so I was spared all of that, but there was still too much sport in the papers — football and rugby. I did so love tossing away the sports section of the *Guardian* before sport was included in the main section. Such a relief not to have to read about sport as well as everything else which, as a newspaper addict, already takes me far too long. Am I doomed to suffer this addiction until my dying day? Probably yes — I am even addicted to yachting magazines, despite their doom and gloom. At least that afternoon I wasn't reading the papers and missing out on the scenery like Thea and Irene. That said, one great plus of cruising with others is not having to be on deck all the time, something I definitely exploit when a reliable crew is on the helm.

We had one reef in the mainsail and were close-hauled south down the Sound of Raasay, going at 6 knots, tacking between the red and green buoys, and then bearing away east past the south end of the island. The sea was flat and the sun came out, a hot sun, all very delightful. It was a splendid reach past the secretive anchorage between the two Crowlin Islands where once we had a barbecue with my older children. It was also the first anchorage on our very first charter trip from Skye in 1976. It is extraordinary how some anchorages are cemented in my memory, for years and years —how to get into them, and what I did there, but usually I can't recall with whom and exactly on which of my many trips.

We shot into Loch Carron in grand style to arrive off Plockton at 5pm. And there was Allegro, the ridiculously small sailing boat containing the Fox family, all five of them crammed into its 25ft length. Again the visitor moorings were too far out, and again no one came to collect any money. We didn't feel the need to go ashore; the Foxes instead came over to us. Izzy, their five-year-old youngest, was very competent on the oars. Tom their nine-year-old had a new fishing rod. And Emily their 11-year-old was very grown-up and taller than ever. Although Patrick their father is quite short, Lisa their mum must be over 6 feet. How they all fit into Allegro, and continue to do so as the children grow but Allegro doesn't, is quite beyond me.

Like Cathie, Patrick too had worked for David Thrush in Plymouth, and they were delighted to see each other again. He is a clinical neurophysiologist and had chosen to work in Inverness, largely for lifestyle reasons like many other consultants there. Some of the Edinburgh neurologists simply could not understand why, after his specialist training, Patrick didn't want to stay as a consultant in Edinburgh and rake in money from private practice, such was their lack of understanding of Patrick and their own desire for private earnings (to fund private schools, expensive holidays, fancy cars, and double garages).

Apéritifs in the cockpit consisted of three bottles of wine, so it all became very jolly … until Thea was stung by a wasp. Of all the people the wasp could choose she was the worst. Not surprisingly, she screamed and shot down below, closely followed by Irene. Eventually all was calm again. Thea has now completely forgotten about what to me was quite a dramatic and very memorable episode. How interesting it is how several people witnessing the same event can have such different memories of it, a phenomenon so brilliantly exploited in Brian Friel's 1979 play *Faith Healer*.

That evening I sat out in the cockpit reading the paper, alone, in peace and quiet (until one of those horrible jet-skis whizzed past, awful things best confined to Poole harbour). The High Court in London had refused a 'locked-in' patient an assisted death, a condition usually caused by stroke in which the patient is fully conscious and sentient, can think and see and smell and hear, but can move nothing except their eyes. The law has got to change. The judges quite rightly have passed the ball to the legislature, who after all are meant to legislate. But our parliamentarians have lacked the courage to develop a humane law to allow mentally competent adults to end their lives when their suffering has become too much to bear, subject of course to having received the best possible care, and with appropriate safeguards against exploitation by family and others. Such is the spinelessness of our MSPs and MPs. The fight goes on, and one day soon the law will change, as it changing in more and more other countries.

To Loch Hourn

Sunday August 19th. I was sorry not to go ashore at Plockton. I had only ever been there once before, after a rather rough sail from South Rona much to Ilona's consternation because my older children were quite small at the time. However, we needed to leave at 8am to catch the strong tide through Kylerhea between Skye and the mainland, the same appointment that John McClintock had to keep 80 or so years ago: 'We had an important appointment to keep at 10 am with the tide at Kylerhea. There is nothing like an eight-knot tide for getting a fellow from his bunk in the morning.'[7] But first we had to stop at Kyle of Lochalsh for provisions.

---

7. John McLintock, *West Coast Cruising* (London and Glasgow: Blackie and Son Ltd, 1938), 133.

There was no wind so we motored over the still and flat-calm sea, a lovely fresh morning, autumnal colours just beginning to appear on land. Within an hour we were under the Skye Bridge, that 1995 monument to the stupidity of PFI, the Private Finance Initiative. It was the first UK, and in many ways the most notorious, example of using PFI to fund a major construction project. It attracted huge local protests because the banks that owned the bridge imposed ridiculously high tolls, and many local people just refused to pay. Eventually in 2004 the Scottish government bought the banks out and the crossing is now, quite rightly, toll-free. The bridge towers over the Stevenson lighthouse on Eilean Bàn and the old keepers' cottages, the final home of Gavin Maxwell.

We tied up to the Kyle of Lochalsh pontoons, very handy for the short walk up to the excellent Co-op supermarket. And to the hotel where the ladies could have showers in vacated but yet-to-be-cleaned hotel bedrooms (just a donation to the RNLI was expected). And it was a handy spot for a bit of deck and heads cleaning too. There were no other visiting boats, until a friendly man from Redcar arrived with his wife, and their Etap 22 on a trailer, ready to be assembled and sailed away. (He told me the Redcar steelworks were back in action, but in 2015 they were closed down again, for ever.) Otherwise it was all deadly quiet, the place dozing in the warm sun, closed on Sundays. The toilets on the station platform were closed on Sundays too. Nae peeing on the Sabbath, let alone passing more substantial excreta.

In the old days before pontoons we used to tie up to the station pier, and Kyle of Lochalsh was a really bustling place because of the ferry to Skye. So the bridge presumably did quite a bit of economic damage to the village, but a lot of good for Skye. Perhaps a bit too much good. In 2017 Skye was jammed with tourists, partly as a consequence of the abrupt fall in the pound against the euro and dollar immediately after the result of the 2016 referendum for the UK to leave the European Union. The gay and deluded Brexiteers, and even sometimes the BBC who should know better, constantly wittered on that an 'overwhelming majority of the British people' voted in favour of leave. Bollocks. 52% of those who *voted* chose to leave vs 48% to stay, and a 4% difference is by no means 'overwhelming'. And 'majority' of what? Of those *eligible* to vote 37% voted for Brexit, or 27% of the population — hardly 'an overwhelming majority' of the British people, rather the opposite.

It is now becoming very clear that the economic and other damage to the UK from leaving the EU is going to be substantially more than foreign holidays complicated by too much red tape. The UK may not have been a completely committed member of the EU but our views were sought and respected by other member states, and we had a say in EU policy. We collaborated more and more with Europeans across so many sectors including medical science. And we were part of a peaceful Europe, a continent that had been ravaged by wars for so many centuries (the Russian invasion of Ukraine in 2022 is a terrible exception). The Brexiteers will have a lot to answer for if, or rather when, it all goes terribly wrong, the rich ones safely off-shore in their tax havens, the poor ones seething in Scunthorpe. The responsible politicians will have long left the scene for lucrative consultancies and directorships.

We had a leisurely lunch in the cockpit. Then slow tacking south between Skye and the mainland, through that delightfully narrow gap at Kylerhea under the power cables, dodging the small ferry gliding across the strong tide between the mainland and Skye. I remembered it all so well, including the emerging view of the Sgùrr of Eigg in the distance. There were more sails around — well, five. Hardly the Solent or Poole Harbour, thankfully. We just caught the tail-end of the ebb, so by the time the tide turned against us at 3pm we were well through and off Sandaig, the island Gavin Maxwell made so famous as Camusfeàrna in *Ring of Bright Water*, his hugely successful book about otters. His house is long gone, burnt down when he was still the owner.

By tea-time it was overcast but there was a nice breeze as we sailed on close-hauled past Glen Uig, to the mouth of Loch Hourn. I had forgotten what an amazing loch it is — long and deep and dark and remote, seldom visited, high mountains reaching down to the water's edge with no intervening roads or hardly even any tracks, clouds touching their tops. The light was reflected and refracted by the dark over-hanging clouds, so much more interesting than the boring cloudless blue skies of the Mediterranean. Even more interesting was a floppy fin meandering in the water ahead of us. At first I thought it was a basking shark. Gavin Maxwell and Tex Geddes never caught very many in their attempts to set up a Hebridean shark fishing industry after the Second World War, described in Maxwell's *Harpoon at a Venture*. I bumped into Tex once, on the island of Soay off the south coast of Skye, which he owned at the time. He was quite some character. 'Where have all the sharks gone, we seldom see any?' I asked. 'No idea, probably killed all the buggers,' he replied. The next day out at sea we discovered Tex again, on his fishing boat. He beckoned us over to present us with a bucket full of langoustines, and we found a bottle of wine in exchange.

But if it had been a shark in Loch Hourn that evening there would have been a tail fin as well as the floppy dorsal fin, and yet there was only the one fin. We got closer, to see a great round thing just under the surface. Surely not a turtle? Turtles have no fins. It was a sunfish! I had never seen one before, apart from the very big and very dead one suspended in the National Museum of Scotland in Edinburgh. We got right up close, maybe too close, and yet it just flopped around, seemingly unconcerned.

We were aiming for a small bay on the south shore of the loch, Poll a'Mhuineil, 24 miles from Plockton, easy of access with plenty of room to anchor with as much chain out as we could possibly need. At 6.30pm it was a lovely spot to stop under the dramatic mountains with cloud still hanging about their tops, a tinkling burn and a small waterfall close by, views across the loch, a pink sunset. And all alone. The crew seemed to be bonding well, a relief. Catherine cooked us fish curry for dinner.

To the Small Isles — Canna and Muck, but not Rum or Eigg

Monday August 20th, the rain overnight cleared away after breakfast leaving ragged clouds and a fresh pre-autumnal and windless morning. Setting off at 10am, we had to motor out of the loch, passing the sunfish still swimming lazily around almost where we had left it the evening before. Soon there was enough wind to sail, close-hauled out of the entrance to the loch, and then in long tacks south down the Sound of Sleat against the 15-knot south-southwest wind, by then needing one reef in the mainsail. The bonxies had disappeared north of Skye to be replaced by Manx shearwaters flying low over the sea from their nests on Rum and Eigg. Butteries had also disappeared from the shops.

Not much had changed in the 40-plus years since I first chartered from Ardvasar on Skye, except the appearance of the in-your-face white buildings of Sabhal Mòr Ostaig, the Gaelic College. Same mountains, same dark skies with scattered sunbeams, same line of white houses spread round the upper reaches of Mallaig, same views of Rum past Sleat Point with the promise of Canna behind. We must have chartered at least 10 times from Ardvasar, probably more. Charles Barrington set up Seòl Alba (Sail Scotland) in 1976 and we were one of his first customers. Ex-navy, ex-school teacher, and definitely ex-public school. Later he became a minister of the Church of Scotland.

He chose Ardvasar because of the convenience of the train from the south to Mallaig, best experienced on the sleeper from London where one wakes up somewhere on Rannoch Moor to look out onto misty mountains and rushing burns, and deer fleeing from the tracks (Scotland, the brand again). At that time Mallaig was very yacht-unfriendly, being dominated by the fishing fleet, but there was an easy and quick ferry across to Skye, right by the Seòl Alba moorings off Armadale pier. In those days it was not roll-on roll-off; rather there was a lift which protested with characteristic grinding and squeaking noises as it deposited cars onto Skye.

Charles had bought four Rival 34s, ideal and tough boats for the Hebrides. His was the only bare-boat charter operation north of Ardnamurchan. Of course, the Rivals are long gone, and I personally don't like their large white plastic replacements, the sort of boats memorably referred to as 'Tupperware bum-hangers' by John Seymour, the 1970s self-sufficiency guru. However, they are what today's charterers seem to desire, with separate cabins and plenty of heads. They were introduced by the very successful Isle of Skye Yachts that eventually took over the business, until closing in 2020. Just south of Ardvasar there is a prominent white house which is where, in 1980, a very-pregnant-with-Ben Ilona spent a week with Kristine, a New Zealand friend, while my mates and I sailed round Skye. Still there, still prominent.

Canna, 35 miles away, was where we were heading. As ever, it's a magnet for me. I so well remember the magical moment in the late-1970s when I first sailed into the harbour, on a charter boat after a rather rough day, and my astonishment at the serene green fields stretching down from the high cliffs which look so formidable from the sea — complete with highland cows (and those squeaky-leather-sounding corncrakes). And again in 1988 when I sailed Calypso into Canna Harbour with my family of slightly frightened small children, and their concerned if not frightened mother. Robert Buchanan had very similar feelings on his first visit in the 19th century: 'It is a difficult job indeed to pick our way through the rocks, in the teeth of wind so keen; but directly we round the corner of the cliffs, the little landlocked bay opens safe and calm, and, gliding into five-fathom water, we cast anchor just opposite the Laird's house.'[8] Canna is where later we spent many family holidays renting an Edwardian house, Tighard, with Calypso bobbing on a borrowed mooring in the bay below us, ready for day-sails. There are not many places to rent on the west coast where you can sleep ashore in comfort and keep your boat safe on a mooring, and within sight.

---

8. Robert Buchanan, *The Land of Lorne, including the Cruise of the 'Tern' to the Outer Hebrides*, vol. 1 (London: British Library, Historical Print Editions, 1871), 211.

Once we got to the Point of Sleat, we could bear away for Canna, but were close-hauled from the north point of Rum. The wind was in the southwest, a direction from where it had almost never blown all summer (so much for that so-called prevailing wind). It had been a very peculiar year. One of the wettest on record in England. By contrast, in Scotland it had been a lovely summer. On the way Irene distinguished herself by repairing the large hole in my jersey — undertaking this sort of task must be one criterion for the perfect crew. Of course there are many others, and no one has them all. But one can live with that. The alternative is to become a very irate skipper with whom almost no one will sail. The art of delegation is certainly the ability to accept second-best, and that applies to giving tasks to the crew. Sometimes, however, they are better than me, as Irene certainly was at repairing jerseys.

Not much had changed in Canna harbour apart from the incorporation of the notorious rock into the roll-on roll-off ferry pier (yes, for a population of less than 20). That rock according to Murdoch Mackenzie is 'about a pistol shot from the shore',[9] a dated but delightful metric superseded by the equally delightful 'biscuit toss', and now by the rather boring but exact number of metres to two or more decimal points on your GPS. He also observed that 'The harbour of Cana is small, but pretty well sheltered, and commodiously situated for vessels bound either northward or southward; and on that account is more frequented than any of the harbours in that neighbourhood.' It's just the same now, and there are even visitor moorings — completely unnecessary in my view if you dig your anchor well in through the kelp.

We arrived at 4.30pm looking forward to a meal at the small restaurant that had opened on the island a few years earlier, but it turned out to be closed on Mondays. Annoying. It had not been there in our renting days and later I learned that the couple running it were leaving. Like so many incomers they had — for whatever reason — got fed up. Coming in to a population of less than 20, many of them from the same family who have been on the island for years, cannot be easy, nor can being managed by the National Trust for Scotland that now owns the island.

There were seven other boats in the harbour, one French. Often on a summer evening there can be 20, such is the safety and convenience of this lovely anchorage (except in an easterly gale, which doesn't happen very

---

9. Mackenzie, *Nautical Descriptions*, 50.

often in summer). Usually all the boats clear out in the morning, with not many staying for their crews to go ashore and enjoy the island.

After our on-board supper I went for a walk all alone down memory lane, first to what we had called the pirate beach, looking over to Rum. The trees behind the beach were dying, the barn was crumbling, the small castle looked even more dangerous to climb up to than it had 20 years earlier. The nostalgia was overwhelming, a function of having a memory. Without memory there could be no nostalgia, so I imagine people with dementia cannot experience it. Here on this beach we buried pirate treasure (sweets mostly) for my older children and their friends to find, here we had picnics, here Ben made up the game of chasing round a complex series of lines he had drawn in the sand, to be washed away by the next tide.

The Round Tower church by the harbour was to be restored, money was being raised. The Roman Catholic chapel, the only working church on this Roman Catholic island, had already been restored and looked lovely. The red phone box was still there outside the farm, but with no phone anymore. Canna House gardens were by then open to the public, but still not the house, and were looking better cared for. Tighard, just above Canna House, had become a bed and breakfast place, still approached by what we called the 'short cut' or the 'short short cut' paths from the shore. The view over to Rum from the garden was as spectacular as ever. No one was around, so I sneaked in. There we were in the visitors' book from 1989, including Oli's four-year-old writing. But the rope swings in the garden had gone, and so had the dreaded Baxi cooker with the back boiler to heat the water, which was so difficult to keep alight.

Tuesday August 21st, not a bad morning, but very little wind when we left at midday, and from the south. However, with the tide we did make progress, slowly tacking down the west side of Rum where the mountains running down to the sea were looking particularly good, in the sun too. Strangely there were no Manx shearwaters around, and typically for that summer no whales. Luckily, as the tide changed against us in the afternoon the wind got up, with heavy squalls and scudding black clouds, the whole scene dramatically lit by occasional shafts of brilliant sunlight.

At 6.30pm, the visibility was not that good as we approached the north anchorage on Muck, perhaps the best managed and most viable of the Small Isles, although Eigg might claim that too. The visibility needs to be good to pick up the leading line from a wall (which looks more like the edge of a cliff) above a barn (the correct one of two). Here of all places the chartplotter is not quite accurate — if you stick to it you go over a reef. As ever, pilotage is best done by eye. We didn't venture ashore as the weather was not encouraging. The day's sail had been a mere 17 miles.

Thea was cheerful, getting used to the sailing and hopefully warming up a bit. Irene emailed me many years later saying that the cruise had changed the course of Thea's life because 'if we hadn't sailed for those two weeks she would never have done her Day Skipper qualification, started racing on J109s, crossed the Atlantic on the ARC,[10] made new Danish and Belgian and Swedish sailing friends — because of which she is now almost at the end of her Masters in Delft, has conversational Dutch and hopes to get a job in offshore engineering.' I was both surprised and terribly pleased.

To Tobermory

Wednesday August 22nd, another pretty good day. The wind was conveniently from the west, 15 knots. Starting at 9.45am, we had a fast reach to Ardnamurchan Point, then turning to port a run into the Sound of Mull. So familiar, these parts. Manx shearwaters swooped over the sea, although there were no waves for them to glide over so effortlessly. As often has been the case, the sea off Ardnamurchan was quiet (more Softnamurchan, as we christened it back in the 1970s when we first rounded it). It was grand to be back in home waters, dashing in to the Sound of Mull, the crew generally cheery. But the mobile phone mast on the Mull cliffs soon deposited a cascade of emails and texts into my phone, which I tried to ignore.

Among them was an interesting text from Cathie, with a photograph of William's arm, which I didn't ignore. There was a thin and angry red line extending from his wrist up his forearm. Lymphangitis, almost certainly due to a bacterial infection spreading from a cut on his hand. Antibiotics, already started. But antibiotics for how long? Seven days? A fortnight? For some conditions they are given for months. Or would three days do for William? Or should they be stopped when he felt better (probably what many patients do irrespective of their doctor's orders). The answer is obviously the shortest time possible without compromising the therapeutic effect and risking reactivation of the infection. This would save the NHS money, and the patient unnecessary hassle and possible side effects. But how short is shortest?

In 2017 this antibiotic dilemma hit the media as though no one had

---

10. The ARC is the annual Atlantic Rally for Cruisers, when rather a lot of mixed-ability sailors cross the Atlantic, more or less together, in a semi-organised way.

ever thought of it before. But they had, and long before. In 1969 when I was working in infectious diseases for the wonderful Harold Lambert (the go-to doctor at St George's for advice about more or less anything medical and indeed anything else), he remarked, 'We just don't know how long to give antibiotics for. It is all a bit random; someone should look into it.' But they haven't. The honest but exasperated 'We just don't know' has not been followed by the more measured 'someone should look into it', in other words do some research. After a ward round Lambert once said, 'Patients are allowed to get better even if we don't know quite what is wrong with them. We had better think more.' A lesson in tolerating uncertainty, while at the same time trying to reduce it. After retirement Harold bought a couple of woods and became a national expert on trees for his next thirty years.

Unfortunately we don't know for how long to give many drugs, not just antibiotics. We may have opinions, guidelines even, but these are not necessarily based on good data. As a medical student I was expected to know the indications for starting treatments for common diseases, but don't remember ever being taught when to stop them. Take epilepsy. Anti-epileptic drugs were once given for life, even if the patient stopped having fits which most do. Of course many patients with epilepsy abandon their drugs, even though they may still be prescribed. Some stop their drugs prematurely because they hate the idea of taking them, or are worried about side effects (real or imagined). On the other hand, some fit-free patients don't want to stop their anti-epileptics and risk another fit. No honest doctor knew what best to do — all there was to go on were anecdotes and so-called expert opinion based on being an expert rather than on any good evidence. This clearly required a randomised trial of stopping the anti-epileptic drugs versus continuing them, and eventually in the 1980s David Chadwick and his colleagues in Liverpool did just that.[11]

We need far more randomised trials of stopping versus continuing drugs, particularly when the aim is to prevent something bad which may or may not happen in the future. Trials of drugs to suppress dangerous heart rhythms, and to control depression. And of aspirin to reduce the risk of heart attacks and strokes, particularly because it may turn out that most of aspirin's useful effect is in the first few weeks of taking the drug, whereas

---

11. Medical Research Council Antiepileptic Drug Withdrawal Study Group, 'Randomized Study of Antiepileptic Drug Withdrawal in Patients in Remission', *Lancet*, 337 (1991), 1175–80.

the side-effect potential probably does not wane with time. Unfortunately, however much it needs to be done, this is not the sort of 'innovative' or 'world-beating' research that appeals to funding bodies, let alone the pharmaceutical industry.

Of course, if a drug's effect is obvious, for example in relieving back pain, or reducing the frequency of migraine attacks, then it is easier to know when it's not working and to try another drug instead. This often requires recording something — such as the intensity and frequency of the migraine attacks — and acknowledging that even when a drug 'works' it may be doing so completely or partially through the placebo effect.

This 'when to stop drugs' problem has become a major cause of concern in the elderly for whom more and more pills are piled up on top of earlier pills that have never been stopped. Many patients end up on 10 or more drugs, all with potential side effects, endlessly repeat-prescribed without anyone taking responsibility for working out if they are all still needed. GPs may not have the time, or be confident enough of their expertise, to review every single drug in a list of 10, or even just five. They are even paid to prescribe some drugs, like statins, which hardly discourages polypharmacy. Specialists might stop 'their own' drug, but hesitate before stopping a different specialist's drug. And many patients resist the idea of stopping what they may have once been told was 'life-saving'. Some may even suspect their doctor is only trying to save the NHS some money, or that they are too old for the NHS to be bothered with. The younger generation will have to sort this out, and preferably before I am on some long-term medication.

We arrived on the pontoons at Tobermory in just under four hours for the 20 miles. Then we sauntered around the small town, as I had done many times before. What a lovely place it is — by far the prettiest town on the west coast of Scotland, with perhaps the best marina of the whole voyage. The anonymous ditty sums it up: 'I've sailed the seven seas and travelled every way but there's nowhere near so beautiful as Tobermory Bay.' While sketching his way around the British coast back in the early 19th century, William Daniell liked Tobermory too: 'The inhabitants of Tobermory, whether from the frequent intercourse with strangers which their situation occasions, or from other causes, are distinguished from other Hebrideans by a greater attention to personal neatness and cleanliness … another agreeable prepossession which a traveller acquires in journeying thither arises from the frequent praise bestowed on the beauty of its females, and this characteristic also is well warranted. There are certainly many pretty women at Tobermory, and their appearance, as well as that of the children and the men, is much improved, by that glow of health which habitual cleanliness never fails to promote.'[12]

The marina and indeed the visitor moorings (as well as the once overcrowded and uncomfortably deep anchoring area close under the trees, now hardly used) have the advantage of being in the midst of the town, close to shops and pubs, with decent showers all within a very short walk. They are also sheltered except from the northeast (when there are other places to escape to), and at that time had friendly Jim Traynor in charge. He told us that many more English boats were visiting, maybe because they prefer tying up to pontoons to anchoring which they are not used to down on the south coast. Unlike local skippers, the English skippers search out Jim after they have arrived, because that is how they have to do it in crowded England, not just turn up and wait for the harbour master to come to them (that laid-back approach might sadly be fading as our Scottish pontoons become more crowded).

The Mull Museum is small and it was crowded that day, but free and informative, better than I remembered it. Most local museums are vastly improved compared with even 10 years before this cruise. More interactive displays, fewer mysterious pieces of rock and stuffed birds with scrawled illegible handwritten 'explanatory' notes, more videos, quizzes for children. But they are still mostly run by voluntary staff, such is the lack of local council funding. Real heroes keep these places going. After we emerged we bought the papers, which don't arrive in Tobermory until midday. They were full of the same stuff — the forthcoming Scottish independence referendum, and the ghastly criminality of some investment bankers, as well as their apparent incompetence and ludicrous salaries.

We came across David and Lynn Wilkie taking a break from their three-year cruise to the Caribbean and east coast of America, a treat for them after retiring from running the Ardfern Yacht Centre for something like 25 years. David was the perfect manager, always around, chatting to customers, knowledgeable about boats in general and your own boat in particular. Late one evening our family had arrived in the dark to find the marina staff had not left our boat keys where I had asked them to, in the cockpit. David emerged out of the dark, listened to the problem, went away and came back with the keys, which had been hidden outside the chandlery. 'How

---

12. William Daniell, *A Voyage round Great Britain Undertaken in the Summer of the Year 1813*, vol. 3 (London: Longman et al., 1818), 70.

did you know where they were?' I asked. 'Ah,' said David. 'Just think like an employee!'

On the VHF radio we heard a pan-pan call, Stornoway Coastguard reporting a 30-foot yacht had passed the Butt of Lewis a few days earlier and was overdue in Iceland. The skipper was not only single-handed but aged 72. And on his way to Iceland! Not my cup of tea. I used to think all coastguard radio stations were much the same. But hearing more of Stornoway and of Belfast now, I appreciate that they are more efficient than Clyde Coastguard was before it was closed down in 2012, and Oban Coastguard which had disappeared 12 years earlier. They are quicker to respond, and to get out the weather forecast.

The 2012 coastguard reorganisation was thanks to my friend Peter Cardy with whom we had had dinner in Gosport. When he became CEO of the Maritime and Coastguard Agency he realised there were an unnecessary number of coastguard stations around the British coast for the new world of quick and easy electronic communication. Each station had to have a minimum number of staff to cover 24 hours a day (I think 14), and often there was simply not enough work for them all. It had also dawned on him that the Coastguard was seriously over-resourced and under-used at the time of their national strikes in 2008 (which he points out were threatened before he started the job), when the entire UK set-up was replicated by a couple of dozen staff at a handful of centres during the busiest weekend of the year. He became even more convinced while skippering a chartered yacht and witnessed a major incident during the Plockton regatta. This was efficiently handled from Stornoway 56 miles to the northwest — local knowledge was held locally by the local rescue teams and the RNLI lifeboat who, of course, worked closely with Stornoway whose highly professional and well-trained team had never been to Plockton.

By then, modern communications meant that the entire coastline could be monitored by one central station, but that would have been a step too far for the politicians. So Peter's plan cut the stations down from 17 to 10, plus the National Maritime Operations Centre which is incongruously located on an industrial estate in landlocked Fareham (which, inter alia, can 'see' every EPIRB — Emergency Position Indicating Radio Beacon — activated in any part of the world). Although there were howls of protest at the time, one of the loudest being the potential loss of local knowledge, there seem to have been few if any problems. A few years later, a senior union man I chatted to at a boat show admitted that he had changed his mind in favour. But there is one loss. With all the coastguard stations now linked together, any one of them can take on the work of any other if it is getting too busy. Talking to 'Stornoway' might now mean you are talking to someone from Humber Coastguard, or from Dover.

But what may be lost is the fascination and interest of the changing coastguard accents around the coast. From 'Estuary' through Yorkshire to Aberdonian to Shetland to Outer Hebridean, on to Northern Irish, Scouse, Welsh and West Country, and back to 'Estuary'. Plus a bit of Irish, often very fast: 'Disismolnheadradiomolnheadradiomolnheadradio'. As for one lady coastguard in Shetland, her diction was so delightful that we wanted to applaud and hear her weather forecast all over again (presumably possible with catch-up radio). Of course, notwithstanding the regional accents, all the coastguards around our coastline speak in English, unlike in the mid-19th century when, while sailing down the Irish Sea, the Reverend Hughes was surprised to be told: 'in the course of a few hours you may hear five languages — English, Gaelic, Irish, Manx, and Welsh, to say nothing of Cornish, which is nearly extinct, spoken as the native tongue in the British Isles.'[13]

But I do hope that the experiment to use text-to-voice technology to broadcast forecasts on the VHF will be abandoned — far too robotic and unfriendly.

To Dunstaffnage, and almost the end of the voyage

Thursday August 23rd, our last day, difficult to believe. Off at 10am down the Sound of Mull, passing occasional CalMac ferries on their way to Coll and the Outer Isles, mostly in sunshine, and a few showers. Long tacks, apart from some motoring when the wind dropped near Loch Aline, and then a broad and fast reach once we rounded the south point of Lismore Island where one day my ashes will float backwards and forwards in the tide. The Sound was 'crowded' by our recent standards. Ten boats, but only ten … in the holiday season.

For some reason I was aware that the English school exam results were out that day. Memories of waiting for the postman and opening the dreaded envelope. There must be just as much dread these days when the results come by email and text. Exams are incredibly heavy on teacher time. I fancied the alternative I heard long ago, for teachers to give their own pupils their best estimates of a mark based on their knowledge of them. If the pupil

---

13. Robert Edgar Hughes, *Hunt's Yachting Magazine*, 2 (1853), 184.

objected he or she could take an exam. That would hugely cut down the work of examining because only the aggrieved would object — those who thought their mark underestimated their abilities (or their parents' hopes), and those who thought they really should not have failed. There would of course be fears of teacher bias (racial, gender, religious or otherwise), even of pushy parents bribing teachers, and loss of jobs for the examiners. Moreover, any performance-related pay for teachers (as does occur in England but not thankfully in Scotland) would obviously have to be abolished because they would mark up their own pupils. Something like this approach had to be urgently adopted when the formal UK school exams were abandoned during the Covid-19 pandemic. However, there was no plan for quickly examining those upset by their allocated marks, or at least not quickly enough to influence their university entrance. And there were serious problems of grade inflation as teachers, encouraged by their ambitious schools tempted to fiddle their place in the league tables, over-egged their own pupils' abilities, perhaps inevitably. Maybe not such a good strategy after all, so back to exams.

Although medical exams are necessary, examining was never my cup of tea, far too boring. But as a university academic how did I avoid them? Tony Mitchell told me what he did. Just say 'no, sorry'. This was a surprising tip given that he was the first professor of medicine at the Nottingham medical school, a charismatic and blunt man who made major contributions to thrombosis research. Nowadays, continuous assessment has become all the rage, but is more like continuous harassment. It provides a golden opportunity for students to swot up a small chunk of something quickly, and forget equally quickly. Was the old way of learning everything for a grand final exam, and then forget, any better? Later, Objective Structured Clinical Examinations (OSCEs) came in. Here the examiner watches and assesses every student, all given exactly the same task to perform, in another attempt to avoid biased assessment. Out of curiosity I did once examine an OSCE, the experience of which nearly put me to sleep. I was told to give the students one mark out of the total of 10 if they managed to introduce themselves to the patient — a far too easy 10%. The most recent trend seems to be to mark yourself, a dotty idea, which must have been dreamt up by an educational psychologist. As for reading through trainees' ePortfolios — what a waste of my and their time. I knew trainees were or were not competent after working with them for a few days, but who knows what biases lurked in my subconscious.

We did that last 25 miles in five hours, and at 3pm picked up our mooring in Dunstaffnage Bay, just north of Oban. Pickle and I had gone not quite all the way round Great Britain, but as good as. There was no brass band playing on the pontoons, no fluttering scarves, no dusky maidens offering floral garlands, no 21-gun salute, no family even, no sponsors, no spraying champagne over everyone, no brandishing of hand-flares, no drama at all. It was clean-up time. The crew were very keen so I let them get on with it even though I knew I could do it better. However, Irene did do a spectacular job on the heads, and David on the decks. Probably better than me on a bad day, but not as good as Cathie on even her worst day.

Dunstaffnage looked the same as ever. With our own mooring we had little to do with the marina. How they got Five Golden Anchor status is a mystery, perhaps another meaningless metric. We felt we should have a final dinner ashore, as it would not have done to mess up the well-cleaned galley. Without a car we went local, to the Wide Mouth Frog above the pontoons. It was a disappointment — the fish soup gloopy, the scallops cold. It is such a shame because that restaurant must have a huge potential clientele tied up to the pontoons and moorings. I often wonder what makes a successful restaurant, or hotel. To me it is having the boss out front, keeping an eye on everything, a familiar face welcoming old customers and encouraging the new. Take Poppies café next door to the marina, where Marion McPherson is so obviously visible and in charge (unfortunately it is not open for dinner, but it does the best meringues in Scotland — in my opinion).

Friday August 24th, up early, morning coffee at the Frog but no scones available (typical), taxi to Oban station, train to Glasgow, changing at Queen Street station for the Edinburgh train. So familiar. There is something reassuring about familiarity, like the label and shape of a Marmite jar, the Cadbury Crunchie bars even though they are smaller than when I was a child, Rowntree fruit gums (they have shrunk too), and Dennis the Menace who hasn't shown any signs of ageing for the last 70 years. Despite the rickety trains, that journey between Oban and Glasgow is one of the most attractive in the UK, best on a sunny winter's day when there are no leaves on the trees to obscure the spectacular views. The passengers chat away, probably because many are on holiday, at least in the summer, or they are local and know each other. The conductor is usually cheery too, but not on that August Friday morning. She was grumpy. Maybe she wanted to sail round Britain and was envious. If so she was right to be. I had had a great time.

And finally, from Dunstaffnage to Ardfern

To properly complete the circumnavigation I still needed to sail Pickle back to our winter quarters at Ardfern. So, on Monday October 1st at 3pm one very sunny afternoon, with Steve, again, and Malcolm Stewart with whom he had shared their Sigma 33, we set off south from Dunstaffnage. We had picked our weather window carefully. What a beautiful day it was, but given the lack of wind we had to motor all the 12 miles south to Easdale. We were relaxed, very much in home waters, not needing either the chartplotter or the chart. There were only a couple of other boats out, but we were right at the end of the season. Most boats had disappeared for the winter, many to the Clyde.

By 6pm we were off Easdale, one of the 'slate islands', which Murdoch Mackenzie said was 'of difficult access, and only fit for small vessels that draw not above eight feet of water. The creek is not frequented by any vessels, but such as go to take in slate in the island; and these vessels, by throwing out their ballast in the anchorage, have made it shallower than it used to be formerly; and in time will render it incapable of floating the smallest vessels at low water.'[14] Eight feet was not a problem, but a lot of slate on the seabed was worth a thought as we let down the anchor in a flat calm between the tiny island of Easdale and Ellenabeich on Seil (itself an island attached to the mainland by the late 18th-century hump-backed Clachan Bridge, the so-called Bridge over the Atlantic). These islands are where much of Scottish slate was quarried for centuries, until more or less everything closed down after the first world war. Another major quarrying area was at Ballachulish further north, to where one of my medical school teachers, John Batten, bought a train ticket at the end of the second world war. He told me that demobbed servicemen were given a free ticket to wherever they wanted to go, and he reckoned Ballachulish was about as far from London as he could reasonably get.

At that time of year we didn't expect any other boats in the anchorage, and there weren't any, despite the lovely autumnal weather. Nor was there any visible person on Easdale, maybe because the ex-slate miners' houses are mostly now holiday homes and the holiday season was over. It was all deadly quiet. Charming, but a blank. We went ashore in the other direction, to Ellenabeich, to see if there was any food at the quite cosy Oyster pub, but there wasn't. There were only two other customers who soon left. Apparently trade had been very poor all summer despite the good weather. So we rowed back to the boat for a sausage casserole, followed by whisky. And bed. The west coast has a real problem with such a short tourist

---

14. Mackenzie, *Nautical Descriptions*, 40.

season — only a matter of weeks in the summer plus Easter and maybe the October school half-term. No wonder pubs, cafés and restaurants are mostly closed from the end of September to April, their temporary staff dispersed far and wide, possibly to return the following year.

The next morning we went ashore to Seil again. It was a bright blue day, sunny, with a light breeze. A fabulous autumnal day. I wanted to see the gardens of An Cala, which did not disappoint. We had the place to ourselves to admire the tinkling waterfall, the ponds and streams, the charming house made up of three 19th-century cottages knocked together, and the millennium fir-cone installation in the summerhouse by the lily pond. It is a garden clearly loved and cherished by Mrs Downie, open to the public for far less than it must cost her to look after it, at just £3 a head. How sad, and deeply irritating, that three gardens on this part of the coast which used to be open to the public had been closed by their new owners: Jura House gardens by that Australian hedge fund manager, Achnacloich on Loch Etive by I believe a London banker, and Torosay on Mull by a Swiss family. 'Who owns Scotland?' A good question. Not, it seems, the Scots. It is high time something is done about this. Naturally we also viewed the eccentric Highland Arts Centre (now closed) that was full of tartan tat, and much frequented by coaches full of eager tourists, seduced again by 'Scotland the brand'.

We set off again at 2.30pm, wind from the southeast, looking out for Dorothea, my Contessa 32 co-owner Richard's new boat, also heading from Dunstaffnage to her winter quarters in Ardfern. We had been co-owners for 22 years without a cross word between us, although perhaps a few cross thoughts. What was the secret of our success? It was partly because we had similar jobs as neurologists, so understood the stresses and strains we were both under; partly because we probably had a similar disposable income; partly because we were equally obsessional, not too obsessional, but always leaving the boat in good order for each other; and partly because we sat down with our families at New Year and decided exactly which weekends and weeks in that year we were each going to take the boat. We seldom sailed together. Only once did one of us — Richard in unanticipated bad weather — not return the boat to where it was supposed to be in time for me to take over. Each boatyard bill was daunting on first viewing, but became much less daunting when divided in two. On our retirement we arranged an amicable divorce. Calypso was sold to a friend who took the boat back to the south coast to race her. She was later sold again to Peter

Webb, and refurbished by Jeremy Rogers in Lymington who had made her in the late 1970s. Last seen in Orkney in 2021 she was looking immaculate.

As we headed south towards the Sound of Luing, Dorothea appeared to the north of us. We slowed and she caught up. Richard was sailing with his wife Jacquie. They had met as undergraduates in Oxford, after which she became a social worker and eventually CEO of the Scottish Commission for the Regulation of Care. Initially she was quite keen on Calypso but gradually became less so, maybe to do with getting older and not so willing to put up with the boat's discomforts. In the end she ventured onto Calypso only once a year — so infrequently that she used to sign the visitors' book making pithy remarks about Richard whom she referred to as Captain Birdseye. Dorothea is more spacious, comfortable and light down below, and has been so much better for her, and so for Richard too — an inspired choice. She threatens to write an article about sailing wives; it may not be complimentary about sailing husbands and their co-owners, but we shall see.

It was a grand afternoon, the two boats making long and leisurely tacks backwards and forwards between the islands of Scarba and Luing until we could turn east through the tide race of the Dòrus Mor and into Loch Craignish, arriving off Ardfern at 6pm as the sky was darkening. A lovely evening. A complete circumnavigation of Great Britain. We celebrated with Richard and Jacquie on Dorothea, toasting our boats with gin and tonic, and then went for a meal in the local pub where we joined the quiz. 'The highest mountain in the USA?' Richard knew but wasn't quick enough to see off the other team. By the time we left it was raining, and the weather window had closed.

CANNA

Chapter 12

Epilogue

Rather pleasingly I had sailed right round Great Britain without any serious mishap. There had been no Covid-19 pandemic back then, or any international disaster, to force us to delay, or even abandon the whole project. We had changed crew where we expected to change crew (Harwich rather than Walton-on-the-Naze was a trivial variation). We never had to turn back because of bad weather or breakages (the closest was between the River Deben and Lowestoft). No crew walked away. There were no life-changing arguments. And — perhaps surprisingly given the average age of the crew — no one got really ill. The worst medical issue was Steve's swallowing problem. John's, Neil's and my bruises soon got better, as did my irritating vertigo, but not the hernia. And the family coped at home. Which all perhaps makes for a dull read, as Henry Reynolds remarked about his own cruise in 1904: 'Yet, thoroughly enjoyable as the cruise was throughout, the account of it, through lack of incident, makes, probably, insipid reading. The better the cruise, the less interesting its history.'[1] People usually do indeed prefer to read about a great disaster like a dismasting survived, or a man overboard retrieved. But not everyone. Arthur Ransome did not believe he was 'alone in finding that the sailing books I take most often from their shelves are those that mention the sands, the headlands,

---

1. Henry Reynolds, *Coastwise—Cross-Seas: The Tribulations and Triumphs of a Casual Cruiser* (London: J. D. Potter, 1921), 189.

the lightships and perhaps the very buoys with which in my own small vessels I have been familiar'.[2]

The weather may not have been all that bad in the sense of keeping us battened down in harbour, but it certainly wasn't brilliant. As I've mentioned, this was actually quite helpful because with more wind we had to do very little motoring compared with many who sail round Britain in the summer. The whole journey was about 2540 nautical miles, we were at sea for around 560 hours, and so we averaged 4.5 knots. We were sailing for about 80% of the time, which is pretty good considering we had to get to the end of each of leg on time to change crew. This is not much different to Hilaire Belloc's suggestion, a century ago: 'When you are on a long passage, even with steady weather, you had better bank on three to four knots and no more. For what with beating, fishing perhaps, the falling of wind, over-reefing in terror, and the rest of it, you will not do more.'[3] The marina and harbour fees came in at £1641, quite a lot for one person but not so bad when shared among the crew.

So, job done, or 'mission accomplished' as the banner behind the puffed-up President George W. Bush so over-confidently and wrongly proclaimed in 2003 at the end of the Iraq War. However, my own mission was certainly not done — too many places unvisited, and too much interesting detail left out of the ones I had visited. Hence two further circumnavigations in 2015 and 2018 to plug the gaps, including the great coastal cities of London, Liverpool, Bristol, Hull, Plymouth and Newcastle upon Tyne. And surprises like Chatham with its outstanding naval museum, diminutive Peel Island in Cumbria with its King, and Lundy Island to view but not to climb the Devil's Slide (I left that for Oli and Ben to tackle). But there are some tempting gaps still left to fill: Chichester Harbour where I had raced Fireflies for my school; distant Foula off Shetland which still hangs on to a small population; and Solva where my two attempts were thwarted — first by my venerable Tinker inflatable sinking under us, and then by lack of time. But I don't fancy the crowds of Lymington, or indeed anywhere else in the Solent.

---

2. Arthur Ransome, introduction to *The Cruise of the Kate* (London: Rupert Hart-Davis, Mariners Library Number 23, 1953), in *Blue Water Sailing* (Christina Hardyment, Amazon Publications, 1999), 43.

3. Hilaire Belloc, *The Cruise of the Nona* (London: Constable & Co. Ltd, 1925), 311.

Looking astern

Looking back (or astern as we mariners say), it is truly astonishing how far medicine has come during my professional lifetime, despite all the problems in medical research — incompetence, bias, fraud, ethics roadblocks and red tape, competing interests, non-randomisation, waste. CT and MR scanners have made investigating patients so much quicker, easier, safer and cheaper largely because hospital admission is hardly needed. The downside is that more investigations are carried out, the modern young doctor forgetting always to ask first, 'Is this test really necessary — will the result change the patient's management?' If not, don't do it, even if it is cheap and easy and safe. You can be so easily tripped up by an incidental abnormality that is nothing to do with the patient's problem.

When I was a student, successful kidney dialysis had only just started, as had the use of immunosuppression drugs to prevent kidney transplants being rejected. Heart, lung and liver transplants came later. Hip joint replacements were in their infancy, and knee and now shoulder replacements were hardly dreamt of. Interventional radiology had not been invented, and even diagnostic cardiac catheterisation was regarded as risky. No ultrasound for obstetrics existed outside Glasgow. There were no artificial lenses to replace cataracts. Modern anaesthetics have made operations safer, laparoscopic surgery has made recovery quicker, and operating robots are already here. When my mother had her gall bladder removed she was in hospital for over a week whereas I was in for less than a day.

In my student days we didn't necessarily tell patients that they were dying of — or even had — cancer. Now perhaps we tell too much. There was little if any shared decision-making between patients and their doctors. The slightly trite but reasonable slogan 'No decision about me without me' is the only good thing that came out of Andrew Lansley's time as the worst Health Secretary we have ever had. His reforms[4] to increase competition between healthcare providers, and to not just encourage but enforce outsourcing to the supposedly more efficient private sector, have been catastrophic in a system that depends on healthcare providers working together for the benefit of patients, not needlessly competing against each other. Besides, the transaction costs of monitoring the multitude of service providers with newly set-up regulators, and of the initial tendering with legal challenges

---

4. Health and Social Care Act 2012. http://www.legislation.gov.uk/ukpga/2012/7/contents/enacted.

thrown in, are a huge waste of NHS money. David Cameron, the Prime Minister at the time, may have 'regrets' now. He should have had them a lot earlier.[5]

When purchasers of healthcare are forced to accept the lowest bid, the private provider cherry-picks the cheapest patients to care for, and then attempts to keep to their unrealistic budget by cutting corners and laying off staff after they their pay and benefits have already been reduced. When things go wrong, the patients are dumped back into the NHS. Complaints mushroom, and lawyers' letters are exchanged, costing everyone even more money, and wasted time. Then the private provider withdraws or goes bust, or catastrophically fails in some way, again leaving the NHS to clear up the mess. After all, their priority is to their shareholders, not the patients.

A more welcome advance is that letters between doctors are routinely copied to patients. There are only two rules: never put anything in the letter you have not already discussed with the patient, and send it to the right address. The suggestion of writing a second letter to the patient in plain English would be over-burdensome, so a third rule might be to avoid too much medical jargon and abbreviations in letters between doctors. It has even been suggested that consultants should write to their patients and copy the letters to the referring GP. I am not so sure, but then I am well retired.

When I was a student there was no way stroke patients could or would be admitted to St George's Hospital at Hyde Park Corner. We were far too important to dirty our hands with them. It was to some dark and distant geriatric hospital they went. Ironically, the first stroke I saw actually occurred in St George's, caused by a botched operation on the carotid artery in the neck. Maybe I can claim some credit in helping to turn around this terrible and old-fashioned view of stroke, and contributing to the falling incidence of stroke too. Ironically again, St George's now has one of the best stroke units in the country.

Patients these days arrive in clinics with their print-outs from the internet, which may or may not be a welcome development. Video consultations are now commonplace, not just in remote areas but anywhere, saving patient journey time and cost but probably not much doctor time, if any. Cathie no longer needs to rush into the hospital to see an acute stroke patient, but can sit at home and with video conferencing on her laptop she can take a history from a patient in a distant hospital, ask a local doctor to examine the patient in front of the camera, look at their brain scan, and then discuss

---

5. David Cameron, *For the Record* (London, William Collins, 2019), xiv.

treatment 'face-to-face' with the patient, family and local doctor — all in just minutes where minimising time-to-treatment really counts.

Also mainly after my time came the tsunami of emails, available on your phone as well as laptop, at work or on holiday. Cathie gets more than 100 every day (excluding spam), an impossible number to read and respond to. Paperless hospitals and general practices are now almost universal, and no longer do doctors have to leaf through several volumes of handwritten and misfiled notes bursting out of their increasingly tatty folders. The downside is trying to find an unoccupied computer terminal on the ward, remembering one of a variety of passwords to log on with, dealing with different software systems in different hospitals and practices, and hopefully find what you are looking for.

A mixed blessing has been the loss of 'Nightingale wards' which had maybe 10-20 beds down each side where just one nurse could keep an eye on everybody, and where a patient might alert her (not many hims in those days) to another patient in trouble. While there is more privacy in a single room, and perhaps less risk of cross-infection, patients are out of sight of the nurses, a risky situation. And there is none of the camaraderie that you can find in a larger ward. Perhaps four-bed areas are a reasonable compromise. Having gone to a boys' boarding school where we all had to dress and undress in front of each other has probably given me a more relaxed view of this difficulty.

The loss of medical 'firms' in hospitals has been a disaster. As has the general loss of collegiality, the feeling that everyone is working together to help patients, that we know who is who, who can be trusted and who not, who knows what and who doesn't. It is ironic that just when Edinburgh rebadged its School of Medicine, which was spread over several sites, as the College of Medicine, the regular meetings of all the professoriate from across town were axed and the previous collegiality which that facilitated disappeared.

Sailing too has come a long way since I started. The boats are now mostly built in easy-to-maintain fibreglass which is much cheaper than wood (but so difficult to dispose of). They have stanchions and lifelines, sprayhoods, electric navigation lights and anchor winches, VHF radio, chartplotters and AIS, radars too. Larger boats have fridges and hot running water, even TV. Ashore there are marinas almost everywhere around our coastline, and almost hardly anyone dries out against harbour walls anymore. Looking further back it is impossible to imagine cruising without an engine, although some diehards still do. Or without decent weather forecasting, or Sailing

Directions, or an echosounder, or a seriously waterproof outer layer to keep out the wind and rain. We have inflatable dinghies, and don't have to tow unwieldy wooden ones, which can so easily be lost in a heavy sea. The future will see electric engines (already on the way) and some easy alternative to the dangers of gas cookers. Our predecessors were as tough as old boots, and I salute them. Our descendants might think the same about us, or maybe not.

Ruminations

Fourteen years after retiring I have completely cast off the role of neurologist, doctor, researcher, dotty professor. Cathie who has similar roles, more or less, keeps me vaguely in touch, as does superficial reading of her *BMJ*. It has been sad to abandon and so perhaps 'waste' my talents such as they were, and more importantly the knowledge I once had. No longer on the front line, I am well out-of-date, a danger to friends and relatives who unwisely seek my informal medical opinion. I would be an irritation to active and younger researchers. In any case, one must move over for the next generation. It is such a relief not to have to keep up with the rapidly escalating numbers of scientific papers, even within just one field like stroke. It takes so much time to read a paper properly to detect any nonsense, which is more likely than not, particularly if the research is rushed without proper scrutiny (as so much was during the Covid-19 pandemic). In any event, most research results turn out to be wrong sooner or later — like beta-blockers being harmful in heart failure. Scientific 'truth' is a slippery and transient beast.

Was I a good doctor, a good enough doctor even? I do brood about that. I certainly always strived to do better at doctoring, and am sure most doctors do. One can always make anything better given time and resources. For me, the incentive to do better was not fear of litigation, which was less of a problem than it is now. Or money, although I was certainly very well paid. I only ever worked for a salary, never in commercial (aka private) practice. Being a patient certainly gave me insights that changed my practice, and I hope made me a better doctor: the chill feeling of a cancer diagnosis; irritation at being left on a trolley in a corridor waiting for an X-ray; looking forward to the reassuring consultant bedside visit; appreciating good nurses and avoiding catching the eye of bad nurses; and welcoming doctors who sat on my bed — now banned for fear of I know not what — rather than towering above me. (Professor Douglas in Aberdeen used to squat by the bed for lack of a chair, not a bad idea.). Worrying needlessly about secondary cancer, deep vein thrombosis, Parkinson's disease, motor neurone disease, and mouth cancer, all helped my own doctoring. I have long supported assisted dying for patients who are suffering unbearably despite the best possible care, but unfortunately some unimaginative doctors, and others, do have to experience a friend's or relative's difficult and unpleasant death before they too come to support it.

Was I a good teacher? Again I don't know. We had very little feedback from undergraduate students in my day. Most of my graduate research fellows did well, so I must have been a reasonable mentor. My research probably made a difference although it will surely be superseded: aspirin reduces the risk of heart attacks and strokes; well-targeted carotid surgery reduces the risk of stroke too; we know much more about stroke from the Oxfordshire Community Stroke Project and from the Oxford Vascular Study, its worthy successor. I certainly asked questions arising out of my clinical work, and answered a few of them. It is so important in medicine to be able to admit that you don't know, but then go and find the answers: look in the literature, ask an expert, and if that fails then do some research. And never be surprised if quite common medical truths are based on nothing more than mutating theories without any empirical proof. I once thought of giving a lecture 'Causing trouble by asking questions, a poke in the eye with the best of intentions', but I ran out of time. Maybe it could be my epitaph.

Having fun while still being deeply serious about doctoring, research and teaching is important too — which is why I was no good at management which although serious is no fun at all. All that management-speak: transformational-change-moving-forwards, zero-sum game, key performance indicators, delivering outputs, bla bla and bla. Working with people you respect as well as like is also important. I can't imagine putting up with, for example, being a medical advisor to a cognitively challenged and dishonest government minister.

Of course I am wistful, and feel guilty not to have a proper job, not being part of a team. Sad not to be useful anymore, at least not as a doctor, teacher and researcher. I must work on being a better parent, a task I had delegated to Ilona with my first three children when I was forging my career in Oxford, and whose efforts I have only come to fully appreciate by spending far more time with my two youngest children. And I must be a better friend to my friends. One downside of having made friends at work is that so many are far away, and without going to conferences anymore I don't see them. Getting to London is bad enough, Penzance is worse,

Europe even worse, and New Zealand much, much worse although it is a kind of paradise when you get there.

So here I am, still standing but with no gall bladder, half a colon, no appendix, no tonsils, mesh controlling my hernias, and three implanted teeth — all thanks to surgery. And on no regular drugs, nor with any artificial joints.

And finally was I, am I, a good sailor? I can't have been too bad to have sailed where I have, not across oceans but into rocky anchorages, around shifting and hidden sandbanks, and in and out of marinas. I haven't gone aground very often, and never disastrously. Only that one call for a lifeboat, off Kinsale. Have I frightened the crew and myself? Yes, quite often, but I have got away with it. So far.

Retirement

Retirement sinks people who don't have another purpose in life, an interest of some sort, and a plan. Maybe that is why some people just go on working. I know many colleagues who do but then it is easier as an academic than in most other occupations. Out-of-work interests are best developed when you are younger and then carried on into retirement, which, crucially, also stops work intruding into every corner of family and home life. When I was working I didn't give up photography despite the brush-off from the *Sunday Times*, or sailing despite the time it took up. As a result, since retiring, I could combine the two by developing my Scottish anchorages website (scottishanchorages.co.uk). It keeps me busy, because it has to be kept up-to-date. Hotels, pubs and restaurants change, often at surprising speed. Cathie once said to me as we were driving across to the west coast, 'You are a different person out here.' Indeed I was — I was away from the stresses and strains of work.

In retirement, boutique tourism to Antarctica, the Taj Mahal, Machu Picchu, the Grand Canyon, the Himalayas and the Galapagos Islands is not sustainable for our steadily warming planet that has to absorb all those aircraft emissions. Besides, I still have one child to look after and must stay near to home. My last long-haul flight was in 2009 and I don't plan any more of them. I will never see those distant sights, but don't feel disadvantaged. I feel guilty enough about having flown so much when working. If at the time I thought about it at all, it seemed justified — but I was not then alerted to the high likelihood and now fact of global warming.

Why oh why did we — I —think it macho to fly to Australia, give a lecture, and then fly straight back? Was it really such a good idea to accept so many lecture and other invitations, to 32 countries over the years? My successors can — and should — spend far more time video-conferencing to distant places, rather than sitting in airport lounges. The trouble is that distant places are attractive and fun. 'This is the life for a medical researcher,' remarked my friend and colleague of many years, Peter Sandercock, as we sipped cappuccinos on a terrace in Perugia one sunny spring morning. Difficult to dispute that. But at least you can get to Italy from Edinburgh by train, with a lot of reading done on the way. You don't have to fly. Flying should become as socially unacceptable as smoking, unless it is really necessary — which certainly doesn't include stag weekends in Prague. Every single new central and local government law or initiative should be scrutinised not just for gender imbalance and racial discrimination (as they are now) but also for effects on the climate.

Finale

At the age of 18 I thought I could do anything with a bit of effort — doctor, photographer, glider pilot, engineer — anything. Too late now. I shall never be President of the Royal College of Physicians, not that I wanted to. I did once try to head up NICE (The National Institute for Health and Care Excellence) but the job was stitched-up for the incumbent who unbeknown to me had to reapply for his own job (some civil service rule). I applied to be Chief Medical Officer for Scotland but now realise I would have hated it. I was once encouraged to apply to be chairman of the Stroke Association. I told the head-hunters they needed not me but someone in or near London, good at fund-raising, with connections, and preferably with a knighthood too. Which is what they got.

Now pushing towards 80, I will stick with what I know and try and get better at that, or at least no worse, while I await the 'Last scene of all, that ends this strange eventful history, is second childishness, and mere oblivion, sans teeth, sans eyes, sans taste, sans every thing'.[6] What upsets me most is that I will never know if the human race destroys itself by global warming, or by nuclear weapons, or by some terrible plague, or is wiped out by an asteroid. Or even how my children get on. Maybe we have already passed 'peak civilisation', a disturbing thought from Steve Druitt. I won't be able to surreptitiously turn over the remaining pages of the story of the human

---

6. William Shakespeare, *As You Like It*, Act 2, scene 7, lines 166–70.

race on Planet Earth to peep at the last page of all, to find out what happens at the very end.

I hope the themes in this book have not been too depressing — ageing, a life well past halfway, with assorted bees in my bonnet about medicine, politics, and other things. That was not my intention, which was rather to describe a cruise, and parts of a life which for the most part has been rewarding. And very definitely fun. I am not ready to 'swallow the anchor', as mariners say when they abandon sailing for good. But when I do I shall reflect on the words of Hilaire Belloc, perhaps the best writer about sailing: 'Under that failing light, all alone in such a place, I shall let go the anchor chain, and let it rattle for the last time. My anchor will go down into the clear salt water with a run, and when it touches I shall pay out four lengths or more so that she may swing easily and not drag, and then I shall tie up my canvas and fasten all for the night, and get me ready for sleep. And that will be the end of my sailing.'[7]

Like almost everyone, I won't leave a footprint that lasts forever, not like those fossilised stegosaurus footprints on Skye. Nonetheless, it would be nice to leave something behind, not just a wake to be lost moments later in the waves. But even if I am remembered for anything at all, my own memories will die with me. Meanwhile there is still more sailing to be done, not abroad but nearer home, because like Belloc I too have 'made discoveries close at hand, and have found the island of Britain to be infinite'.[8] Having sailed round our coast three times, I know for sure that the Hebrides and the west coast of Scotland are the very best cruising grounds in our 'island of Britain'. I will mainly stick to them, I think. Fortunately, I enjoy still being on the sailing learning-curve, a fact all too familiar to my crew who refuse to leap across that gradually widening gap on to pontoons, particularly now they are mostly old themselves.

Anyone with a suitable boat, or who can crew on someone else's, should sail round Britain at least once. Don't bother with the Mediterranean or the Caribbean, or even further afield. You will learn so much about your own country, will see so many interesting things, and will meet people you would never otherwise have met. For novelty or a purpose, you could connect with famous writers as you meander around the coast — Dickens

---

7. Hilaire Belloc, 'On Dropping Anchor', in *On Sailing the Sea: A Collection of the Seagoing Writings of Hilaire Belloc*, ed. W. N. Roughead (London: Rupert Hart-Davis, 1951), 157.

8. Belloc, *Cruise of the Nona*, 32.

for London and the Thames, Thomas Hardy for Dorset, George Mackay Brown for Orkney — or with artists — Turner for Margate, Constable for Essex, more or less everyone for Iona. Or you could focus on castles of which there are far too many to list, or on maritime museums, or on historic ships. For wildness savour Shetland, for summer warmth the Scilly Isles, for the warmth of people call in on Northern Ireland, for marine domesticity try the Essex-Suffolk border, for 'left-behind' Britain brood on Maryport and Hartlepool. And definitely go with friends, to share all the fun.

Glossary

abeam off to the side of a ship, usually at its widest part
amidships *see* midships
antifouling a type of paint for the underwater parts of boats to discourage marine organisms attaching themselves to the hull and slowing the boat down
autohelm *see* tiller-pilot

bar the sand and mud which tends to collect at the mouths of rivers and estuaries, making them shallow, and often with breaking water over them as a result
beam the width of a boat at its widest point
bearing away letting the sails out more, and heading away from the wind
beating if you are beating you are close-hauled, and may have to tack backwards and forwards; *see also* tacking; close-hauled
Bermudan sloop a sailing boat with one mast and typically a headsail (foresail) in front of the mast, and a triangular mainsail behind the mast
bilge(s) the lowest part of the interior of the hull of a boat, where any water collects
boards *see* tacking
boom the horizontal spar (pole) attached near the bottom of the mast, and to which the bottom of the mainsail is attached
bottlescrew (turnbuckle) the adjustable connection between the shrouds (which support the mast) and the deck, as well as between other parts of the rigging
bow (bows) the pointy bit at the front of a boat
bow-thruster a motor in the bows (usually electric on yachts) with a propeller mounted sideways, so the bows can be turned to port or starboard when manoeuvring in tight spaces
bulkheads vertical barriers built across the hull to strengthen it, and to divide

the boat into different functional areas like the saloon, forecabin, etc.

chain-plate the strong connection between a shroud, or any other stay that supports the mast, and the hull

cill an underwater gate which can be fixed or movable, to keep water within (for example) a marina basin when the tide falls

cleat that T-shaped device on the deck, or on pontoons, around which you can quickly wrap and secure a mooring or other rope without having to find the end and thread it through anything

close-hauled sailing as close to the wind as possible, with the sails pulled tightly in; *see also* tacking.

cockpit the part of a sailing boat from where the boat is steered and where the crew can lounge around in the open air

companionway the steps down from the cockpit into the saloon

crosstrees the horizontal bits on masts, to which shrouds are attached to keep the mast standing

cruising shute a balloon-like lightweight sail flown from in front of the mast in relatively light airs (a bit like a spinnaker but without a boom so easier to manage)

diesel bug a horrible bacterial infestation that can occur in diesel fuel contaminated by water, changing it into a sludge which stops the engine, gradually or suddenly

dory a small seaworthy boat, like a dinghy but bigger

ebb tide when the seawater level is falling, and the tide is going out

echosounder electronic device for displaying the depth of water

ensign the flag worn usually at the stern of a ship to indicate its country of origin

fairway buoy a red and white vertical-striped safe-water mark which can be passed on either side, often indicating the entrance to a river or harbour

fender a device (usually an air-filled soft plastic cylinder) that protects the hull from damage by a pontoon or harbour wall

fender-board a wooden plank hung over the side of the boat between the fenders and a harbour wall or piling, so better protecting the hull if the wall is rough and irregular, or if the piles are well separated

fetch means sailing almost close-hauled towards one's objective, and with no need for tacking

fine reach sailing relatively close to the wind but not close-hauled

finger-berth a narrow berth between two floating 'fingers' on a pontoon

flap-gate a barrier to water flow which opens to allow boats to enter a harbour when there is enough depth of water, and shuts to keep enough depth of water

inside a harbour for boats to float as the tide falls
flood tide when the seawater level is rising, and the tide is coming in
force *see* wind-speed
forecabin the cabin in the bows of the boat
foredeck the triangular-shaped deck in front of the mast.
foresail (headsail) the sail in front of the mast, usually triangular and can be called a jib

gaff a spar (pole) near the top of a mast and angled upwards, to which a four-cornered mainsail is attached. Tends to be confined to traditional sailing boats.
genoa a large foresail (or jib) that extends behind the mast and so overlaps the mainsail
grab bag a container for essentials that may be needed if one has to abandon ship in an emergency — flares, chocolate, a knife etc.
guardrails (lifelines) usually horizontal wires rather than fixed rails, they are attached to the stanchions, pulpit and pushpit to run right round the boat. The idea is that they stop you falling overboard.
gybe when the wind is from behind, the mainsail is usually out as far as it can go, and the boat is running. When making a turn towards the direction in which the boom is pointing, the wind can then get behind the sail, so the boom has to be taken across to the other side of the boat — i.e. gybed. This can be a fraught procedure in heavy seas with a lot of wind (and a crew who don't know what they are doing).

halyards ropes to pull the sails up — main halyard for the mainsail, and jib halyard for the foresail
hanks metal clips to attach sails to the wire up which they run
heads the toilets on boats
headsail *see* foresail
heave to a method to stop the boat sailing by backing the foresail (i.e. pulling it across to the windward side of the boat) and keeping the mainsail where it is. This can be surprisingly comfortable even in a heavy sea and provides respite for the crew who may want to make a cup of tea or visit the heads.
helming steering the boat standing at the 'helm', which might be with a tiller or a wheel
high tide (high water) when the seawater is at its highest

impeller the small rubber circular part of the pump which rotates and pumps cooling water around the engine
inflatable shorthand for an inflatable dinghy, or 'tender', carried on a boat so the crew can get ashore when at anchor

jackstay a tape or wire, usually the length of the boat, fixed along the side deck, to which crew can clip themselves when moving around and so avoid being swept overboard in a heavy sea

jib see foresail

jubilee clip circular metal ring which can be placed around flexible tubes around pipes and then tightened with a screwdriver to prevent the tubes falling off

kicker the diagonal strut (or rope) from the bottom of the mast to the boom, which prevents the boom rising up when running before the wind, and when adjusted in length controls the shape of the sail

knot measure of speed, defined as one nautical or sea mile per hour

leading line the imaginary line between two marks which indicates the direction in which to approach

leech the back edge of a fore-and-aft sail

lee shore the shore on to which the wind is blowing, to be avoided by sailing boats for obvious reasons

lifelines *see* guardrails

lighters flat-bottomed barges used to transfer cargo and passengers to and from larger moored ships

liveaboards people who live on boats, not sailing across oceans but likely tied up to the bank of some river, or in a harbour. Cheaper than living in a house, particularly in a city, and very romantic until you have to find somewhere to pump out your poos.

low tide (low water) when the seawater is at its lowest

luff the forward leading edge of a fore-and-aft sail

mainsail the sail behind the mast of a single-masted sailing boat, but not necessarily the largest sail — the spinnaker will be larger, and often the genoa too

marina a collection of pontoons with services such as electricity and fresh water

Mayday the international call signal for emergencies

midships (amidships) the middle part of the boat, often the widest part.

nautical mile *see* sea mile

neap tides when the range of tide between high and low water is least, and the flow of the tide is least too; it coincides with the half moon.

osmosis an affliction of fiberglass hulls, less of a problem now than in the early fiberglass boats. Water gets under the outer surface where it forms blisters that can then permeate the hull to weaken the structure. Expensive to fix.

outboard engine an engine usually driven by petrol, or sometimes electricity, which is mounted usually on the stern of a boat. Depending on its size, it may

power anything from a high-speed boat to a small inflatable dinghy.
overfalls turbulent water in a tidal race

pan-pan signal indicating the need for help but not a dire emergency (one step down from Mayday)
pick-up strop thin rope, usually supported by a small buoy, with a loop which can be picked up with a boathook, attached to thicker rope or chains on a mooring buoy
pilotage the business of navigating a boat close to the shore and in and out of anchorages, rivers and harbours
pilot-gig (rowing-gig) a narrow four- to six-oar rowing boat, originally used as a lifeboat and for taking pilots out to ships, but now for recreation and racing
pipe-cot a sleeping berth made of canvas stretched between two poles, and which can be folded away when not in use
PLB personal locator beacon, which when activated provides the distant emergency services with the exact position of the beacon by virtue of its GPS signal
pontoon a floating, usually wooden platform anchored to the seabed, to which boats can be tied. Pontoons may be attached to a harbour wall as in a marina, or be anchored away from the land.
port to the left of a boat
Practical Boat Owner a UK sailing magazine which tends to attract the more DIY characters. A friend once said it was full of articles on 'How to knit your own spinnaker'.
preventer a rope which is attached to the boom when it is swung out for running before the wind, and which prevents it unexpectedly gybing which can be dangerous — crew have been killed by the boom hitting their head during an unexpected gybe (I once broke a wooden mast in a poorly controlled gybe).
pulpit the metal tubular structure at the bows of a sailing boat
pushpit the metal tubular structure at the stern of a sailing boat

quarter berth a single or double berth towards the stern of a boat, and often tucked away behind the chart table or galley. It can be difficult to get into and to extract oneself from but is snug and impossible to fall out of in a heavy sea.

raft up when there is not enough room for boats to tie up directly to a pontoon or harbour wall, they have to lie against each other or 'raft up'. Sometimes these rafts can consist of six or more boats (which is tricky when the inner boat wants to leave at 5am).
reach (reaching) sailing with the wind coming from the beam (the side)
Reeds Almanac the bible and almost as thick, updated annually, containing all you need to know for sailing round the British Isles — tide times, harbour

lights, emergency procedures etc.

reef to reduce the size of a sail to cope with increasing wind-speed

roadstead a place close to the land where ships can safely anchor sheltered from waves, tide, currents and wind

rowing-gig *see* pilot-gig

run (running) sailing with the wind coming from behind the boat

sacrificial anodes small lumps of zinc placed on hulls, propellers and engines to protect their metal from galvanic corrosion in seawater. Zinc will corrode before bronze, steel etc.

Sailing Directions contain information about the coastline, harbours and anchorages.

saloon the main cabin in a sailing boat, usually with a table and bunks each side to sit on

seacocks valves set in the hull through which water can flow into the sea from the galley sink, heads etc., and which allow water into the cooling system for the engine

sea mile (nautical mile) defined as equal to one degree of latitude, which works out at 1.15 land miles or 1.85 kilometres

sheets ropes that pull in or let out the sails once they have been raised by the halyards — mainsheet to pull in the mainsail, jib sheet to pull in the jib

shore-power 240v electricity supply from the shore, usually from a socket on a pontoon to which a lead is taken to the boat. Same sort of thing for caravans.

shrouds wires (or ropes on traditional boats) which run from the mast to the deck on each side of the boat to hold the mast up

slack water when the tides are changing and there is no tidal flow, either as a high tide is beginning to ebb, or a low tide beginning to flood

slipway a sloping hard surface from the shore down into the water, useful for launching small boats (or swimming)

snatch-block a type of pulley (sheeve) which is opened from the side and slipped onto a fixed rope and so used to redirect the fixed rope's direction of pull

spinnaker a big balloon-like sail flown in front of the mast when the wind is coming from behind or the side. It is held out on a boom and can be difficult to manage when the wind gets up — hence the look of horror on family faces when the skipper mentions the word 'spinnaker'.

splicing to avoid making knots which weaken a rope's strength, it is better to splice the rope to make loops to attach things to like shackles, or to join two ropes together, provided that a permanent fix is required. This is done by partially untwisting short strands at the end of the rope and then reinserting them further along the rope.

sprayhood usually made from canvas stretched over a collapsible steel frame at the front of the cockpit, this protects the crew from wind, rain and spray.

spring a rope attached to the midships of a boat, either angled forwards to an attachment on the land or a pontoon, or backwards. It stops the boat surging backwards or forwards respectively.
spring tides when the range of tide between high and low water is maximal, and the flow of the tide is greatest, coinciding with the full or new moon
stanchions the upright metal poles along the edge of a sailing boat to which the lifelines are attached
starboard to the right of a boat
stern the back end of a boat
sweep old-fashioned term for an oar

tack (tacking) when the wind is blowing from the direction one wishes to go in, to get there one has to tack in zigzags as near to the wind as possible, i.e. close-hauled. Each tack was called a 'board' in earlier times.
tell-tales small pieces of wool or other material attached to sails which indicate whether there is the desired laminar flow across them
tidal race where the tide flows very strongly either over an uneven seabed, or down a narrow channel. Eddies and hazardous currents form, with erratic and steep waves. Everything gets worse if the wind or the swell are against against the direction of the tide.
tides *see* high tide; low tide
tiller-pilot (autohelm) an electronic and mechanical machine connected to the tiller to make the boat steer on a preordained compass course
tiller steering using a tiller rather than a wheel to steer a boat
tombolo a sandbar or spit which connects one island to another, or an island to the mainland, so forming a double beach
traffic separation zones to avoid collisions where shipping is very crowded, these are internationally agreed one-way systems, as in the English Channel and between Northern Ireland and Scotland. Ships must stick within their designated 'lanes', and cross them only if necessary, and then at as near right angles as possible.

vane self-steering (windvane self-steering) a wonderfully simple piece of machinery mounted on the stern which, once the boat is set up to sail in the required direction, uses the flow of air over the vane to keep it at the same angle to the wind and then using rope or other connections the tiller or wheel are moved appropriately

warps ropes to pull the boat where you want it to go, or to connect a boat to the shore, either to a pontoon or harbour wall
weigh anchor to pull up the anchor prior to setting sail
weatherboarding a traditional way of building the wall of a house with

horizontal, overlapping wooden boards
wheel-steering using a steering wheel rather than a tiller to steer a boat
wind-speed measured in knots, miles per hour or kilometres per hour, and also by the Beaufort Scale from force 1 (calm) to force 12 (hurricane force)
windvane self-steering *see* vane self-steering
windward where the wind is blowing from

Yachting Monthly a slightly more upmarket UK sailing magazine compared with *Practical Boat Owner*
yawl a sailing boat with two masts; the one at the back is mounted behind the rudderpost and its boom generally overhangs the stern.

References

Bacon, Francis, *The Advancement of Learning*, book I, v, 8 (1605).
Bathurst, Bella, *The Lighthouse Stevensons* (London: Harper Collins, 1999).
Batstone, Tim, *Round Britain Windsurf, 1800 Miles on a 12ft Board* (Newton Abbott: David and Charles, 1985).
BBC Science Focus Magazine, 15th February 2022.
Beckett, Samuel, *Murphy* (London: G. Routledge & Co., 1938).
Belloc, Hilaire, *On Sailing the Sea: A Collection of the Seagoing Writings of Hilaire Belloc*, ed. W. N. Roughead (London: Rupert Hart-Davis, 1951), 231.
Belloc, Hilaire, *The Cruise of the Nona* (London: Constable & Co. Ltd, 1925).
Belloc, Hilaire, 'The North Sea', in *The Hills and the Sea* (London: Methuen and Co., 1906).
Betjeman, John, *John Betjeman's Collected Poems* (London: John Murray, 1958).
Boswell, James, *The Journal of a Tour to the Hebrides with Samuel Johnson, LL.D.*, ed. R. W. Chapman (orig. 1785; Oxford: Oxford University Press, 1970).
Brandreth, Gyles, *Have You Eaten Grandma?* (London: Penguin Random House, 2018).
Brown, V. T. et al., 'Appraisal and Revalidation for UK Doctors—Time to Assess the Evidence', *BMJ*, 370 (2020), m3415.
Buchanan, Robert, *The Land of Lorne, including the Cruise of the 'Tern' to the Outer Hebrides*, vol. 1 (London: British Library, Historical Print Editions, 1871).

Cameron, David, *For the Record* (London, William Collins, 2019), xiv.
Campbell, Denis, 'The Mid Staffs Hospital Scandal: The Essential Guide', *Guardian*, 6 February 2013.
Campbell, Lewis and William Garnett, *The Life of James Clarke Maxwell* (London: Macmillan and Co., 1882), 297.

Carroll, Lewis, *Through the Looking-Glass and What Alice Found There* (London: Macmillan, 1871).
Cobb, L. A. et al., 'An Evaluation of Internal Mammary-Artery Ligation by a Double-Blind Technic', *New England Journal of Medicine*, 260 (1959), 1115–18.
Collins, Greenvile, *Great-Britain's Coasting Pilot* (London: 1693).
Colloca, L. and A. J. Barsky, 'Placebo and Nocebo Effects', *New England Journal of Medicine*, 382 (2020), 554–61.
Coppen, Allen and John Bailey, '20 Most-Cited Countries in Clinical Medicine Ranked by Population Size', *Lancet*, 363 (2004), 250.
Cowper, F., *The Vagaries of Lady Harvey* (Kirkwall: W. R. Mackintosh, 1930).
Cowper, Frank, *Sailing Tours: The Yachtsman's Guide to the Cruising Waters of the English and Adjacent Coasts*, parts 1–5 (London: Upcott Gill, 1892–6).
Cowper, Frank, *Sailing Tours: The Yachtsman's Guide to the Cruising Waters of the English Coast*, part 1: *The Coasts of Essex and Suffolk* (London: Upcott Gill, 1892), ix.
Cowper, Frank, *Sailing Tours: The Yachtsman's Guide to the Cruising Waters of the English Coast*, part 2: *The Coasts of Kent, Sussex, Hants, The Isle of Wight, Dorset, Devon, Cornwall and the Scilly Isles* (London: Upcott Gill, 1893), 35.
Craven, Lawrence L., 'Experiences with Aspirin (Acetylsalicylic Acid) in the Nonspecific Prophylaxis of Coronary Thrombosis', *Mississippi Valley Medical Journal*, 75 (1953), 38–44.

Daniell, William, *A Voyage round Great Britain Undertaken in the Summer of the Year 1813*, vol. 3 (London: Longman et al., 1818), 70.
Daniell, William, *A Voyage round Great Britain Undertaken in the Summer of the Year 1813*, vol. 5 (London: Longman et al., 1821), 8.
Defoe, Daniel, *A Tour through the Whole Island of Great Britain* (orig. 1724–6; London: Penguin, 1971).
Dependence and Withdrawal Associated with Some Prescribed Medicines (Public Health England, 2019).

Eastcott, H. H. G., G. W. Pickering, and C. G. Robb, 'Reconstruction of Internal Carotid Artery in a Patient with Intermittent Attacks of Hemiplegia', *Lancet*, 264 (1954), 994–6.

Ferriar, John, 'An Affection of the Lymphatic Vessels hitherto Misunderstood', in *Medical Histories and Reflections*, vol. 3 (London: Cadell and Davies, 1810).
Fry, J., *Profiles of Disease: A Study of the Natural History of Common Diseases* (Edinburgh and London: E. and S. Livingstone, 1966).

Goodwin M. and Colmer R., *Blue Star Adventure: a Circumnavigation of Britain* (Independent Publishing Network, 2021).

Haswell-Smith, Hamish, *The Scottish Islands: A Comprehensive Guide to Every Scottish Island* (Edinburgh: Canongate Books, 1996).
Havard, Robert, *Wellington's Welsh General: A Life of Sir Thomas Picton* (London: Aurum Press, 1996).
Heckstall Smith, S., *Isle, Ben and Loch, from the Clyde to Skye* (London: Edward Arnold, 1932).
Hill, Austin Bradford, 'Aims and Ethics', in A. B. Hill (ed.), *Controlled Clinical Trials* (Oxford: Blackwell, 1960), 3–7.
Hine, Alfred, *Magnetic Compasses and Magnetometers* (London: Adam Hilger, 1968).
Hine, Ian, *A Cumberland Endeavour — Hine Bros. of Maryport: The People, the Ships, the Town* (Words by Design, 2012).
Hoeritzauer, I. et al., 'Scan-Negative' Cauda Equina Syndrome: A Prospective Cohort Study', *Neurology*, 96 (2021), e433–e437.
Holt, Geoff, *Walking On Water: A Voyage round Britain and through Life* (Rendlesham, Suffolk: Seafarer Books, 2008).
Hore, Peter, *HMS Pickle: The Swiftest Ship in Nelson's Trafalgar Fleet* (Stroud: The History Press, 2015).
Huxley, Thomas, 'President's Address to the British Association for the Advancement of Science, Liverpool Meeting, 14 Sept. 1870', *The Scientific Memoirs of Thomas Henry Huxley*, vol. 3 (1901), 580.
Hughes, Robert Edgar, *Hunt's Yachting Magazine*, 1 (1852); 2 (1853).
Hunter, John, 'A Treatise on the Blood, Inflammation and Gunshot Wounds', in *The Works of John Hunter*, ed. J. F. Palmer (London: Longman et al., 1794).

Inglis, John, *A Yachtsman's Holidays or Cruising in the West Highlands* (London: Pickering and Co., 1879).

Johnson, Samuel, *A Journey to the Western Isles of Scotland*, ed. R. W. Chapman (orig. 1775; Oxford: Oxford University Press, 1970).

Kay, Adam, *This is Going to Hurt: Secret Diaries of a Junior Doctor* (London: Picador, 2017).
Kingston, William H. G., *A Yacht Voyage round England* (orig. 1870; London: The Religious Tract Society, *c.*1879).
Kmietowicz, Z., 'Cystic Fibrosis Drugs to be Available on NHS in England within 30 Days', *BMJ*, 367 (2019), l6206.
Konstan, Angus, *Jutland 1916: Twelve Hours to Win the War* (London: Aurum Press, 2016).

Le Fanu, James, 'Mass Medicalization Is an Iatrogenic Catastrophe', *BMJ*, 361 (2018), k2794.

Lynam, C. C., *The Log of the 'Blue Dragon', 1892–1904* (London: A. H. Bullen, 1907).

MacCarthy, Dermod, *Sailing with Mr Belloc* (London: Collins Harvill, 1986).

Mackenzie, Murdoch, *Nautical Descriptions of the West Coast of Great Britain from Bristol Channel to Cape-Wrath* (London: 1776).

McLintock, John, *West Coast Cruising* (London and Glasgow: Blackie and Son Ltd, 1938), 133.

McMullen, R. T., *Down Channel* (orig. 1869; 3rd edn, London: Horace Cox, 1903; London: Grafton Books, 1986).

McMullen, R. T., *Down Channel* (orig. 1869; London: Grafton Books, 1986).

McPherson, Ann, 'An Extremely Interesting Time to Die', *BMJ*, 339 (2009), p. 175.

Matthews, W. B., *Practical Neurology* (Oxford: Blackwell, 1963).

Medical Research Council Antiepileptic Drug Withdrawal Study Group, 'Randomized Study of Antiepileptic Drug Withdrawal in Patients in Remission', *Lancet*, 337 (1991), 1175–80.

Meehan, Patricia and Malcolm Brown, *Scapa Flow: The Story of Britain's Greatest Naval Anchorage in Two World Wars* (London: Pan Books, 2002).

Middleton, E.E., *The Cruise of the Kate* (London: Longmans, Green and Co., 1870).

Middleton, E. E., *The Cruise of 'the Kate'* (2nd edn, self-published, *c.*1888).

Miller, Henry, 'Facial Paralysis', *BMJ*, 3 (1967), 815.

Miller, Henry, *Medicine and Society* (Oxford: Oxford University Press, 1973).

Molyneux, A. et al., 'The Durability of Endovascular Coiling versus Neurosurgical Clipping of Ruptured Cerebral Aneurysms: 18-year Follow-up of the UK Cohort of the International Subarachnoid Aneurysm Trial (ISAT)', *Lancet*, 385 (2015), 691–7.

Monro, Sir Donald, *Description of the Western Isles of Scotland called Hybrides* (Edinburgh: Birlinn Edition, 1994)[combined with 'A Description of the Western Islands of Scotland Circa 1695' by Martin Martin].

Murray, Sarah, *A Companion and Useful Guide to the Beauties of Scotland, and the Hebrides*, vol. 2 (3rd edn, London: 1810) [p. 74 in the version printed and bound by Pranava Books, India].

O'Brian, Patrick, *The Commodore* (London: Harper Collins, 1995).

Osler, William, 'Books and Men', *Boston Medical and Surgical Journal* (1901).

Ozieranski, Piotr et al., 'Exposing Drug Industry Funding of UK Patient Organisations', *BMJ*, 365 (2019), l1806.

Palmer, W., 'Is the Number of GPs Falling across the UK?', Nuffield Trust blog, 8 May 2019.

Pattenden, Ron, *Land on my Right: A Sail round Britain Single-Handed on a Laser, Unsupported* (self-published, Lulu Enterprises Inc., 2008).
Pharmaceutical Compounding and Dispensing (2nd edn, London: Pharmaceutical Press, 2012), chap. 2 'Solutions'.
Pickering, George, *High Blood Pressure* (2nd edn, London: Churchill, 1968).
Private Eye, 1556 (Sept. 2021), 10.
Purves, Libby, *One Summer's Grace: A Family Voyage round Britain* (London: Grafton Books, 1989).

Raban, Jonathan, *Coasting: A Private Journey* (orig. 1986; New York: First Vintage Departure Edition, 2003).
Ransome Arthur, introduction to *The Cruise of the Kate* (London: Rupert Hart-Davis, Mariners Library Number 23, 1953), in *Blue Water Sailing* (Christina Hardyment, Amazon Publications, 1999), 43.
Rawles, John, *The Matter with Us: A Materialistic Account of the Human Predicament* (Brighton: Pen Press, 2011).
Reynolds, Henry, *Coastwise—Cross-Seas: The Tribulations and Triumphs of a Casual Cruiser* (London: J. D. Potter, 1921).
Robertson, A., 'Flotsam and Jetsam', *Marine Quarterly*, 35 (2019), 13–15.
Rose, Geoffrey and Linda Colwell, 'Randomised Controlled Trial of Anti-Smoking Advice: Final (20 Year) Results', *Journal of Epidemiology and Community Health*, 46 (1992), 75–7.
Rothwell, P. and C. P. Warlow, 'Is Self-Audit Reliable?', *Lancet*, 346 (1995), 1623.

Scott, Catherine, Linxin Li and Peter Rothwell, 'Diverging Temporal Trends in 21st Century Stroke Incidence in Younger versus Older People: Population Based Study and Systematic Review', *Stroke*, 51 (2020), 1372–80.
Scott, Walter, *The Voyage of the Pharos: Walter Scott's Cruise around Scotland in 1814* (Hamilton: Scottish Library Association, 1998).
Shelley, Mary, *The New Annotated Frankenstein*, ed. Leslie S. Klinger (New York: Liveright Publishing Corporation, 2017).
Silverman, Mark, T. Jock Murray and Charles Bryan (eds), *The Quotable Osler* (Philadelphia: American College of Physicians, 2008).
Smith, Richard, 'Neurology for the Masses', *BMJ*, 319 (August 1999).
Spall, Shane, *The Voyages of the Princess Matilda* (London: Ebury Press, 2012; pbk edn 2013).
Spall, Shane, *The Princess Matilda Comes Home* (London: Ebury Press, 2013).
Steele, Sam, *UK and Ireland Circumnavigator's Guide* (2nd edn, London: Adlard Coles Nautical, 2011).
Stevenson, Robert Louis, 'Letters to His Mother from the Lighthouse Steamer, 18–22 June, 1869', in *Stevenson's Scotland*, ed. Tom Hubbard and Duncan Glen (Edinburgh: Mercat Press, 2003).

Stevenson, Robert Louis, 'Memoirs of Himself', book 1, p. 149, in *Memories and Portraits, Memoirs of Himself, Selections from his Notebook* (orig. 1887; London: William Heinemann, 1924).

Stone, Jon, Chris Burton and Alan Carson, 'Recognising and Explaining Functional Neurological Disorder', *BMJ*, 371 (2020), m3745.

Strathern, Marilyn, '"Improving Ratings": Audit in the British University System', *European Review*, 5 (3) (1997), 305–21.

Theroux, Paul, *The Kingdom by the Sea: A Journey around the Coast of Great Britain* (orig. 1983; London: Penguin, 1984).

Tudor Hart, Julian, 'The Inverse Care Law', *Lancet*, 297 (1971), 405–12.

Voelcker, Adam, *David Lea: An Architect of Principle* (London: Artifice Press, 2015).

Wakefield, A. J. et al., 'Ileal-Lymphoid-Nodular Hyperplasia, Non-Specific Colitis, and Pervasive Developmental Disorder in Children', *Lancet*, 351 (1998), 637–41.

Warlow, C. P. and P. Hinton, 'Early Neurological Disturbances following Relatively Minor Burns in Children', *Lancet*, 2 (1969), 978–82.

Warlow, Charles, 'A (So-Called) Mild Head Injury', *Practical Neurology*, 13 (2013), 260–2.

Warlow, Charles, 'Circumnavigation of Britain', *Marine Quarterly*, 28 (2017), 98.

Warlow, Charles and John Garfield (eds), *Dilemmas in the Management of the Neurological Patient* (Edinburgh: Churchill Livingstone, 1984).

Warlow, Charles and John Garfield (eds), *More Dilemmas in the Management of the Neurological Patient* (Edinburgh: Churchill Livingstone, 1987).

Wilde, Oscar, *Lady Windermere's Fan* (1893).

Wise, J., 'NHS and Vertex Remain Deadlocked over Price of Cystic Fibrosis Drug', *BMJ*, 364 (2019), l1094.

Woodcock, Percy, *Looking Astern: A Ditty-Bag of Memories* (London: Frederick Muller Ltd, 1950), 176.

Worth, Claud, *Yacht Cruising* (3rd edn, London: J. D. Potter, 1926).

Worth, Claud, *Yacht Navigation and Voyaging*, chap. 31: *From Hampshire to Rockall and Round the British Islands* (London: J. D. Potter, 1928).

Yeh, R W, at al., 'Parachute Use to Prevent Death and Major Trauma when Jumping from Aircraft', *BMJ*, 363 (2018), 463.

Young, Archibald, *Summer Sailings by an Old Yachtsman* (Edinburgh: David Douglas, 1898).